Management Control in Hospitals

For years, problems related to health-care efficiency have been at the top of the priorities of many hospital systems and governments. The growing cost of health care, and particularly hospitals, is a significant factor in the increasing pressure for improvement of hospitals' efficiency while maintaining a high quality of services. Hospitals are recognized as organizations in which waste, unnecessary administrative burdens, failures of care coordination, failures in execution of care processes, and even fraud and abuse are frequently identified issues.

Adoption of management control as a response to hospital problems is consistent with the conviction that control is a critical management function that has the greatest impact on organizational performance. Research proves that the lack of adequate control, adapted to modern organizational solutions, causes many harmful consequences, such as faulty services, dissatisfied patients and employees, inability to effectively compete on market, low flexibility and innovativeness, and, consequently, poor performance of the organization.

This book comprehensively presents issues related to management control and develops a breakthrough theory about management control in hospitals. It is the result of many years of research and outlines the concept of control and related theories, which are discussed in detail, taking into account the unique characteristics of medical services, the health-care market, and hospitals as higher public utility organizations.

Research has shown that the main elements of management control in hospitals are information systems, diagnostic control, interactive control, innovativeness, manager's trust in physicians, and perceived uncertainty. And that proper relationships between these elements positively influence the hospital's performance. This book describes how the success of the entire control process is based on the hospital's top management and its interaction with clinical managers, department heads, and directors of other medical departments as well as clinicians. After reading this book, the implementation of the solutions suggested will help hospitals improve their performance, including the quality and effectiveness of the provided medical services and patient care.

Management Control in Hospitals

A Breakthrough Approach to Improving Performance and Efficiency

Roman A. Lewandowski

Routledge
Taylor & Francis Group

A PRODUCTIVITY PRESS BOOK

First published 2024
by Routledge
605 Third Avenue, New York, NY 10158

and by Routledge
4 Park Square, Milton Park, Abingdon, Oxon, OX14 4RN

Routledge is an imprint of the Taylor & Francis Group, an informa business

© 2024 Roman Andrzej Lewandowski

ISBN: 978-1-032-43272-4 (hbk)
ISBN: 978-1-032-43271-7 (pbk)
ISBN: 978-1-003-36655-3 (ebk)

DOI: 10.4324/9781003366553

Typeset in Garamond
by Deanta Global Publishing Services, Chennai, India

I dedicate this monograph to my wife Danusia as a thank you for her love, patience, and persistent presence with me, and for her constant support. She is the inspiration of my life and my work. It is thanks to my wife that I have been able to work long hours without losing my home hearth all these years, which I have dedicated to my work at the hospital and at the university as well as to research and publications.

Contents

Contents ix

About the Author

Roman A. Lewandowski is an assistant professor at the University of Warmia and Mazury in Olsztyn, Faculty of Economics, Institute of Management and Quality Science and director of Voivodesship Rehabilitation Hospital for Children in Ameryka, Olsztynek, Poland. With his primary research interests in management control in health care, performance management systems, person-centered care implementation, trust, hybridity, and quality. Roman combines his extensive real-world management experience with academic expertise to explain fundamental management and control theories, concepts, methods, and tools, and how to apply them in health-care organizations.

Roman has published over 60 studies, including two books on management control, and he is a recognized expert in his field. He has contributed to several international projects, including the COST Action IS0903: Enhancing the Role of Medicine in the Management of European Health Systems – Implications for Control, Innovation, and User Voice; the COST Action TD1405: European Network for the Joint Evaluation of Connected Health Technologies (ENJECT); and the Polish National Science Centre project: The model, the typology, and methods of measurement of control systems in public hospitals where he served as the Principal Investigator. He was involved in the Artificial Intelligence, Enhanced Person Centred Care in Neurosurgery project, which was financed by the Ministry of Health of Montenegro. Roman has also served as Vice Chair for the European Network for Cost Containment and Improved Quality of Health Care (COST Action

CA15222) and is a member of the governing council of the Polish Federation of Hospitals, which is part of the European Hospital & Healthcare Federation (HOPE).

Overall, Roman is a researcher and expert in his field, with a passion for improving health-care systems and patient outcomes through his research, teaching, and involvement in international projects and organizations.

Introduction

More than two decades ago, a famous management researcher, H. Mintzberg, stated: "I have long suspected that running even the most complicated corporation must almost be child's play compared to managing almost any hospital" (1997, p. 14). On the whole, hospital management is extremely complex. Extant studies have shown that transferring the results of research in commercial enterprises to hospitals, which function in a multifaceted institutional environment, without taking into account hospitals' specificities, is ineffective (de Harlez & Malagueño, 2016, p. 2; Cardinaels & Soderstrom, 2013, p. 649). Although for years the efficiency issues in hospitals have been at the top of many countries' priorities, results of previous reforms have been poor. Yet, this research indicates that the proper use of management control appears to be the key solution for improving the efficiency of hospitals' delivery of medical services (Yu et al., 2018, p. 2). However, control cannot be designed in the traditional way – comparing facts with benchmarks and drawing conclusions from these comparisons – but should be understood in the modern way as all instruments, activities, and systems used by top management to increase the likelihood of favorable adaptation of the hospital to the environment, which is measured by the hospital's performance. Attention should be paid to seeing control as a function that supports not only the implementation of approved plans and strategies, but also their modification.

The choice of management control as the answer to hospitals' inefficiencies is in line with the belief that control is a critical management function and has the greatest impact on organizational performance (Merchant & Van der Stede, 2017, s. 1; Eisenhardt, 1985, s. 134; Kanthi Herath, 2007, s. 896). The lack of adequate control, adapted to modern hospitals' organizational arrangements, causes many harmful consequences, such as defective services, dissatisfied patients and employees, inability to compete effectively in the market, low flexibility and innovativeness, and, consequently, poor organizational performance (Kanthi Herath, 2007, s. 898). The above observations are consistent with the author's experience as a long-time director of a hospital and a researcher of hospital operations.

In the scientific literature, there are many general approaches, concepts, and models describing management control in a comprehensive manner in commercial companies (e.g., (Flamholtz i in., 1985; Simons, 1995; Flamholtz, 1996; Otley, 1999; Kanthi Herath, 2007; Ferreira & Otley, 2009; Malmi & Brown, 2008; Merchant & Van der Stede, 2017), while with regard to hospitals, such exhaustive concepts are lacking. This constitutes a significant research gap. Reasons for the difficulty of studying management control in health care include the fact that hospitals operate in a dynamic and intricate regulatory environment and are characterized by the high complexity of core operational processes overseen by medical professionals endowed with broad autonomy. Additionally, important elements that differentiate the functioning of hospitals from business companies is a more complex institutional environment, consisting of a number of external stakeholders, such as public and private payers or insurers, national and local governments, and health workers and patient associations, creating a highly politicized operating environment (Abernethy i in., 2006, s. 805; de Campos i in., 2017, s. 291). All parties pursue separate goals and possess great power to influence hospital decisions that affect every aspect of cost, revenue, and quality functions (Eldenburg i in., 2017, s. 53). Therefore, two research perspectives were adopted: institutional and organizational.

According to institutional theory, organizations such as hospitals must obtain legitimacy for their actions in order to secure their development and survival (Andreasson i in., 2018, s. 26; DiMaggio & Powell, 1983, s. 148–149). They can achieve such legitimacy by copying solutions in the area of management and control, which, while widely regarded as rational and effective, may, in fact, be nothing more than a socially accepted myth. The same is true for solutions that have worked in other organizations but are not suited to hospitals (Åberg & Essen, 2010, s. 16; Meyer & Rowan, 1977, s. 346). In such an environment, hospitals cannot control their activities, as "incompatible" control methods can generate inconsistencies and be perceived by internal actors as irrational, making control nothing more than a ritual. Thus, studying institutional factors is important to understand how they interfere with management control, since changes in management control can result from both institutional factors and motives for achieving efficiency. After all, hospitals may adopt a particular package of management control not only to improve their performance, but also to appear well managed and gain legitimacy in their environment.

From the perspective of organizational theory, control problems arise primarily from the interaction of two human characteristics: bounded rationality and opportunism (Wilkes i in., 2005, s. 1056). Bounded rationality refers to people's inability to take in and process all available information, which prevents them from making the most effective actions and optimal decisions (Eicher, 2017, s. 342; Simon, 1957). Opportunism is defined as "self-interest seeking with guile" (Williamson, 1975, p. 255). It is worth noting that both traditional institutional theory (e.g., DiMaggio & Powell, 1983; Meyer & Rowan, 1977) and the organizational approach (e.g., Flamholtz, 1996; Merchant & Van der Stede, 2017; Ouchi, 1979; Wilkes i in., 2005) see the organization as homogeneous and irrational, which, however, is at odds with contemporary views of how hospitals function. Only the emergence of theory introducing institutional logics (Friedland & Alford, 1991, s. 232; Thornton i in., 2012) changed the attitude to organizations, challenging the view of homogeneity and limited rationality. The perspective of institutional logics explains not only homogeneity, but also heterogeneity. The fundamental difference between the organizational and institutional perspectives based on the theory of institutional logics is that the former sees the hospital as a homogeneous cybernetic system, while the latter sees it as a historical accumulation of past practices and understandings, forming a heterogeneous environment of coexisting institutional logics that determine the behavior of organizational actors.

Previous studies of management control in hospitals have tended to be conducted separately in the organizational and institutional streams, thus providing a fragmented and incomplete picture, while hospitals, as hybrid organizations in their day-to-day functioning, feel the pressure of different institutional logics, face limited rationality and opportunistic behavior of their employees, and yet have to implement effective and possibly consistent strategies. Thus, underpinning the study of management control in hospitals from both the organizational and the institutional perspective, as well as taking into account the coexistence of multiple institutional logics, enables a deeper understanding of the essence of the functioning of management control in hospitals and its connection with other elements of the management system.

The above considerations underlie the goal of the book, which is to identify the main elements of management control and the links between them, as well as to develop a coherent model of management control in hospitals.

This research, analyzing management control and its impact on hospital performance, focuses on the perspective of the top management, and, in doing so, takes into account the key role of information systems, innovativeness, environmental uncertainty, and trust. The research focuses on the interaction between top management and middle managers, i.e., between clinical managers of medical departments and the medical professionals subordinate to them or, rather, working with them. This is because the majority of physicians working in modern hospitals are autonomous professionals taking full responsibility for their work. For this reason, references to medical professionals mostly refer to physicians as the only group of medics with the right to make important diagnostic and therapeutic decisions, which has a key impact on the quality of services provided and on the costs and revenues of a hospital. The high degree of physicians' autonomy means that the controlling role of the ward manager (head of department) is often limited to being a representative of the medical team of a particular specialty rather than a supervisor in the traditional sense.

This study made it possible to create a coherent, transparent, and thoroughly researched theoretical construct of management control in hospitals, contributing to the development of the theory and the practice of managing hospitals. In the first instance, it has provided broad insight into how management control functions, paving the way for recognizing the interdependence between the way the information system is used and the performance of a hospital, and it has provided an opportunity to identify specific practices for improving hospital efficiency. This represents new knowledge that will enable both theoreticians and practitioners to better understand the functioning of management control and the role of managers in this control and to improve actions that respond to emerging challenges.

The research is elaborated in seven chapters. Chapter 1 discusses the unique characteristics of the health-care market, medical services, and hospitals. It also highlights the role of the medical profession (especially physicians) as a major organizational resource and the complex relationship between medical professionals and managers and discusses the implications of the existence of two bureaucratic orders in hospitals: Weberian and professional. Attention is also paid to the institutional perspective in the social sciences and, in particular, to the concept of institutional logics, which further illuminates the relationship between physicians and hospital managers. The chapter goes on to summarize the effects of past efforts by various countries to improve the efficiency of the health-care system, especially hospitals.

Chapter 2 introduces the concept of control and related major theories, considering, among other things, the division between performance and behavioral control, agency theory and coupled information needs in the perspective of hospital management. Attention is given to the links between the development of control and the evolution of approaches to understanding organizational strategy, and, in this context, the concept of levers of control is discussed. Chapter 3 examines the extant body of knowledge concerning elements of management control identified as fundamental during the research, such as information system, diagnostic control, interactive control, innovativeness, manager's trust in physicians, environmental uncertainty, and employee rewarding. It also synthesizes the previous research about the interrelationships between these elements. Chapter 4 addresses the research methods used in the study, namely, the sequential exploratory mixed-methods design. In this study design, the quantitative phase of data collection and analysis follows the qualitative phase of data collection and analysis. In this chapter, the research samples for both phases are described.

Chapter 5 is devoted to the qualitative research report. It contains a discussion of elements of management control, i.e., second-order themes (constructs) identified in the procedure of thematic analysis of materials collected during field research in hospitals. The identified elements of control are illustrated with numerous examples of their functioning in the hospitals. The quoted statements of directors are intended to enable readers to form their own view of the functioning of management control and thus reduce the impact of the potential subjectivity of the author, a long-time hospital director. As a result of the theoretical considerations and the results of the qualitative research, 14 interrelated hypotheses are put forward, which, together with the identified constructs, make it possible to formulate a conceptual model of management control in hospitals.

Chapter 6 discusses the results of statistical tests related to the estimation of the path model proposed in Chapter 5. In this part of the work, the meaning of the variables in the process of their operationalization is clarified. At this stage of the research, the theoretical constructs that emerged from the qualitative research are linked to the specific indicators identified during operationalization, which became the basis for the development of the questions and statements included in the research questionnaire. In the next section of Chapter 6, given the existing research limitations, the choice of the PLS-SEM estimator is justified, and a report on the validation of the measurement model of variables and the estimation of the structural model of management control in hospitals is presented. Given the characteristics of the PLS-SEM estimator, great importance is given to assessing the predictive power of the model, and the problems associated with evaluating the model's fit to the data are characterized. Extended structural model analyses of non-linear relationships between variables are also described, and observable and unobservable heterogeneity in the data are estimated.

The work closes with Chapter 7 and the Ending summarizes the research achievements. Chapter 7 evaluates the hypotheses posed in Chapter 5 and analyzed in Chapter 6 and interprets the results obtained in light of previous research, taking into account the paradigmatic dualism, providing an interpretation of the research results from two perspectives: organizational and institutional. The final section of the publication also presents implications for theory and practice, research conclusions, and it discusses the limitations of the proposed model and directions for further research. The final subsection of Chapter 7 should be especially interesting for health-care managers of all levels, including heads of medical departments and lead nurses.

List of Abbreviations

Accreditation   Ministry of Health (Quality Monitoring Center (QMC) in Krakow) Accreditation – Polish version of hospital accreditation similar to some extent to the Joint Commission on Accreditation of Healthcare Organizations (JCAHO)

DRG   Diagnosis Related Groups, case-mix system (pl. Jednorodne Grupy Pacjentów)

Head physician (clinical manager)
the formal leader/manager of the hospital ward (head of the medical department)

HIS   Hospital IT systems

ICC   Individual cost center(s)

IPHI   Independent public health-care institution

LLC   Limited liability company

NHF   National Health Fund (pl. Narodowy Fundusz Zdrowia)

Overruns   The amount of services performed over the limit stipulated in the contract between a hospital and the National Health Fund.

PCoMSM   Path coefficients of the modified structural model (final model)

PCoPSM   Path coefficients of the preliminary structural model

TCA   Medical costing – treatment cost accounting

ToR   Terms of reference (description of the parameters of products and services purchased under public procurement and term of their delivery)

Ward lead nurse (or lead nurse)
> A nurse who manages all the nurses in a particular hospital ward. At the same time, she or he reports to the head of the department (head physician) and the director of nursing.

Chapter 1

The Essence and Nature of Hospitals and Their Environment

1.1 Characteristics of Hospitals

The scientific output in the field of management control in hospitals is relatively small, so the base of theoretical considerations for the creation and adaptation of new solutions in hospitals has be the body of knowledge relating to other organizations. This is in line with the approach that says that the essential processes of managing hospitals do not deviate fundamentally from the logic of general management, especially strongly recognized in the commercial sector, although this requires a critical approach and consideration of their specifics. Management in health-care organizations, and, in particular, the management of hospitals, is perceived as more complex than management in the private sector, and, according to many researchers, the complexity of management in health care is constantly increasing (Firth-Cozens & Mowbray, 2001, pp. ii3–ii7; Nash, 2003, pp. 652–653; Smith, 2001, pp. 1073–1074; Waldman & Cohn, 2007, p. 33). This unique complexity of hospital management is influenced by the combination of a number of already problematic elements:

- affiliation of hospitals with higher public utility units;
- the multiple and often contradictory goals imposed on hospitals by both internal and external stakeholders;

DOI: 10.4324/9781003366553-1

- the materiality of the politicization of the environment;
- the unique nature of medical services;
- peculiarities of the health-care market characterized by the separation of the consumer of services from the payer;
- the complexity of basic operational processes;
- dominance of the control of basic operational processes by medical professionals.

A hospital, as a unit of higher public utility, is subject to influences different from a commercial organization. This is because the hospital does not have the ability to decide on all the goals it must achieve. Some of them are externally imposed, and these goals require process management that differs from that of enterprises. The hospital is not subject only to economic conditions, but social and political factors also play an important role, and it should be evaluated in this context – in social rather than economic terms.

Factors that increase the complexity and difficulty of hospital management also include less transparent transaction outcomes, more dispersed direction and control, and unclear signals from the environment (Durán et al., 2011, p. 27; Hodges et al., 1996; Lynn et al., 2000). In addition, hospital executives typically have less control over core business functions (e.g., pricing, shaping offerings and service delivery, etc.) than their corporate counterparts. This generates a number of problems, including the inability to take appropriate actions (e.g., referring patients, raising prices, closing unprofitable operations, etc.) to increase the efficiency of hospital operations (Pizzini, 2006, p. 184). At the same time, the continuous development of knowledge and technological innovations, including new drugs that provide improved disease treatment options, also requires more extensive multidisciplinary medical teams and technical support, generating ever new treatment costs (Bodenheimer, 2005, p. 932; Mintzberg, 2012, p. 4; Rye & Kimberly, 2007). Restricting access to new treatments to contain cost increases is impossible in practice, due, in part, to the fact that knowledge of medical advances is widely available, and societies demand access to treatments based on the latest medical knowledge. On the other hand, the same societies protest against increases in health-care premiums. In addition, the decision to use certain medical technologies is made autonomously by medical professionals, mainly doctors, who are obliged to use current medical technologies.

According to current legislation, in most European countries and Canada the state is responsible for delivering universal health insurance programs and the availability of medical services, using an appropriately organized network of providers located at different levels of health care: primary health care (PHC), outpatient specialized care (OSC), and inpatient treatment in hospitals. A different situation is found in the United States, where a significant part of the responsibility is shifted to private insurance organizations. In Europe, most hospitals are owned by central or local governments, while in the United States, hospitals are mostly owned by non-government organizations and state and local governments. Thus, even in the United States, 76% are not-for-profit hospitals. However, regardless of the ownership and for-profit or not-for-profit status, the operation of hospitals is affected by the unique nature of the services provided by these organizations. Medical services – unlike other types of public and private services – have their own specificity in that (Shortell & Kaluzny, 1997):

- norming and measuring work results is more difficult;
- the work is more diverse and comprehensive;
- most of the work is immediate and cannot be postponed;
- work allows for little ambiguity or error;
- activities at work are highly independent of each other and require a high degree of coordination between different groups of specialists;
- the work requires an extremely high degree of specialization;
- organization members are highly specialized and are more loyal to their professional groups than to the organization;
- physicians, i.e., the group most responsible for generating services and expenditures, have little effective organizational and managerial control;
- there is a great deal of freedom in the choice of methods and means of treatment;
- treatment does not always result in a full recovery of the patient, and then there is no way to determine whether the result obtained was optimal, taking into account the current level of medical knowledge, the severity of the disease, and the physical and mental state of the patient;
- when a full cure occurs, it is not possible to determine the level of economic efficiency from both the patient's and the provider's point of view;
- there is a large knowledge gap between medical professionals and patients;
- the contact of doctors, psychologists, and other medical professionals with patients is largely shrouded in professional secrecy, which limits the possibility of ongoing verification of the quality of these services.

It should be noted that each single characteristic considered may also characterize an organization other than a hospital. Undoubtedly, immediacy of action characterizes the fire and police departments. High specialization is found in high-tech service companies. A small margin for error is found in aviation services. However, it is only in medical services that all the factors mentioned interact simultaneously, which significantly hinders the provision of services by hospitals.

The specificity of the processes undertaken in hospitals is also determined by the following characteristics:

■ the obligation to maintain constant readiness to assist patients seven days a week and 24 hours a day, despite the fact that in many situations the cost of this readiness is not funded (the state fire department is not funded based on the number of fires in a given month, and the hospital is paid for the number of births over which it has no control);
■ in most countries the inability of the majority of hospitals to set pricing policies and make the price dependent on the quality of the service, as well as the inability to choose a target market – the hospital must treat all patients whose conditions match its medical profile;
■ the fact that most of the personnel providing health-care services are medical professionals (e.g., doctors, nurses, laboratory diagnosticians), who have a special legal status that protects them in the labor market through a system of licenses, called professional rights, granted by a professional corporation;
■ restricting access to information on the work process (medical confidentiality) for managers and others outside the medical profession;
■ the need to reconcile higher, abstract social goals (e.g., "the pricelessness of life") and individual goals (e.g., "health regardless of cost") with real economic constraints.

The characteristics indicated are the reason for the relatively significant limitation in the ability to control subordinate personnel, in conditions where up to 80% of hospital resources are under the control of physicians who have broad autonomy over diagnostic and therapeutic decisions (Doolin, 2002, p. 370; Goes & Zhan, 1995, p. 508). In other words, managers have no control over what diagnostics and therapy doctors order for patients, and it is these orders that create the costs of medical services.

In the market for hospital services, the costs of providing medical services are not financed directly by the patients themselves, but by an external financing institution, a so-called third party. Indeed, while in outpatient care, especially specialized care, some patients pay out of their own pockets for the health services they receive. This is rarely the case in hospitals due to the much higher unit costs of services. This type of financing system transforms the nature of economic exchange, changing the paths of money flow and making it difficult to define the customer of medical facilities. The difficulty arises from the question: is it the one who pays or the one who uses these services? This separation of the function of the payer from the consumer should also be considered one of the main peculiarities of the market for medical services, since in the standard market model a group of consumers determines the demand for services with certain characteristics, and a group of companies is mobilized by this demand to invest and create supply. In the market for hospital services, on the other hand, patients receive care, but they do not directly pay for it, while insurance companies and government institutions, which neither consume nor provide services, finance the operation of hospitals, spreading the risk among citizens or insured. Thus, it is the payers for medical services or/and the parliament, government, and government institutions that shape the boundary conditions for private and public providers to enter the system. In other words, it is not patients, but institutions, that decide which provider will receive money for their treatment. In this arrangement, beneficiaries also do not have as much influence over the performance of hospitals in terms of quality of care as the clients of commercial companies do. In addition, institutions that purchase services on behalf of patients determine not only hospitals' revenues, but in many countries also the cost of treatment by setting minimum requirements in many areas, including the number of medical professionals employed and the medical technologies used, including drugs. This approach limits innovation, especially in the use of more efficient forms of work organization (Porter, 2010a, p. 2478).

From the structure of the market for health services also comes the extent of hospitals' autonomy. This is because embedding hospital management in the health-care system results in a significant limitation on hospital autonomy. This means that, compared to free market enterprises, hospitals can be semi-autonomous at best, since the scope of operational decisions made is limited by insurers and government policies related to, among other things, the financing of hospital services and the freedom to create relationships with medical workers and social policies. This problem also applies to private, for-profit hospitals, which, although characterized by much greater operational freedom, are also conditioned by a number of guidelines for the provision of medical services.

1.2 Hospitals' Structure and Management

Today's hospitals are large organizations employing from several hundred to even tens of thousands of employees, and trends observed in developed countries indicate consolidation and a continuous increase in the size of hospitals (Durán et al., 2011, p. 16). As a result, the coordination and control of such large and complex organizations requires a hierarchical structure and bureaucratic tools, as neither the market mechanism nor the collegial clan mechanism, based on shared values, socialization, and direct supervision (Ouchi, 1980), can meet the challenge of managing hundreds or even thousands of people organized into a single institution. However, on the other hand, the identified unique characteristics of hospitals, such as the performance of highly complex activities, the inability to clearly assess the efficiency and desirability of these activities, and the prevalence of multi-disciplinary work teams, which makes it difficult to assess the individual contributions of employees and a functional structure consisting most often of more than a dozen separate medical specialties, all make centralized planning, assessment of the efficiency of activities, standardization of work processes, and decision-making characteristic of bureaucracies impossible (cf.: Mintzberg, 1980, p. 332). In addition, knowledge-intensive work, such as that performed by doctors in a hospital, creates a conflict of loyalties between professional affiliation and organizational responsibility, compounding the difficulty of maintaining bureaucratic means of control (Alvesson & Willmott, 2002, p. 623). As a result, hospital management differs significantly from corporate management not only because of its specificity, but also because of the determinants of clinical management, which involves interactions between management and physicians, relying on balancing management control and physicians' professional autonomy.

Hospital services involve the treatment of the most serious diseases, often requiring the coordinated action of many specialists from many fields and a complex infrastructure adapted to the work processes specific to each medical specialty. An aging population means that hospital patients, in addition to the so-called "acute" illnesses for which they are admitted to the hospital (e.g., an open fracture), also suffer from many "chronic" illnesses that further complicate and increase the risk of providing services. In addition, an increasingly demanding society expects an individualized approach and a focus of treatment not only around the underlying condition, but also consideration of the multiple needs of both the patient and his or her family participating in the care process. Thus, the idea of coordinated, patient-centered care and even the integration of the patient's environment (family, friends) and their more active participation in the process of their treatment is becoming increasingly popular. This approach is called person-centered care (more in: (Ekman et al., 2011; Lewandowski et al., 2021)).

A hospital is generally responsible to numerous external stakeholders, such as the government, the community, the payers and accreditation agencies. In most European countries as well as in the United States, a hospital is run by a general director also called chief executive officer (CEO), who is responsible for the hospital's operations. In large hospitals, directors have several senior executives, who often carry the title of vice director or vice president responsible for various key service areas, such as nursing services, rehabilitation services, human resources, finance, and so forth. In Europe, the medical director is often in the position of a deputy director, while in the United States, this medical director creates a more parallel organizational structure to the administrative one.

Estimating the number of hospitals and comparing them with one other in each country is a complex task, as hospitals vary widely not only in size, but also in the complexity of the services provided. It is difficult to compare small hospitals specializing in one field of activity with several beds, e.g., maternity hospitals and large university hospitals with a thousand or more beds and a very wide range of specialties. Moreover, acute hospitals that perform surgical procedures have a different structure, number of employees, and costs compared to those focused on psychiatry or rehabilitation.

The analysis based on OECD statistics shows that in most developed countries, the majority of beds are in publicly owned hospitals (Table 1.1). And in those countries where there are not many publicly owned hospitals, such as in South Korea, the majority of beds are in not-for-profit hospitals (90.3%). From the statistics, it appears that only in three countries – Germany, Greece, and Italy – for-profit privately owned hospitals have just over 30% of beds. What is important, on average, publicly owned hospitals are larger in terms of the number of beds than privately owned, no matter whether for profit or not for profit. Summarizing the data contained in Table 1.1, it can be concluded that public hospitals play a major role in most developed countries of the world. While in the United States public hospitals account for just over 20% of all beds, when we consider not-for-profit hospitals, they already account for over 80% of the beds nationwide. Therefore, in the rest of the book, we will mainly focus on public and not-for-profit hospitals. In this case, Polish, Lithuanian, Irish, and British hospitals can be good examples.

Table 1.1 Comparison of hospitals in selected OECD countries

Country	Number of hospitals				Number of beds in:			
	Publicly owned hospitals	Not-for-profit privately owned hospitals	For-profit privately owned hospitals	Total	Publicly owned hospitals	Not-for-profit privately owned hospitals	For-profit privately owned hospitals	Total
Australia	695	116	543	1 354	61 797	13 552	17 477	92 826
Austria	143	42	82	267	43 121	10 244	9 508	62 873
Belgium	38	125		163	16 730	47 117		63 847
Canada	695		7	702	96 220		629	96 849
Chile	216		131	347	29 856		9 263	39 119
Czech Republic	164	3	96	263	58 906	240	10 344	69 490
Estonia	20	3	6	29	5 539	152	244	5 934
Finland	164		85	249	14 930		696	15 626
France	1 347	670	972	2 989	237 941	55 625	93 352	386 918
Germany	762	914	1 330	3 006	261 027	184 177	204 963	650 167
Greece	123	4	143	270	29 472	823	14 522	44 817
Iceland	8			8	1 039			1 039
Ireland	67		19	86	12 697		1 715	14 412
Israel	37	26	21	84	18 384	5 657	2 861	26 902
Italy	420	34	611	1 065	120 529	7 286	61 536	189 351
South Korea	222	3 884		4 106	63 417	592 471		655 888
Latvia	45		15	60	9 025		1 020	10 045
Lithuania	69		9	78	16 580		222	16 802
Mexico	1 514	20	3 375	4 909	92 011		34 438	126 449
New Zealand	83	26	50	159	10 784	440	1 460	12 684
Poland	**747**	**25**	**464**	**1 236**	**186 322**	**3 683**	**44 412**	**234 417**
Portugal	113	57	71	241	24 424	7 175	4 733	36 332
Slovenia	26		3	29	8 893		101	8 994
Spain	342	121	308	771	96 759	17 281	25 893	139 933
Türkiye	950		584	1 534	193 942		57 240	251 182
United Kingdom	1 921			1 921	162 723			162 723
United States	1 418	3 098	1 574	6 090	198 242	559 761	161 556	919 559

Country	Percentage of beds in:			Average number of beds in:			
	Publicly owned hospitals	Not-for-profit privately owned hospitals	For-profit privately owned hospitals	Publicly owned hospitals	Not-for-profit privately owned hospitals	For-profit privately owned hospitals	All hospitals
Australia	66.6%	14.6%	18.8%	89	117	32	69
Austria	68.6%	16.3%	15.1%	302	244	116	235
Belgium	26.2%	73.8%		440	377		392
Canada	99.4%		0.6%	138		90	138
Chile	76.3%		23.7%	138		71	113
Czech Republic	84.8%	0.3%	14.9%	359	80	108	264
Estonia	93.3%	2.6%	4.1%	277	51	41	205
Finland	95.5%		4.5%	91		8	63
France	61.5%	14.4%	24.1%	177	83	96	129
Germany	40.1%	28.3%	31.5%	343	202	154	216
Greece	65.8%	1.8%	32.4%	240	206	102	166
Iceland	100.0%			130			130
Ireland	88.1%		11.9%	190		90	168
Israel	68.3%	21.0%	10.6%	497	218	136	320
Italy	63.7%	3.8%	32.5%	287	214	101	178
South Korea	9.7%	90.3%		286	153		160
Latvia	89.8%		10.2%	201		68	167
Lithuania	98.7%		1.3%	240		25	215
Mexico	72.8%		27.2%	61	0	10	26
New Zealand	85.0%	3.5%	11.5%	130	17	29	80
Poland	**79.5%**	**1.6%**	**18.9%**	**249**	**147**	**96**	**190**
Portugal	67.2%	19.7%	13.0%	216	126	67	151
Slovenia	98.9%		1.1%	342		34	310
Spain	69.1%	12.3%	18.5%	283	143	84	181
Türkiye	77.2%		22.8%	204		98	164
United Kingdom	100.0%			85			85
United States	21.6%	60.9%	17.6%	140	181	103	151

Despite the different legal and systemic solutions adopted in each country for several decades, if we consider medium and large hospitals, essentially only two models of hospitals have taken shape around the world. The first, prevalent in Anglo-Saxon countries, is characterized by the role of physicians as consultants, in the United States often employed and paid outside the hospital. In these hospitals, the management of resources (beds, operating rooms, ancillary staff) is handled by administrative staff, who are carriers of managerial culture (logic), while the actual and most important work processes are carried out mainly by physicians, who are carriers of professional culture (logic) (Lewandowski & Sułkowski, 2018, p. 152). This creates "hybrid organizations" (Lewandowski & Sułkowska, 2017) with at least two clear dividing lines (two hierarchies) – a separate one for doctors and a separate one for managers and other hospital employees. For example, this type of hospital operates through academic departments and institutes. Each department has a high degree of autonomy, operating within a matrix structure. The model is market-oriented, that is, the method of financing is used as a tool to influence doctors' behavior. F. Lega and C. DePietro (2005, p. 263) call this type of hospital a "decentralized two-headed hospital" (decentralized two-headed hospital).

The second model, more common in Europe, is characterized by salaried physicians and centralized responsibility. Resources are allocated by top management to specialized units (clinics and/or wards). All of the department's resources are uniformly managed by the physician-director of the specialty (head of department), who is endowed with a high degree of autonomy in this regard. This type of hospital is therefore more oriented toward bureaucratic mechanisms, reducing the importance of market mechanisms. This type of hospital can be referred to as a "centralized single-headed hospital" (centralized single-headed hospital) (Lega & DePietro, 2005, p. 263). The common feature of the two types of hospitals discussed is a functional organizational structure centered around medical specialties.

In this context, it seems important to note that although for years many scholars have been calling for a remodeling of the structure of hospitals into a process-oriented one, which should improve the efficiency of hospitals and the quality of the services they provide (Vera & Kuntz, 2007, p. 55), hospitals are still organized into functional structures, centered around particular medical specialties, and there is no indication that the organizational form of hospitals will change significantly in the foreseeable future.

The reasons for the functional organization of hospitals are many (du Gay & Pedersen, 2020, p. 222). First, it stems from making efforts to match hospitals to the predetermined outcomes of a standardized treatment program for particular groups of conditions, in accordance with the principles of evidence-based medicine. Second, the functional structure makes it possible to organize the work process around the skills and knowledge of medical specialists – physicians who are responsible for categorizing and diagnosing patients' needs and executing a tailored treatment process. Such a division ensures a high specialization of personnel and knowledge, leading to high-quality treatment of specific, separate conditions (e.g., the cardiology department perfectly treats cardiovascular diseases, but already has difficulty treating the digestive system damaged by the cardiovascular drugs administered). As a result, functional division enables standardization of knowledge and skills, which is the primary coordination mechanism in professional bureaucracies such as hospitals. Third, organizing around skills allows for the promotion of the development of individual specialties and related knowledge, which is an important part of the culture of the medical profession. If one considers the autonomy of each medical specialty, with its scientific associations and regional and national consultants and its rather loose ties to other specialties, it becomes logical to think in terms of an individual strategy for each specialty in hospitals. Specialists do not make their choices about patients and treatment methods randomly; they are the result of the many years of training a specialist undergoes, often starting as early as in college or well before he or she began working in a particular department of a particular hospital. This means that the skills required in a given specialty and the standards set by professional associations and training institutions outside the organization play an important role in determining the strategies preferred by professionals. Hence, to an important extent, all hospital departments in a specialty have similar strategies, but rather separate from departments in other specialties.

The aforementioned factors make it extremely difficult to change the functional model of hospital organization from one focused on individual specialties to one focused around the needs of modern patients, who often suffer from multiple conditions simultaneously. Such a transformation would require systemic changes that ensure the influence of citizens as potential patients on the formation of state policy and organizations of medical professionals. This has been partially done through legal regulations that increase the rights of patients and the obligations of hospitals, an example of which is the introduction of legislation that facilitates the determination of compensation and redress in the case of medical events, which has increased the possibilities of patients in actions to prove malpractice, i.e., deviation from the treatment procedure adopted for a given condition. This has had a strong impact on adherence to medical procedures and has made the distribution of medical work and the way doctors organize their work even more focused on specialization and departmentalization of treatment, reducing the area of responsibility of doctors to their chosen specialty and the likelihood of medical error due to better alignment of skills and infrastructure. However, these changes have resulted neither in relatively significant improvements in the coordination of care and treatment nor in the efficiency of hospitals.

In summary, it should be said that the hospital has features characteristic of all organizations, but it is distinguished by a specific system of values and goals, as well as intra-organizational relations and relations with the environment. As a unit of the higher public utility units, it is subject to different legal regulations, forcing the reconciliation of efficiency with the legalism of action and the realization of higher social goals. It can be said that the peculiarities of medical services, the health-care market, and the organization of hospitals lead to difficulties in the management of these facilities, particularly in the area of management control. This peculiarity makes the adaptation of management and control techniques used in commercial organizations to hospitals complex, and the results obtained from such transfer are not obvious. Another important factor affecting the complexity of hospital management – in addition to the peculiarities of hospitals indicated thus far – are the medical professionals who dominate the main "production" processes in hospitals. Thus, to study the mechanisms of management control in hospitals, which is the subject of this work, it is necessary to understand what role professionals play in them, how they obtain power, how large this power is, and what interactions it has with the jurisdiction of managers and other members of the organization.

1.3 Medical Profession and Professional Bureaucracy

The literature on professionalism dates back to the early 20th century; however, due to social changes in the second half of the 20th century, the modern approach to professionalism has changed significantly (Noordegraaf, 2020, p. 206). Professionalism is no longer viewed functionally, as a collegial organization of experts whose main attribute is the asymmetry of knowledge and experience, requiring clients to trust and professionals to respect clients and colleagues (Abbott, 1988, p. 5), and as a buffer to defend the common good against the overexpansion of capitalism (Durkheim, 1960, p. 116). Today, professionalism is treated as a form of control, assuming that it does not serve existing social needs, but rather dictates to a distracted society the definitions of needs and how to meet them, although "the shortcomings of protective professionalism are increasingly clear [and] protective professionalism and protected professionals are becoming outdated" (Noordegraaf, 2020, p. 207).

Thus, a profession is a highly specialized and collectively knowledge- and skill-based group of individuals who are given special status within the workforce, whose members are certified through a formal educational program controlled by the profession; its qualified members have exclusive jurisdiction to perform certain activities vis-à-vis society and protection in this regard in the labor market (Freidson, 2001, pp. 127–128). In this approach, the attributes of the profession are self-regulation, self-control, and social duty, but also dominance and autonomy, which means that the profession performs two mismatched functions in society – "servant" and "supervisor." Professionals should have an ideology that gives priority to doing valuable and necessary work, rather than economic profitability and self-satisfaction. Thus, within the profession, there is a contradiction between altruism and self-interest.

Some researchers (Berlant, 1975; Larson & Larson, 1977, p. 309) attribute the goals of creating economic monopolies to professionalism, an overt focus on market interference aimed at intellectual and organizational domination of a certain sensitive social sphere in order to achieve wealth and prestige. On the one hand, the professions attack and destroy "charlatans," while, on the other hand, they force concessions from unorganized clients and the state (Abbott, 1988, p. 87), as manifested, for example, in the treatment of advanced cancers, when the therapy provided by academic medicine (doctors) in many cases leads to death, and the takeover of the treatment process by someone outside the medical profession (a quack) is punishable. Consequently, professionalism can serve to protect members of the profession in the labor market, giving them status, power, and money. At the same time, the social construction associated with professionalism is so important in the organization of relationships between transactors (Freidson, 2001, p. 60) that it is mentioned on par with the market relationship described by Adam Smith, in which consumers exercise control over the work done by suppliers, and on par with Max Weber's bureaucratic relationship, where control is exercised by managers (Andreasson et al., 2018, p. 25). The profession differs from these two forms of relationship in that it is the professionals themselves, i.e., the performers, who control the tasks they perform. Professionals, who are mere technicians, must serve their clients. They can practice as "freelancers," and they can advise clients based on their knowledge, but they must largely follow the instructions of those who pay them and accept their choices. In contrast, members of the true profession can modify the requirements of their clients and even make decisions for them and act against their will (Freidson, 2001, p. 122; Salvatore et al., 2018, p. 776). An example of the latter action is asking the court to incapacitate patients when they refuse to undergo necessary medical procedures.

The professional ideology of service thus goes much further than fulfilling the wishes of clients; it serves higher goals and derives its legitimacy from serving higher values, such as justice, truth, health, and life. Therefore, the profession can claim the right to act independently and evaluate its effects, instead of faithful service (Freidson, 2001, p. 122). It should be noted that in the remainder of the monograph, reference to the profession will usually mean the professional group of doctors; nurses, pharmacists, and laboratory technicians are strictly subordinate to doctors and must be commissioned by doctors to do their work, since mostly doctors can prescribe reimbursable drugs and order diagnostics and therapeutic technologies.

As mentioned, despite the differences between the two distinguished forms of hospital organization (centralized single-headed and centralized double-headed), their common feature is that they are organized along the lines of bureaucratic institutions, with a functional diversified structure. However, hospital bureaucracies, due to the nature of the tasks they perform and the characteristics of the main performers of these tasks, i.e., medical professionals, differ significantly from this traditional bureaucracy. The first to point out this difference was H. Mintzberg, distinguishing between mechanical bureaucracy and professional bureaucracy (1980, p. 333), and M. Lipsky, calling it street-level bureaucracy (1971; Lipsky & Hill, 1993). Although initially M. Lipsky referred to the provision of professional services to the mass customer, such as security (police) and education, the concept also partially reflects the relationship in health care (Hupe & Hill, 2016, p. 61). The distinction between two types of bureaucracy – Weberian, also called machine bureaucracy, and professional bureaucracy, including street-level bureaucracy – is crucial, as it is the type of bureaucracy that has a significant impact on how management and management control are carried out.

Weberian bureaucracy and professional bureaucracy differ primarily in the source of the origin of standardization. Traditional bureaucracy generates its own standards by creating a technical structure and designing work standards and various types of organizational (internal) laws. Professional bureaucracy standards, on the other hand, derive largely from generally available scientific knowledge and recommendations from self-governing professional associations, which are located and legally empowered outside the organization's structure. Employees of professional bureaucracies have similar goals and standards to their colleagues in other professional bureaucracies. Thus, while machine bureaucracies rely on authority of a hierarchical nature – the power of the office – professional bureaucracies emphasize authority of a professional nature – the power of knowledge (Abernethy & Stoelwinder, 1990, p. 20; Mintzberg, 1993a, p. 192).

Professional bureaucracy therefore requires coordination in terms of skill standardization, training, and socialization. This is the situation in hospitals, where professionals have well-defined skills and have learned how to expertly perform their tasks. As a result, the work is highly specialized horizontally. Control over one's own work means that the specialist works relatively independently of his colleagues but closely with the clients he serves (Mintzberg, 1993a, p. 190). For example, a doctor works alone in his office, relatively hidden from his colleagues and superiors, so he has wide autonomy in dealing with patients. Especially since access to medical records, one of the outcomes of the patient encounter, is severely restricted not only for superiors in the administrative line, but also to some extent professionally. In such a decentralized environment, it is crucial to ensure an adequate level of control to monitor, at least to some extent, what medical professionals are doing, what results they are achieving, and how they can be motivated and disciplined (Hupe & Hill, 2016, p. 61).

Therefore, training within the professional bureaucracy has one goal – to internalize standards that serve clients and coordinate professional work. Therefore, a professional bureaucracy has a clear bottom-up method of decision making, in which both independent professionals and strategic managers must accept proposed changes (Andreasson et al., 2018, p. 26). This means that a professional bureaucracy can be a highly democratic structure, at least for professionals. In fact, professionals can not only control their own work, but also take collective control over administrative decisions that affect them, such as the hiring of colleagues, their promotion, and the distribution of resources. This results in the emergence of parallel administrative hierarchies: a bottom-up, democratic one for professionals and a top-down, hierarchical one for support staff (Mintzberg, 1993a, p. 198). With regard to hospitals, P. du Gay and K.Z. Pedersen (2020, p. 222) argue that classical bureaucratic dependencies are not incompatible with the exercise of professional autonomy.

In general, managers in professional bureaucracies, especially those at higher levels, play key roles at the boundaries of the organization, between professionals inside the organization and external stakeholders, i.e., representatives of the governing bodies – owners, the government, patient associations. On the one hand, professionals expect managers to protect their autonomy and "buffer" them from external pressures, and, on the other hand, they expect managers to solicit external support for the organization, both in terms of gaining external legitimacy and in terms of raising funds for operations. Thus, the manager's role largely consists of maintaining external contacts, acting as a public relations spokesperson, and negotiating with external agencies, such as public and private contributors. This leads to a situation where doctors' ability to order expensive diagnostics and therapies depends on the manager's effectiveness.

The considerations outlined above indicate the complex nature of the relationship between professionals and managers in hospitals, which leads to tensions between the manager and medical professional. This is because in enterprises, the top management has the authority to accept or reject the recommendations of the managers of the various functional departments and professionals to ensure the integration of these functions to achieve compatible and purposeful management control. In health care, on the other hand, the top management has neither the authority nor the right to interfere in the activities of specialists. Nor is it in a position to either evaluate or inspect the diagnosis issued and treatment recommended, no matter how costly it might be. These tensions are considered by some researchers to be the reason for the inability to improve quality and reduce costs in health care (Garelick & Fagin, 2005, p. 241; Waldman & Cohn, 2007, p. 27). They call for dialogue and cooperation between professionals and managers, pointing to their shared values of altruism, service, and overcoming challenges (Waldman & Cohn, 2007, p. 40).

The tension between professionals and managers is largely due to the strong political pressure to increase efficiency and reduce costs in hospitals as well as to the significant differences in the nature of the work and areas of responsibility between the two roles (Witman et al., 2010, p. 478). Managers are more interested in organizational aspects, such as efficiency, cost savings, and cost containment, while professionals are more focused on providing medical care (de Campos et al., 2017, p. 293). Studies have shown that the differences between the doctor's role and the manager's role are significant. The doctor's role is to focus on individual patients, solve current problems quickly, and take a scientific approach, while the manager's role is to focus on groups, politics and human motivations, seek efficiency, and accept situations where some problems are unsolvable (Table 1.2). Thus, professionals are autonomous reactive "doers" and decision-makers prepared to react immediately, and managers are participatory designers prepared to collaborate, delegate tasks, and share responsibility (Les MacLeod, 2012, p. 13).

In general, a certain level of conflict between managers and doctors is directly related to the structure of modern health-care systems. The task of senior hospital managers is to bring stronger public control of professionals into health care, based on performance indicators, management by objectives, and medical processes based on evidence and clinical guidelines (Kuhlmann et al., 2013, p. 2). Managers also have a powerful weapon in the form of integrated information systems capable of collecting and processing

Table 1.2. Differences between the role of a physician and the role of a manager

Physicians	Managers
Focus attention on individual patients	Focus on population groups
Not primarily concerned with costs	Focus on efficiency and resources
Contact patients face to face	Rarely meet patients or their families
Are expected to solve all problems	Choose the problems to be solved
Are trained to be independent and competitive	Expect to share responsibility
Present a scientific approach	Deal with politics and human motivations
Poorly tolerate unsolvable problems	Tolerate many unsolvable problems
High loyalty to a professional group	Low loyalty to a professional group
Loyal to patients	Loyal to the organization
Significant clinical autonomy	Little autonomy, dependence on rules and procedures
Evaluation of work results confidential (medical confidentiality)	Evaluation of work results available to the public
High social and professional status	Medium social and professional status

Source: Adapted from (Les MacLeod, 2012, p. 13; Davies, 2000, p. 116).

large amounts of medical and cost data, the use of which is capable of creating "disciplined doctors" (Reich, 2012, p. 1021).

Pressure from governments to contain cost growth is leading to a situation where top hospital management is trying to carry this pressure deep into the organizational structure and force medical professionals to reduce costs and increase productivity and efficiency. In hospitals, it is not managers, but medical department managers (heads) in professional roles and subordinate bedside professionals who must take these pro-efficiency measures. Thus, managers involve physicians in bureaucratic mechanisms (e.g., developing guidelines, implementing clinical pathways), as well as economic matters related to management, revenue, and hospital costs. Managers push doctors to engage not only in individual patient problems, which they are trained to do and which is the essence of their work, but also to have the survival of the entire organization in mind. Under these conditions, it is expected that tighter control will increase the responsibility of professionals for the safety of society (Lambert et al., 2006) and the cost of health care, reducing or at least limiting the rate of their growth, which has been higher than the rate of GDP growth in the EU-15 and in the United States for many years (Oliveira Martins & de la Maisonneuve, 2013). However, it is difficult to find evidence that neoliberal policies based on the principles of new public management and the introduction of professional managers into the roles of hospital leaders increase control over doctors, limit the high autonomy and independence of specialists employed at the operational level (Salter, 2007; von Knorring et al., 2010), and improve the efficiency of health care (Bach, 1994; Manning, 2001; Kuhlmann et al., 2013). It seems fair to say that new regulatory tools, such as clinical guidelines, and evidence-based medicine may also increase the power of the profession, since doctors are the experts who develop the scientific evidence and medical guidelines on which policy decisions are made (Kuhlmann & Burau, 2008).

As mentioned, one of the relatively frequently mentioned fields of conflict between doctors and managers is the focus on different areas of hospital management. G. Laffel and D. Blumenthal (1989, p. 2871) state that most quality assurance programs in health care focus exclusively on the technical knowledge and interpersonal skills of physicians, and little attention is paid to other ways of creating quality, such as effective organization and the ability to mobilize internal or external resources. In addition, it is noted that cultural differences between physicians and managers in hospitals are related to how quality management initiatives are accepted and implemented, which is reflected in hospital performance levels (Klopper-Kes, 2011, p. 14).

The relationship between physicians and managers can also be considered from an institutional perspective, which makes an important contribution to understanding the behavior of important professional groups in a highly institutionalized setting, such as health-care organizations, among others (Andersen, 2008, p. 55; Eldenburg et al., 2017, p. 60). It is pointed out that each of the most important orders of modern societies has a central logic, that is, a set of material practices and symbolic constructs that constitutes its organizational principles (Powell & DiMaggio, 2012, p. 248). In health care, there are at least two competing logics: the logic of the medical profession and the logic of management (Andersson & Liff, 2018, p. 72). The logic of the medical profession is also called professional logic or medical logic, and it basically applies only to physicians (cf.: (Ramsdal & Bjørkquist, 2019, p. 1723; Reay & Hinings, 2009, p. 630)). Managerial logic is also often interchangeably referred to as business logic (Reay & Hinings, 2009, p. 630). The two logics are quite different from each other (more in: (Lewandowski & Sułkowski, 2018)), which is particularly important in analyses involving hospitals.

Institutional theory in the study of management control mainly focuses on isomorphic pressures and irrationality (Lounsbury, 2008, p. 350), but this is at odds with contemporary views of hospital performance (Lewandowski & Sułkowski, 2018). With the advent of theories on institutional logics, the view of the organization through the prism of homogeneity and bounded rationality could be replaced by a combination of organizational heterogeneity and rationality. In this sense, the perspective of institutional logics encompasses organizations and explains not only homogeneity, but also heterogeneity, which it is able to explain in terms of organizational practices, providing a more conclusive perspective of causality (Damayanthi & Gooneratne, 2017, p. 525).

The concept of institutional logic, which evolved from institutional theory, is an important theoretical construct that explains the creation of a sense of common purpose and unity within a certain area, referring to a set of belief systems and related practices that shape people's cognition and behavior, being "the basis of rules taken for granted" (Reay & Hinings, 2009, p. 629). Institutional logics can be defined as "socially constructed, historical patterns of cultural symbols and material practices, assumptions, values and beliefs through which individuals produce and reproduce their material existence, organize time and space, and make sense of their daily activities" (Thornton et al., 2012, p. 51). In addition, institutional logics are "practices and symbols that are available to individuals, groups and organizations, which can be further developed, manipulated and used for their own benefit" (Friedland & Alford, 1991, p. 232). Each institutional logic consists of elementary categories (building blocks) that represent the cultural symbols and material practices characteristic of the individual. These building blocks define the organizational rules that shape individual and organizational preferences and interests, and the behavioral repertoire through which interests and preferences are achieved in the sphere of influence of a particular order. Theoretically, these elements categorize how individuals and organizations, influenced by any institutional order, can understand their sense of self-identity and identification, that is: who they are, their logic of action, their vocabularies of motives, and what language is most relevant to them (Thornton et al., 2012, p. 54). Institutional logic gives identity and meaning to actors operating within an area, such as treatment or management (Skelcher & Smith, 2015, p. 437), and influences the strategy, structure, and practices of organizations (Greenwood et al., 2011). Institutional logic, having material, cultural, and symbolic elements, can provide normative guidelines for social actors and explain how to interpret organizational reality, e.g., what constitutes appropriate behavior, what constitutes success, what are its symbols? The logic of the medical profession, for example, may emphasize autonomy and the pursuit of quality without necessarily drawing attention to efficiency and cost, while business logic may emphasize efficiency as well as quality, but in direct relation to the strategic position of the product or service in the market and its price (Lewandowski & Sułkowski, 2018, p. 149; Reay & Hinings, 2009, p. 630).

In Poland, until the 1990s, doctors ruled hospitals indivisibly, dominating hospitals with their institutional logic – the logic of medical professionals. The placing of managers at the head of hospitals and the change in the health-care financing formula in 1999, from budget financing to financing based on the number and type of services provided, resulted in the entry of business logic into the jurisdiction of medical professionals (Lewandowski & Sułkowski, 2018, p. 152). Funding on the basis of services rendered is intended to encourage hospitals with monetary "rewards" to allocate resources in a more "market-based" manner, thereby introducing business logic, albeit in a highly indirect and decentralized manner (Abernethy et al., 2006, p. 807). The introduction of business logic has redefined and expanded the perception of health care, no longer just as a social issue, but also an economic one. Health care is no longer a medical issue belonging exclusively to medical professionals, but it has become an economic issue in which economists, managers, financiers, and accountants also play major roles. This results in a situation where hospitals, to a large extent, acquire the characteristics of businesses and must focus on reducing costs and increasing revenues. Although managerial logic contradicts the traditional humanitarian role of medicine, it is not possible to exempt medical professionals from management control based on economic performance, since they are the main operational staff, and it is primarily on their activities that the performance of medical entities depends.

Currently, doctors have to deal with the conflicting demands of professional and managerial logic (Ramsdal & Bjørkquist, 2019, p. 1723; Reay & Hinings, 2009). For example, some hospitals use case-mix tariffs (JGPs) to screen patients and then pressure physicians to admit only those patients deemed "profitable" under this approach (Lewandowski, 2014, p. 132). Managers at some hospitals are also implementing specialized software to advise and control physicians on the use of optimizing hospital length of stay and appropriate medical procedures for patients in the context of their clinical condition (diagnosis codes) to maximize revenue from the payer (Samuel et al., 2005, p. 250).

When discussing the concept of professionalism, it is also important to note that it is built on two basic assumptions. First, the work is so specialized that it can only be performed by those who have specialized (very extensive) training and relevant experience, and second, the work cannot be standardized or rationalized because it is too complex (Freidson, 2001, p. 17). These assumptions not only limit the performance of certain work to members of the profession, but also give the profession the exclusive right to supervise this work and evaluate its results (Freidson, 2001, p. 84; Noordegraaf, 2020, pp. 206–207).

The domination of professions in the labor market is only possible if there is a widespread belief that the work that professionals do is so different from the work done by others that autonomy in daily work and the resulting self-control are justified. The dominance of the professions is as strong as their clients will allow them to be, and as strong as the professionals are protected by legal arrangements (Abbott, 1988, p. 141). Formal institutions and regulations determine the economic and social conditions under which professionals can control their own work. Ideology, on the other hand, is what makes society tolerate and even support the institutionalization of the profession. For neither economic power nor political power is inherent in knowledge and skill (Freidson, 2001, p. 105). In hospitals, doctors' autonomy in daily practice includes control over four main areas:

1. diagnosis and treatment – decisions on the choice of methods of diagnosis and treatment, to whom to refer and where, which drugs and procedures to use;
2. evaluation of care – judgments about the appropriateness of care for a particular patient or general patterns of care provided;
3. the type and number of medical tasks – the ability of doctors to avoid control, decisions on the extent to which doctors can independently set their own work schedule, priorities and workload;
4. independence related to taking up work – refers directly to features of doctors' employment contracts, decisions on the extent to which clinicians have autonomous rights to take up activities outside their main duties, such as research, teaching, work in scientific associations, private practice, especially during working hours (Davies & Harrison, 2003, p. 647).

The aforementioned areas have a significant impact on both the direct costs of treating patients associated with the medical technologies used and the productivity of the specialists employed by the hospital. Broad autonomy within the aforementioned four scopes makes it very difficult, and sometimes even illusory, for managers to exercise control over doctors. The problem of measuring the performance of the profession is all the more complex because medical professionals defend their autonomy precisely against the possibility of measuring their performance. This defense stems from the fact that an important element affecting the position of the profession in the workplace and society is precisely the measurability of results. When the results of work are easily measurable, giving those outside the profession the opportunity to evaluate them, the risk of losing the profession's control over an area increases, as it makes it easier for competitors to demonstrate the superiority of their treatment, if, of course, such an advantage exists (Abbott, 1988, p. 46). The example relatively most often cited in this context is the increasing annexation by physiotherapists of areas until recently reserved only for rehabilitation specialists.

The previously indicated recognition by professionals of the control of a course of action (treatment) as one of the most important principles leads to a situation where more complex methods of action are easier to defend, and professions try to apply unique courses of action (treatment), even when the results of individual methods of action cannot be measured and when a universal approach would suffice. In many cases, when doctors fail to make an appropriate diagnosis, they do not abandon the field of activity, admitting their inability to solve the problem, but they give specific recommendations such as "please avoid stress, get plenty of rest, eat healthy, reduce excess weight, take moderate physical activity at least an hour a day (walking out-doors or cycling) and come see me in a month." In this approach, even the complete ineffectiveness of specialized treatment does not lead to its aban-donment. It is needed for competitive reasons, as it allows the area of medi-cal activity to be defended against all sorts of quacks and healers (Abbott, 1988, p. 46).

The profession constantly needs to justify its privileged position. It must neutralize oppositional ideologies that provide arguments in favor of solu-tions aimed at controlling the work of professionals by the market or the bureaucracy, i.e., managers (Freidson, 2001, p. 106; Noordegraaf, 2020). This is due to the belief that the mere possession of exclusivity in a certain area already gives enormous power to the extent that the public accepts the definitions of a medical problem and good treatment results proposed by the incumbent (incumbent) profession (Abbott, 1988, p. 136). An example of such a state can be found in physiotherapy, which has developed its own methods of diagnosis and treatment, but is at a disadvantage in relation to the incumbent medical profession. According to the solutions adopted in Poland, a physiotherapist can provide publicly funded outpatient therapy on the basis of a referral from a family doctor, who often does not have the appropriate competence (training) in physiotherapy. In this case, although other doctors are not able to demonstrate their positive contribution to treatment, the very legal entrenchment of the profession gives them a huge advantage. Thus, maintaining the impediments to performance measure-ment, especially from outside the profession, is crucial for the profession, since its power comes precisely from the right to define the problem and to measure the results and quality of treatment as well as from the lack of comparisons.

1.4 Past Efforts to Improve Hospital Efficiency

The unique characteristics of hospitals described earlier make increasing efficiency and limiting the growth of health-care costs very difficult. For example, total (public and private) health spending in the European Union has been steadily increasing and consumes a significant portion of member states' resources. On average, this spending has increased from 7.1% of GDP in 1980 to 9.9% in 2017. A steady increase in spending is also observed in inpatient treatment (Schwierz, 2016), which is a significant problem when hospitals consume the largest share of all health resources in most European countries, averaging 36.3% of €1.3 trillion (EU-27 in 2017). In Poland, the share of health spending in the GDP has fluctuated around 6.5% in recent years, with spending on inpatient treatment slightly exceeding 30% of all health spending (Miszczyńska & Antczak, 2020, pp. 27–29). Additionally, hospitals, like health care as a whole, are recognized as organizations where phenomena such as waste, unnecessary administrative burdens, errors in the implementation of treatment processes, and even fraud and abuse are relatively frequently identified (Covaleski et al., 1993, p. 74; Samuel et al., 2005, p. 250; Schwierz, 2016; Stadhouders et al., 2019, p. 71). These dysfunctions can lead to significant overspending on health care, which seems to be borne out by the situation in the United States, where it has been estimated that this is about 20% of all health spending (Berwick & Hackbarth, 2012, p. 1513).

Already in the second half of the last century, due to the systematic increase in the cost of health care, especially hospital care, major changes were initiated in both the organization of health care systems and approaches to hospital management (Saltman et al., 2011, p. 2). Some of these were modeled on management strategies used in private companies. These reforms were aimed at introducing more flexible solutions in the area of management that could stimulate greater institutional autonomy, and thus more effective integration of different types of services and increase the overall efficiency of the health-care delivery process (Saltman et al., 2011, p. 3). In many countries reforms were initiated to implement a neoliberal way of managing public hospitals, which can be encapsulated in the concept of new public management (NPM) (Hood, 1991, 1995) or new public administration (more on this issue: (Greenwood et al., 2002)). However, the measures carried out so far to reduce the cost of hospital treatment have yielded unclear results, particularly in the long term (Schwierz, 2016).

As already mentioned, until the 1980s in western Europe (von Knorring et al., 2010, p. 2) and until the 1990s in most post-communist countries, hospitals were indivisibly managed by physicians. However, due to the rising cost of hospital treatment and unsatisfactory quality of services, professional managers were invited to manage these organizations. As a result, cost reduction initiatives were undertaken in two areas. The first concerned reducing the number of patients who end up in hospitals. In Germany alone, it is estimated that 20% of hospitalizations could be avoided if effective prevention and treatment of chronic diseases in outpatient care were implemented (Sundmacher et al., 2015, p. 1422). The second area concerned the introduction of initiatives to stimulate hospitals to be more efficient in providing services. In this regard, such measures have so far been taken:

- entrusting the management of hospitals to professional managers;
- introducing payment systems for hospital services of the case-mix type (e.g., DRG);
- co-payment of patients for certain hospital services;
- linking payments to productivity improvements;
- optimization of employee compensation;
- promoting good practices in public procurement;
- optimizing spending, such as through group purchasing;
- improving staff structure;
- reducing the number of hospital beds;
- strengthening competition among hospitals;
- strengthening the autonomy of hospitals;
- hospital privatization;
- supporting mergers and creating hospital networks;
- promoting public-private partnerships.

Improving the efficiency of health-care delivery by introducing a corporate management structure in medical facilities has given managers formal authority over medical professionals, who previously had undivided control over decision making in hospitals for many decades. However, the results of this initiative are still unclear (Lewandowski & Sułkowski, 2018). Similarly, attempts to contain costs by privatizing hospitals have not clearly proven their effectiveness. Studies in Germany have produced divergent results: either that private ownership is associated with better financial performance than public ownership (Schwierz, 2011) or, conversely, that for-profit hospitals are less efficient than public hospitals (Tiemann & Schreyögg, 2009). In contrast, Y.-C. Shen et al. (2007) found only a small difference in revenue and profitability in favor of for-profit hospitals, although they found no systematic differences in terms of costs and efficiency. However, it should be remembered that encouraging private investment in health care forces greater transparency in the processes of allocating funds and the value of medical services provided, further complicating the health-care system (Klopper-Kes, 2011, p. 12). Other reforms were introduced in Russia but also did not bring positive effects (Lewandowski, 2011).

The aforementioned case-mix (prospective) payment systems, which typically base the number and type of services on the definition of cost clusters – often so-called diagnosis-related groups (DRGs) (Eldenburg et al., 2017, p. 57) – also have some dysfunctions and drawbacks. The system encourages more services, efficiency, and transparency, but it does not necessarily drive hospitals to provide a higher quality of care, as quality is not considered a factor in funding for most systems. Unintended negative consequences of case-mix-based hospital payments include, but are not limited to, selecting the most "profitable" patients, referring remaining patients to other facilities, over-treatment and frequent readmissions, coding additional diagnoses in patients, using the wrong diagnosis or a diagnosis that does not fit the case description, miscoding (reporting treatments or procedures that were not performed), and reordering diagnoses or reporting a secondary diagnosis as the primary diagnosis in cases where this would result in higher reimbursement (Christensen et al., 2006, p. 35).

Patient co-payment mainly contributes to lower overall public spending on health in the short term, with most of the available studies looking at spending on drugs discharged in outpatient care (OECD, 2015). The introduction of co-payments has, on the one hand, reduced the number of hospital visits in almost all countries (Qingyue et al., 2011) but, on the other hand, risks limiting access to care, and thus may have a detrimental effect on the health of entire populations, particularly when demand for many health services is relatively price inelastic (Cutler & Zeckhauser, 2000).

A mechanism designed to increase the efficiency of hospitals is also the introduction of competition among them (Rüsch, 2016, p. 138), which, by design, should improve efficiency, such as through consolidation and reallocation of services, leading to a reduction in excess beds and lower costs for the operation of hospitals and, ultimately, the entire health-care system. However, health-care markets deviate significantly from the theoretical notion of perfectly competitive markets due to, among other things, information asymmetry occurring at as many as three levels (patients, providers, and payers), the wide variety of hospital services, the difficulty of objectively assessing the quality of services, oligopolistic market structures, and barriers to entry and exit (Getzen, 2022). Therefore, achieving the desired benefits requires careful design of the competition framework, especially since its effects depend on a number of health system variables, which include the degree of competition among insurers, the centralization of the health system, the role of insurers, the extent of private hospital services, the range of choices for patients, hospital autonomy, hospital size and market concentration (OECD, 2012). The concept of competition has been exploited in the United States by managed care organizations, which have achieved savings by negotiating prices for services and packages offered by competing hospitals and enrolling patients who can benefit from potentially lower premiums within a specific network of managed care services provided. In the case of the United States, there is some evidence that purchaser competition combined with selective procurement has reduced spending growth (Zwanziger et al., 2000). Increased competition among hospitals resulted in cost containment, higher efficiency, and quality of health care only in the United Kingdom (OECD, 2015). In contrast, no significant effects were observed in the Netherlands and Germany (Schut & Van de Ven, 2011; Shmueli et al., 2015).

However, it should be noted that the conditions for relatively fair competition between public and private hospitals are, in particular, the separation of purchaser and provider functions at the health system level, equal remuneration, and the same approach to the deficit of private and public facilities (Expert Panel on Effective Ways of Investing in Health, 2015). In these efforts, ensuring equal remuneration can be achieved through case-mix (DRG) systems, but this requires careful and continuous calibration to discourage providing services only to "profitable" patients. In a competitive environment, a significant degree of autonomy is also needed for hospitals to make politically difficult decisions, such as restructuring. In addition, hospital market concentration must be well monitored to limit the exploitation of a dominant position in a specific area. In this aspect, attention should be paid to the possibility of strengthening competition between public and private hospitals by allowing private patients to be treated in public hospitals. However, this is a solution with a number of advantages and disadvantages. The advantages of such a solution are the possibility of providing additional income to public hospitals, increasing the spectrum of choices for patients, and making employment more attractive for medical professionals. The main disadvantage, on the other hand, is that treating private patients in public hospitals limits access to care and increases waiting times for public patients (OECD, 2020).

Larger hospitals stand a good chance of lowering their unit costs and providing better quality of care and, thus, achieving better financial results through higher volumes. Because of the effect of scale, larger hospitals can have lower unit costs. However, economies of scale are already fading in hospitals with more than 100 beds. This is a result of problems arising from increasing organizational complexity, which can cause management inefficiencies (Schwierz, 2016, p. 58). Research in this area shows that mergers have not resulted in increased technical efficiency (Kristensen et al., 2010), nor have they resulted in economies of scale and significant quality improvements, although they have had an impact on promoting cooperation between specialties (Ahgren, 2008). Based on an international comparison, there is limited evidence that hospital consolidation has improved hospital quality and efficiency (Nolte et al., 2014), although the latter is explained by the fact that most hospital markets are geographically small and thus merged hospitals can abuse their dominant position (Ashenfelter et al., 2011). By taking advantage of their dominant position, hospitals can force increased funding, which can counteract cost containment.

Some countries also introduce nationwide standards (most often in the form of mandatory measures) that medical facilities should adhere to, otherwise they are penalized financially. An example is the rate introduced in the United Kingdom of patients waiting no longer than four hours in hospital emergency departments. However, studies have shown that setting ambitious goals in one area leads to reduced activity in another (Glasziou et al., 2012, p. 2). In the case of the United Kingdom, the introduction of this indicator resulted in the shifting of staff from other areas of the hospital to emergency departments and the cancellation of some planned operations, among other things. Thus, it should be noted that, to date, a number of different tools have been introduced to reduce operating costs and improve hospital efficiency. However, there is a lack of scientific evidence on the impact of individual tools or combinations of tools on better hospital performance. Many of the reforms mentioned above are widely used and have been proven to help control costs in the short term, but their long-term impact is more difficult to determine.

An important factor that makes it difficult to assess the effects of the introduced reforms is the permanent development of health care, including hospitals, which makes the historical data used in the study as a reference point for comparison rather imprecise. This is because it should be remembered that the aforementioned development is also associated with the expansion of the number of medical specialties and their dynamic development (e.g., cardiac surgery, neonatology, interventional cardiology, transplantation), as well as with changes in the level of quality and an increase in the number of non-medical personnel. In recent decades, some hospitals in Poland have developed into powerful organizations with up to several thousand employees, with budgets reaching hundreds of millions of zlotys (Table 1.1). In most Western countries, hospitals are even larger, employing up to tens of thousands of people each and disposing of sums well in excess of a billion euros a year.

In Poland, too, there have been many reforms in recent decades aimed at improving the quality and efficiency of hospital care. In the first phase of Polish reforms, by 1999, hospitals were transformed from budgetary establishments directly subordinate to the state into independent public healthcare institutions (IPHI) subordinate mostly to local governments. They are legal entities largely similar in structure to commercial companies, however, with one key difference – they cannot go bankrupt. Any debts of the IPHI that threaten its operation must be covered by the creating entity, in most cases the local government.

In contrast, from the perspective of hospital financing, the reform introduced two major changes. First, paying hospitals based on the number and type of services provided, instead of funding based on historical budgets. Second, competition among hospitals. To access public funds for treatment, hospitals had to participate in competitions. These changes triggered quasi-market mechanisms in place of purchasing services based on planning. The correlation of hospital revenues with the number and type of services provided introduced great pressure to provide more and more existing medical services and introduce new ones, on the one hand, and to reduce costs and be more efficient, on the other. This quasi-market pressure has forced hospital developers to abandon the previously used hospital management based on clinical leadership in favor of a more productivity and economic performance-oriented approach. This approach has paved the way for managers to become hospital CEOs. This does not mean that physicians cannot manage hospitals in Poland, but those physicians who still wanted to do so were forced to complete their education in the areas of economics and management and to significantly reduce their clinical role in favor of a managerial role since the efficacy of managers in hospitals depends not on formal training but on certain key competencies (Wysocka & Lewandowski, 2017).

In order to increase the pressure on the management and employees of hospitals, some creating entities, with intense encouragement from the government, have decided to convert IPHI into commercial companies. This solution, from the point of view of the owning entity, has several advantages; it frees the owning entity from liability for debts, opens the way to bankruptcy, and increases the pressure on the manager (CEO) of such a hospital-corporation by imposing certain property liability in the event of the hospital's insolvency. Years later, however, it can be concluded that none of the solutions applied have resulted in a clear improvement in the performance of hospitals. Both in the group of hospitals transformed into commercial companies and in the group of those still remaining in the legal form of IPHI, there are those that balance their costs with revenues and those that are permanently in debt. Similar results were obtained in the present study (Table 4.5).

The lack of visible improvement in the performance of hospitals converted to companies prompted the next government to move away from further commercialization of hospitals, and a reduction in the intensity of competition among hospitals, in favor of a greater role for planning the structure of services and more stable financing through the introduction of a system of basic hospital provision of health-care services, the so-called hospital network. This approach is in line with Post-New Public Management, characterized by a shift away from pressure for privatization and marketization of public services, toward greater oversight and broader regulation (Hood et al., 1999, pp. 191–193). This manifests itself in a shift toward "enforced self-regulation," reflecting a new "soft bureaucracy" in which central control is exerted through protocols and guidelines and less through centralized top-down management over the operational details of hospital operations (Dent, 2005, p. 626). In Poland, this approach reveals itself in the imposition of staffing standards (e.g., the number of nurses per bed) or the centralized setting of salary levels for an increasing number of professional groups in hospitals. However, these solutions, so far, have not had a fundamental impact on improving the financial performance of Polish hospitals (Table 1.1 and Table 1.2). The research concerning identification of different control areas and mechanisms, which have been used by hospital managers to ensure delivery of high-quality cost-effective patient care and balance the hospital budget, shows that managers can control four generic areas (354Lewandowski, 2014, p. 133):

1. Input control, associated with the appropriate selection of patients: (a) control of the selection in the emergency room of "instant," "urgent," and "elective"; (b) training of primary care physicians on how to properly diagnose and classify patients for treatment; (c) control of the cost-revenue balance of elective patients;
2. Legitimacy of medical procedures control during the process of care: (a) consumption of drugs, in terms of treatment process – its necessity; (b) necessity of applied diagnostic procedures (oversupply avoidance);
3. Revenue control: (a) control of completeness of reporting to the payer; (b) control of the possibilities of optimal settlement depending on the

department (medical specialties), in which the patient could be treated; (c) control of the possibility of obtaining the payment from the payer for patients treated over the limit in a lawsuit;

4. Control of the overall hospital costs, including: (a) cost of drugs and other medical materials, focusing on the use of lower-cost substitutes and on negotiating lower prices from suppliers; (b) downward pressure on the reduction of cost of employed staff, maintenance of medical equipment, cost of capital, etc.

The considerations presented above show that it is difficult to find a single factor or group of factors that are unambiguously related to the financial situation of hospitals. Hospitals, as it has been pointed out, are extremely complex institutions enmeshed in a complex network of interrelationships of the health-care system, so the search for simple relationships and correlations between factors makes it much more difficult to obtain and deepen knowledge in this area. Therefore, it is reasonable to undertake efforts to search for a new scientific perspective that will enable the construction of multidimensional models, at least in part corresponding to the complex nature of hospitals. If we consider the unsuccessful initiatives presented in earlier subsections regarding the operation of hospitals, one of the essential areas for improving the efficiency of hospitals' delivery of medical services appears to be the proper use of management control.

Chapter 2

Control in Management Sciences

2.1 Origins and Definitions of Control in the Literature

Although control as a separate management function was identified by H. Fayol in the first decade of the last century (Wren et al., 2002, p. 916), there is still no consensus in the scientific community on its definition. There is also the concept of coordination in the literature. To some extent, control and coordination have different meanings, as in the case of controlling performance or the degree of achievement of objectives as opposed to the coordination and synchronization of activities. However, in this work, control and coordination will not be distinguished. Indeed, it has been accepted as correct to say that "Although much of the organization behavior literature uses the term co-ordination rather than control, co-ordination involves control as much as co-ordination and can be considered 'to be the same in principle'" (Abernethy & Stoelwinder, 1990, p. 19). Over the course of the century, a considerable number of definitions of control have emerged within the management and quality sciences.

H. Fayol, conceptualizing the functions of management, understood control as monitoring whether everything is done in accordance with the adopted plan, issued instructions and established rules (Wren & Bedeian, 2009, p. 227). This definition of control is also in line with the scientific management promoted by F.W. Taylor, assuming that in most management situations one should be guided by causal logic and economic objectives, and that problems related to the organization of work, control and relations

DOI: 10.4324/9781003366553-2

in the enterprise should be treated as "technical" problems (1903). A common feature of the early definitions of control was its restriction to checking whether the output[1] is in line with the accepted standards (2004). In the first half of the 20th century, control tended to be seen as separate processes for individual organizational tasks, for example, financial control, cost control, production control, sales control, inventory control, personnel control (Eilon, 1961, p. 13).

Early theories of control include Max Weber's theory of bureaucracy, which has made a substantial contribution to the development of management science and is still relevant today (du Gay & Pedersen, 2020; Cockerham, 2015; Weber, 2009). Weber pointed out that organizations arranged along bureaucratic lines base control on a set of rules and norms of behavior, as well as personal supervision and direction by superiors (those higher up the organizational hierarchy) within the framework of their formal authority. Formal authority (also called rational-legal authority) gives the person holding it the right to give orders and exercise control. These standards and rules can be changed only through a well-defined process, also described in this set of rules. These rules may include standards for the quantity and quality of the work to be done and instructions on how to proceed with particular tasks. The right to exercise control in a bureaucracy is vested in those people – the officials (this is what Weber called the employees of a bureaucratic organization) who are at the appropriate hierarchical level, according to the principle of superiority and inferiority, or who perform the relevant control functions as defined in the rules and norms assumed in the organization – who have formal authority.

Decisions taken in a bureaucracy are scrutinized for their compliance with rules and norms regardless of who issued them and at what hierarchical level. Thus, before execution, each decision is checked for legality, i.e., for compliance with the institution's rules and whether the official at a given hierarchical level had the right to issue it (Ritzer, 2020). In an ideal bureaucracy, employees are only subject to their superiors higher up in the hierarchy, and only to the extent that this is specified in the organizational rules and in the roster of their job duties. Thus, it is control within the hierarchy, based on formal rules, that is the key element of bureaucracy, ensuring its effectiveness. Bureaucracy and bureaucratic control can function as an irresistible force of high rationality that is able to dominate and absorb all other forms of control, and, once established, it is very difficult to overcome (Barker, 1993, p. 410).

In the bureaucracy model, control is an implicit element, sewn into the organizational structure (hierarchy, authority, and impersonal rules). However, if one looks at the organization from a broader perspective, the control system appears to consist of two parts: (1) a set of preconditions governing the form of control to be applied, and (2) the control system itself, which mainly consists of a process of monitoring and performance evaluation. The preconditions determine the reliability and validity with which comparisons can be made (information system). From this perspective, management control is essentially a process of monitoring something, comparing it to some standard, and then providing selective rewards and adjustments (Kruis, 2008, p. ii).

It was not until the late 1950s that control was recognized as a separate subject area with its own distinctive research and conceptual apparatus. Previously, control principles were most often developed for a specific factory and then propagated, whereas in the 1950s research began to be conducted in many organizations simultaneously, comparing the control systems found there and building models of control (Deverell, 1967; Strong & Smith, 1968; Villers, 1964). While conducting research in many organizations, A.S. Tannenbaum rightly paid attention to the interactions between people in the organization, in particular between different hierarchical levels (1956, p. 53). He argued, similarly as R. Likert, that more intensive control does not necessarily mean blocking the creative invention and commitment of employees (Tannenbaum, 1962, p. 256); on the contrary, the large number of interactions resulting from control leads to a more integrated social system (McMahon & Perritt, 1973). More contemporary research has also reached similar conclusions that:

> controls implemented in the organization that already had many procedural controls were generally perceived more positively than those implemented in the organization that had less in place. Finally, controls implemented in departments accustomed to them (e.g.: R&D) were perceived more positively than controls implemented in departments with less (e.g.: marketing).
>
> **(Tessier & Otley, 2012, p. 175)**

R. Likert also drew attention to two aspects related to control: the total level of control in the organization and the system of interaction and influence. Indeed, it turns out that organizations with higher levels of control and more interaction between managers and subordinates and horizontal interactions show greater sensitivity and openness on the part of each member of the organization to the influence of others, resulting in better performance (1960). At the same time, an increase in people's ability to control their work does not result in a decrease in supervisory control over them by managers. Thus, an increase in the intensity of control in an organization results not only in higher levels of morale within groups, but also in increased commitment, motivation, and productivity (1958). This finding has proven true for most large service and manufacturing organizations.

In general, however, an increase and wider spread of control in the organization helps to distribute a sense of commitment to the organization. On the whole, the diffusion of norms, measured in terms of homogeneity in employee behavior, is more pronounced in departments with high levels of total control (Tannenbaum, 1962, p. 256). The relationship between the total intensity of control in an organization and its effectiveness makes the focus on control a source of satisfaction and a basis for the psychological integration of individuals into the system. Exercising control reinforces participation, which can increase motivation, commitment, and loyalty; moreover, it makes participants more submissive to control, since identification with the organization and loyalty resulting from participation are the reasons for individuals' favorable response to attempts to act for the good of the organization that might otherwise be ignored (McMahon & Perritt, 1973, p. 626).

It can be noted that as early as the late 1950s, control was also viewed as an interdependent system involving the entire organization. However, this view framed control in a very formalized way and distinguished three phases: (1) the legislative phase; (2) the administrative phase, which is related to the distribution of legislative decisions; (3) the sanction phase, which consists of punishment for actions that do not comply with the adopted legislation (Tannenbaum, 1956, p. 52). Referring to research in this area, A.S. Tannenbaum also pointed out that control carries two fundamental consequences: pragmatic and symbolic. Pragmatically, control signifies something a person must do or something he or she cannot do, the constraints to which he or she is subject, and defines his or her areas of choice and freedom. In the symbolic area, on the other hand, it characterizes a person's place in the system of control, indicating who controls whom and by whom they are controlled, and it can imply their superiority or inferiority, dominance or submissiveness, and exposure to criticism (1962, p. 240). Thus, control also has a particular psychological significance for those involved in it and is emotionally charged.

Many authors have pointed out that control is inseparable from power and domination. For example, A. Etzioni regarded control as the equivalent of power and distinguished between three means of coercion to control people's behavior: physical punishment, material means, and symbolic means, such as prestige, respect, love or acceptance. Consequently, he defined control as "a distribution of means used by an organization to elicit the performances it needs and to check whether the quantities and qualities of such performances are in accord with organizational specifications." (Etzioni, 1965, p. 650). Similarly, G. Salaman and K. Thompson, D.T. Otley and A.J. Berry, and A. Giddens emphasized the importance of the nature of power in organizations, how it is distributed and where it comes from, and the dominant nature of control-inducing submission (1980, p. ix; 1980, p. 231; 1984).

In principle, however, it should be recognized, as early research in this area has already shown, that control is one of the essential information processes that explains the progress made in implementing established plans and the obstacles that occur and how they can be removed (Dornbusch & Scott, 1975). In addition to serving objectives, it is a tool to ensure the organization's effectiveness and efficiency. In effect, control should be regarded as a process by which managers ensure that resources are obtained and used effectively and efficiently in achieving the organization's objectives (Ansari, 1977, p. 102; Anthony, 1965b, p. 17). Significant to this definition is the focus on the coordinating function of control and the emphasis on the need to ensure alignment of employee and organizational goals (Flamholtz et al., 1985, p. 36; Ouchi, 1979, p. 846). From this also follows the recognition of control as the process by which managers ensure that resources are obtained and used effectively and efficiently in pursuit of organizational objectives (Anthony, 1965a, p. 245).

The last definition presented seems to take into account and respond to the needs of the professional bureaucracy in hospitals. Resource acquisition can refer to both internal resources, i.e., increasing the efficiency of medical professionals, and external resources, enabling the acquisition of support for the creation of attractive working conditions in order to retain professionals in the organization and thus achieve its goals. However, although this definition is rather broad and, on the whole, covers a large part of managerial activities, it is still limited to operational control and excludes the control of strategy formulation from the jurisdiction of management control (Langfield-Smith, 2007, p. 754).

An important point regarding the definition of control is the observation that, in principle, only two elements can be controlled: behavior and the output from behavior. In this view, control is "an evaluation process that is based on the monitoring and evaluation of behavior or outputs" (Ouchi, 1977, p. 95), whereby "regardless of whether the control process is based on behavior or on output, it is always the behavior that is the ultimate object of feedback and change" (Ouchi, 1978, p. 175). Indeed, even when the output is measured, true control is still about behavior, since evaluating or rewarding an employee for the results obtained leads to a modification of his/her behavior (Govindarajan & Fisher, 1990, p. 97). This dichotomy of areas of control has already been pointed out by M. Weber, J.G. March, and H.A. Simon, writing that, within a bureaucratic organization, control can be exercised through personal observation or through relevant documentary records (2009, 1958, pp. 136–171).

Given the two variables that characterize the tasks performed by employees – knowledge of transformation processes and the ability to measure work performance – it is possible to determine the control strategy to be used to achieve the objectives (Eisenhardt, 1985, p. 135; Ouchi, 1977, p. 98). When the measurement of work output can be precise and the task can be programmed, meaning that the activities that the worker should perform to achieve satisfactory results can be predicted, and there are no significant deviations during the execution of the task, i.e., the tasks are routine, control can be exercised both on the basis of behavioral assessment and on the basis of the final work output (upper left quadrant in Figure 2.1). This means that if knowledge of the transformation process is high, behavior leading to satisfactory results can be clearly defined. As the knowledge decreases, the control of the behavior becomes more difficult, as an effective behavior cannot be unambiguously defined.

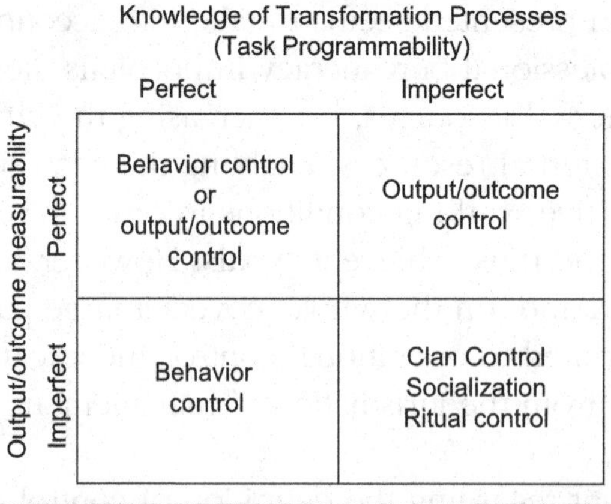

Knowledge of Transformation Processes
(Task Programmability)

	Perfect	Imperfect
Perfect (Output/outcome measurability)	Behavior control or output/outcome control	Output/outcome control
Imperfect (Output/outcome measurability)	Behavior control	Clan Control Socialization Ritual control

Figure 2.1. Types of controls according to the types of tasks performed

When tasks become less programmable, i.e., more stochastic, many non-standard situations may arise that require autonomous decision making based on multiple variables. In this case, only the end result of the completed task can be used as a control strategy. However, outcome-based control can be used only under the assumption that the measurement of these outcomes, i.e., the output of the process, is valid and reliable. If the results are unobservable or unreliable, and therefore not a good predictor of behavior, outcome-based control is not appropriate (Eisenhardt, 1985; Ouchi, 1977, p. 98).

If, on the other hand, performance measurement is ambiguous and tasks are programmable, then the only available control option is to evaluate the behavior (e.g., of registrars in a hospital) of people who have strictly routine tasks to perform and whose performance depends on how many patients turn up at the hospital on a given day and only marginally on their actions. Behavior will, therefore, be assessed here, that is, for example, whether the registrars do not leave their place of work, whether they are polite and helpful, whether they know the procedures in force (bottom left quadrant in Figure 2.1).

When both the outcome measurement is ambiguous and the tasks are complex and non-programmable, i.e., neither outcome nor behavioral control can be carried out, then only ceremonial or ritual forms of control are possible (bottom right quadrant in Figure 2.1).

The approach outlined also identifies situations where rational control is impossible. When performance measurement is ambiguous and tasks are complex and non-programmable, neither performance nor behavioral control can be exercised because the use of incentives to reinforce desired behavior or expected outcomes is impossible, due to the fact that they cannot be identified. This is the area that is relevant to the consideration of the monograph topic. Indeed, hospitals are relatively the most frequently cited organizations in which control of behavior or outcomes is impossible or at least ambiguous (Ouchi, 1979, p. 837). However, it should be emphasized that, in this context, outcome control means that behavior is influenced by specific rewards that are given for the achievement of redefined goals, i.e., the outcome is monitored and behavior is not evaluated as long as it leads to the right outcome. Behavioral control, on the other hand, means that it is the behavior itself that is observed and directly modified. In most organizations, it is difficult to identify situations where the desired behavior or outcome can be unambiguously defined; then organizations can use a mixture of behavioral control and outcome control.

In the context of the considerations carried out, significant importance should also be attributed to the insight of H. Mintzberg, who pointed out that organizational structure involves two basic issues: (1) the division of work into separate tasks, and (2) the achievement of coordination between these tasks. In this approach, coordination is a more complex issue, requiring various measures, such as control, communication and coordination, where five mechanisms for coordinating work in an organization should be distinguished: (1) mutual alignment, (2) direct supervision, (3) standardization of work processes, (4) standardization of work results, and (5) standardization of employee skills (1993b). The coordination mechanisms and components identified here are clearly applicable to hospitals.

Mutual alignment refers to the control of doctors' work by the clinical manager (head of department) through a simple process of informal communication on the hospital ward. In contrast, at a higher hierarchical level, senior management makes one person responsible for the work of others, giving them instructions and monitoring their activities. Standardization of the work process, i.e., the programming of work content, including procedures, standards, and guidelines for medical procedures, is also an example of coordination activities. The standardization of work results, on the other hand, is related to the fact that it enables the indication of a goal, without specifying how to reach this goal. In a hospital, an example would be surgical procedures that may be performed using different methods but lead to a similar outcome. Coordination through standardization of work and standardization of results can be compared to outcome control and behavioral control in Ouchi's model, respectively. However, as business practice shows, there are situations where neither the work nor the results can be standardized, but coordination through standardization may still be required. In such a situation, the skills and knowledge needed to perform the work may be standardized, as is evidenced in the work of doctors (Mintzberg, 1993b, p. 6). This case largely relates to a situation where knowledge of the transformation process is imperfect and measurement of outcomes is very difficult (fourth quadrant in Figure 2.1).

It is important to emphasize that coordination through mutual adjustment, direct supervision, standardization of the work process and work results, and through standardization of knowledge and skills is consequently also behavioral control, except that in each way of coordination there is a different control mechanism. In coordination through mutual adjustment, the control mechanism is the social interaction of the workers with each other. If the work team notices that one of its members is displaying opportunistic behavior, not putting in the right effort for the good of the team, it is likely to take appropriate sanctions against him or her. This is a different approach to the one used in coordination by direct supervision, where the manager is obliged to enforce appropriate behavior, inter alia through the use of formal (rational-legal) authority (in the sense of M. Weber), which is based on the belief in the legality of enacted rules and the right of those in positions of authority under those rules to give orders (Cockerham, 2015, p. 129).

In contrast, in the other three modes of coordination, i.e., standardization of work processes, standardization of work outcomes, and standardization of workers' skills, behavioral control is enforced by the person doing the work. A form of self-control is used here, except that in this self-control it refers to external norms, rules, and codified knowledge (Salvatore et al., 2018, p. 775). In coordination by standardized work processes, it is the instructions and guidelines (usually developed by people other than the performer) that are the reference point for the performer in the self-monitoring process. In coordination by standardized outcomes, knowledge and skills are required to achieve the goal. In medicine, it is often possible to use several approaches to cure a specific disease. In this case, it does not matter which method the doctor has chosen, as long as he or she has achieved the desired result. So here, the result itself is the control mechanism, more specifically, the comparison of the achieved result with the assumed one. The standardization of skills and knowledge comes from external training and an education process based most often on codified knowledge (the formal education process of medical professionals), which the performer refers to when carrying out his or her duties.

Mutual adjustment and direct supervision are based on the social control of colleagues and on the control of the supervisor, who, due to the small size of the team, is able to control the behavior and performance of his subordinates, in principle regardless of the complexity and programmability of the tasks they perform. The problem of conducting control arises with the standardization of work processes, with employee performance and skills, and with the control of non-programmable tasks for which neither performance nor behavioral assessments can be used (Ouchi, 1979, p. 843) – and, as such, occur in hospitals.

As mentioned, coordination based on the standardization of processes and performance as well as knowledge and skills of employees includes a self-monitoring component. This means that an organization cannot easily control the extent to which employees comply with the principles set out in the standard of behavior, performance, or knowledge and skills. This is particularly difficult in health care, where all the specific features of health-care services listed in Chapter 1 are present. In these modes of coordination, the goodwill of employees is implicitly assumed, for while the way of working itself, i.e., adherence to standards, may be less prone to opportunistic behavior, it is the efficiency of the execution of tasks, i.e., the amount of energy and effort, that may be subject to this negative phenomenon in a significant way.

The problem of coordination based on the standardization of work processes and outputs as well as the knowledge and skills of employees is partly solved by agency theory, extending the control models described by W.G. Ouchi and H. Mintzberg to include the concepts of the cost of acquiring information (information as a commodity), the risk associated with the uncertainty of the environment, and the way in which the employee (agent) is remunerated. In W.G. Ouchi's conception, information about the programmability of tasks or the possibility of measuring an outcome is directly derived from the nature of the tasks (1979, p. 843), such as the work of a registrar in a hospital. Similarly, in H. Mintzberg's model of coordination, the possibility of measurement stems from the programmability (codification) of behavior, outcomes, and knowledge and skills. In agency theory, on the other hand, information about an agent's behavior and the results he or she achieves can come from the information system as designed and implemented (Carabalí, 2017, p. 125; Govindarajan & Fisher, 1990, p. 261).

Agency theory, involving the search for the optimal form of control of the agent (in this thesis it is identified with the medical professional) giving maximum benefit to the principal (manager) (Govindarajan & Fisher, 1990, p. 261), highlights two aspects. The first concerns the situation where the objectives of the principal (manager) and the agent (professional) are in conflict, and where it is difficult or expensive to control what the agent actually does. The second relates to the sharing of risks that arise during the execution of tasks. The principal and the agent may prefer to act differently because of the difference in risk attitudes. In general, the relationship between principal and agent (between organization and employee) is considered under the following assumptions:

■ people are focused on their own goals, show limited rationality and are risk averse;
■ in an organization, there are divergent goals among its members;
■ the information needed to conduct inspections is a commodity that can be obtained for a price. (Eisenhardt, 1989a)

In health care, the principal can be identified with the external stakeholders of the hospital, such as the public or private owner or the payer for health-care services. In this configuration, the hospital management acts as an agent (Jiang et al., 2012, p. 145). The principal may also be the top management of the hospital, which has to take countermeasures to increase the transparency of the actions of medical professionals (agents) in order to increase the efficiency of health service delivery (Carabalí, 2017, p. 126; Kerpershoek et al., 2014, p. 420). However, the health-care delivery process is complex and involves clinical and non-clinical staff from different disciplines, and patients treated in hospitals may represent hundreds of different conditions. The clinical processes of care may, therefore, vary considerably depending on the type of condition. Furthermore, patient outcomes are influenced not only by the quality of treatment, but also by other factors, such as genetic predisposition, general health status, and the severity of the patient's illness, among others. Nevertheless, to reduce the potential risk of opportunism by professionals, the directorate must monitor both the process and the outcome of treatment. To do so, it must obtain a broad spectrum of information on various aspects of the hospital. J.V.J. Carabalí and C.R. Thompson and M. McKee have shown that there will always be agency problems in health-care systems because information is naturally asymmetric on many levels when considering the uncertainty that exists in the demand for services and the new technologies that will be available for use in the future (2017, p. 126; 2011).

The problem of control of the principal (manager) over the agent performing the task (medical professional) always arises when the two parties have different goals and there is asymmetry of information. In agency theory, it is the agent who has more information, with the result that the principal cannot directly control whether the agent is acting in his or her best interests. The agency model considers the divergence of preferences among members of an organization (often referred to as "effort aversion"). It assumes that people have preferences for their own actions that are not necessarily consistent with the actions of other members of the organization. In this political view of the organization, the role of control is to provide the means and benefits that allow individuals pursuing their own interests to pursue the collective interest as well (Eisenhardt, 1985, p. 137).

When information about the employee's behavior is readily available, i.e., both the employee and the director know what the employee is doing, then the employee's behavior is a commodity that can easily be valued, for example, a day's work of a registrar in a hospital or an hour's work of an anesthetist in an operating theater. In contrast, in the case of more complex medical activities, such as those related to the treatment of rheumatoid diseases, the time and cost of making a proper diagnosis and treatment cannot be determined. In this case, information about the employee's behavior is not readily available; the employee is aware of his or her behavior, but not the organization. The organization cannot determine whether the employee is behaving appropriately and then tries to control the employee by assessing the employee's performance. Not being able to confirm that the employee's behavior is in line with expectations can lead to a situation where the employee reduces his or her performance. The organization in this situation is unable to discover whether the poorer performance is due to the employee's reduced effort or to unforeseen obstacles that arise in the course of the employee's work, i.e., the uncertainty of the environment.

One way to reduce information asymmetries is also to use participatory control systems, with the assumption that participation is a negotiation process. The employee, having more information about the task being performed than the organization, by participating in the negotiation of the control system, gives the organization part of the information he or she has, which can be included in the standards or budget (Baiman & Evans, 1983). Innovative solutions to increase the efficiency and quality of the tasks performed can also be developed during negotiations.

Agency theory draws attention to the fact that both information about performance and information about the behavior of the organization's members (the agent) have a cost. Thus, in the case of incomplete information, the organization has two options:

- it can buy information about an employee's behavior and reward appropriate behavior.
- it can reward for results, for example, performing a certain number of surgical procedures, reducing the level of in-hospital infections, achieving a certain level of profit or reducing costs.

"Purchasing information" means paying for some kind of oversight mechanism, such as increasing the number of managers at a given management level or levels in the organizational hierarchy or implementing a performance measurement system that allows for the monitoring of multiple metrics, particularly non-financial ones. In the latter option, these results are a substitute for observing behavior.

Ostensibly, rewarding for outcomes that are readily available, such as the number of treatments performed or profit, is less costly than increasing managerial oversight. In the case of pay for performance, the organization does not know how this result has been achieved, e.g., whether more treatments have been performed at the expense of a reduction in service quality, which is not easy to detect in the short term and may jeopardize the organization's existence in the future. In this solution, as a result of the uncertainty of the environment, an employee may be rewarded or penalized for results that do not depend entirely on him or her, e.g., a high profit may depend on the fact that the medical specialty the doctor is dealing with is very well priced by the public payer (for many years interventional cardiology was priced very high in relation to costs), and a loss may result from the fact that patients who came to the department during a given period suffered significant complications, which drastically increased the cost of treatment. The number of procedures performed may also depend on the condition of the patients rather than the effort of the surgeon. These examples direct attention to two issues: the way the employee is remunerated and the sharing of risk between the parties to the relationship.

Opportunistic behavior may increase as goal divergence increases, where actions beneficial to the organization require a great degree of effort and are costly to the employee, and where control of the employee's actions is ambiguous and resource intensive.[2] When comparing the models described earlier, it is important to note that in this situation, the agency theory introduces the remuneration modality as a method to reduce the divergence of interests and goals between the parties to the relationship. It is important to note that if there are no diverging interests between the parties, neither the measurement of this behavior nor the measurement of the results obtained is needed to ensure appropriate agent behavior. Thus, by constructing the right way to reward the employee, the agent can be induced to behave as expected (Merchant & Otley, 2007, p. 786). One way to ensure alignment between the goals of the organization and employees is to introduce performance-related pay (e.g., task-based contracts for doctors, which is in a sense piecework pay linked to the number of procedures performed or the number of DRG points "completed") or to use penalties (e.g., threat of termination). However, since remuneration based on outcome assessment is less costly for the organization than measuring behavior, this reduction in control costs entails transferring some of the risk to the agent (Eisenhardt, 1985, p. 137). Thus, an organization, when looking for the optimal way to reward employees, must consider the level of uncertainty, i.e., the risk of achieving a certain outcome.

In many hospitals, there is remuneration for doctors, particularly surgical specialties, based on civil law contracts, in which the doctor's fee is a certain percentage of the revenue received from the payer for the patients he or she operates on, except that the variable costs of performing the procedures (the cost of the disposable materials used, medicines, the time of the nursing team, the anesthetist, etc.) are deducted prior to calculating the remuneration. In this situation, the doctor is responsible for optimizing the use of disposable materials and medicines and for the length of the procedures. Often, the cost of the team's salary is taken as a working day, while the doctor, the "lead operator," decides on the number of procedures performed that day, and thus regulates the team's unit cost per procedure. Of course, with this type of remuneration, doctors can earn more revenue, except that they take on the risk, for example, of a patient being absent or disqualified for a procedure, as well as of using a higher number of or more expensive disposables and medicines. For the organization, on the other hand, the choice of remuneration method depends on the relationship between the revenue received and the costs in the application of behavioral or outcome controls plus the additional remuneration demanded by the doctor for the risks he or she incurs.

Thus, as can be seen from the considerations so far, management control can be effective when the performance of employees can be measured or when employee behavior can be identified and observed (Eisenhardt, 1985, p. 135; Mintzberg, 1993b, p. 4; Ouchi, 1977, p. 98, 1979, p. 843). The problem arises when both performance measurement and task programmability are imperfect. Such a case occurs, among others, in the knowledge- and skill-based coordination mechanism of employees found in hospitals (Eldenburg et al., 2017, p. 58). While it is possible to standardize and certify staff knowledge and skills through training and licensing systems, controlling the effective use of knowledge and skills during task performance is problematic. This is the situation in the fourth quadrant of Figure 2.1. Here, agency theory proposes investing in a measurement system and, on that basis, shaping incentives to stimulate the achievement of set outcomes or adherence to certain behaviors. Agency theory thus supports the search for an answer to the question of whether contracts oriented toward the use of incentives shaping professional behavior, e.g., remuneration for working time and control using hierarchy and authority, are more effective than contracts oriented toward outcome control, e.g., commissions on the number of JGP billing points performed, a share of the excess of revenue over branch costs, etc. The axis of agency theory is, therefore, to know what is less costly for the organization – controlling employee behavior or measuring performance – considering the cost of the information system and the possible risk premium for the employee. Because measuring performance and rewarding the employee for performance involves transferring the risk of a good outcome to the employee although the employee does not always have a significant influence on the outcome, as the outcome can be determined by many factors, including the work of other departments in the hospital, pricing of services, and time-consuming and expensive-to-treat complications in patients. Performance appraisal can also introduce the danger of an employee taking "shortcuts," leading to an underestimation of the quality of services or seeking savings in areas that are unacceptable to the organization. Agency theory considers the phenomenon of risk aversion, analyzes the level of risk borne by the organization and the employees, and draws attention to the dependence of the multiplicity of risks borne by the parties to the relationship on the shape of that relationship.

In summary, the following assumptions can be made about the context in which the role of principal is played by managers and the role of agent by employees:

■ Employees are mainly driven by their own selfish goals;
■ There is always some level of goal conflict between employees and the organization, but also between employees;
■ The employee's behavior depends on the forms of control and incentives used by the organization (e.g., forms of employment and remuneration);
■ There is uncertainty in the result obtained regardless of the employee's efforts (e.g., an organizational unit may make a profit or incur a loss regardless of employee commitment and effort);
■ The employee and the organization are risk averse and each party tries to shift the risk to the other;
■ An employee's risk increases when he or she is controlled on the basis of performance (e.g., performance-based task contracts for doctors carry a legal risk of liability in addition to the financial risk arising from variable remuneration);
■ The control and performance measurement system influences the employee's behavior, but also the pattern of risk distribution between the employee and the organization;

■ There is an asymmetry of information between the organization (manager) and the employee. The employee has more information regarding the task at hand (moral hazard);
■ Information is an asset that can be acquired at an appropriate cost (e.g., by investing in management accounting, budgeting, additional levels of management, a reporting system, medical consiliums);
■ There is an "agency cost," i.e., the difference between the expected and actual behavior of the employee.

Analyzing agency theory from the perspective of management control in hospitals, it can be concluded that in the absence of certainty of an adequate outcome (mainly as a result of external circumstances, e.g., a change in the valuation of a given procedure) and in the absence of risk aversion on the part of the parties to the agency relationship, the choice between a form of control related to the agent's behavior and a form of control focused on the organization's results comes down only to a comparison of measurement costs (Eisenhardt, 1985, p. 137). In this context, another aspect differentiating outcome and behavioral measurement should be recalled – behavioral (process) measurement. Although useful in health-care settings, it cannot replace outcome measurement because any complex system, such as a hospital, that attempts to control behavior without outcome measurement limits progress and innovation to only small improvements (Porter, 2010b, p. 2478). This is because controlling behavior forces employees to replicate programmed activities, which can lead only to small improvements, e.g., resulting from greater proficiency. In contrast, when results are controlled, then radical and disruptive innovations can occur. In management practice, the choice of form of control also depends on the manager's preferences and his or her subjective assessment of the effectiveness of the various forms of control. It is also worth signaling here that the form of control used in an organization, especially a public organization, may also depend on organizational isomorphism (DiMaggio & Powell, 1983, p. 149; Meyer & Rowan, 1977, p. 346), i.e., what forms of control are considered appropriate by the main external stakeholders.

In general, the approach derived from organizational theory (e.g., Mintzberg, 1993b; Ouchi, 1977, 1979) and the approach derived from economics represented by agency theory (e.g., Carabalí, 2017, p. 125; Eisenhardt, 1989a; Ross, 1973) are complementary. The organizational approach emphasizes the importance of task characteristics, especially the possibility of standardizing them in terms of performance evaluation and the required behavior, skills, and knowledge of employees. It also raises the theme of employee relations in the form of social control as an alternative to control through performance appraisal or behavior. Agency theory, on the other hand, complements the organizational approach with the mercantile use of information systems, the impact of uncertainty, and risk-sharing and remuneration modalities as tools for regulating the extent of divergence between the goals of the organization and its employees. The combination of agency and organizational perspectives shows that organizations can improve the effectiveness of management control under uncertainty through improved information systems or social control related to trust and socialization, among other factors (Eisenhardt, 1985, p. 135). It should be noted, however, that the direct application of organizational and economic theories developed from enterprise research has important limitations in health care, as health-care facilities are less, if at all, focused on profit maximization.

2.2 Management Control at the Operational and Strategic Levels

Viewing control as a cybernetic process based on a negative feedback model makes it possible to see that it is implemented through the following stages: setting objectives and standards for their achievement, measuring the achievement of objectives and adherence to standards, providing feedback on undesirable deviations of the controlled process, and, if there are deviations, adjustments to the process (Collier, 2005, p. 323; Kanthi Herath, 2007, p. 900; Malmi & Brown, 2008, p. 292). Hence, there are also references to *feed-forward* activities as an alternative to control. In this case, it is assumed that interventions to correct the implementation of the plan are foreseen and planned in advance, which, firstly, deviates considerably from the primary function that control performs by focusing attention on the planning function, and, secondly, is fraught with low probability of application in most practical management situations.

In the indicated cybernetic paradigm, attention is drawn to the stochasticity of phenomena managed within an organization and the need for the goals of individual organizational actors and the organization itself to converge (Flamholtz et al., 1985, p. 36). Since phenomena occur randomly within an organization, standards of human behavior cannot be clearly defined, but through the application of appropriate techniques and processes, the goals of the organization and its employees can be made to converge. This increases the likelihood that in random situations they will behave in a way that supports the organizational goals. The task of control in this approach is to enhance organizational agility, which is defined as the ability of an organization to effectively achieve multiple goals that may be set by the dominant coalition or imposed on the organization by other stakeholders. This model greatly extends the views of control described earlier. While previous work on the identification of essential forms of control (behavior or performance) (Ouchi, 1977, p. 96), modes of coordination (mutual alignment, direct supervision, standardization of work processes, standardization of work outcomes, and standardization of employee skills) (Mintzberg, 1993b, p. 4), the applicability of information systems, the impact of uncertainty risk-sharing and ways of rewarding, with the consequent reduction of the mismatch between the objectives of the organization and its employees (Eisenhardt, 1985, p. 137, 1989a, p. 59) indicated the existence of disconnected and generic elements of control, the integrated model (Figure 2.2 and Figure 2.3) combines all these elements, confirming the stochastic nature of the phenomena occurring in organizations.

The integrated control model is a solution that bridges the gap among management control, strategic planning, and operational control. It is intended to combine strategic planning, understood as the setting of goals for the entire organization in the long term, and operational control as an element that ensures the proper execution of day-to-day tasks. The distinction between these activities comes, inter alia, from the work of R.N. Anthony, who, although he saw management control as a process combining strategic planning and operational control (1965b, p. 17), drew a clear line

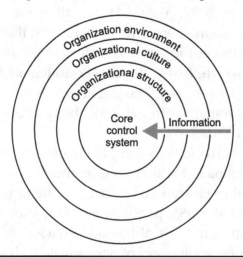

Figure 2.2.   Diagram of the organizational control system

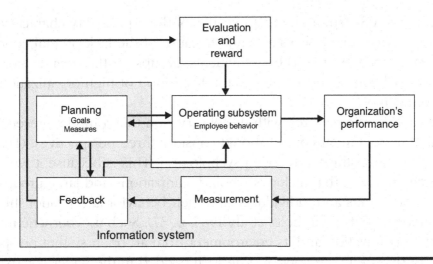

Figure 2.3. Core control system

between organizational control and strategic planning and between organizational control and operational control. This appears to have encouraged a narrow view of management control, failing to capture the wealth of issues and relationships involved in the design and use of management control, and resulting in a focus on formal (and usually accounting) forms of control without placing them in a wider context.

In this context, the integrated approach of E.G. Flamholtz, T.K. Das, and A.S. Tsui was a significant step forward in the development of management control (1985, p. 38, 1996, p. 599). Also R.N. Anthony, in his later work, tried to discover universal patterns of middle management control that could be generalized for many types of organizations. In his later work he stated that management control is a tool for managers to use in their interactions with each other and with subordinates. It is a people-oriented process. Line managers are the focal point of management control. They create the plans for implementing strategy and achieving goals, and they are the people [line managers] who must influence others and whose performance is evaluated (Anthony, 1988, p. 12). This shows that R.N. Anthony, like A.S. Tannenbaum, saw control as a hierarchical element, that is, that the different levels of management control subordinate units and that within this hierarchy, top-down, a predefined strategy is implemented.

As a result, the momentousness of exerting influence through management control to increase the alignment of organizational actors' goals with those of the organization should be emphasized, considering it as a stronger theoretical basis for organizational effectiveness, rather than the congruence of an action or achieved outcome with prior assumptions. E.G. Flamholtz,

T.K. Das, and A.S. Tsui argue that because of the equifinality characteristic of open organizational systems and because of the lack of total control over performance (exercised by individuals, groups, or the organization as a whole), goal congruence increases the likelihood of high organizational effectiveness most.

One can, therefore, agree with the observation that a model presenting integrated management control should consider three perspectives: (1) sociological, (2) administrative, and (3) psychological. This is because it will allow a research approach that includes whole organizations and large groups, organizational units and individuals, and their behavior and relationship to organizational goals (Flamholtz et al., 1985, p. 37). Such a cybernetic model views the organization and its environment from an open system perspective. It consists of a core control system embedded in the wider context of organizational structure, organizational culture and non-organizational factors, i.e., the organization's environment (Figure 2.2). The core control system has to be fed with information from all levels. The purpose of the mechanisms embedded in management control is to influence the behavior of people as members of the formal organization (Flamholtz et al., 1985, p. 38). The center, on the other hand, is the core control system, which is a cybernetic structure consisting of four subsystems: (1) planning, (2) operations, (3) measurement, and (4) evaluation and reward (Figure 2.3). The subsystems are connected through feedback and feed-forward loops. The next circle contains the structure of the organization, i.e., the set of rules and their interrelationships. The outer circle represents the culture of the organization. These three elements of the control system are bounded by the organization's environment (Flamholtz et al., 1985, p. 3, 1996, p. 599).

Complementing the model presented are the insights of S. Kanthi Herath, who listed among the elements of a control system:

- core package of controls, representing the organization's core control practices and mechanisms,
- an organizational structure, consisting of an organizational hierarchy, rules and regulations, and reporting relationships,
- organizational culture, defined as the set of values, beliefs, norms, and behavioral patterns of participants that characterize an organization,
- information systems, consisting of formal and informal information systems for managers,
- strategy understood as organizational goals and ways to achieve them. (2007, p. 905)

The contextual variables (structure, culture, and environment) in which the primary control system is embedded can either facilitate or limit the effectiveness of the primary control system in coordinating human efforts toward the achievement of organizational goals. Examples include the level of formalization, centralization, standardization, and social norms in the organizational culture or standards of professionalism found in the external environment of the organization (professional associations or cross-organizational trade unions). The control context may limit the effectiveness of the main control system if it is incompatible with norms, values, or management philosophy or practices in the wider context (Flamholtz et al., 1985, p. 45). In this view, the level of formalization denotes the extent to which duties, responsibilities, reporting, and communication relationships are detailed in writing, in opposition to informal arrangements; while the level of standardization characterizes the extent to which processes are governed by procedures describing standards of operation, and the extent to which these processes are controlled on an ad hoc and discretionary basis (Kanthi Herath, 2007, p. 904).

The core control system of the model of E.G. Flamholtz, T.K. Das, and A.S. Tsui assumes that management control begins with planning, involving the setting of objectives and standards in each key functional area for which an individual or organizational unit is responsible. From a control system perspective, the function of objectives is to help focus and direct human effort.

The operational system, an important subsystem in the model, refers to the day-to-day system of performing the functions required in the day-to-day operations of the organization (1996, p. 601). It can refer to any level of organizational analysis: individuals, teams, departments, organizational units, and the whole enterprise. This means that a core control system can be designed for any component of the organization – from the individual employee to the whole enterprise. As a result, a generic control system scheme has four key elements: measurement, planning (objectives and measures), feedback, and an evaluation and reward system (Figure 2.3). Planning involves adopted and emerging strategies accepted by top management. Measurement refers to the regular and reliable reading of the actual results obtained by the unit under review. Feedback, which is the result of comparing measured results with planned ones, as well as evaluation and reward, provides a motivational system to induce employees to behave appropriately. The operational subsystem is, therefore, where the actual work processes take place.

Importantly, for control systems to be able to motivate people to behave in a way that is consistent with organizational goals, they must perform four related tasks (1996, p. 597). First, they must be able to motivate people to make decisions and take actions that are consistent with organizational goals. Without control systems, people are likely to take actions or decisions to satisfy their own needs rather than the organization's goals. Therefore, a control system, by generally linking rewards to organizational goals, keeps people focused on achieving organizational goals.

Second, control systems need to integrate the efforts of many different parts of the organization. Even if people are trying to act in the best interests of the organization, they may find themselves having to pursue conflicting objectives. In particular, this may manifest itself in a divergence of goals between different parts of the organization. A classic example is the different goals of the sales department and the production department. The former is interested in fast and as customized deliveries as possible to increase sales, while production is most effective when it produces long series of similar products.

The third task of the control system is to provide information on the results of operations and the performance of people. This information enables the organization to assess performance while allowing people to work on a daily basis without subjecting every decision to review. This is referred to as "autonomy with control" and allows decentralization of day-to-day operations while ensuring that organizational goals are achieved. The idea is for managers to run day-to-day operations as they wish, while assessing the results of their decisions and actions against the organization's objectives. This allows managers a high degree of autonomy, while at the same time enabling top management to control the objectives of operational management. This leads to optimization of the degree and extent of control.

Fourth, the role of control is to facilitate the implementation of strategic plans and the planning process (1996, p. 597). This is because in many organizations it is mistakenly believed that planning is complete when a written plan is developed. For, as the theory of management science and business practice shows, this is only the end of the beginning, and an effective control system is required if the plan is to be implemented. In other words, planning must actually be part of the control process and not a stand-alone system.

It seems understandable that the evolution of the perception of management control has been influenced by advances in many areas of management science and quality, mainly in the understanding and application of strategy. Until the 1970s, strategic planning reigned supreme in organizations, which, due to the change to a more turbulent environment, was replaced by strategy formulation. This newer approach focused less on the detailed management of companies' growth paths and more on positioning the company in markets and in relation to competitors in order to maximize potential profits (Mintzberg, 1994, p. 112). This shift from planning to strategic management was associated with an increasing emphasis on competition as the main feature of the environment and competitive advantage as the main goal of strategy, which saw the external environment as the main area of potential profits.

Strategy was not explicitly used as a variable in management control research until the 1980s. With the field of business strategy or business policy becoming increasingly important since it emerged in the 1950s, such an approach seems difficult to justify. Much of the empirical research in this area is based on a contingent approach and involves the search for systematic relationships between specific elements of management control and organizational strategy (Govindarajan & Gupta, 1985; Merchant, 1985). Case study research has also been undertaken to identify the role of management control in supporting and influencing strategic processes in organizations (Archer & Otley, 1991; Roberts, 1990; Simons, 1990). The focus was, therefore, primarily on business strategy at the senior management level of the organization. However, since the mid-1980s, interest has grown in operations management literature in exploring how manufacturing strategies can be used to gain a competitive advantage (Langfield-Smith, 1997, p. 207). In the 1990s, instead of pursuing similar strategies in search of attractive markets and a favorable competitive position, organizations placed emphasis on finding unique strategies through which they could exploit their unique advantages (Porter, 1980). In the 21st century, in the face of rapid technological development, constant change, and relentless competition, strategies have already permanently shifted away from building a position focused on sustainable competitive advantage and focused attention on developing responsiveness and flexibility to create further temporary advantages. Indeed, the creation of temporary advantages forces rapid modification of strategies. In this context, the strategic planning process should, therefore, be defined as "a more or less formalized, periodic process that provides a structured approach to strategy formulation, implementation, and control" (Wolf & Floyd, 2013, p. 1758). Under conditions of permanent change, including regarding strategy itself, control of the strategic process has become a key function of any organization. This has given rise to two approaches related to the relationship between strategy and control.

The indicated changes in the perception of strategy were also related to the scope of the research conducted. Until the 1980s, research on control systems tended not to refer explicitly to organizational strategies and viewed strategy from the perspective of top management in static terms. Strategy was understood in terms of:

1. the position an organization can occupy in the market relative to its competitors (e.g., total cost leadership, differentiation and concentration) (Porter, 1980);
2. the pace of product and market development (defenders, prospectors and analyzers) (Langfield-Smith, 1997, p. 221);
3. attitude toward innovating their products (conservative or entrepreneurial companies) (Miller & Friesen, 1982, p. 16);
4. approaches to gaining market share and maximizing short-term profits (build, hold, "harvest," divest) (Gupta & Govindarajan, 1984, pp. 26–27).

The above conceptualizations treated strategy as a fixed element of the organization and considered it from the perspective of the content it contained. Under this assumption, the control system focused on the implementation of strategy and was regarded as the last step in the strategic management process. The task of management control in such a situation was to exert pressure resulting in the content of the strategy not being changed, and monitoring involved using the most important elements of the strategy in the decisions and actions taken. Thus, this approach referred to the traditionally understood one-way process of strategy planning, implementation, and control.

The approaches to management control identified at the time assumed, albeit not explicitly articulated, that the strategic objectives of the organization have been properly established and fully understood by the members of the organization (Kanthi Herath, 2007, p. 897). However, as business practice has shown, such an assumption is very difficult to meet for several reasons. First, it requires a presumption that the strategy, as well as the objectives, can be developed and communicated in such a precise way that they can be understood by the employees and at the same time can provide a basis for control. However, as is well known, it is unlikely, if not impossible, that all members of an organization, or even just key organizational actors, understand strategy in the same way as top management. The result may be that different interpretations emerge in the decision-making space at different levels and in different areas of the organization. Second, the way strategy is interpreted is conditioned by different actors' uneven reading of the uncertainty of the environment. Third, the determination of the level of desired organizational performance in many areas (sectoral strategies or sub-goals) will also be different, as what some consider a success, others may consider unambitious or even a failure. Fourth, the same discrepancies will touch on the identification and interpretation of the causes of organizational successes or failures.

In addition, it should also be noted that in this approach, the process of informing the management about changes in the environment would have to be fast and precise enough to allow the strategy to be adequately updated to the changing environment. Thus, the approach assuming that management control also covers the implementation of strategy determines the assumption that the top management of an organization should be able to (Kanthi Herath, 2007):

▪ determine the desired results;
▪ establish predictors of these outcomes;
▪ set standards for predictors and outcomes;
▪ create an information system to provide feedback;
▪ evaluate the feedback and take appropriate corrective action.

In essence, however, it should be noted that while this approach was acceptable in a stable environment, increasing competitive pressures and increasing volatility of the environment, particularly as a result of developments in communication and information technology, necessitated a change in approach to the strategy development and implementation process.

One of the tasks of top management is to ensure the long-term development of the organization. This entails the duty to develop and implement a strategy, or at least to develop its main ideas. However, in the economic reality, managers are not in a position to analyze a large number of internal and external signals on an ongoing basis or to effectively communicate the resulting strategic changes deep into the organization. In hospitals, the difficulties in communicating strategy by managers are compounded by the bottom-up method of decision making, characteristic of professional bureaucracies, in which both independent professionals and strategic managers have to accept changes proposed by professionals (Andreasson et al., 2018, p. 26). Hence, to keep up with external changes – the environment – and internal changes – resulting from bottom-up implemented or proposed changes and innovations – management must cede some of the strategy-forming competences to employees (Schaefer & Guenther, 2016). At the same time, however, it cannot relinquish control over this process.

One solution under these conditions is to appeal to the dominant organizational coalition (Abernethy & Chua, 1996, p. 573). This means that the process of strategy and goal formulation itself may also be subject to negotiation, as often the signals coming from the environment may be ambiguous, on the one hand, which may cause a difference of opinion among the key organizational coalition partners, and, on the other hand, the formulation of goals may also violate the interests of individual groups, which may lead to a breakup of the coalition and changes of coalition partners. Coalition changes in such circumstances usually arise to challenge previous goals and strategies. Thus, management, to reduce the divergence of objectives and the resulting possibility of opportunistic behavior, needs to align objectives with the dominant coalition in the organization in such a way that its interests are not too strongly compromised. However, it should be borne in mind that it may not be possible to agree on unambiguous goals because organizational actors may use different institutional logics (Lewandowski & Sułkowski, 2018, p. 152). However, it should also be remembered that "the management control system is designed to help the organization adapt to the environment in which it is embedded and to deliver the key outcomes desired by stakeholder groups," with "almost everything in the organization being included as part of the overall control system" (Merchant & Otley, 2007, p. 785). Indeed, in this approach, attention is paid to the external environment, while there is a shift away from seeing the system as being directed at changing the behavior of subordinates by superiors (Anthony, 1965a, p. 245). The aim becomes to make the organization adapt to the environment in which it is embedded. The objective becomes the adaptation of the organization to the changing environment, which can be carried out both by actions at the operational level and by changing strategy. However, information about changes in the environment usually reaches top management through lower-level employees who are in direct contact with customers. Only on this basis can top management develop a new strategy, which, in the traditional top-down model, has to be propagated back through the organizational structure. However, this route of strategy modification is very time-consuming and imprecise, as disruptions occur both in the cycle of communicating changes in the environment and in the propagation of the strategy.

2.3 The Concept of Levers of Control

An answer to the complexity of strategy formulation and implementation in hospitals can be found, among other things, in the four levers of control approach (Simons, 1995), which includes both control of strategy formulation and control of strategy implementation. Control of strategy formulation mainly concerns that which emerges at lower hierarchical levels as part of everyday working practices. Indeed, referring to R. Simons's definition that: "management control systems are the formal, information-based routines and procedures managers use to maintain or alter patterns in organizational activities" (1995, p. 5), it should be noted that in this concept, performance measurement and evaluation systems, such as the balanced scorecard, or management accounting systems, budgets can be used as information systems. In this view it is possible to use information systems in a diagnostic, interactive way and to build belief systems and boundary systems.

The diagnostic use of information systems refers to the traditional cybernetic approach to control, when these systems are used to monitor the degree to which objectives are being met and to make sure the organization is on the right track. The interactive approach involves the regular involvement of senior managers in the decision-making process of subordinates based precisely on information from the information system. Considering information systems as control systems involves top management creating belief systems to search for new organizational opportunities and strategies and boundary systems to limit the search area, so that the organization does not waste resources or energy entering domains where there is no competitive advantage.

It follows from the considerations made that organizations relatively often include control not only in the stage of implementation and possible modification of the strategy, but also in the stage of its formation. In this approach to control, almost everything in the organization is covered by it, including the processes of learning, innovation, and adaptation (Merchant & Otley, 2007, p. 785), and control itself can be seen as managing the inherent tension in organizations between creative innovation and anticipated goals, considering the fact that these processes contribute to the success of the organization. The inherent tension mentioned here comes in three types, which must be reconciled and balanced to enable effective strategy control: (1) unlimited opportunities versus limited employee attention, (2) intentional versus emergent strategy, and (3) protection of employee self-interest versus willingness to contribute to the organization (Henri, 2006a, p. 533). According to J.-F. Henri, managers use management control as positive and negative forces to create a dynamic tension that contributes to managing these inherent organizational tensions. Under these conditions, effective strategy control involves the need to create the conditions for freedom of innovative action and to ensure that people are committed to achieving goals (Simons, 1995, p. 29). R. Simons's theory of control is built on the assumption that organizations are complex social systems, collections of individuals linked together to satisfy not only their personal, but also their social needs. In other words, organizational actors seek to balance personal well-being with the needs of the organization, and, in this process, group norms and patterns of power and influence internal decision-making processes (1995, p. 13). One of the essential tasks of control under these conditions is to balance the contradictions within the organization between freedom and constraints, employees' autonomy of action and their responsibility, learning and control, advice and support and prohibitions, motivation, and coercion, and between innovation and experimentation and efficiency (Tessier & Otley, 2012, p. 173). These different areas of tension are often understood as a struggle between short-term and long-term policies, and between the bottom-up freedom of creativity, manifested in emergent strategies, and the top-down rigidity of implementing intentional (deliberate) strategies.

Strategy can be formed and implemented in two distinct ways: (1) it can be formulated by top management and implemented down the organizational structure, and (2) it can result from the day-to-day activities of employees at all levels (Mintzberg & Waters, 1985). In the first case, top management is responsible both for analyzing opportunities and threats from the environment and the resources, competences, weaknesses, and strengths of the organization itself and for setting the organization's strategic objectives and communicating them to employees and other stakeholders. In the second case, strategy emerges directly from the actions of individual employees, which is known as emergent strategy or spontaneous strategy. Emergent strategies are autonomous strategic decisions or actions taken by employees located deep within the organization, in response to changes in their working environment or as a reaction to a perceived opportunity or threat (Mintzberg & Waters, 1985, p. 258). In fact, the two modes of strategy formulation coexist, simultaneously complementing and competing with each other, resulting in a situation where the strategy actually pursued by the organization is the product of intentional and emergent strategies.[3]

In the defined control environment, it therefore seems justified to implement the solutions of the levers of control (LOC) concept proposed by R. Simons, which shifts the focus within management control from the control of internal processes to increase their efficiency and alignment with organizational strategy to a control focused on strategic efficiency and control of strategy formulation. The author himself defines his approach as an "action-oriented theory of control" (1995, p. ix). Four key concepts are associated with the LOC concept: (1) core values, (2) risks to be avoided, (3) critical performance variables and (4) strategic uncertainties. Each of these is directly controlled by one of the systems of the LOC concept:

- Core values are controlled by belief systems that guide the process of creatively seeking new opportunities for organizational development and instilling widely shared beliefs;
- Risks to be avoided are controlled by boundary systems to limit the search area for new solutions;
- Critical performance variables are controlled by a diagnostic control systems, whose functions are to monitor, evaluate and reward performance in key performance areas;
- Strategic uncertainty is controlled by an interactive control systems, designed to stimulate organizational learning and the creation of new ideas, concepts and strategies (2014, p. 302).

R. Simons argues that successful strategy execution requires companies to use all four levers in the right combination (2014, p. 303). Positive control techniques (belief systems and interactive control) motivate, reward, show the way, and promote learning. Negative control techniques (boundary and diagnostic control systems) coerce, punish, command, and control. Positive and negative techniques must coexist as they create opposing forces that create dynamic stresses that ensure effective control of strategy formulation and implementation. R. Simons compares these opposing forces to the Yin and Yang forces of Chinese philosophy, describing them as a balancing act between freedom and constraints, between employee empowerment and accountability, between hierarchical management and bottom-up creativity, and between freedom of experimentation and productivity (1995, p. 4). Complementing the thoughts indicated is the aforementioned observation that the essence of management control is to manage the inherent organizational tension that also exists between the levers of control.

Belief systems form a control mechanism based on the creation of a shared vision and values among employees. They thus constitute an explicit set of organizational definitions that senior managers formally communicate and systematically reinforce to ensure the organization's core values, goals, and directions. Belief systems reinforce the organization's core values and increase the alignment of employees' actions with the organization's goals. They can increase the level of transparency, especially the degree to which employees understand their tasks, responsibilities, and objectives, thereby increasing the likelihood of achieving desired organizational goals (Yu et al., 2018, p. 6). An illustration of this type of control is the vision or mission statement, which should be formulated in such a way so as to indicate a deep and enduring value system that inspires employees to seek out new opportunities for organizational development. The strategic goals of the organization should be derived from these values.

Boundary systems define the scope of employees' authority and decision-making freedom, thereby limiting the area of exploration of new opportunities. The idea is to make sure that the search for new opportunities by employees does not go beyond the scope of the organization and thus does not carry too high a risk of wasting organizational resources by taking actions that have no chance of being realized (Yu et al., 2018, p. 8). These boundaries are created by imposing restrictions in the form of rules and regulations and guidelines for appropriate behavior and defining penalties for exceeding these boundaries. Boundary systems, on the one hand, reduce the risk of taking inappropriate actions but, on the other hand, may constrain managers from taking actions that are actually necessary or could be appropriate (Simons, 1995, p. 160). Boundary systems are often constructed as a list of prohibited activities.

Diagnostic control systems are a fundamental element of control in any organization. Thus, the diagnostic control perspective is the backbone of traditional management control designed to ensure that planned objectives are met (Simons, 1995, p. 59) and that employees are motivated, controlled, and evaluated. They are the formal control systems that managers use to monitor organizational performance and correct deviations from established performance standards (Bisbe et al., 2019, p. 130). The quality of such a system depends on the ability to link the results (performance) achieved to service delivery processes, the availability of measurements of current performance and evaluation standards, and the ability to intervene proactively when deviations between current performance and the standard are observed. Thus, any formal information system can be used diagnostically. However, this is contingent on being able to set targets in advance, measure performance, calculate deviations from targets, and use deviation information as feedback to change inputs and/or processes to produce results in line with set targets and standards.

The described use of the information system indicates that diagnostic control is cybernetic in nature, serving to communicate relevant performance variables and monitor the implementation of strategy, providing insights into organizational performance, and allowing for the correction of emerging deviations (cf. Simons et al., 2000, pp. 208–209). The essence of the corrective information required here relates to the measurement and reporting of operating system performance and deviations from an accepted standard or set target to help reconfigure operations in an effort to improve expected performance (Yu et al., 2018, p. 8). Thus, diagnostic control systems relate to virtually all "traditional" formal management control systems with feedback.

Interactive control systems, on the other hand, stimulate organizational learning and the creation of new ideas and new strategies by involving managers in the decision-making process of subordinates. They enable the organization to focus its attention on strategic uncertainty and questioning of assumptions made. These systems, therefore, operate by permanently checking that the data they generate are correct, that managers and other employees are focusing their attention appropriately on the data, and that they are regularly discussing and challenging assumptions and current plans (Bisbe et al., 2019, p. 130; Simons, 1987a, p. 351). As a result, through diagnostic control systems, top management seeks the right answers and, through interactive control systems, the right questions in order to broaden the range of information collected and analyzed by members of the organization. Hence, interactive control makes it possible to narrow the gap between the information the organization has and the information that is available but requires creativity to acquire. This expanded information gained by asking the right questions makes it possible to reduce the uncertainty of actions taken, which is the gap between the information that is needed to perform a task and the information held by the organization (Galbraith, 1977). Indeed, as mentioned, diagnostic control systems are compared to a thermostat that maintains a set temperature at the same level, responding to deviations by turning the heating system on or off. Interactive control, on the other hand, is compared to the operation of the National Institute of Meteorology. According to R. Simons's observation: "In order not to be blind–sided in rapidly changing markets, the search for relevant information must not be limited by diagnostic routines and procedures. Instead, senior managers need a measurement system more like the one used by the national weather service. Ground stations all over the country monitor temperature, barometric pressure, relative humidity, cloud cover, wind direction and velocity, and precipitation. Balloons and satellites provide additional data. These data are monitored continuously and fed to a central location where they can be used to search for patterns of change. Based on this intelligence data, forecasts of impending conditions can be made or revised in light of changing circumstances" (1995, p. 92). Hence, in health care, interactive control systems are used in, among others, profit planning systems, brand revenue budgets, intelligence systems, and human resource development systems (Simons, 1991, p. 53).

However, the use of interactive control requires attention to two specific features of the system. First, such a system must be monitored personally by top management. Second, only one control system is used by top management at any given time as an interactive control system (Simons, 1995, p. 103). As a result, one agrees with the view that, in general, there is no single, special system that can be described as an interactive control system. It is the way in which some system is used that makes it an interactive control system. Interactive use of a given control system requires management to focus on that control mechanism and identify strategic uncertainties, i.e., threats and opportunities that challenge the implementation of current strategic plans (cf. Demartini & Mella, 2014, p. e5). When implementing this type of solution, managers are required to obtain a greater number and range of information on these strategic uncertainties and discuss them with their subordinates in order to adapt previous plans to the identified strategic uncertainties. From this interaction, a new strategic plan emerges. Thus, what distinguishes a diagnostic control system from an interactive control system is not the system itself, but the way in which managers use the system in question. An information system can be a diagnostic control system if it is used in the traditional way to identify differences between achieved and planned results. But the same information system can be an interactive control system if it is used as a tool for dialogue and learning involving several groups or organizational levels. Consequently, the discursive framework of the interactive perspective facilitates decision making at the strategic level and presupposes the active participation of managers at all levels.

The choice of an interactive control system, i.e., a system that is used in an interactive way, need not be a conscious decision by top management and often is not (Bisbe & Otley, 2004, p. 717). A system becomes a system of interactive control when top management, through this system, regularly and personally participates in the decisions of subordinates, allowing them to question data, assumptions, and action plans and, thus, stimulating dialogue, organizational learning, and strategy formulation. The choice of an interactive control system sends a signal to subordinates about which aspects to pay attention to and when to propose and test new ideas. This activates organizational learning, and new strategies emerge over time through the debate and dialogue that surrounds interactive controls. Indeed, organizations within the same industry may face the same set of strategic uncertainties; however, the managers' choice of which uncertainties are most relevant to the organization, and therefore also the choice of appropriate interactive and diagnostic control systems, may differ (Langfield-Smith, 2007, p. 773). For a system to qualify for use as an interactive control system, it must meet the following criteria:

1. The information generated by the system should meet the validity requirement and be regular;
2. The information contained in the interactive control system must be easy to understand if the debate and dialogue is to be productive, everyone must work with the same data and believe in its accuracy;
3. The system should be used frequently and regularly by operational managers at multiple levels of the organization;
4. The data generated by the system should be interpreted and discussed in personal meetings between supervisors and subordinates;
5. The system should be seen as a catalyst for continuous questioning and debate about data, assumptions, and action plans (Simons, 2014, p. 238).

As already mentioned, top managers typically only use one system interactively. It is important to bear in mind that the use of interactive control systems is linked to uncertainty and is a way of dealing with the increased information processing demands associated with that uncertainty (Ezzamel & Bourn, 1990). The more strongly top managers perceive the potential negative effects of uncertainty, the more they use information systems interactively (Janke et al., 2014, p. 255). The more they use information systems interactively, the more they use them. What is clear, however, is that while only one system is usually used interactively, there may also be situations where managers use multiple control systems interactively or not at all. Rather, multiple systems are used by top management only during short periods of crisis and when the organization is in transition, and they do not use any system at all when they do not have a strategic vision or do not feel the need to create one (Langfield-Smith, 2007, p. 773). This follows directly from the role that interactive control should play. This is because its function is to give relatively early warning that a particular strategy is no longer appropriate and needs to be revised (Merchant & Otley, 2007, p. 789).

The bottom line, therefore, is that interactive control systems stimulate the creative search for new initiatives to deal with emerging opportunities and threats. They cover both present and future timeframes, leading to a reassessment of objectives. At the same time, through interactive control, senior managers seek to motivate subordinates, make sure that the data generated by the system forms a valid and recurring topic of conversation with them, and ensure that subordinates and other managers across the organization regularly pay attention to the designated areas. This allows information to be collected at the point of origin and this information to be directed to the appropriate places in the organizational hierarchy, creating connections between members of the organization at different hierarchical levels (Widener, 2007, p. 764). This use of interactive control leads to constant interaction between senior managers, lower-level managers, and other members of the organization and facilitates the flow of information as it nullifies hierarchical and functional barriers.

The control levers structure ensures that strategic uncertainty and risk influence the selection and application of control systems, which, in turn, influences the organization through organizational learning and effective use of management attention. Diagnostic control systems act as tools to reduce the need for top management attention, allowing the organization to function without constant monitoring by directors. Therefore, control levers theory is not a system that identifies which control is related to which strategies, but deals with the distribution of management attention across control systems. In this context, control systems are not seen as tools to constrain and monitor activities to ensure that organizational goals are achieved, but play a role in maintaining or changing patterns of organizational activity.

Previous research has shown that an organization's performance measurement systems, e.g., the balanced scorecard or budgeting, can be used in all four levers of control, i.e., it is possible to use performance measurement systems to support control through belief systems and boundary systems, in addition to their use in a diagnostic or interactive manner (Abernethy & Brownell, 1999; Demartini & Mella, 2014; Tuomela, 2005, p. 298). However, it should be kept in mind that, in some organizations, such as subsidiaries, belief and boundary systems may largely extend beyond the control domain of the subsidiary (Ferreira & Otley, 2009, p. 266). This is reflected in business practice. Indeed, public hospitals are in a similar situation, with significantly reduced strategic autonomy. For example, in the United Kingdom, all public hospitals belong to the National Health Service (NHS) and the directions of their development must be approved by the NHS management. Also, in Poland, all investments with public funds, which constitute a significant part of investments in hospitals, have to be assessed for expediency by the governors competent for the location of the hospital. This is done through the Instrument for the Assessment of Investment Applications in the Health Sector. Furthermore, any investment in a public hospital that introduces new health services or merely increases the number of existing services must be financed by the NFZ, which usually requires prior approval of such an investment by this institution. Similarly, the purchase of new services in the United Kingdom must be approved by the hospital's relevant Clinical Commissioning Groups (CCGs).

Another weakness is that the meanings of the concepts embedded in the theory of control levers (e.g., values held in the organization), on which belief systems and boundaries can be based, are scattered and leave much room for subjective interpretation (Ferreira & Otley, 2009, p. 266). Thus, diagnostic control systems and interactive control systems seem to be the most relevant control systems in relation to hospitals (Demartini & Mella, 2014, p. e2).

On the whole, a significant number of strengths and weaknesses can be identified in the control levers theory. In terms of strengths, it has been noted that levers of control have a strong focus on strategic issues and their implications for the control system (Ferreira & Otley, 2009, p. 266). Furthermore, control levers theory offers a broad approach to the control system, looking at the range of controls in place and how they are used by organizations. Linking specific uses to particular controls enables a better understanding of management control systems. Importantly, the control levers framework provides a taxonomy of alternative uses of management controls, which is seen as a significant and helpful contribution to control theory. In contrast, a weakness of the control lever is that it does not place sufficient emphasis on socio-ideological controls, covering issues such as group norms, socialization, and culture.[4] While to some extent implicit in belief systems (Collier, 2005, p. 336), control levers theory recognizes that culture permeates the entire control system influencing choices and behavior, but it excludes both culture and external contextual factors from the study, dismissing them as contingent variables that can explain effectiveness rather than features of the control system itself. In this view, therefore, it can be seen that R. Simons's concept is strongly oriented toward the highest level of management and that it does not deal well with the range of informal controls that exist in organizations, especially small ones, or in the operation of control at lower hierarchical levels (Collier, 2005, p. 336). However, this allegation is only partly accurate, as the author of the concept of levers of control himself points out: "I am concerned primarily with formal routines and procedures – such as plans, budgets and market share monitoring systems – although we will also examine how these stimulate informal processes that affect behavior" (Simons, 1995, p. 5). Thus, control levers are unlikely to adequately explain the operation of the entire control system, which can be a problem when informal control mechanisms are particularly important in an organization. In relation to hospitals, this limitation of control levers theory may have a different impact on the quality of research based on the concept depending on the level at which control is studied. If control was studied in groups of professionals at lower levels, where a collegial, informal control system prevails, the results of the analysis could be unreliable. In contrast, at the level of control exercised by top management, where informal and collegial mechanisms are much less important, due, for example, to the conflict between medical professionals and managers described earlier and to the different institutional logics, analyses based on the levers of control theory could contribute significant cognitive value.

2.4 Levers of Control in Hospitals – An Assessment of the Results of the Previous Research

The theoretical considerations carried out so far clearly accentuate the importance and the need to understand the interdependencies between the different elements of management control and, at the same time, show that the levers of control perspective is a suitable perspective for the study of this phenomenon in hospitals. R. Simons's concept may be a good fit for hospitals, particularly when seen as an instrument for balancing multiple organizational challenges without relying on overly formal or overly informal controls, allowing the different control systems to be considered together and their main roles in the organization to be identified in the search for balance. In this context, it is crucial to recognize how hospitals measure and manage their performance and how the information system and management controls are used to deal with specific management challenges.

It is worth noting, however, that the results of studies to date directed at identifying the manifestations of the use of particular levers of control in hospitals and their impact on hospital efficiency provide an inconclusive picture. This is partly due to the fact that some studies have misidentified managers' use of diagnostic control or interactive control, resulting in incorrect conclusions about their effectiveness. As an example, studies conducted in two of the five Norwegian regions into which the country's health system is administratively and financially divided, i.e., Health Region East (non-deficit region) and Health Region West (deficit region), showed different approaches to the use of control levers and different results (Østergren, 2009, p. 179).

The eastern region emphasized cooperation between subordinate hospitals, which was done by conducting various health projects. In this region, a platform for dialogue was created between managers of medical departments, which should be interpreted as interactive control. In contrast, the top management of the western region placed direct emphasis on leveling the budget deficit, which meant that the system of management control was more diagnostic in nature. Similarly, in the declarative layer, hospital managers in the western region tried to pay special attention to cost-effectiveness and a balanced budget. Managers of medical departments in the eastern region perceived the strategy as focusing on capacity for change and on patients, while the strategy of the western region was seen as focusing almost exclusively on financial performance. The actual data, however, showed that the eastern region had a more intensive follow-up, with the finance department meeting at least once a month with most medical ward managers, maintained frequent phone calls and email contact, and required clinical managers to prepare monthly financial reports. The priority in this region was to maintain intensive monitoring activities so that overruns of the medical wards' budgets would never be allowed. In contrast, monitoring activities in the western region were less intensive than in the eastern region. Most medical ward managers did not have to meet with the finance department at least once a month. Although most medical ward managers had to send financial reports every month, the financial directors in the western region emphasized autonomy rather than close involvement. This contrasted with the situation in the eastern region, where hospital managers also met regularly with medical ward managers, regardless of their economic performance (Østergren, 2009, p. 186).

The research described above, therefore, showed that, although theoretically there were differences in the controls used (interactive or diagnostic), in reality diagnostic controls were used in both cases, but in the case of the western region in a much less intensive way; more contact between clinical managers and top management does not automatically mean interactive control. One of the manifestations of the use of interactive control, in the opinion of the investigators, in the eastern region was the intensive monitoring (follow-up activities) of the medical wards by the finance department and the creation of ways of operating based on the principle of "sitting in the same boat" (Østergren, 2009, p. 191), which meant that if one ward was operating in deficit conditions, it was fed by some resources from other wards.

The misinterpretation of the results here is a consequence of incomplete consideration of the requirements of levers of control theory. In particular, this is related to the requirements included in the characteristics of this system already discussed, as well as the observation that it is diagnostic control that emerges as top-down processes for implementing an adopted strategy or action plan, whereas interactive control is characterized by more bottom-up processes (Solstad & Petterson, 2020, p. 88) implemented by involving employees in decision making and goal-setting processes, which are then successfully implemented (Yu et al., 2018, p. 7). However, as can be seen from the description of the above studies, top-down activities were used in both regions. It is also evident that, while the first three characteristics of interactive control can be found in the research findings, there is no evidence of a continuous debate on challenging the assumptions of the adopted strategies and the implementation of bottom-up processes. It is also questionable to treat the frequent and face-to-face meetings between CFOs and medical heads to monitor their performance (follow-ups) as a catalyst for ongoing questioning and debate about data, assumptions, and action plans when the author cites the following statements from eastern region CFOs as an example of this: "Consequently, the means are to keep emphasizing finance so that it is never acceptable to have a budget overrun" and "We are just as strict as before" (Østergren, 2009, p. 185).

Doubts about the type of control exercised were also raised in the indicated studies by the possibility of questioning assumptions and setting own targets. In the eastern region, there was more intensive and more frequent supervision by financial directors directly over medical departments, increasing the intensity of control, but not changing its nature to interactive control. It would, therefore, seem more correct to refer to intensive hierarchical and bureaucratic control (Ouchi, 1980). In addition, in the eastern region there was social (clan) control (Ouchi, 1980) associated with close direct supervision based on shared values, linked to unity based on destiny, and, as a result, balancing budgets was the result of fear of criticism from other branch managers, rather than questioning assumptions and seeking other solutions. This can be explained by feeling the stronger impact of peer pressure, characteristic of clan control, rather than the pressure associated with the possibility of losing one's job. In this context, there was no horizontal pressure coming from managers of other medical departments in the western region, where, despite the relatively greater emphasis on balancing budgets, the actual direct pressure was less, and medical department managers enjoyed much more autonomy than in the eastern region. It can, therefore, be inferred that it is difficult to find evidence in the studies discussed (Østergren, 2009) to support the idea that it was the interactive use of management control that influenced budget balancing by the eastern region.

The researchers' assertion that the application of diagnostic control in the western region failed to prevent financial deficits is also controversial. This is because, as the analysis of the interviews cited in the study shows, the achievement of set targets and measures was not monitored regularly, in contrast to diagnostic control, which is characterized by the setting of measures, providing comparative parameters of actual performance against planned performance and taking corrective action on this basis. As a result, this draws the problem of too little management control over the divisions, which may alter the perception of the research results.

Relatively similar observations were made in a field study carried out in a large Norwegian university hospital, where the use of departmental budgets was considered an application of diagnostic control, and, at the same time, it was found that the introduction of budgets in the hospital did not result in a significant increase in the effectiveness of management control, as the hospital budget was still exceeded (Nyland & Pettersen, 2004, p. 77). However, it should be noted that in this hospital, despite the director's declaration indicating the importance of economic performance also for clinical managers, in reality budgets were not part of the management control system. Data on budget implementation, and in particular information on overruns, were identified but did not trigger any management reaction, so budget deficits were also not interpreted as unacceptable, even in the opinion of the director general, and, as such, they did not have a negative impact on the performance evaluation of clinical department managers. This was because, despite the official rhetoric about the need to balance the hospital, budget overruns were seen as a way of getting more money from the hospital owner. Thus, budget responsibility was formally declared, but, in reality, it was beneficial for the hospital to exceed the budget.

Similar phenomena were identified in a study of two large Swedish hospitals – Sahlgrenska University Hospital (16,400 employees) and Sodra Alvsborgs Regional Hospital (4,000 employees) (Kastberg & Siverbo, 2013). Although management accounting systems were originally designed for diagnostic control, they were used as such only to a certain extent, when a committed senior manager at Sahlgrenska Hospital used accounting information to put pressure on his subordinates. So, there were examples of diagnostic control, but these attempts failed and weakened after some time. In contrast, at Sodra Alvsborgs Hospital, measures related to targets in the management accounting system were regularly monitored, but failure to achieve targets did not lead to anyone being held accountable (Kastberg & Siverbo, 2013, p. 264).

An important area of consideration to be identified in the analysis of the research to date related to the concept of levers of control is the influence of other organizational factors on the effectiveness of individual levers of control. A quantitative study of the interactive use of the budget, understood as an information system, during strategic change in hospitals showed that hospital performance was better if budgets were used interactively at a time when hospitals were undergoing a strategic reorientation (Abernethy & Brownell, 1999, p. 199). Such a relationship was identified under conditions of "significant" strategic change, while, in the case of smaller changes, better results were obtained when budgets were used in a diagnostic manner. This means that the choice of budgeting mode should be tailored to the scope of activities undertaken. This is justified to some extent by studies in Spanish hospitals. Indeed, an analysis using partial least squares (PLS) regression shows that the broad scope of the management accounting system is positively associated with strategic change for organizations aiming for prospector positions in the sense of the strategy typology (Miles & Snow, 1978). In contrast, the interactive use of the management accounting system is not associated with strategic change for organizations moving toward defender positions, but it is positively associated with strategic change for organizations moving toward prospector positions (Naranjo-Gil & Hartmann, 2007, p. 751). The above research may also explain the inconclusive results for the interactive use of management accounting systems in Swedish hospitals (Kastberg & Siverbo, 2013), as the authors did not indicate which phase of strategic change these hospitals were in or what information systems they had in place.

Also relevant to the issues discussed here are the results of a survey of Australian hospital executives, which showed that both diagnostic and interactive controls had a direct positive impact on staff-related outcomes and on outcomes related to performance and patient care (Yu et al., 2018, p. 21). Interactive control use also shows a positive direct relationship with medical infrastructure and staff resources. This allows attention to be drawn to the research of M.Z. da Silva et al., who, rather than identifying how the use of individual levers of control affects organizational performance, investigated how the accreditation process affects the strengthening of individual levers of control (2020). The results of these studies confirmed that the implementation of accreditation standards in hospitals strengthens all levers of control (2020, s. 245. This is because, in the process of bringing a hospital into compliance with accreditation requirements, a number of bylaws and policies have to be put in place, which strengthens both boundary systems and belief systems. In the accreditation process, the monitoring of a number of processes related to the quality and safety of patient treatment must be demonstrated, which, in turn, strengthens diagnostic control. Also, the preparation for the implementation of individual accreditation standards is itself an important long-term program handled by top management representatives, which is a catalyst for continuous questioning and debate about data, assumptions, and action plans. The accreditation process also requires frequent and regular attention from operational managers at all levels of the organization, and the interpretation and discussion of information from hospital systems in face-to-face meetings among superiors, subordinates, and colleagues. All these activities exhaust the characteristics of interactive control in the sense of the R. Simons's approach. However, while these studies show that the accreditation process strengthens the levers of control, they say nothing either about the use of these control mechanisms or about how their possible use would affect hospital performance.

Summarizing the existing body of research on the levers of control in hospitals, it is possible to conclude that the problem described at the beginning of the subsection with accurately identifying interactive and diagnostic controls and assessing their effectiveness may be due not only to the features identified in the cited studies, but also to the decoupling of formal structures from day-to-day practices in hospitals (Meyer & Rowan, 1977, p. 340). A vivid example of this phenomenon is the decoupling described by K. Nyland and I.J. Pettersen of the rhetoric of top and middle managers about the importance of budgets from day-to-day practices, i.e., the use of information contained in budgets to evaluate the performance of clinical department managers (2004, p. 77). This was due to the fact that, despite the official rhetoric about the need to balance the hospital budget, overruns were seen as beneficial, as it was a way of getting more money from the hospital owner. The occurrence of this phenomenon can also be identified in studies of two Norwegian regions, the eastern and western regions. In the western region, managers and medical professionals in the official, rhetorical layer were in conflict around the issue of balancing the budget, but, in practice, they cooperated in the field of obtaining more funding for hospitals from the Ministry of Health (Østergren, 2009, p. 192). The above observation prompts attention to an institutional perspective that deals with the phenomenon of decoupling everyday practices from formal structures and rhetoric.

2.5 Management Control from an Institutional Perspective

The traditional approach indicates that control problems are primarily due to the interaction of two human characteristics: bounded rationality and opportunism. Bounded rationality refers to people's inability to take in and process all available information, preventing optimal decisions and actions (Eicher, 2017, p. 342; Simon, 1957). This leads to an inability to attend to more than a few things at once, i.e., to take in and process a large amount of available information, preventing optimal decisions and actions (Lebas & Weigenstein, 1986, p. 260; Simon, 1957, 1995, p. 16). Opportunism, on the other hand, is defined as "self interest seeking with guile" (Williamson, 1975, p. 255), which results, among other things, in missing out on development opportunities and forgoing opportunities to innovate, leading to a loss of resources or damaging the organization's reputation. The effects and consequences indicated depend on the tasks performed by employees and the configuration of the environment in which they work. It can lead to a waste of resources when employees act in their own self-interest, for example, using much more expensive materials than patients need and counting on the gratitude of manufacturers or distributors (Dixon-Woods et al., 2011). These problems involve deforming or blocking the flow of information to make the right decisions or assess performance. It is clear, however, that not all people act opportunistically at every opportunity. However, the very possibility of this phenomenon occurring, even for certain situations, creates the need to introduce controls. It should also be noted that it is not only people who can behave irrationally, but also entire organizations, which, when making decisions and solving problems, can perform only one or, at most, several actions at a time, using a small fraction of the information stored in their memory (Miner, 2005, pp. 43–48; Lebas & Weigenstein, 1986, p. 260).

Hospitals, where multiple and conflicting objectives are the norm, are similarly prone to irrationality.

From the traditional perspective of organizational theory, which sees hospitals as homogeneous cybernetic systems, and similarly from the perspective of economic agency theory, certain phenomena can be interpreted as opportunism and irrationality, although they are not, in fact, such. The appropriate interpretation here is only provided by institutional theory, which abandons opportunism, bounded rationality, and organizational homogeneity in favor of heterogeneity and rationality, while referring to institutional logics that can differentiate the perception of the problem (Damayanthi & Gooneratne, 2017, p. 525; Thornton et al., 2012). Instead of following self-interest, institutional theory can see the opposition of organizational actors to the institutionalization of external pressures to implement incompatible performance procedures (Damayanthi & Gooneratne, 2017, p. 526). Of course, these insights do not exclude the need for control (Merchant & Van der Stede, 2017, p. 8), as it must protect organizations from what people can do that the organization does not want to do, or what they may not do that the organization believes is necessary.

Applying an additional institutional perspective will make the understanding of the problems associated with perceived "opportunism" and "irrationality" deeper and closer to reality. While from the perspective of organizational theory certain phenomena may be considered deviations requiring the reinforcement of control, from an institutional perspective the answer is to seek new understanding and new practices, which, consequently, may mean seeking new innovative solutions instead of reinforcing the tools of control. In this context, opportunistic and irrational actions may be taken for granted, not because the rational choice process has found them to be the most appropriate for the technical requirements of the task, but because they are "old" institutionalized habits. Perceived irrationality may also be a manifestation of conflicts and rivalries between the institutional logics of influential groups (Lewandowski & Sułkowska, 2017). Heterogeneity of logics and their goals, on the other hand, can induce intergroup conflict and lead to bargaining, coalition formation, and disintegration as well as different kinds of political phenomena and actions, and the control system has to deal with these phenomena (Kuhlmann et al., 2011; Lebas & Weigenstein, 1986, p. 260; Lewandowski, 2013).

The aforementioned need to implement control systems is, under these conditions, the result of the observation that it is a tool through which organizations can achieve their objectives, whereby the acquisition by organizations as specific as hospitals of the resources necessary to achieve their objectives requires a constant accentuation of their social utility. This is because it gives them external legitimacy and access to resources (Meyer & Rowan, 1977, p. 340). However, in many situations, external social or political objectives may conflict with the expectations of the members of the organization or with the requirements for the effective implementation of their daily tasks (Knezevic et al., 2022). Meyer and Rowan (1977, p. 356) have noted that, in such situations, to avoid dysfunction, organizations often respond to external forces by decoupling their externally visible activities and formal structures from their internal daily working practices. In other words, organizations decouple the externally recognizable structures and activities that are expected and accepted by society, thus ensuring their legitimacy and access to resources, from the internal, behind-the-scenes practices that allow the organization to actually perform its daily work (1977, p. 341). This means loosely linking or even decoupling the formal structures of the organization, which often perform ceremonial activities, from the daily work performed.

What constitutes legitimate goals and how organizations can achieve them is shaped not only by external pressures, but also by the institutional logics of internal actors. Therefore, in recent years, academics have taken an interest in the perspective of institutional logics, including the problem of their coexistence, in the context of management control, examining issues such as budgeting (Ezzamel et al., 2012), performance measurement and evaluation systems (Carlsson-Wall et al., 2016), management accounting in the non-profit sector (Järvinen, 2016), the impact of individual subjectivity on the institutionalization of new accounting practices (Ancelin-Bourguignon et al., 2013), and health-care reforms (Reay & Hinings, 2009), among others.

Over the years, management control has evolved from a more formal approach, which provides quantified information to support management decision making, to a sociological approach, which provides a much broader range of information for management decision making, giving individuals the power to achieve their own objectives (Chenhall, 2003, p. 129). A similar character is represented by the operational definition of control adopted in this study, which refers to all the instruments, activities, and systems used by top management to increase the likelihood of the hospital adapting favorably to its environment and thus achieving satisfactory results. In this view, management control should be understood as a reflection of wider social and political interactions.

The use of institutional theory in the study of management control emphasizes isomorphic pressures and irrationality (DiMaggio & Powell,

1983, p. 149; Lounsbury, 2008, p. 350), which interferes with contemporary hospitals operating in a hybrid regime of different institutional logics (Lewandowski & Sułkowski, 2018). The theories of management control described earlier understood hospitals as homogeneous organizations with bounded rationality and opportunism. Looking at hospitals from the perspective of institutional logics allows one to see heterogeneity and rationality instead of homogeneity and irrationality, as commonly postulated by organization theory (Simon, 1957). The perspective of institutional logics allows one to look at organizations in a different light and observe not only homogeneity, but also heterogeneity (Thornton et al., 2012). Heterogeneity in the context of management control means that organizations cannot be seen as a homogeneous set of actors with the same understanding of goals and the feedback provided to them, regardless of their institutional logics.

Generally, at least two institutional logics are considered to be at work in hospitals: the logic of medical professionalism and the logic of business (Leotta & Ruggeri, 2012, p. 436; Reay & Hinings, 2005, p. 358). The logic of medical professionalism is characterized by a patient-centered approach, acting in accordance with clinical expertise but without paying sufficient attention to cost containment. Business logic, on the other hand, is mainly focused on cost and efficiency (Reay & Hinings, 2005). However, the only way in which managers are able to achieve at least part of their business objectives is through collaboration with professionals, as doctors are the only professionals certified to actually deliver health care and thus generate revenue for hospitals. Therefore, in the external symbolic layer, doctors followed their professional logic geared toward the unfettered provision of health care to patients regardless of cost, and managers followed government rules. At the operational layer, however, where the day-to-day work is actually done, these two logics were modified to create space for compromise and collaboration. The result of this compromise was the emergence of managerial logic and hybrid professional logic.

The idea of this carve-out stems from the observation that managers are unable to reduce medical costs because they do not have the competence to assess clinical work or the ability to limit doctors' autonomy in diagnosis and therapeutic decisions to order costly diagnostic tests and expensive therapies (Knezevic et al., 2022). Thus, it is only together with the doctors that managers can appeal to the relevant decision-makers "in support of physicians' requests for better funding" (Reay & Hinings, 2009, p. 641). Otherwise, they would not be able to balance hospital budgets. At the same time, the increase in the number of unnecessarily highly reimbursed medical services and procedures provided is problematic in this solution. In addition, managers, when unable to obtain the required resources, were able to encourage doctors to use their medical expertise to increase hospital revenues and financial margins in exchange for less managerial pressure on other areas of doctors' autonomy. The actions indicated, however, relatively rarely led to reforming the way health services were delivered (Lewandowski & Sułkowski, 2018). In this context, it is worth noting that solutions involving doctors in hospital management do not bring improvements either. This is because doctors who become managers do not perform better in managing doctors than managers from other backgrounds (von Knorring et al., 2010, p. 11).

The phenomenon discussed above, therefore, involves the decoupling of formal structures, actions, and narratives visible to those outside of the organization from everyday working practices, which are an organizational response to external pressures and the hybridization of the organization associated with the presence of multiple institutional logics. Decoupling carries the risk that efforts to strengthen external legitimacy may negatively affect perceptions of legitimacy within the organization. This may result in the institutionalization of inappropriate behavior and ultimately lead to a loss of external legitimacy for the organization (Schäffer et al., 2015, p. 297). Avoiding this negative phenomenon requires the use of alternative responses, mainly selective linking, defined as "the purposeful enactment of selected practices among a pool of competing alternatives" (Pache & Santos, 2013b, p. 994). Indeed, this action, like decoupling, allows hybrid organizations to reduce symbolic concerns, but with a lower risk of being perceived as an organization pretending to be conformist. Selective amalgamation is often considered less costly than compromising around institutional logics, as it does not require organizational members to come up with alternative ways of doing things. It should be noted, however, that instead of selective merging or changing practices, organizations may also carve out subunits that are dominated by one particular institutional logic. However, this can lead to undermining cooperation between different subunits of the organization and fragmenting the organization, resulting in a less efficient division of labor, lack of cooperation, and ultimately hampering control and coordination activities (Schäffer et al., 2015, p. 298).

Management control, therefore, plays an important role in the daily practices of the hospital, as it contributes to the creation of organizational reality. At the same time, it is required that this control is constantly adapted to the changing demands of the environment, so that it is compatible with the requirements of different audiences, specific contexts, etc. (Ahrens & Khalifa, 2015; Lewandowski, 2013). Indeed, in hybrid organizations where several institutional logics coexist, organizational actors may find it difficult to interpret organizational reality, in terms of appropriate behavior and success criteria (Thornton, 2004, p. 70). When organizations are exposed to different, sometimes competing institutional logics, they have to cope with different interpretations of reality, different norms of appropriate behavior, and multiple criteria for success. It should be noted, however, that this coexistence of multiple institutional logics presents not only a challenge, but also an opportunity for managers to find new and innovative ways of dealing with them (Johansen et al., 2015, p. 726).

Complementing the definitions of institutional logic already cited in the study with the concept of institutions allows for the inclusion of regulatory, normative, and cultural-cognitive elements, which, together with related activities and resources, provide stability and meaning to social life (Scott, 2014, p. 56). This combination should be considered a model of institutional logic, which distinguishes three institutional pillars: regulatory, normative, and cultural-cognitive (Scott, 2014, s. 60–82; Johansen et al., 2015, p. 727). Each of these creates challenges for top management.

The main managerial challenge within the regulatory pillar is efficiency, assessed through economy, expediency, and legality. The logic in the normative pillar is geared toward relevance, and the main managerial challenge concerns legitimacy derived from doing the right thing in relation to prevailing values, norms, and obligations. This legitimacy in business concerns the pursuit of profit, while in public institutions it focuses on equality and justice. In the cultural-cognitive pillar, by contrast, the dominant logic is orthodoxy, seen as the correctness and rightness of the ideas underlying action.

This pillar is governed by routines and templateness, taken for granted and "the way we do things here" (Scott, 2014, p. 68). Thus, the main challenge managers face related to the cultural-cognitive pillar of the institution is meaning-making. Meaning is created through the sharing and shaping of categories, typologies, causal explanations, cultural codes, social routines, and scripts (Zilber, 2008, p. 152). A decisive step in meaning-making is the internalization of these elements to such an extent that they are largely taken for granted (Johansen et al., 2015, p. 728).

The phenomena indicated, therefore, also apply to hospitals as organizations with different institutional logics, where managers will encounter challenges related to different forms and different definitions of performance, legitimacy, and relevance. In exercising management control, managers here are obliged to interpret and set adequate standards of performance, ensuring that they are relatively consistent with different definitions of organizationally relevant categories. Indeed, under these conditions, the way in which the concept of efficiency is understood (more in economic or medical terms) requires, for example, a decision related to canceling or postponing a planned procedure or performing it despite exceeding budget limits and risking less payment in a degressive form of funding. Under these conditions, too, the concept of the patient's well-being may be understood differently in a situation of strong economic pressure imposed by various reforms. It can be seen as the good of the individual and the uncompromising satisfaction of their needs regardless of cost, or as the good of the local community and ensuring the sustainability of the hospital. Maintaining and developing legitimacy and relevance can, therefore, be more challenging for managers in hybrid organizations than ensuring efficiency. Legitimacy and relevance tend to be the result of long-term efforts, whereas efficiency appears to be easier to achieve in a shorter time frame, making managers' responses more likely to be seen as a set of strategies adapted to different configurations of institutional logics (Johansen et al., 2015, p. 728). As a result, one of the key challenges is to analyze and evaluate managers' responses in relation to different institutional logics. These responses in the coexistence of multiple institutional logics can vary from deletion, compartmentalization, aggregation, and integration (Johansen et al., 2015; Pache & Santos, 2013a).

Removal in hybrid settings means that the manager deliberately rejects the values, norms, and practices defined by a given logic (Johansen et al., 2015, p. 728; Pratt & Foreman, 2000, p. 29). Rebellious reactions may vary in their degree of resistance, from refusing to conform to the dictates of a given logic to more active attempts to deny or attack in order to annihilate them (Pache & Santos, 2013a, p. 13). In compartmentalization, managers apply different logics to different situations or conditions, with the result that the same manager follows an economic logic for specific decisions, but a patient welfare logic for other decisions (Johansen et al., 2015, p. 728). Compartmentalization can occur in time and/or space, as individuals may choose to play competing logics in the same place at different times (for example, when interacting with different people) or in different places (for example, in different organizational contexts). In the face of competing logics, compartmentalization allows individuals to secure legitimacy by demonstrating compliance with multiple logics, even if they are incompatible (Pache & Santos, 2013a, p. 13). An important feature of compartmentalization is the absence of the pursuit of any synergy between logics (Pratt & Foreman, 2000, p. 26). Aggregation of multiple logics involves the preservation of all logics while creating linkages between them (Pratt & Foreman, 2000, p. 32). In a hospital, this may include the development of new organizational practices that combine economic and patient welfare logics. Such a phenomenon occurs when doctors and managers change their logics in order to establish more effective collaboration (Lewandowski & Sułkowski, 2018, p. 152). Integration, on the other hand, means combining multiple logics into a distinct new whole (Pratt & Foreman, 2000, p. 30), leading to the creation of an overall logic encompassing the different logics and causing the multiple logics to no longer be seen as different, but rather as a single logic (Johansen et al., 2015, p. 728). This can be achieved by recruiting employees with weaker affiliations to one of the logics and socializing them in a hybrid environment.

Understanding how managers interpret and respond to the coexistence of different institutional logics is a prerequisite for gaining insights into hospital relationships and for better understanding the limitation of the functionality of certain control mechanisms in hospitals. Indeed, control tools that are effective in other organizations, in hospitals, due to their hybrid nature, can be used only ceremonially (Schäffer et al., 2015, p. 396). Additionally, control effectiveness in hospitals relates also to each country's context (Kuhlmann et al., 2013).

2.6 Operational Definition of Management Control

The overview presented in this chapter of the fundamental issues and definitions related to management control shows that, over time, more and more areas of organizational management have been included in the domain of control. This is reflected, among other things, in the definitions of control – ranging from the definition of control as comparing whether everything is done in accordance with the approved plan, issued instructions, and established rules to the statement that "almost everything in the organization is included as part of the overall control system" (Merchant & Otley, 2007, p. 785).

On the basis of the discussion so far, taking into account the academic body of work on management control and the unique characteristics of hospitals, it should be considered that **management control encompasses all instruments, activities and systems used by top management to**

increase the likelihood of favorable adaptation of the hospital to the environment, which is measured by the hospital's performance.

The definition indicated has been adopted in the work as **an operational definition of control** because, despite its brevity, it encompasses a wide range of possible activities, instruments, and systems, which corresponds to the observation that "almost everything in the organization is included as part of the overall control system" (Merchant & Otley, 2007, p. 785). At the same time, however, and this is an important difference in relation to most definitions to date, there is movement here away from an emphasis on the direct influence of superiors on employee behavior, relatively often treated as the main control mechanism. This feature of the proposed definition is due to the fact that in hospitals the main "workforce" is made up of professionals with a high degree of autonomy, using work procedures mostly created and legitimized outside the organization in which these professionals work. In such a situation, intensive attempts to influence subordinate professionals would lead to conflicts rather than to the smooth implementation of objectives, both strategic and operational.

In this area, it should also be noted that existing definitions of control largely treat the organization as a homogeneous organism, focusing on minimizing deviations of employee behavior from accepted rules on the way to achieving organizational goals (Kanthi Herath, 2007, p. 895). This approach, which treats employees as individuals with limited rationality and mainly oriented toward the achievement of their own goals (Kruis, 2008, p. 16), suggests that without control systems, human decisions would be oriented more toward the satisfaction of one's own needs (Wilkes et al., 2005, p. 1056). This discrepancy is grounded in the fact that, although hospitals have their own individual strategies, these are usually not unique ideas to achieve unique goals but, due to external legal and political constraints, relate to goals set by the public owner, payer, and government. Consequently, hospitals are limited to adapting optimally to the framework set by these institutions (Merchant & Otley, 2007, p. 785).[5] The proposed definition, through its generality, allows for the separate objectives of different groups of employees to be taken into account, including within different institutional logics.

The aforementioned peculiarities of the hospital environment have also led to the need to include the issue of "adapting to the environment" in the management control of hospitals, which means that a reactive approach based on responding to current local opportunities and threats may prevail in these organizations. Importantly, such an approach, oriented toward the implementation of local and ongoing strategies, may enable the hospital to achieve the best results. This is because the interdependencies indicated here are due to the fact that the complex environment in which hospitals operate and, above all, the ambiguity of objectives make (Abernethy et al., 2006, p. 813) it relatively more difficult and problematic for hospitals to relate to common and fixed objectives. This is because, due to dynamic political processes and frequent changes in funding priorities for services by the public payer, which affect the bargaining power of individual medical specialties, changes in objectives can occur very quickly and sectorally. In a situation of limited resources, individual medical specialties may, therefore, succumb to pressure to develop their own local strategies.

It is noteworthy, however, that even relatively new literature takes a conservative approach to management control, treating it as packages of control instruments to coordinate work and provide incentives through reward and punishment (Kruis, 2008, p. ii) or as a process by which senior managers influence lower-level managers to implement the organization's strategy (Anthony et al., 2014, p. Kindle Locations 595–596). This view of control assumes a hierarchical implementation of strategy and does not consider emergent strategies coming from within the organization, which contradicts the proposed operational definition of control.

Notes

1. Although there are many differences between the definitions of the words "output" and "outcome," in this book, in many cases, they will be used interchangeably – also with the word "result."
2. The difference between the real behavior of the agent and the expected behavior of the principal is called agency costs.
3. More about the strategy can be found, among others, in: Burgelman, R. A. (1996). A process model of strategic business exit: Implications for an evolutionary perspective on strategy. *Strategic Management Journal, 17*(S1), 193–214; Mintzberg, H. (1994). The fall and rise of strategic planning. *Harvard Business Review, 72*(1), 107–114; Mintzberg, H., & Waters, J. A. (1985). Of strategies, deliberate and emergent. *Strategic Management Journal, 6*(3), 257–272.
4. More about this type of control is in Lewandowski et al., 2020, 2017.
5. Examples include not only the conversion of wards in individual hospitals or entire hospitals for the treatment of COVID-19 patients, by order of the provincial governor, with limited or no involvement of the hospitals' senior management in this decision. It also includes the amalgamation of hospitals carried out through a resolution of the local government by the owner of the hospital, rather without the participation of the senior management of the hospitals.

Chapter 3

Main Elements of the Management Control Model

3.1 Information System in Management Control

A common feature of the vast majority of control definitions mentioned in the previous chapter is the centrality of information systems (IS) to management control. The information systems included in control can be those used by top management to influence the behavior of lower-level managers or employees, as well as those used by lower-level managers and employees in the operational core of the organization to support decision-making processes, often creating emergent strategies (Mintzberg & Waters, 1985, p. 258). In this context, control is understood as the rules, procedures, mechanisms, and practices that provide the information needed for decision making (Tucker et al., 2009, p. 129), with the understanding that decisions about corrective actions (traditional diagnostic control) are only part of the set of all decisions made as part of management control. In addition, a distinction must be made between decision support systems and control systems. Although they are the same information systems, such a distinction is due to the difference in their use. Information systems are decision support systems when they provide information to managers and allow them to make autonomous decisions. In contrast, when decision making based on an information system is monitored by superiors, the information system is part of management control, as can be seen in the four forms of using information systems in the service of control already mentioned, i.e., diagnostic and interactive, and boundary and belief systems.

DOI: 10.4324/9781003366553-3

Early models of control assumed that managers set a pattern of behavior or standard of performance, and then, through observation or measurement, acquire information about whether the adopted standards of behavior are being followed or whether the assumed results are being achieved (Ouchi, 1977, p. 96; Taylor, 2004). Agency theory, which is still considered the dominant theory in the area of information systems in organizations (Kerpershoek et al., 2014, p. 422; Zhang, 2018, p. 632), points out that information acquisition is a deliberate activity that requires specific inputs (Eisenhardt, 1989a; Govindarajan & Fisher, 1990). Organizations "buy" information by building, often complex, information systems that consist of a set of interrelated technological components, organizational environment, and people. The appropriate configuration of these components allows information to be collected, processed, stored, and distributed to support decision making and control within the organization (Au et al., 2008, p. 46; Müller-Stewens et al., 2020, p. 1). In the context of agency theory, information systems serve as tools for managers (principals) to reduce opportunistic behavior by employees (agents). In addition, however, information systems can also provide valuable information about the performance of the organization itself, not only to managers, but also to its employees. This increases internal transparency, enabling the organization to learn, innovate, and improve processes.

Taking into account the specifics of the cybernetic model of management control (Figure 2.3), it can be pointed out that the information system (IS) consists of three basic elements: (1) planning, (2) measurement, and (3) feedback, and its potential is measured by, among other things, its ability to generate accurate and timely key information about the functioning of the organization and its availability. In the adopted system, planning is the process of deciding on the goals of the organization (and/or its members), as well as the means to achieve those goals. Planning is also defined as the recurring procedures of routinely disseminating planning assumptions, gathering market information, providing details of relevant analyses, and encouraging managers to estimate resource needs and performance targets and milestones (Simons, 2014, p. 7).

The realization of the planning function understood in this way requires the use of appropriate measurement mechanisms to enable the implementation of controls to determine the degree to which goals and milestones are achieved. In this view, planning is the process of preparing assumptions for an organization, providing a framework for setting aspirations through performance goals, and ensuring that the right level and mix of resources are available to achieve those goals. The term "goals," on the other hand, refers to the relatively broad definition of what an organization wants to achieve in a given "performance area" (products, personnel, financial performance, etc.). In the context of an information system, goals are relatively most often thought of as a quantitative level of aspiration, a certain standard, defining a state that an organization or individual considers successful. The plan also clarifies the level of effort and behavior expected of the members of the organization, while allowing coordination by adjusting goals in the functional areas of the organization, and thus becoming the basis for controlling the actions of groups and individuals to ensure their compliance with the desired results of the organization as a whole.

Planning is a form of *ex ante* control because it provides the information necessary to guide individual and group activities. It is the main tool for promoting coherence between the goals of employees and the organization (Malmi & Brown, 2008, p. 290). This observation makes it possible to identify a number of approaches that allow us to distinguish short-term and long-term planning (depending on the time perspective), as well as operational, tactical, or strategic planning (depending on the importance to the organization).

Over the years, it has become established that if something cannot be measured or is not measured, it cannot be managed or improved (Kaplan & Porter, 2011). The list of reasons why measurement should be used is also relatively extensive, coming in the following set of statements (Halachmi, 2002, p. 65):

■ If you cannot measure it, you will not understand it;
■ If you cannot understand it, you cannot control it;
■ If you cannot control it, you cannot improve it;
■ If they know you intend to measure it, they will get it done;
■ If you do not measure results, you cannot tell success from failure;
■ If you do not see success, you cannot reward it;
■ If you cannot reward success, you are probably rewarding failure;
■ If you will not recognize success, you may not be able to sustain it;
■ If you cannot recognize success or failure, you cannot learn from it;
■ If you cannot recognize failure, you will repeat old mistakes and keep wasting resources;
■ If you cannot relate results to consumed resources, you do not know what is the real cost;
■ If you cannot tell the full cost you cannot get the best value for money when contracting out.

One of the reasons behind the popularity of using performance measurement systems in organizations is the observation that measurement, which involves assigning numbers to objects according to rules, influences employee behavior (Neely et al., 1995, p. 95). This influence takes place through the information that the measurement itself produces, as well as through the act or process of measurement. This constitutes a kind of control mechanism (Flamholtz et al., 1985, p. 40; Zábojník, 2014, p. 341) in which the information function of measurement provides the basis for *ex post* control, allowing the results achieved to be compared with the plan. Conversely, when measurement is used to indicate the expected level of achievement, it performs a function similar to planning, influencing the behavior of employees as they strive to achieve their goals, becoming *ex ante* control (Flamholtz et al., 1985, p. 40). However, for the act of measurement to induce behavioral change, the results of the measurement must be made available and presented. Presenting an organization's achievements and comparing them with plans creates feedback information, which, as a feedback loop, can enable comparison of actual and expected achievements of the organization and, in the case of deviations, trigger corrective actions (Flamholtz, 1996, p. 601; Merchant & Otley, 2007, p. 786).

Cybernetics views feedback as a signal, mechanism, and process that controls the system itself, or, if it applies to human performance, triggers self-control mechanisms, and thus enhances both performance and motivation (Ashford & Cummings, 1983, p. 370). Feedback is, therefore, an essential resource for organizations and, as loops between performance and goals, can induce at least three processes: (1) keeping controlled individuals on intended paths of development, i.e., leading to goal attainment; (2) directing individual behavior toward organizational goals, ensuring that individual and organizational goals are aligned; (3) stimulating learning and change as the organization and its members seek to improve their performance by revising previously adopted goals (Pitkänen & Lukka, 2011, p. 127). The human behavior-oriented approach to organizational behavior (cf. Flamholtz, 1979, pp. 75–77) points out that the information system:

■ can serve as a criterion function, operationally defining the goals and standards of actions that should be achieved, which has three psychological effects: it directs the efforts of employees, helps organize thoughts and directions of analysis, and provides a model of the appropriate set of variables to which actions should be adjusted (simplifying reality);

■ acts as a catalyst, increasing the propensity of managers to plan systematically;

■ influences managers' perceptions, as it creates a set of indicators that serve as inputs to generate alternatives for decision making and problem-solving, with alternatives for decisions and behaviors usually limited to the set of information generated by the system (Flamholtz et al., 1985, p. 41);

■ through measurement affects both the direction and the strength of motivation, as members of the organization, while focusing efforts in areas where results are measured, often ignore areas that are not measured or rewarded.

The information system can use both financial measures used in traditional financial and cost accounting and budgeting systems as well as non-financial measures of organizational performance, including indicators of capacity utilization, product, or service quality (e.g., patient satisfaction rate, bed utilization, average length of patient treatment, reoperation, hospital infection rate, etc.) (Flamholtz, 1996, p. 601). The effectiveness of the impact of the measurement system on work behavior and performance depends mainly on the adequacy and reliability of the information generated by the measurement system. Hence, a key task of the measurement system must be to ensure transparency to stakeholders through a systematic internal and external credibility acquisition process (Austen, 2010, p. 123). Thus, an important feature of the measurement system should be behavioral adequacy and reliability. The behavioral adequacy of an information system refers to the extent to which the measurement process leads to the behavior it is intended to induce or reinforce. Behavioral reliability, on the other hand, refers to the degree to which the behaviors produced by the measurement process are consistently produced, that is, they are repeatedly replicated (Flamholtz et al., 1985, p. 41).

It should be noted that while there are many benefits to performance measurement, there are also some problems associated with it, since the introduction of measurement in specific areas can lead to a shift of focus from major organizational goals to those that have been "measured" (cf. Hopwood, 1972, p. 159; Liedtka et al., 2008, p. 75). As a result, the introduction of metrics that induce specific behaviors to achieve isolated specific goals can result in a reduction in efficiency in achieving important organizational goals in favor of achieving a given indicator. This is supported to some extent by the observation: "For in a situation where the number of possible actions for attaining a given end is severely limited, one acts rationally by selecting the means which, on the basis of the available evidence, has the greatest probability of attaining this goal and yet the goal may actually not be attained. Contrariwise, an end may be attained by action which, on the basis of the knowledge available to the actor, is irrational (as in the case of "hunches")" (Merton, 1936, p. 896).

It is worth noting that some authors directly equate management accounting systems, including systems for measuring and evaluating achievements, with management control (Eldenburg et al., 2017, p. 52; Ferreira & Otley, 2009; Otley, 1999, pp. 363–364). Such an approach, however, should be considered inappropriate. While management accounting systems certainly encompass a broader scope than financial accounting (which is primarily used for external reporting, among other things, for tax purposes), and are considered to include systems for measuring and evaluating achievements, such as the balanced scorecard (Aidemark & Funck, 2009, p. 256), they are only one component of the control system (Simons, 1995; Otley, 1999, p. 367), particularly when the control system is understood broadly, as in the concept of the four levers of control (Simons, 1995). D. Otley believes that a formal performance measurement system can be seen as the main mechanism that can be used to make the set of relationships between goals and decisions, actions and processes explicit, that is, the measures that an organization has developed as methods used to control the strategic direction (Otley, 1999, p. 367). However, the main task of the information system that comes before the management control system (Naranjo-Gil, 2016, p. 866) is to support control by providing information not only on the performance of each department of the organization, but also on planning and measurement, and providing an assessment of top management (Kanthi Herath, 2007, p. 905). The relationship between performance measurement and strategy has been extensively analyzed in the strategy literature (Lachmann et al., 2013; Langfield-Smith, 1997, 2007; Tucker et al., 2009), but it does not point to aspirations or insights that justify replacing management control with performance measurement and evaluation systems.

Feedback information in the context of management control has its basis in systems thinking and cybernetics as a form of feedback (Lachmann et al., 2013; Langfield-Smith, 1997, 2007; Tucker et al., 2009). Cybernetics views feedback as a signal, mechanism, and process that controls itself and simplifies and mechanizes the functioning of an organization, although in principle it can also be used to analyze complex human systems. Feedback can be defined as the return of information about variability from the output of a process to the input or stages of the process, providing the opportunity to make adjustments to maintain desired levels of performance or control the stability of the system (Simons, 2014, p. 4).

In the context indicated, feedback is defined in two ways, narrowly or broadly. From a narrow viewpoint, it is seen only as retrospectively oriented comparative information between actual results and predetermined goals, deviations revealing the need for action (*ex post* control). From a broader point of view, feedback is considered future-oriented anticipatory information that can be used to forecast the need for action before observed deviations, with an eye to changes that may occur in the environment (*ex ante* control) (Pitkänen & Lukka, 2011, p. 127). Often, however, in a hospital, for example, the implementation of a contract with the payer must include both monitoring of actual results (*ex post*) and planning and forecasting for the future (*ex ante*) related to, for example, seasonal fluctuations in patient morbidity. In some areas of activity, feedback also serves as a control mechanism, for example, with regard to information on employee behavior and performance being part of the incentive system (Leung & Trotman, 2005, p. 538; Pitkänen & Lukka, 2011, p. 127).

The recipient of feedback can use it for corrective action, can interpret it as a reward or punishment or as a promise of future reward or punishment. Thus, the informational function of feedback should be considered the most appropriate for a control system. At the same time, it seems reasonable to consider that the impact of feedback on performance is positive when the information is frequent, from a reliable source, delivered in a timely manner, understandable, relevant to the tasks performed, and specific. At the same time, negative feedback is rejected more often than positive feedback (Flamholtz et al., 1985, p. 42).

As a primary control mechanism, feedback can directly guide individual efforts toward achieving group or organizational goals (Flamholtz et al., 1985, p. 43). In other words, performance measures, budgets, and other diagnostic control systems produce specific, directional, and comparative feedback on how an organization or its units are achieving their strategic, operational, and financial goals. Along with an associated system of organizational rewards or personal supervision, feedback is intended to motivate desired behavior (Pitkänen & Lukka, 2011, p. 127). Feedback is also crucial for learning, as it allows managers to fine-tune, and sometimes radically change, the organization's strategies (Simons, 2014, p. 46). In the area of strategy, this information is of two types: information about progress toward goals and information about emerging threats and opportunities.

Both of these types of information provide feedback – information about actual events or results that can be compared with expectations or standards (Simons, 2014, pp. 71–72). In this context, too, feedback can serve three functions: to keep controlled entities on planned development paths (goal attainment), to guide individual behavior toward organizational goals (goal congruence), and to enable learning and change when organizations and individuals seek to improve their performance (goal verification) (Malmi & Brown, 2008, p. 292; Pitkänen & Lukka, 2011, p. 127). The performance of such important functions by feedback makes the provision of feedback based on evaluation, including subjective evaluation, one of the three main goals of performance evaluation (Zhang, 2018, p. 633). This is an important observation, but it should be remembered that the information system, including planning, measurement, and feedback, while performing control functions, cannot be equated with fully developed management control. Instead, they are a key prior element (*antecedent*) to management control.

Over the decades, a number of integrated models of organizational performance measurement and management systems (PMS) have emerged, combining planning, measurement, and feedback into a single system. Examples include the Balanced Scorecard (Kaplan & Norton, 1992), the French proposal Tableau de Bord (Epstein & Manzoni, 1998) or the Total Performance Scorecard (Rampersad, 2004). As mentioned earlier, it happens that these systems are equated with management control or, conversely, some researchers equate management control with information systems (Otley, 1999, p. 364). While PMS can perform important control functions and are key elements of management control, they cannot fully replace it. B. Pešalj, A. Pavlov, and P. Micheli point out a clear difference between performance measurement and management (performance appraisal) systems and organizational control. They define PMS as a formal process whose purpose is to obtain, analyze, and communicate information about the nature of a process or activity, while they define organizational control as formalized procedures and processes that use information to maintain or change patterns in an organization's activities (2018, p. 2172). In most organizations, formal feedback and measurement systems (e.g., budgeting systems, project management systems, management accounting systems, balanced scorecards, and other performance measurement systems) are an important subset of the broader management control systems (Bisbe et al., 2019, p. 124).

It is also important to note the inconsistencies in nomenclature found in the scientific literature. The most common names used are performance measurement systems and performance management systems, and by some authors these systems are defined separately (Table 3.1). Other authors combine these two systems into one, calling it performance management and measurement (PMM) (de Waal & Kourtit, 2013; Yetano et al., 2020), use these terms interchangeably (Austen, 2010, p. 102), or give them other names as well, for example, contemporary performance measurement systems (Franco-Santos et al., 2012, p. 79) or comprehensive performance measurement systems (Hall, 2008, p. 141).

It should be noted that the word *performance* is ambiguous and difficult to define (Otley, 1999, p. 364). The word *performance* in management sciences is understood in many ways, including efficiency, execution, result, achievement, and accomplishment. In addition, terms such as "efficiency" and "results" are often used interchangeably (March & Sutton, 1997), even though organizational efficiency is more about the consumption of resources to achieve organizational goals, and results are more about the achievement or failure to achieve those goals. Thus, results can be achieved efficiently

Table 3.1. Classification of the organization's performance measurement and management systems

Performance measurement systems:	Performance management systems:
• "the process of quantifying action, where measurement is the process of quantification and action leads to performance." (Neely et al., 1995, p. 80) or • "(1) provide information that allows the firm to identify the strategies offering the highest potential for achieving the firm's objectives, and (2) align management processes, such as target setting, decision-making, and performance evaluation, with the achievement of the chosen strategic objectives." (Ittner et al., 2003, p. 715) or • information systems that managers use to track the implementation of business strategy by comparing actual results against strategic goals and objectives. A performance measurement system typically comprises systematic methods of setting business goals together with periodic feedback reports." (Simons, 2014, p. 7)	"PMSs as the evolving formal and informal mechanisms, processes, systems, and networks used by organizations for conveying the key objectives and goals elicited by management, for assisting the strategic process and ongoing management through analysis, planning, measurement, control, rewarding, and broadly managing performance, and for supporting and facilitating organizational learning and change." (Ferreira & Otley, 2009, p. 264)

when relatively few resources are consumed, or inefficiently when a greater amount of those resources are consumed. In this book, the word *performance* will be understood mainly as "results" or "achievements," although it can also be understood as "productivity," "efficiency," or "effectiveness."

This is because different categories, such as efficiency and effectiveness, which may be defined differently, may be considered in the process of measuring performance. Effectiveness can be defined as the degree to which goals were achieved within a specified time frame (Otley, 1999, p. 367) or the extent to which customer requirements were met (Neely et al., 1995, p. 80). Efficiency refers to what level of resources are required to achieve certain results (Otley, 1999, p. 367). In other words, it may be defined as the result of the activities undertaken, described by the ratio of the results obtained to the value of the inputs. There are three elements associated with performance measurement:

- the process of quantifying the efficiency and effectiveness of an action,
- metric used to quantify the efficiency and/or effectiveness of an action, and
- the set of metrics used to quantify both the efficiency and effectiveness of actions. (Neely et al., 1995, p. 80)

Some light is shed on this terminological heterogeneity by the typology of PMS developed by M. Franco-Santos, L. Lucianetti, and M. Bourne (2012, p. 81). These authors identify four types of PMS on the basis of two criteria: components, i.e., the building blocks of PMS, and key objectives (Table 3.2).

It should be noted that the different types of PMS do not incrementally develop further components or objectives, as is the case, for example, in the three-element typology on the balanced scorecard developed on the basis of a study of German-speaking organizations (Speckbacher et al., 2003, pp. 363–367). Indeed, these studies show that organizations use three different versions of the balanced scorecard. Type I contains only financial and non-financial performance measures grouped into perspectives. Type II is a Type I scorecard that uses a specific approach to describe an organization's strategy using sequential cause-and-effect logic to link tangible and intangible assets. These cause-and-effect linkages are called strategy maps (Kaplan & Norton, 2004) and success mapping (Neely et al., 2002, pp. 178, 199, 240, 249). Type III is a Type II scorecard with an additional feature that makes bonus payments contingent on performance. In practice, however, it turns out that many organizations tie financial and non-financial performance

Table 3.2. Types of performance measurement

	Type A	*Type B*	*Type C*	*Type D*
Components	Financial and non-financial performance measures implicitly or explicitly linked to strategy	• Financial and non-financial performance measures explicitly linked to strategy • With explicit cause-and-effect relationships among measures	Financial and non-financial performance measures explicitly or implicitly linked to strategy	Financial and non-financial performance measures explicitly or implicitly linked to strategy
Use/purpose	• Inform decision making • Evaluate organizational performance	• Inform decision making • Evaluate organizational performance	• Inform decision making • Evaluate organizational and managerial performance (without links to monetary rewards)	• Inform decision making • Evaluate organizational and managerial performance • Influence monetary rewards

Source: Adapted from Franco-Santos et al., 2012, p. 82.

measures to rewards, but they do not analyze the cause-and-effect relationships between these measures (Franco-Santos et al., 2012, p. 81). Thus, it can be concluded that the use of different names may be due not only to the desire of the authors to "stand out," but also to different configurations of PMS. In the context of hospitals, performance measurement and management system may be defined as an instrument that facilitates:

- assessing the degree to which the hospital's goals are being met;
- taking corrective action in cases of significant deviations from the plan;
- motivating employees to work toward the hospital's goals;
- identification of areas of hospital operations that need improvement (Hass-Symotiuk, 2011a, p. 19, 2011b, p. 63).

Previous research shows that health-care organizations are using various systems to measure and evaluate achievements, mainly the balanced scorecard (Aidemark & Funck, 2009; Jaworzyńska, 2015; Lachmann et al., 2013; Lewandowski & Cirella, 2022; Rahimi et al., 2017; Ritchie et al., 2019; Raposo et al., 2022). Such complex systems allow for comprehensive measurement and evaluation of hospital achievements in a number of areas, relating to internal processes, including quality improvement, patients (e.g., initiatives to improve patients' satisfaction and experience of their interactions with the facility), and financial aspects (Lachmann et al., 2013, p. 346). In this context, it is important to keep in mind that in addition to these complex systems, there are also information systems specialized in providing decision-makers with information to make rational decisions; these are most often referred to as: (1) management information systems (Cygańska, 2018, p. 43; Kanthi Herath, 2007, p. 905)72, (2) accounting information systems (Romney & Steinbart, 2018), (3) formal information systems (Simons, 1995, p. 39; Lill et al., 2020, p. 2), or (4) cost-systems (Pizzini, 2006). These systems are also widely used in health care, particularly in hospitals as the sector's most complex organizations (Abernethy et al., 2006, p. 806; Aidemark & Funck, 2009, p. 256; de Campos et al., 2017, p. 292; Cygańska, 2018; Engin & Gürses, 2019).

Contemporary hospital information system consists of a set of interrelated sources of information, aimed at processing information and systematically supplying management bodies and other interested units and individuals in the organization with the necessary information. One should also agree with the observation that, due to the close connection between medical and management activities, the information system should meet the needs of both management and medical personnel. To meet these needs, the information system should provide information to comprehensively coordinate the management process, create a network of information necessary for planning, control, and decision making, and use information systems that enable the collection, processing, retrieval, and transfer of information, which requires, among other things, ensuring the appropriate scope, level of aggregation, timeliness, and integration of information (Chenhall & Morris, 1986, p. 17; Hammad et al., 2010, p. 766; Hammad et al., 2013, p. 319; Nguyen, 2018, p. 42; Ghasemi et al., 2019, p. 195).

The scope of information stored and made available by information systems can be characterized by a number of features. It can be narrow or expanded, depending on whether the information is internal or external to the organization, financial or non-financial, only quantitative or also qualitative, whether it concerns cost information or also medical information (Chenhall & Morris, 1986, p. 19). Information can be provided at different levels of aggregation – from basic unprocessed data to various aggregations, depending on the area and period of interest, for organizational units, business units, and the entire organization, respectively, on a monthly, quarterly, or annual basis (Chenhall & Morris, 1986, p. 21; Ghasemi et al., 2019, p. 195). Timeliness of information enhances AI's ability to report on the latest events and provide rapid feedback on decisions and their effects (Chenhall & Morris, 1986, p. 20; Ghasemi et al., 2019, p. 195). Integration refers to the ability to generate information that crosses functional boundaries, such as a single department, which can support coordination of goals that take into account interdependencies between functional areas (Chenhall & Morris, 1986, p. 22; Ghasemi et al., 2019, p. 195). It should be noted that medics' access to relevant information promotes cost reduction and improved quality of treatment (Dick et al., 1997, p. 3; Haux, 2006, p. 270).

Analyzing the definitions relating to PMS and management information systems (MIS), one can see that there is a great deal of overlap between these concepts. This is particularly clear when MIS is compared with the PMS typologies proposed by M. Franco-Santos et al. and by G. Speckbacher et al. (2012, p. 81) i (Speckbacher et al., 2003, pp. 363–367). Indeed, this comparison shows that type A, but also type C PMS (Table 3.2), completely overlap with the functionalities of management information systems. Similarly, the Type I balanced scorecard overlaps with MIS as far as its functions are concerned. The only elements that distinguish the more advanced of the systems in question are the causal relationships assumed in the PMS and the systemic linking of goal achievement to remuneration, although the use of MIS does not exclude such a link to employee and team performance in certain scopes or periods. Due to the existence of an obvious convergence between PMS and MIS, some authors, more attached to the traditional association of information systems with management accounting, use the term "strategic management accounting systems" (Naranjo-Gil, 2016, p. 866).

Thus, given the definitional and nomenclatural ambiguities around PMS and MIS cited in this chapter, in the remainder of the monograph systems that provide useful information for control and promote efficiency and effectiveness in achieving organizational goals will be generally referred to as **information systems (IS)**. From the point of view of the purpose of the study and the hospital's top management, information systems should provide information in two main areas at least: quality and safety, and the cost of health services provided. Combining and comparing indicators from these two areas makes it possible to create more complex measures of hospital performance.

3.2 Measurement of a Hospital Performance

As mentioned, a prerequisite for the management and control process in a hospital is ongoing measurement and evaluation of achievements (performance). However, it is important to note an important difference between measuring various types of activities and processes taking place in the hospital and measuring the performance of the hospital as a whole. This is because efficient implementation of a process does not mean that this process positively affects the performance of the entire hospital (Lewandowski & Cirella, 2022). An example would be scientific activities. The result of efficient implementation of this process may be a large number of scientific publications in high-scoring journals; however, this may be at the expense of time devoted to patients, and thus the quality of treatment. Therefore, on the one hand, a hospital's achievements should be measured either as a summary indicator or as a bundle of performance indicators, and, on the other hand, the selection of appropriate indicators and their relevance as measures of a hospital's achievements should take into account the influence of external factors on the variability of performance and include practical as well as social and political considerations (Raposo et al., 2022).

Noting that management theory based on the experience of the business sector emphasizes the need to ensure a positive correlation between management and efficiency, it should be assumed that such a relationship also exists in the case of hospital management. What is important here, however, is the need to consider the peculiarities of the health-care sector, requiring consideration of a broader context, primarily involving more intricate stakeholder relationships. This means that the efficiency of hospitals can be studied, for example, from the point of view of acquiring resources from the environment, especially valuable and scarce resources (funds for investment and treatment, specialists, knowledge, innovation, reputation), transforming resources into products, i.e., treating patients, and transferring the outputs of the system to the environment, i.e., organizing further treatment of the patient after hospitalization. However, the use of quantitative performance measures common to business organizations should be approached with caution.

In addition, the evaluation of achievements first requires the definition of specific performance objectives. Meanwhile, as already mentioned, in hospitals, the problem of consistency of objectives is relatively unclear and there are serious difficulties in ensuring it, which is due, among other things, to the fact that the decision-making process in public organizations is far from economic rationality, as it is dictated largely by a political component related to the influence of various types of stakeholders, including medical professionals (Marinkovic et al., 2022). At the same time, one must agree with the observation that profit is not the primary goal of public hospitals (Austen, 2010, p. 104; Hass-Symotiuk, 2011b, p. 67; Hensel, 2008, pp. 11–52), and, therefore, it is not an adequate indicator of hospital performance. A. Kożuch and B. Kożuch even warn against the use of financial indicators, especially profit, as an indicator for measuring the performance of public organizations, noting that "relating the profit category to non-business organizations causes the negative phenomenon of excessive economization of the provision of public services and irregularities in management" (Kożuch & Kożuch, 2008, p. 34). An example of such irregularities may be the introduction of financing of hospitals through casemix systems (DRG, DRG), strictly linking the payment received by the hospital to the health status (illness) of patients, the procedures that were performed, and the length of stay in the hospital (Schwierz, 2016, p. 35). Such strict monetization has led some hospitals to select patients for profitability, adjust the length of hospital stay based on the amount of funding instead of medical criteria, and "creatively" code patients to bill them in a higher group (DRG) (Christensen et al., 2006, p. 129; Covaleski et al., 1993, p. 75; Schwierz, 2016, p. 35).

Finding accurate measures of achievement for health-care organizations is, therefore, a major challenge, particularly due to the fact that these organizations use economic resources to achieve a social effect that is difficult to measure in precise terms (Greenberg & Nunamaker, 1987, p. 332; Jones & Pendlebury, 2000, p. 105; Raposo et al., 2022; Van Peursem et al., 1995, p. 36). The solution here seems to be to make assessments on the basis of both objective indicators, such as those determined by cost accounting, and subjective ones, based on perception measurements (Austen, 2010, p. 118). In the area of quality, measurement systems based on both patient (Anhang Price et al., 2014; Groene et al., 2015; Isaac et al., 2010; Wheat et al., 2018) and medical professional opinions (Ball et al., 2017; McHugh & Stimpfel, 2012), as well as objective indicators, such as hospital readmissions (Fonarow et al., 2017; Tsai et al., 2013) and mortality rates (Jha et al., 2007; Krumholz et al., 2013), are highly applicable. However, here too, objective measurement is very difficult, and patient experience cannot be the main criterion for assessing quality either, because, as studies have shown, patients evaluate quality mainly on the basis of their interactions with nursing staff (Tasso et al., 2002).

However, due to the difficulty of applying objective performance indicators (Lewandowski & Cirella, 2022), the use of subjective indicators is advocated. Importantly, the benefits of such a solution are pointed out even in areas concerning financial performance, which in this situation is assessed by key employees, mostly members of top management, in relation to either surrounding organizations or the industry average (Abernethy & Brownell, 1999, p. 196; Abernethy & Stoelwinder, 1991, p. 111; Baird et al., 2017, p. 206; Gong & Ferreira, 2014, p. 508; de Harlez & Malagueño, 2016, p. 9; Widener, 2007, p. 774).

The difficulties flagged make it necessary to pay attention to indicators for determining efficiency in general, especially adapted to the activities of non-profit organizations. In this regard, it is important that (Herman & Renz, 1999, pp. 110–121):

■ the efficiency of the organization was evaluated only by comparing either with other organizations in the same group or against historical data of the same organization or against some model of an ideal organization;
■ organizational agility has been treated multidimensionally and has never been reduced to a single indicator (although it is already less clear what dimensions should be considered);
■ boards have been able to influence the efficiency of the organization (although it is not clear how they do this);

- organizational agility was considered a social construct;
- more agile organizations have had the opportunity to identify and apply sound management practices;
- outcome indicators for single areas as a measure of organizational performance had significant limitations, and they may be dangerous to assess as a whole in this view.

It is important to point out that the use of outcome indicators can generate pressure to engage in practices that will produce inappropriate or unintended consequences (Herman & Renz, 1999, p. 121). Using PMS in hospitals may also bring problems with strategy development and implementation (more in (Lewandowski & Cirella, 2022)). This has been reflected, among other things, in vocational training social assistance programs, for which recipients who were most ready to benefit were qualified instead of those who were most in need, resulting in significant improvements in indicators. What is clear is that the fundamental problem in such circumstances arises when such evaluations become the basis for future funding decisions. Similar effects in health care are caused by the use of financing based on casemix systems. For years, it has been observed in this solution that hospitals, to gain more funding, use various ways to "move patients" to better-funded groups. These ways include misdiagnosis, miscoding (reporting treatments or procedures that have not been performed), and reordering of diagnoses (reporting secondary diagnoses as primary diagnoses in cases where this results in higher reimbursement, etc.) (Hsia et al., 1988; Schwierz, 2016, p. 35). It should be remembered that after several decades of using casemix systems, payers are aware of the use of such practices, and while they do not have the character of serious abuse (it is not always easy to resolve which condition is primary and which is comorbid), this phenomenon is already considered in the pricing of individual groups. In general, however, despite the well-known problems of financing hospitals using casemix systems for decades, more and more medical services are being paid for in this way (Kahn III et al., 2015; Thomas Craig et al., 2020, p. 2).

Based on what has been discussed so far, it can, therefore, be concluded that a comprehensive information system is necessary to help managers and key employees plan and monitor hospital services efficiently and effectively (Ramani, 2004, p. 210). A study conducted by M.J. Pizzini on a sample of 277 U.S. hospitals showed that hospitals with systems that provide more cost details are significantly more profitable, generate more cash flow, and have proportionately lower administrative costs (2006, p. 203). The results of these studies support the assumption that more functional cost-systems provide managers with data more appropriate for making decisions that improve hospital performance. However, no relationship has been observed between data detail and costs per patient treated. The reason for the lack of relationship may be that physicians are responsible for the cost of treatment, and managers' decisions have little impact on their clinical decisions. This means that cost containment has been focused on administrative processes rather than the clinical process. At the same time, in the perception of managers, better cost classification is associated with higher ratings of the relevance of the data received, as well as with actual financial performance. Similarly, positively associated with managers' beliefs about the relevance and timeliness of data is increased reporting frequency, which is also unrelated to financial performance. As a result, hospitals with systems that identify more actual deviations from assumed costs have significantly lower profits and relatively higher administrative costs (2006, p. 203). This may be indicative of reverse causality because, while poorly performing hospitals may engage in deviation analysis to identify and correct problems, tests controlling for past performance result in higher administrative costs at these hospitals. In summary, therefore, it should be recognized that a system that enables analysis with greater detail and has the ability to partially disaggregate costs has a positive impact on hospital performance, but even an improved detail function does not have the potential to reduce clinical costs.

An important element that strengthens the quality of information available in hospitals, and thus the role of the information system, is the degree of use of information systems. Indeed, there is a direct positive impact of the quality of information obtained from management accounting systems, as measured by their scope, timeliness, and aggregation capabilities, on the satisfaction of its users in hospitals (Chun Cheong Fong & Quaddus, 2010, pp. 173–174). On the other hand, the ability to obtain, analyze, and distribute information is understandably closely related to the degree of computerization of hospitals. Indeed, as business practice shows, the informatization of hospitals affects not only revenue growth and cost reduction, but even such indicators as mortality rates. Lower mortality rates result from increased adoption of computerized physician orders, more accurate ordering and delivery of drugs, and better clinical decision support (Menon et al., 2009, p. 298).

The observations presented here allow us to accept as true the statement that managers of business units in hospitals, who are responsible for both costs and achieving other goals, need more up-to-date information in terms of frequency and speed of reporting (Hammad et al., 2013, pp. 325–326). Up-to-date information is also badly needed by clinical unit managers who deal with more specialized services, such as clinical wards, operating theaters, and laboratories, where patients' lives have the highest priority. Clinical unit managers are more likely to use information aggregated by different criteria, such as time, functional areas, or decision-making models, and this correlates with the greater autonomy their units receive. They also use more integrated information to coordinate among their subunits in a highly decentralized hospital and to clarify the impact of their decisions on other subunits throughout the hospital. On the other hand, however, to reduce information overload in decision making, subunit managers try to limit the amount and scope of information to only the most important when it relates to other sections, functional areas of the hospital, the external environment, and when it is non-financial and future-oriented (Hammad et al., 2013, p. 325).

The conceptual model, linking information system design to performance, is usually presented in terms of a cause-and-effect chain in which more effective IS produces more relevant and useful data that improves decision making at various levels of the organization, thereby leading to improved performance. Up-to-date, relevant, and understandable information has the potential to improve management decisions in areas such as cost control, product quality, and performance evaluation (Baines & Langfield-Smith, 2003, p. 681). This is a direct result of the nature of a manager's job, which involves recruiting, training, and implementing innovative changes based on the right information (Laitinen, 2009, p. 551), especially since there is a significantly positive relationship among broad coverage, timeliness, aggregation, and integration and management actions, including but not limited to planning, control, and problem-solving (Soobaroyen & Poorundersing, 2008, p. 202).

In this context, it is also important to note that the extent and timeliness of information provided are significantly positively related to managers' actions in such areas as coordinating, representing, evaluating, supervising, and planning (Hammad et al., 2013, p. 324). Similar results were obtained in a study of two Norwegian health-care regions (Health Region East and Health Region West). The east region (East) kept its spending within the planned budget, while the west region (West) exceeded its planned budget year after year. One significant difference noted was precisely the frequency with which financial matters were discussed. In the region that was within budget, financial matters were discussed more frequently (Østergren, 2009, p. 185).

Thus, based on the considerations made, it can be concluded that IS generates a wide range of information and ensures its timeliness improves management activities, including at the level of clinical unit managers, and can lead to improvements in hospital performance. However, objective measurement of the performance of the hospital as a whole is difficult, indicating that business practice should pay attention to an approach using subjective indicators, whereby it is important to distinguish the evaluation of hospital performance from the evaluation of employee performance and behavior.

3.3 Evaluation and Reward of Hospital Employees

Performance and behavioral evaluations, which are the basis for reward or punishment, are a critical link in management control, as their criteria indicate to employees what top management considers important and necessary (Ferreira & Otley, 2009, p. 272). Appraisal involves evaluating the performance of individuals or groups in achieving organizational goals and is usually based on some system of measures. In this view, it is relatively most often a type of *ex post* control that involves comparing achieved performance against predetermined goals and standards, based on information provided by the measurement system and personal observation of the superior. Rewards are given either for appropriate behavior or for achieving results that are desirable for the position or from a particular team or group (Flamholtz et al., 1985, p. 43; Ouchi, 1977, p. 96). Established negative deviations require improvement actions. Positive deviations, or the absence of deviations, require motivating actions to continue behaving in the same way or to ensure repetition of results. In doing so, it is important to keep in mind that behavior that is not followed by a reward is less likely to be repeated in the future (Flamholtz, 1996, p. 602), and rewarding increases the likelihood that the same behavior will be repeated. In doing so, it is worth noting that there are formal and informal rewards and punishments in organizations. Formal ones are awarded on the basis of objective evaluation criteria and are included, for example, in the salary regulations of the organization. They can also be assigned subjectively, based on the individual evaluation of the superior or possibly the collective opinion of colleagues. Informal rewards and punishments are not listed in organizational documents, but they too can be allocated based on objective criteria. In practice, it can look like this: information about an employee's performance from the information system is available to members of the organization and on this basis the employee gains respect and recognition from those around him (Idemobi et al., 2017). Informal rewards and punishments can also be administered on the basis of subjective evaluation (Zhang, 2018, p. 633). Studies show that the closer the link between employee performance and incentive rewards, the better the organization's results and the greater the satisfaction obtained by employees (Lin et al., 2014, p. 12).

Generally, however, the terms "reward system" or "rewards" refer to levels of compensation and other benefits provided to employees based on their performance, which can also be referred to as "performance-based rewards" (Nguyen et al., 2017, p. 206). Thus, evaluation and rewards can be both formal and informal, tangible or intangible, and granted on the basis of objective and subjective considerations (Zhang, 2018, p. 633). In contrast, the very use of punishment and rewards is different. Rather, rewards are used to reinforce positive behavior, to achieve increasingly better results, while punishments are used to eliminate undesirable behavior. The idea is to instill in the employee the hope of gaining benefits when they act in accordance with the organization's goals, and to create a sense of fear of punishment when they violate accepted norms and work below the set minimum (Lange et al., 2014). Thus, control in this area serves to reinforce behavior that coincides with the organization's goals and discourage harmful or unproductive behavior. A prerequisite for the proper functioning of the behavior control system is the acceptance of the applied means of influence by the majority of the workforce. One can speak of the possibility of controlling behavior only when, in the perception of the employee in question, but also of those around him, the incentives applied have been judged as deserved, that is, coinciding with the effort made (the employee knows exactly for what behavior he has been rewarded), fair and not contradictory to the legal, ethical, and moral norms adopted in a given environment (Franco-Santos et al., 2012, p. 93).

What is clear here is that a formal system of measuring and evaluating performance is usually seen as the main mechanism that can be used to establish how employees are rewarded (Flamholtz, 1996, p. 601; Otley, 1999, p. 367). In doing so, it should be noted that, in fact, many organizations conduct subjective evaluations of their employees, using them to provide feedback to employees (Zhang, 2018, p. 633). However, such evaluations are only fair if managers understand the contribution made by subordinates under certain conditions. Measurement-related evaluation systems in hospitals, on the other hand, are mainly constructed based on cost accounting or measurement of medical indicators (Hass-Symotiuk, 2011b).

One of the essential requirements of appraisal systems is the generation of feedback, both influencing the behavior of organizational members and being one of the determinants of managers' actions. In fact, they are a tool at their disposal to motivate, reward, and guide the actions of subordinate employees (Ashford & Cummings, 1983, p. 371; Zhang, 2018, p. 633). In this approach, however, it is important to distinguish between formal procedures for evaluating performance and thus creating feedback (often coordinated by the human resources function) and procedures that are informal and subjective, but actually performed by senior managers. Informal and subjective appraisal often safeguards "gaming" activities with the formal appraisal system (Franco-Santos et al., 2012, p. 93) or when the quality of information obtained from formal information systems is insufficient. This is because bonuses for employees based on subjective assessments of performance are used in situations where objective evaluation of performance or behavior is difficult and complex (Baker et al., 1994) and, as the previous discussion shows, this group includes the evaluation of the performance and behavior of medical professionals. In this case, the level of remuneration or the granting of other rewards depends on the superior's perception of the quality and quantity of the work performed by a subordinate or team (Prendergast, 1999, p. 29). It is assumed here that rewards or punishments are given in a subjective manner, when the decision to give them is made by the manager, based on his own assessment of the situation, usually judging some facts, but often using intuition as well (Lange et al., 2014). The subjective form of awarding rewards and punishments gives managers considerable power, and thus control, over the behavior and actions of employees. However, it should be kept in mind that evaluation based on subjective measures is usually accepted only when there is a high degree of trust between the evaluator and the person being evaluated (Flamholtz et al., 1985, p. 44). The trust of subordinates stems not only from a belief in the goodwill of superiors, but also from a belief in their competence (Yeşilbaş & Çetin, 2019), in the fact that they know the industry in which the organization operates very well, that they are able to assess the context of the actions and decisions taken by subordinates, the size of the field of freedom in taking these actions and decisions, and the potential results of these activities (Fleig-Palmer et al., 2018, p. 71) but also resistance to stress, courage, and authority (Wysocka & Lewandowski, 2017, p. 180). The indicated solutions confirm the insights of R. Simons (Simons, 1995, p. 117), who, in describing an interactive control system, noted the importance of formal incentives awarded by managers subjectively, rather than on the basis of predetermined criteria. For taking certain actions, "for trying," rather than for specific results.

Subjective forms of rewards and punishments are particularly important for activities that cannot be programmed before they are carried out, nor can they be evaluated after they are carried out, as they are based on individual commitment to seeking new opportunities. Thus, subjective rewards for employees are one of the conditions for the flexibility necessary to ensure that employees are engaged in those processes that superiors believe can bring the greatest development opportunities to the organization (Pierce & Sweeney, 2005, p. 364; Zhang, 2018, p. 632). Rewarding for contributions to the search for new solutions, rather than for results, also stimulates organizational learning, since commitment – unlike results – is dependent not on the environment, not on general economic or political trends, but on the individual efforts of individuals. This kind of reward dynamizes the search for and sharing of new knowledge, as well as the flow of information up the organizational hierarchy. Importantly, this also applies to negative information, about poor performance or trends, since remuneration is not dependent on it.

Given the above arguments, the subjective form of reward is one of the key solutions in controlling the process of formulating a strategy or correcting a currently operating one, since it is through rewards that managers can encourage the search for new ways to develop the organization in their preferred areas. In interactive control systems, rewards based on subjective considerations are even a necessity, since, as mentioned earlier, it is practically impossible to use objective criteria to control innovative activity. It is also obvious that rewarding commitment and innovative activities can also cause disadvantages, just as rewarding for performance can deform employees' behavior, directing their efforts to take only actions that improve short-term achievements and harming the long-term development of the organization. In addition, a manager's subjective criteria can be incomprehensible to other employees and raise suspicions of unfair treatment of subordinates (Langfield-Smith, 2007, p. 772). Rewarding commitment, on the other hand, may encourage employees to do only those activities that are visible to their superiors, regardless of whether they are ultimately likely to improve performance. Employees knowing that they are being evaluated for their contribution will try to portray it as more important and performed under more difficult conditions than it actually was, such as frequently staying at work "after hours," without it translating into actual results.

However, business practice shows that in many situations it is not possible to accurately assess performance or evaluate behavior either objectively or subjectively. Under these conditions, the task of managers is to seek the right combination of the two methods, using both objective and subjective means of measurement, in order to achieve the maximum control under the given conditions and the probability of achieving the set goals (Baker et al., 1994, p. 1125). Therefore, in real-world conditions, usually objective and subjective incentives are combined and applied simultaneously (Prendergast, 1999, p. 9; Zábojník, 2014, p. 359). The strength of the subjective reward incentives is limited by the quality of the objective measurement. When it is inaccurate or unreliable, subjective evaluations can have only weak motivational effects (Zábojník, 2014, p. 359).

In the context of the considerations carried out, it seems important to refer to the possibilities of applying formal economic and non-economic incentives, conditioned by the specifics of hospitals (in particular, related to the already discussed strong regulation of the environment). There are two basic forms of employment in Polish hospitals that determine the possibility of rewarding employees. The first form of employment is the so-called full-time employment, regulated by the Labor Code, and the second is employment based on a civil law contract, regulated by the Civil Code. The basic document regulating how full-time employees are rewarded is the salary regulations and possibly the bonus regulations. Both of these bylaws must be approved by trade union organizations operating at the hospital. In the case of full-time employment, pay may consist of a base salary, fixed allowances related to overtime, work on Sundays and holidays, night work, a degree, a seniority allowance (it is mandatory for full-time employment and follows from the Law on Medical Activities), as well as a regulatory or incentive bonus, rewards, including jubilee awards. In recent years, several important legal regulations affecting remuneration conditions in hospitals have been introduced, the most important of which include the manner of determining the lowest basic remuneration of medical and some non-medical employees. Employment based on a civil law contract, on the other hand, is based on the fact that a health-care institution enters into a civil law contract with a person engaged in registered business activity. The method of remuneration in this case is determined by the concluded contract.

The solutions indicated thus draw attention to the key problem of management control here, which is to link the performance of individual employees and/or groups providing medical services. Indeed, financial incentives are usually seen as a method of increasing the number of services provided per unit cost. In public organizations in general, and in health care in particular, the context in which financial incentives operate is complex, and it is rare that the sole objective is to increase the number of services or throughput without regard to quality of care. This is important when there are multiple dimensions of hospital performance that are difficult to measure and monitor, and therefore also difficult to attribute to specific activities and individuals (Institute of Medicine, 2021). In addition, there may be tensions between intrinsic motivation and external financial incentives (Levy et al., 2017, p. 206).

The results of studies on the impact of financial incentives are inconclusive, which may be due to the fact that they can relate to a wide range of different aspects. Research in this area must take into account the importance of various incentives, literal and symbolic, money, promotions, co-workers' dislikes, which may be intentionally or accidentally related to financial incentives in the context of individual attitudes toward money, employee comparison, group norms, organizational structure, and so on. Since many factors influence the estimation of the overall link between financial incentives and individual and group achievements, it is very difficult to isolate and estimate the impact of financial incentives and the extent of distortions caused by individual non-financial factors. While despite the lack of conclusive evidence on the effectiveness of financial rewards, these rewards in companies are widely regarded as an important and effective mechanism for influencing employee behavior, resulting in improved organizational performance, these incentives are less frequently used in health care. This is due not only to a lack of confidence in their effectiveness, but also to a concern that efficiency-maximizing incentives may negatively affect the quality of medical services provided (WHO, 2008).

It is worth noting here that, in general, outside of health care, financial incentives increase employee motivation and productivity, but this finding does not hold true when applied to complex systems (Franco-Santos et al., 2012, p. 89), which manifest themselves in the lack of a link between financial incentives and quality, with their correlation with the amount of work done (Jenkins et al., 1998, p. 777). In addition, some cases identified a mixed effect of financial incentives on the number of consultations or appointments, with an overall improvement in processes and an increase in referrals and admissions, and a reduction in prescribing costs (Flodgren et al., 2011). By referring to only a few cases, it can be noted that there is insufficient evidence to support or reject the hypothesis of the effectiveness of the use of financial incentives in complex organizations, in the area of improving the performance of primary care (Scott et al., 2011, pp. 7–19). It should be noted here, however, that studies on the impact of financial incentives on the efficiency of medical service delivery in hospitals rarely consider the issue of the quality of patient treatment (Scott et al., 2011). In general, there are relatively few studies on this problem in European hospitals. The reason for this may be that in European countries the most common form of remuneration for doctors employed in public hospitals is a fixed monthly salary (Materna, 2010, p. 125).

Importantly, when there is strong intrinsic motivation, there is less need for strong financial incentives, and even strong extrinsic incentives can "crowd out" or reduce intrinsic motivation, thus leading to lower quality (Flodgren et al., 2011, p. 3). The introduction of strong financial incentives for medical professionals by hospital directors usually stems from the incentives already described that have been introduced at the level of the healthcare system, such as financing hospitals based on the number of services performed of a certain type (casemix payment systems). Such a financing system forces hospital directors to stimulate professionals to perform more services or better-paid services. They then use financial incentives aimed at either increasing patient throughput or raising the proportion of better-funded patients – both of which are aimed at increasing revenue, but may not be linked to providing quality care (Schwierz, 2016, p. 35). In some cases, the strength of the incentive may have no bearing on its effectiveness, as a weak incentive used to motivate performance of a worthwhile task may be more effective than a strong incentive for behavior that is not perceived by the physician as important (Flodgren et al., 2011, p. 3). At the same time, misaligned goals and associated extrinsic rewards can actually reduce the intrinsic motivation and results achieved by medical professionals (Glasziou et al., 2012, p. 2). These issues are addressed in the extensive literature (Cerasoli et al., 2014; Tak et al., 2017; Benabou & Tirole, 2003; Tung et al., 2020) on the issue of intrinsic motivation, but they are not the primary focus of this book.

3.4 Innovations and Innovativeness in Hospitals

Scholars define innovation in a variety of ways, "ranging from very broad and impressive generalizations to a very specific focus on technical innovation" (Sušanj, 2000, p. 350). From a more universal view, defining innovation as the application of new ideas, processes, products, or procedures that benefit an individual, group, or society (Yoon et al., 2016, p. 413) to an organization-centered approach, where innovation is defined as changes that help organizations cope with "environmental change or means of bringing about change in an organization. Organizations can cope with environmental changes and uncertainties not only by applying-new technology, but also by successfully integrating technical or administrative changes into their organizational structure that improve the level of achievement of their goals" (Damanpour & Evan, 1984, p. 393).

In contrast, the OECD and Eurostat *Oslo Manual 2018* defines innovation in two areas – product innovation and business process innovation – as "a new or improved product or business process (or combination thereof) that differs significantly from the firm's previous products or business processes and that has been introduced on the market or brought into use by the firm." In this view, a product innovation is "a new or improved good or service that differs significantly from the firm's previous goods or services and that has been introduced on the market," and a business process innovation is "a new or improved business process for one or more business functions that differs significantly from the firm's previous business processes and that has been brought into use by the firm" (OECD & Eurostat, 2019, pp. 20–21). The creators of this publication believe that their proposed definitions of innovation are applicable to all sectors of the economy, including government and non-profit organizations. In this approach, innovation in health care should also be considered the adoption of best practices that have proven to be effective and whose implementation, while ensuring safety and the best outcomes for patients, can affect the performance of the entire organization (Thakur et al., 2012, p. 564). In other words, health-care innovations are changes that help physicians focus on the patient, helping health-care professionals work smarter, faster, better, and more cost-effectively. It is also important to remember that hospitals, as public institutions, are subject to external evaluation, and innovation may be seen by employees as one form of gaining external legitimacy. Then, the implementation of innovation may be more of a symbolic process directed at meeting public expectations than an actual action to improve the organization and the services provided (Ramsdal & Bjørkquist, 2019, p. 1720).

It should be emphasized that innovation is not the same as creativity or invention. Innovation includes such activities as implementation, dissemination, replication, and gaining economic and social significance for the invented element (Ramsdal & Bjørkquist, 2019). Innovation should also be distinguished from inventiveness. Innovation can be seen as the result of innovation, and innovation itself is the ability to create and implement innovations, the degree to which an organization or even an individual innovates. It can also be a kind of yardstick for determining the ability to create and implement innovations (Kamaruddeen et al., 2010, pp. 71–73).

Innovativeness in hospitals can be viewed from two perspectives, as the adoption of innovations created outside the hospital and as the ability to generate, develop, and implement new ideas generated within the hospital (Jin et al., 2004, p. 257). Earlier observations relatively often viewed hospitals as major consumers of health-care innovation (Kimberly & Evanisko, 1981, p. 691). Today, hospitals are viewed from both perspectives, with hospitals increasingly seen as generators of innovation (Salge & Vera, 2009, p. 62). Although still "the innovation effort in hospitals is underestimated or even, in some cases, wholly unrecognized" (Djellal & Gallouj, 2005, p. 818).

In this context, the goal of increasing innovation in organizations is also an important issue. One may agree with the observation that the main purpose of implementing innovation is to achieve strategic goals in a competitive environment (Sankowska, 2011, p. 132), although this also requires viewing the role of innovation in the delivery of medical services mainly as a factor in increasing the value of health care, particularly as expressed in efficiency gains (Paulus et al., 2008, p. 1236). This is because sustainable value in health care is created only when inefficient steps in the care process are eliminated, automated, appropriately transferred to cheaper but capable workers, or otherwise innovatively improved. This is due to the fact that innovative change in the care process occurs when (Paulus et al., 2008, p. 1236): (1) consumers actively engage in behaviors that mitigate illness or improve purchasing; (2) safer and more effective drugs or devices are developed and adopted; (3) clinicians provide faster, appropriate, and reliable care; (4) unnecessary tests and therapies are eliminated; or (5) supply chain costs are systematically reduced.

Hospital innovativeness can be viewed from four perspectives (Djellal & Gallouj, 2007). In the first, hospitals are considered in terms of production functions. In this approach, the hospital is seen as a "black box," a separate economic entity consisting of capital inputs (buildings appropriately arranged for bed wards, operating and diagnostic rooms equipped with medical equipment), the supply system (drugs and medical supplies, food, energy), various types of employees (nurses, doctors, medical technicians, administrators, etc.) and patients, since patients themselves are participants in their care (co-production). In this view, innovations are considered as shifts in the production function (Djellal & Gallouj, 2005, p. 819, 2007, p. 182; Phelps, 2016, pp. 213–218). In the second perspective, hospitals are viewed as a collection of technological and biopharmacological capabilities, defining their innovativeness mainly through the prism of changes in the ways they treat patients, focusing on the introduction of new therapeutic substances, medical equipment, diagnostic and therapeutic strategies (Djellal & Gallouj, 2005, pp. 819–820, 2007, p. 182). The third perspective focuses on innovations carried out mainly in terms of information systems used in hospitals (England et al., 2000; Djellal & Gallouj, 2007, p. 186; Thakur et al., 2012, pp. 566–567; Cranfield et al., 2015, 2016). The fourth perspective views hospitals as providers of comprehensive services and key centers in the health-care system (Djellal & Gallouj, 2007, p. 188; Phelps, 2016, pp. 239–242). Here, more emphasis is placed on the service delivery process itself and internal and external relationships. The patient, together with his or her family, is a consumer of a complex set of services, which is additionally part of a chain of other services provided within the health-care system, an example of which is the coverage of primary health care before hospital treatment and referral to rehabilitation after hospital treatment.

Using the first two perspectives, it can, therefore, be seen that innovations in hospitals are changes in technology, structure, administrative system, and medical services that are relatively new to the industry as a whole and newly adopted in a particular hospital (Goes & Park, 1997, s. 674183). In a similar vein, then, they should be considered significant changes in terms of a new product (Salge & Vera, 2009, p. 55), such as a drug, medical technology, or information system, an innovative service (e.g., a clinical procedure or non-medical offering such as hotel services), a new process (e.g., a therapeutic strategy or patient pathway), or a new organizational structure (e.g., an organizational form or "corporate" structure). Hospital innovativeness, broadly considered here, is most often associated with process innovation (Demartini & Mella, 2014, p. e7), which also corresponds to the requirements of the *Oslo Manual 2018* definition. Process and product innovations can be understood and refined to different extents. Studies show that the scope of innovations in hospitals, in addition to technological innovations, can include organizational innovations, management innovations, service delivery innovations, and external and social relations (Djellal & Gallouj, 2007, p. 189).

Also worth noting is an approach that distinguishes between science-based innovativeness and practice-based innovativeness (Salge & Vera, 2009, p. 56). Science- (technology-) based innovativeness typically builds on codified scientific and technical knowledge, looking for opportunities to expand it. Science-based innovativeness projects are mostly carried out by a small group of highly skilled employees and are often conducted and formally managed as research and development (R&D) projects directed at clinical technology development. Practice-based innovativeness is usually induced by rather mundane challenges encountered in daily operations. Therefore, it largely thrives on learning by doing and on tacit, highly localized knowledge. Because practice-based innovativeness is deeply rooted in the daily activities of employees, it is not limited to a specific hierarchical or technical subset, but it is highly dispersed throughout the organization. Moreover, such innovation projects are often carried out informally, making it difficult to clearly separate innovation from ordinary work. As a result, practice-based innovation projects, in particular, are ubiquitous, but they often remain hidden even to those inside the organization. In a hospital setting, practice-based innovations are highly inclusive and potentially created by employees at all levels of the hierarchy and in all functional areas.

As a result of the discussion so far, it can be pointed out that there are at least six areas in which hospitals innovate: (1) technological, (2) organizational, (3) management, (4) in service delivery, (5) social, and (6) external relations. Technological innovations refer to the implementation of new or significantly new pharmaceuticals, disposable materials, diagnostic and therapeutic equipment, and treatment and diagnostic methods (Djellal & Gallouj, 2007, p. 188; Ramsdal & Bjørkquist, 2019, p. 5). However, it is important to note that the vital phenomenon here is the shift in focus from technological innovations to organizational innovations, as empirical studies show that organizational change is the key to transforming technical innovations into economic results (Dias & Escoval, 2013, p. 270).

Organizational innovation involves any attempt to modernize the organization and improve the functioning of the medical and non-medical organizational units of a hospital through the implementation of new organizational methods, including by leveling boundaries between organizational units, increasing cooperation between them, and modifying the organizational structure (McConnell, 2005). The scope of organizational innovations also includes solutions involving the creation of new units to develop or assume responsibility for new functions and changes in the organization of health-care delivery, such as creating new types of clinics, moving some services "home" or changing treatment from inpatient to day or outpatient forms (Djellal & Gallouj, 2007, p. 189; Kamaruddeen et al., 2010, p. 70; Sankowska, 2011, p. 209).

Management innovations include new management techniques and methods, such as new accounting and financial techniques and procedures, including costing, incentive systems, ways to hire and pay employees, and techniques to improve quality and patient safety. Included in this type of innovation are new management practices, such as the development of strategic approaches, patient segmentation, and quality management solutions (Young et al., 2001; Madorrán García & de Val Pardo, 2004; Kamaruddeen et al., 2010, p. 70; Ramsdal & Bjørkquist, 2019, p. 5).

Innovations in service delivery include all innovations that affect the ways in which providers communicate with service users and their families, such as improving the conditions of patients and their families, the hospital admission process, reducing waiting times, accommodations for patients' families, etc. (Midttun & Martinussen, 2005; Djellal & Gallouj, 2007, p. 189; Ramsdal & Bjørkquist, 2019, p. 5). Social innovations are most often carried out through processes based on social negotiations and formal and informal compromises leading to changes in coordination provisions and incentives. Thus, these innovations are shaped by the development of new attitudes in work organization, governance and decision-making processes, e.g., experiments with internal communication, volunteering outside paid work hours, flexible time management, etc. (Djellal & Gallouj, 2007, p. 189)

Innovations in external relations include the implementation of new ways of establishing relationships with suppliers, with other medical facilities or partners, e.g., in the purchase and use of expensive equipment, support in the treatment of complex cases, coordinated transfer of patients, but also in catering, laundry, and logistics services, training, consulting, etc. (Djellal & Gallouj, 2007, p. 190; Kamaruddeen et al., 2010, p. 70).

The basic requirement for innovation is that it must be significantly different from previous solutions. The term "significantly different" is subjective, so also the assessment of whether a solution is innovative will vary depending on the context and the criteria adopted. Innovations can also vary in scope. Some may only be new to a particular organization but are already known and applied elsewhere, others may be groundbreaking in a particular country, and thus they may affect an entire national industry, and still others may be groundbreaking on a global scale (Price, 1997, p. 396; Walker, 2014, p. 23). The specifics of the research conducted in this monograph mean that in what follows, solutions that are new to a particular hospital will be considered innovations.

Looking at the hospital that is part of a broader, highly politicized and institutionalized environment such as the health-care system, it is apparent that innovation can come from a variety of sources. Innovations can be externally imposed by the government or public institutions. An example of such innovation is the introduction of professional managers into hospitals,

in a wave of new public management. L. Fuglsang argues that organizations that have to adapt to and adopt these "innovations" not because they
have been proven to be effective, but in order to maintain the legitimacy
of their operations, introduce a separation between actual operations and
the adopted "innovations" (2010, p. 70). This leads to a decoupling between
formal structures and day-to-day operations (Fuglsang, 2010, p. 70; Meyer &
Rowan, 1977; Powell & DiMaggio, 2012), which, as business practice shows,
leads to a situation in which hospitals sometimes brandish adaptation to new
structures.

In this context, it is worth noting the processes by which innovations
are created. Among other things, it is pointed out that innovations can
be created in three types of processes: (1) at a separate planning stage,
in which innovations are pre-planned activities or projects; (2) as part of
rapid application, in which planning and innovation creation occur simultaneously, that is, as part of a trial-and-error process, in which prototype
innovations are tried and corrected in practice; (3) as part of a retrospective innovation recognition process, in which certain solutions that work
in practice are recognized in retrospect as innovations (Toivonen et al.,
2007, p. 374).

On the other hand, from the point of view of top management involvement, innovation creation processes can be considered (Fuglsang, 2010, p. 76):

1) As an intentional top-management initiated abstract interest-creating and
   employee-involving activity around a new idea (for example a new
   health care centre that has to be created).
2) As a management mediated problem driven formalising activity around
   concrete problem-solutions (for example a new way to shop for the
   elderly or an elderlymen get-together).
3) As bricolage and ad hoc innovation (services are continuously adjusted in
   relation to clients leading to an expansion of routines).

Purposeful action, thus, involves initiatives taken by determined managers
often as a response to imposed ideas and political requirements (Fuglsang,
2010, p. 76). In this approach, sometimes abstract challenges of the environment are interpreted by top management, and innovation is a practical way
of dealing with them. For innovation to be implemented, key personnel
must be interested in and committed to these ideas, so the manager here
plays the role of a visionary, a heroic entrepreneur taking the risk of challenging deeply entrenched ways of organizing work, while demonstrating

a determination to win employee support for new organizational concepts (Andersen, 2008, p. 55). The top-down direction adopted here often results in radical innovations behind it. The second approach refers to innovations that are partly intentional and partly emergent (Fuglsang, 2010, p. 78), in which problems or challenges are identified by employees and reported to top management, which, in consultation with employees, formalizes the process of solving the problem in question, usually in the form of a project (e.g., a pilot project) and supports its implementation. In contrast, *bricolage* innovations occur without an overall "grand design" or abstract concepts that require concretization and implementation, but rather as a response to practical problems (Ramsdal & Bjørkquist, 2019, p. 4). The concept of *bricolage* was originally developed by French anthropologist C. Lévi-Strauss to conceptualize the practical use of the human mind (Levi-Strauss, 1966). C. Lévi-Strauss believes that the "wild mind" is constantly collecting and applying structures wherever they can be used. He contrasts the scientific mind, which asks questions and tries to design an optimal or complete solution, with the "wild mind" resembling the do-it-yourselfer (fr. *bricoleur*), which constructs things from whatever materials are available. According to C. Lévi-Strauss, the scientist and the *bricoleur* assign opposite functions to events and structures, treating them either as ends or as means. The scientist creates events (changes the world) by means of structures, while the *bricoleur* creates structures by means of events (Levi-Strauss, 1966, p. 22). This can be compared with the planned innovations of managers and the bottom-up, emergent innovations of workers.

In organizations, specific practical problems or challenges for improving daily work are identified on a daily basis, and employees try to solve them in some way by making various practical improvements. These small emerging innovations are then solidified over time as a routine through frequent exchanges between employees. Emerging ideas are discussed and transferred from one employee to another, although often only part of the idea is transferred (Fuglsang, 2010, p. 82). Such innovation processes are also observed in organizations characterized by "strong institutionalization," such as hospitals (Andersen, 2008, p. 55). These innovations emerge from daily work with patients rather than being a deliberate action. In hospitals, these are innovations related to the development of medical knowledge, which not only improve the quality and safety of treatment, but can also give rise to the introduction of new forms of work organization.

The last two of the approaches discussed focus on practice as a source of innovation. From this perspective, innovations can be seen as constantly being created in an evolving practice in which problems are discovered, and to which the response is to look for innovative solutions. Incorporating this perspective into the analysis of innovations makes it possible to spot and reveal innovations that might not otherwise be created. The *bricolage* model also makes it possible to pay attention to ad hoc innovations that arise, which can be generally defined as the interactive (social) construction of a solution to a specific problem posed to employees, often in the course of interaction with the patient. This is a very important form of innovation in professional services, where available knowledge and experience are accumulated over time and synergistically used to create new solutions and new knowledge that changes the patient's situation, but also work processes, in a positive and original way (Gallouj & Weinstein, 1997, p. 549). Furthermore, emergent innovation, although mostly smaller in scope, avoids the uncertainty associated with discrepancies between the original plan and actual implementation.

Of particular importance is that *bricolage* innovation can also be supported by management. Top management, noticing bottom-up innovation activities, can organize meetings where problems and solutions are discussed in a more systematic and formalized way, leading to the dissemination and replication of ideas (quality circles). Support can also consist of allowing employees to spend more time on development and innovation activities. In this way, formalizing *bricolage* can be a systemic tool to support organizational innovation. Management intervention can sometimes mean more control and can be counter-productive, but it can also ensure that ideas are remembered, developed, and replicated (Fuglsang, 2010, p. 83). Overall, it appears that the various forms of innovation mediated by both top management and employees occur side by side in a complex interaction that is difficult to explain and measure, and that must be observed and understood from a process and practice perspective.

The innovative behavior of organizational members tends to depend on the skills of management (Thakur et al., 2012, p. 564), although, importantly, many studies on innovation have ended up with inconsistent results. Indeed, as has been observed, factors that influence innovative behavior in one context may be perceived as having little or the opposite effect in another context (Zmud, 1982, p. 1421) and, additionally, that the implementation of innovation in medical organizations becomes more effective when the organization believes in interactivity between employees (Fitzgerald et al., 2002). It is worth remembering that the implementation of innovative ideas becomes ineffective when it is forced on employees. To effectively innovate in an organization, managers should encourage interaction between different departments in the organization, which in health-care organizations becomes more effective when the following insights are taken into account (Fitzgerald et al., 2002, p. 1444):

1. The process of determining the credibility of evidence is interpretive and negotiated;
2. New knowledge must be accepted before it can be used, but some knowledge is ambiguous and contested;
3. Professional organizations are an extreme case in terms of the complexity of innovation diffusion processes;
4. Decisions to implement innovations involve active rather than passive employees;
5. The progress of innovation diffusion is influenced by the complementary characteristics of the members of a medical organization and the interactions between them;
6. Some of the factors that influence decisions to adopt or reject innovations are not rational, but political;
7. The community of practice may be reluctant to accept the efficacy of a novel treatment because it threatens the established skill base, thereby jeopardizing the status and professional standing of its members;
8. Financial incentives can act as both facilitators and inhibitors of adaptation.

The relationship between innovation and innovativeness and the performance of health-care organizations has been the subject of much research in recent years (Chen et al., 2014; Cucciniello & Nasi, 2014, p. 96; Dias & Escoval, 2013; Hernandez et al., 2013; Leidner et al., 2010; Moreira et al., 2017; Salge & Vera, 2009; Tsai, 2013). While there is probably no doubt in anyone's mind that innovation means progress and improvement, both empirical and theoretical cases of a direct and positive relationship between innovativeness and performance remain less conclusive than is commonly believed (Dias & Escoval, 2013; Salge & Vera, 2009, p. 54; Moreira et al., 2017). In research in this area, the evaluation and measurement of innovation (Cucciniello & Nasi, 2014, p. 91) and the evaluation and measurement of hospital performance (Austen, 2010, p. 104; Hass-Symotiuk, 2011b, p. 67; Hensel, 2008, pp. 11–52; Schwierz, 2016, p. 35) are particularly challenging. Some studies rely on traditional efficiency and effectiveness models (Austen, 2010, p. 104; Hass-Symotiuk, 2011b, p. 67; Hensel, 2008, pp. 11–52; Schwierz,

2016, p. 35), while others suggest broadening the focus and taking more account of the social and ideological effects of innovation in the public sector and the need for stakeholder analysis to illustrate the value of innovation to individuals and understand how they determine the overall outcomes of innovation adoption (Dawes et al., 2009).

Motivations for innovation can include improving productivity, reducing costs, improving quality, including improving clinical outcomes through better diagnosis and treatment, and increasing patient satisfaction, reducing variation in service quality among facilities, regions, and countries, and increasing access to health services. This means that innovation requires not only development and discovery, but also adoption, routinization, and replacement of previous solutions if its benefits are to be fully felt (Williams, 2011, p. 213). It is important to keep in mind that the understanding of innovations and their impact on whatever outcomes are understood depends on the specific context and type of innovation. A particular solution considered innovative at a particular site may not do so in other or changed circumstances or at another hospital, limiting the ability to implement a framework for evaluating innovative practices and measuring opportunity costs. Related to this is the fact that the interaction between innovation and organizational context is unpredictable, as health care contains elements of so-called complex systems (Williams, 2011, p. 214). Thus, where innovation is achieved, it will be done in a multi-directional and iterative manner, which limits the ability to predict the impact of new interventions and practices. This also results in the inability to program innovation. Indeed, as noted, hospital innovativeness is, among other things, strongly positively associated with clinical outcomes in terms of hospital standardized mortality ratio (HSMR) reduction, with patient satisfaction, and, to a lesser extent, with service quality (Salge & Vera, 2009, p. 61) (Table 3.3).

A comparison of science-based innovativeness with practice-based innovativeness shows a relatively stronger positive association of the former with mortality and patient satisfaction, while the use of the latter approach indicates a positive increase in the service quality index.

Administrative performance is much more ambiguously related to innovativeness than clinical performance. Regression coefficients for both types of innovativeness do not consistently confirm a positive relationship between hospital innovativeness and administrative performance. As for innovativeness related to the scientific sphere, a positive and statistically significant relationship is found only for income per bed. However, there is little support for the existence of such a link in terms of return on income or

Table 3.3.   Results of regression analysis of innovation and hospital performance

Type of innovation	Clinical performance			Administrative performance		
	Patient mortality (HSMR)	Patient satisfaction	Service quality rating	Return on income	Income per bed	Resource use rating
Science-based innovativeness	-0.337[4]	0.088[2]	0.306[1]	0.024	1.067[4]	0.006
Practice-based innovativeness	−0.131[2]	0.059[4]	0.630[4]	0.080[2]	−0.081	0.662[4]

[1] $p<0.1$, [2] $p<0.05$, [3] $p<0.01$, [4] $p<0.001$.

Source: Adapted from Salge & Vera, 2009, pp. 64–65.

resource use rating. As for practice-based innovativeness, the situation is the opposite, as there is a positive and statistically significant relationship with the return on income and resource use rating, while the relationship with income per bed is even negative, although not significant.

The results presented here show that hospitals, on the one hand, are important recipients of novelties created elsewhere, whether it is a new imaging technology, a novel drug or a new management tool, and, on the other hand, are important generators of new knowledge and innovation. At the same time, they support the observation about the need to understand innovativeness and hospital performance as complex and multidimensional areas, particularly if attention is paid to the need to increase interest in the relatively less appreciated and often hidden forms of practice-based innovativeness.

It is also important to note that hospitals with greater innovativeness have lower patient mortality, higher patient satisfaction and higher service quality rating than their less active counterparts. Thus, innovation-generating activities in hospitals are mainly driven by the desire to improve the quality of health outcomes and the overall patient experience. At the same time, science-based innovativeness is only positively related to income per bed, the only indicator of administrative performance that does not relate in any way to costs or resource consumption. Hospitals with greater science-based innovativeness, on the other hand, perform significantly better only in terms of income potential. Practice-based innovativeness, on the other hand, shows positive relationships with both return on income and resource use rating.

It is also important to note that organizational innovations are correlated with process and service innovations, and that service and process innovations affect operational performance (Table 3.4), but that innovations in health-care facilities were not found to affect their financial performance (Moreira et al., 2017, pp. 349–350).

As the study results show (Moreira et al., 2017, p. 347), process innovations are correlated with the risk-adjusted readmission rate (0.367, p ≤ 5%). This correlation may mean that introducing innovative treatments increases the number of complications and readmissions, which is a surprising result, as it would indicate that innovations imply a reduction in quality. In contrast, process and organizational innovations are correlated with bed occupancy rates, which may be associated with an increase in the number of patients following the introduction of these innovations. The average duration of hospitalization, on the other hand, is not correlated with either type of innovation.

In doing so, it is important to remember that the links between innovativeness and performance are complex. Innovativeness is not a linear, but a turbulent, dynamic process that can lead to new solutions and can also give rise to new challenges. At the same time, there is a positive correlation between innovativeness and hospital performance (Dias & Escoval, 2013, p. 274), with "innovative and efficient" hospitals having a much greater ability to translate innovation into performance, achieving twice as much as "non-innovative but efficient" hospitals. At the same time, the former are characterized by particularly high levels of organizational flexibility and external collaboration, and the innovations carried out in them translate into productivity and overall quality, including access to services and patient satisfaction. As a result, both efficient and less efficient hospitals focus their attention on activities aimed at providing health care of the highest value to patients, with less concern for reducing costs to the lowest acceptable level. Hence,

Table 3.4. Correlations between the innovation composite measures and the operational performance measures

Type of innovation	Re-admission rate adjusted to risk	Occupation rate	Avg duration of hospitalization (days)
Organizational innovation	0.090	0.335^2	0.039
Service innovation	0.195	0.291	0.136
Process innovation	0.367^2	0.498^1	−0.032

$^1 p \leq 0.01; ^2 p \leq 0.05.$

Source: Moreira et al., 2017, p. 347.

innovation in the hospital sector focuses mainly on medical and organizational outcomes rather than on inputs. Furthermore, C. Dias and A. Escoval (2013, p. 274) found that it was difficult to identify the specific contribution of hospital activities in terms of outcomes, as several external stakeholders were also involved. But they emphasize that the impact of the innovation went beyond organizational performance, increasing value for users as well as society and the economy as a whole.

In the context of the reflections carried out, the observation that there are two fundamental problems, which seem to be in line with the assumptions of institutional theory, distorting the relationship between innovativeness and organizational performance seems relevant: (1) the introduction of innovations that do not benefit hospitals and (2) the participation of external stakeholders in the planning and implementation of innovations. Indeed, as already mentioned, companies operating mainly in an environment dominated by economic and technological requirements ensure their growth and survival through their ability to use these resources. Hospitals, on the other hand, operating in an environment dominated by legal, political, and social requirements, need to obtain external legitimacy of action to ensure their development and survival by fulfilling legal norms, political pressures, and social expectations. This legitimacy, in this case, involves making decisions in line with the expectations of the environment, often in conflict with economic rationality for the organization. It happens, therefore, that decisions conform to the norms of ambient rationality only superficially, but sufficiently to gain this legitimacy. To this end, the organization may perform mostly sham actions in line with the expectations of the environment, e.g., introduce various commonly accepted innovations, without giving any real value to this environment. Such action is particularly easy, and often attractive, for hospitals, for whose activities there are virtually no objective criteria of quality or efficiency.

What is clear here, however, is that public organizations use both approaches. They rationalize actions that are inefficient but in line with the pressures of the environment as well as take rational actions by incorporating a sham environment to gain social legitimacy. In such an environment, it is difficult even for employees to figure out which decisions are rational and which are only made to look that way (Hatch, 2002, p. 98). This is due, among other things, to the fact that organizations that omit elements expected by the environment or create unique structures do not have acceptable, legitimate evidence of their proper activities (Meyer & Rowan, 1977, p. 349). Such organizations are more susceptible to claims that they

are negligent, irrational, or unnecessary. To avoid accusations of careless-
ness and irrationality, hospitals copy from other hospitals or from business
innovations that are considered effective at the time and present the organization as rational and modern, even though the effectiveness of these solutions may only be a socially accepted myth. Moreover, hospitals must not
only succumb to these myths, but also maintain the impression that these
myths actually work (Meyer & Rowan, 1977, p. 356), for example, by taking
part in competitions based on standardized management or quality models,
or when the implementation of certain standards or models is subject to
external evaluation (an example is the use of outsourcing, as most hospital
management models, such as "Portraits of Hospitals – Maps of Opportunity,"
score the use of outsourcing in support services higher than relying on in-
house resources). As a result, in their search for external legitimacy, hospitals may absorb incompatible innovations, not only failing to improve their
performance, but even lowering it.

3.5 Trust between Managers and Physicians

In research work related to organizational control, it is difficult to ignore
the topic of trust, since control and trust are fundamental elements of cooperation between actors in an organization (Long & Sitkin, 2018, p. 725).
And trust in organizations is not only extremely important – it is the most
important – essential element for the success of the organization (Shockley-
Zalabak et al., 2010, p. 1). Moreover, trust-based relationships are considered key to ensuring effective health-care delivery and quality health
outcomes (Brennan et al., 2013; Fleig-Palmer et al., 2018; Graham et al., 2015;
Groenewegen et al., 2019; Solstad & Petterson, 2020, p. 87). Control and trust
are so intertwined that there are researchers who question the theoretical
distinctiveness of the two constructs (Long & Sitkin, 2018, p. 732) or declare
their substitutability as alternative control mechanisms (Gulati, 1995, p. 93).
However, most studies emphasize the distinctiveness of control and trust,
except that they treat these constructs as related ways of managing interdependencies and uncertainties in organizations. Trust is viewed as a more
internal source of reducing the perception of uncertainty, while control is
viewed as a more overt and active means of reducing it (Das & Teng, 2001,
p. 276). When people trust the individuals (e.g., managers) and/or systems
(e.g., information systems) they use, and enforce control, they believe that
these authorities share their values and interests and, as a result, exhibit high

levels of commitment, motivation, cooperation, and productivity (Bijlsma-Frankema & Costa, 2005). Effectively implemented controls clearly define performance expectations and ways to motivate and monitor the pursuit of these goals (Emsley & Kidon, 2007).

Trust is defined in many ways. P. Sztompka defines it as a kind of bet on the future uncertain actions of other people (2007, p. 70). In his view, trust allows us to assume expectations about the properties of other people's actions, such as the degree of predictability, regularity, regularity, rationality, efficiency, or effectiveness. This author also briefly defines trust as an expectation of worthy behavior toward us (1999a, p. 269). F. Fukuyama, on the other hand, treats trust as a mechanism based on the assumption that other members of a community behave honestly and cooperatively, based on commonly held values (Fukuyama, 1997, p. 38). A key element in considering trust is to distinguish it from other similar constructs, such as *hope*. As N. Luhmann rightly pointed out, trust arises only when trusting expectation influences a decision; otherwise, we have simple hope (2017, p. 64). Conceiving of trust as a factor influencing decision making makes trust play an important role in an organization, as it allows it to function regardless of increasing complexity, opacity, and ever-widening areas of uncertainty and risk. Joint action and coordinated individual action based on trust reduce complexity, thereby revealing opportunities for action that would remain improbable and unattractive without trust – in other words, that would not be realized (2017, p. 65).

Depending on the object of trust, it can be divided into interpersonal trust (to a specific person) and trust in abstract objects, such as law, software, information systems, public institutions, administration, medical professionals, health-care system, etc. (Giddens, 2013, p. 87; Gille et al., 2020, p. 2; Luhmann, 2017, p. 99; Maarse & Jeurissen, 2019, p. 300; Sztompka, 1999a, p. 45). Interpersonal trust is characterized by intimacy and closeness, and it refers to people known personally, with whom we interact face to face. Interpersonal trust occurs when there is the possibility of repeatedly testing over time the extent to which a person is trustworthy (Mechanic, 1996, p. 176). In contrast, trust in abstract objects, also known as social or institutional trust, is more distant and is influenced more by general reputation (Mechanic & Schlesinger, 1996, p. 1694). According to A. Giddens, trust in abstract systems provides the security of everyday reliability, but it cannot provide the reciprocity and intimacy that interpersonal trust offers; social trust, on the other hand, implies belief in impersonal principles and can be verified more statistically than in individual interactions (2013, p. 114). P.

Sztompka treats interpersonal and social trust as the outer limits of a certain continuum, within which several social categories of trust fall, such as trust in the social roles represented by the medical profession or trust in institutions, which could include hospitals and payers for medical services or health-care systems (1999b, pp. 42–44). In the context of management control in hospitals, interpersonal trust and trust in social roles (1999b, p. 43) or, as A. Giddens calls it, trust in expertise play a key role (2013, p. 87). Both of these areas include trust in physicians, and trust understood in this way is combined with trustworthiness.

Trust can also be defined as a mental state in which the trustee is convinced that another entity (i.e., usually a person or organization) will reliably act in his or her best interests (Rousseau et al., 1998, p. 395), or as an optimistic acceptance of a situation carrying uncertainty and risk, in which the trusting party believes that the party to be trusted (the trustee) will look out for his or her best interests, regardless of the trustee's ability to control (Hall et al., 2001, p. 615). The above definitions of trust draw attention to the trustee's belief in the attributes of the other party to ensure fulfillment of obligations. These attributes determine the trustees perception of the trustee and, thus, the perception of trustworthiness. Researchers have recognized about ten factors that lead to trustworthiness (Mayer et al., 1995, p. 718). However, there is a fairly widespread consensus in the scientific world that three attributes of a person's trustworthiness have the greatest impact on trust: ability, benevolence, and integrity (Colquitt et al., 2007, p. 910; Fleig-Palmer et al., 2018, p. 70; Mayer et al., 1995, p. 717). "Ability" is the belief that the trusted person has the competence and skills to ensure that the trustee's interests are met. In the context of this research, this means that the manager trusts that the doctor has the right knowledge to effectively carry out the tasks assigned to him. "Capability" includes an element of credibility – "can be done," but this is not enough for the trustee to believe that the trusted person will act in the trustee's best interests.

"Benevolence" is the trustee's assessment of the trustee's willingness to look out for his interests, regardless of his selfish motives (Mayer et al., 1995, p. 718). In other words, it is the trustee's perception of loyalty. "Integrity" is the trustee's belief that he or she holds values that are acceptable and positive to the trustee, and that he or she applies them independently of his or her own interests. The relationship between integrity and trust includes the trustee's perception that the trustee adheres to a set of principles that the trustee considers appropriate. "Integrity" (honesty) of a person can be measured as the degree of adherence to professed values and principles. This means that a person may adhere to professed values, but these values are not considered favorable by the trustee. For example, a person who is exclusively committed to the principle of pursuing profit at all costs may always adhere to this principle, i.e., be a person of high integrity, but the trustee may not like this principle (Mayer et al., 1995, p. 719).

Referring to a hospital, one can imagine a situation in which a doctor follows a rule that they always use only "original" drugs (which are usually more expensive) and never use generic drugs. Although this doctor will be honest to their principles, this rule may not be acceptable because the hospital has a policy of using cheaper generic drugs. It is within this dimension of trust that there may be conflicts between professional logic and management logic. In the literature, all three factors (trust dimensions) have many synonyms. For example, synonyms for "ability" are: skills, competence, perceived knowledge; "benevolence": loyalty, openness, concern or support; "integrity": fairness, consistency, keeping promises, reliability, value congruence, and discretion (Colquitt et al., 2007, p. 913).

Given the organization of the research described in this monograph, focused mainly on the activities of top hospital management, and the vastness of the literature on trust in organizations (np.: Bachmann & Zaheer, 2006; Colquitt et al., 2007; Fleig-Palmer et al., 2018; Gille et al., 2020; Luhmann, 2017; Maarse & Jeurissen, 2019; Mayer et al., 1995; Sankowska, 2011, pp. 28–71; Sztompka, 1999a), the remainder of this chapter will focus on trustee-controller and superior-subordinate relationships in an environment, in which subordinates present a different institutional logic (the logic of medical professionalism) from their superiors using managerial logic (Lewandowski & Sułkowski, 2018, p. 152), and superior-subordinate relationships are complex, as some level of conflict between managers and the medical profession is directly inherent in the structure of health-care systems (Garelick & Fagin, 2005, p. 241; Waldman & Cohn, 2007, p. 27). It is crucial for managers as "government agents" to impose stronger control over physicians through the use of bureaucratic and market-based mechanisms based on performance indicators, management by objectives and medical processes based on scientific evidence and clinical guidelines (Kuhlmann et al., 2013, p. 2), and information technologies that are potentially able to make physicians "disciplined" (Reich, 2012, p. 1021). Such measures have a direct impact on reducing physicians' autonomy, which for centuries has been a fundamental component of their professional status, power, and prestige.

In an environment laden with complex relationships between superiors and subordinates, such as in hospitals, trust is essential for at least two reasons. First, in hospitals, strategy formulation and implementation cannot be embraced by a single individual, a "strategist," or even a narrow group of individuals, such as top management, because these organizations depend on too many educated people (Hatch, 2002, p. 125) with considerable autonomy (VanHeuvelen, 2020, p. 12). And this autonomy, in its essential part, is not given by superiors, but it is based both on academic knowledge gained through formal education and on indefinite, tacit, and empirical knowledge gained in daily practice and on the ability to determine the nature and content of the work themselves (Abbott, 1988, p. 52; Cave, 2020, p. 5; Davies, 2000, p. 116; Les MacLeod, 2012, p. 13). Second, it is very difficult to control both the performance of medical professionals and their behavior (McEvily et al., 2003, p. 92; VanHeuvelen, 2020, p. 13). Top management, when placing the organization's resources at the disposal of medical professionals, particularly clinical leaders, must have a certain level of confidence that these medical professionals are making the best possible decisions regarding cost, quality, and safety of treatment, or the most effective organizational solutions. This is because the manager, in many cases, is unable to understand the medics' explanations and, thus, exercise control over their activities. Even if the chief executive were a medical professional by training, especially a doctor, also not being directly involved in the process of treatment, the effectiveness and efficiency of this process, post factum can evaluate them only on the basis of medical records created by the controlled person. Also, the inspection process, if it were to culminate in some definitive conclusions and significant sanctions, would, in principle, require the establishment of a medical commission, which would be time-consuming and costly. This committee would have to be composed of other medical professionals who have a different institutional logic from the manager. In this situation, trust seems an effective choice (cf: McEvily et al., 2003, p. 92).

Trust does not always require employees to share organizational values and/or those professed by the superior, since, in addition to implicit commitments, such as honesty and loyalty, trust can be based on overt, formal mechanisms such as procedures, budgets, information systems, and systems for measuring and evaluating performance, as long as they are treated as credible (Chenhall & Langfield-Smith, 2003, p. 126; Flamholtz et al., 1985, p. 42). Managers are key actors in these trust relationships, as they are the ones who make decisions and take actions to motivate their subordinates to achieve desired goals. However, this situation can often be challenging for managers, as subordinates may either not want to, or simply not be able to, carry out the goals and objectives that managers direct them to achieve

(Long & Sitkin, 2018, p. 727). Managers must decide in such a situation how much they can trust their subordinates that the subordinates, despite their efforts, were unable to meet the goals set, and how much of the failure to meet the goals was due to their opportunistic behavior. But distinguishing between these two different situations from the point of view of the hospital's top management is very difficult; hence, why the element of trust plays such an important role.

Trust does not apply when there is no situation involving uncertainty and the possibility of misuse of this situation, i.e., opportunistic behavior by the trustee (Mayer et al., 1995, p. 714). In an organization, the greatest uncertainty occurs in a situation of change, especially when the changes are significant and their effects are unknown (Appelbaum et al., 2017, p. 223). Such conditions occur when innovations are introduced. This is when top management bears the greatest risk in accepting the ideas and actions of its subordinates, and this is when trust is needed that those who propose and/or implement innovative solutions have sufficient capabilities (competence), are loyal, meaning they are willing to look out for the interests of top management, and honest, meaning they will act in accordance with their professed values, even against their own interests. We ignore here the differences arising from different institutional logics (Lewandowski & Sułkowski, 2018).

Managers can assess the level of trust in subordinates based on the intensity of conflicts with them around goal achievement, the level of alignment of subordinates' preferences, motivation, and commitment, and the degree to which subordinates resist management orders and generally adhere to values that their organization or manager considers important, as well as observed ability and integrity in previous actions (Long & Sitkin, 2018, p. 739; Williamson, 1993). An important criterion used by managers to assess their confidence is the performance of subordinates. Through this perspective, managers develop perceptions of what level of competence, honesty, and benevolence their subordinates display, and thus whether they are trustworthy exchange partners (Long & Sitkin, 2018, p. 739). To assess trust in the dimension of honesty (integrity), the intensity of conflict related to institutional logics can be considered. C.I. Hovland, I.L. Janis, and H.H. Kelley have argued that trustworthiness can be assessed by estimating the level of motivation (or lack thereof) to lie, analyzing whether the trustee stands to gain something by lying ((1953) w: (Mayer et al., 1995, p. 716).

The design and implementation of management control is the task of managers, and trust is more of a reciprocal phenomenon between managers and subordinates (Swärd, 2016, p. 15). Subordinates may or may not trust their superiors, and vice versa. In the literature, although some research-ers have paid attention to the study of trust on both sides of the superior-subordinate dyad (Brower et al., 2000, p. 228), most empirical studies have focused on only one of these perspectives, namely, the trust of subordinates in their leaders or managers (np. Fleig-Palmer et al., 2018) and, to a much lesser extent, on leader-member exchange (e.g. Dirks & Ferrin, 2002; Dirks, 2006; Scandura & Pellegrini, 2008; Gordon et al., 2014; Engelbrecht et al., 2017; Shao, 2019; Håvold & Håvold, 2019; Yeşilbaş & Çetin, 2019). Only a few studies have examined the trust of superiors in subordinates (e.g. Brower et al., 2008; Kim et al., 2016; Spreitzer & Mishra, 1999), and no such studies have been conducted in health care at all.

The trust of superiors in subordinates is important because low levels of trust can negatively affect organizational performance, as superiors, due to low trust in subordinates, may not give them the necessary autonomy and authority for subordinates to make creative contributions. In their study, H.H. Brower et al. found a strong correlation between a manager's trust in a subordinate and the subordinate's behavior and intentions, in addition to the effect of the subordinate's trust in the manager (2008, p. 338). They discovered a synergistic interaction between a superior's trust in a subordi-nate and a subordinate's trust in a superior. Specifically, they found that the positive relationship between a subordinate's trust in his superior and indi-vidual-directed organizational citizenship behavior became stronger when the superior's trust in the subordinate was high (2008, p. 341). In general, their research suggests that leader-subordinate trust (the degree to which superiors trust their subordinates) may promote better subordinate perfor-mance and be significantly related to subordinates' stated intentions to leave (2008, p. 344). A later study by T.Y. Kim et al. showed that when superior-subordinate trust increased from low to high, task performance and interper-sonal support also increased significantly.[1] With that said, the best results of task performance and interpersonal support were obtained when both the superior's trust in the subordinate and the subordinate's trust in the superior were high (2016, pp. 954–955). According to the study's authors, managers can raise their subordinates' trust levels by delegating power and authority to them. Then their subordinates can feel that their superiors trust them, and thus they can realize the potential benefits of high trust. In general, these studies show a positive correlation between employees' trust in superiors and superiors' trust in subordinates, as well as a positive correlation between mutual trust between employees and superiors and superiors' trust in sub-ordinates (2016, p. 952). This means that, to a certain extent, it is possible to apply the results obtained for subordinates' trust in superiors to a situation in which only superiors' trust in subordinates was measured.

Given the nature of the research described in this monograph, one of the important roles within management control is innovativeness. Innovativeness in an organization can come from many sources. One of the most important factors is the involvement of top management, since innovativeness depends on the successful implementation of creative ideas in the organization (Yoon et al., 2016, p. 413). Top managers can influence organizational innovativeness through:

- identifying new market opportunities and focusing employee's attention around these opportunities;
- deciding on the level and type of innovation-related investments;
- configuring linkages with innovation stakeholders, such as employees, customers (patients), suppliers, research centers, etc.;
- supporting attitudes and practices that promote a culture of innovation within the organization (Dodgson et al., 2013, p. 63).

Research by A. Carmeli et al. has shown that innovative leadership – manifested by behaviors including encouraging individual initiative, clarifying individual responsibilities, providing clear and complete feedback from performance appraisals, maintaining a strong task orientation, and emphasizing high-quality group relationships and superiors' trust in organizational members – has a positive impact on organizational performance (2010, p. 346). Similarly, other authors suggest that an atmosphere of trust is crucial to the development of innovativeness in organizations (Shockley-Zalabak et al., 2000; Dovey, 2009; Shockley-Zalabak et al., 2010), and even that trust is the best predictor of innovativeness (Spitzer, 2007, p. 228; Ellonen et al., 2008, p. 165; Dodgson et al., 2013, p. 209; Williams, 2011, p. 215). The close relationship between trust and innovativeness is confirmed by a study of companies in the Financial Times 100, which found that trust was the first factor distinguishing the most innovative organizations from the least innovative (Shockley-Zalabak et al., 2010, p. 21). Similar results were obtained among medical personnel. They indicate that an atmosphere of mutual trust, shared norms, and social integration encourages individuals to propose new ideas and gain support through strong social ties to implement new concepts (Afsar et al., 2018, p. 163).

S.R. Herting writes that "for individuals to assume the necessary risks of experimentation, they must trust that organizations will reward success and tolerate failure. Likewise, for managers to accept the risks of failure associated with innovation adoption, they must trust subordinates sufficiently to balance discipline with latitude" (2002, p. 292). Risk also exists from top management, as there is a significant knowledge gap in hospitals between managers, who are responsible for control and coordination in the hospital, and physicians, who autonomously lead and oversee treatment processes, including cost and revenue generation. The introduction of innovations by physicians certainly increases the perceived complexity of organizational processes and makes them more difficult to control. In this case, managers may also be used to secure the individual interests of physicians. Therefore, managers' trust in physicians helps to reduce the perceived complexity of the environment and increase the sense of control over the organization (Colquitt et al., 2012, p. 5).

B. Afsar et al. introduced the concept of innovation trust into the scientific discourse, defined as mutual trust between employees regarding innovative ideas. This approach is based on research showing that when employees trust that co-workers listen to and support their ideas, and give weight to any innovative suggestions they initiate, then they tend to exhibit high levels of innovative behavior at work. Trust linked to innovativeness is identified as key to creating a supportive internal environment for innovations, which increases employees' propensity to contribute new insights (2015, p. 108).

People may resist change because it often temporarily disrupts the routine of patient care, and implementing major innovations can be even more cumbersome than making simpler incremental changes (Thakur et al., 2012, p. 567). New ideas and innovations generally require risk-taking, as significant innovative change can also fail (Ellonen et al., 2008, p. 176; Williams, 2011, p. 215). In this context, trust linked to innovativeness is important because it contributes to the readiness of the environment for innovative initiatives and gives employees greater boldness when making suggestions and comments, and is a precursor to creativity, which is a key ingredient in innovative work behavior, helping employees to take more innovative initiatives (Afsar et al., 2015, p. 106). In addition, trust appears to be essential to creating a climate for innovation (Weinert, 2013, p. 44) because it reduces perceived risks and negative reactions caused by employees' innovative behavior (Unsworth & Clegg, 2010, p. 90).

The introduction of innovations is often associated with organizational change, which creates resistance to change (Amarantou et al., 2018; DuBose & Mayo, 2020; Grol & Wensing, 2020). In this case, trust proves to be a key factor in helping to reduce resistance to change. S. Oreg found that of all the factors he studied that affect resistance to change, such as power and prestige, job security, intrinsic rewards, trust in management, social influence, and information about the change, trust in management was the only variable that had a significant effect on all three components of resistance (i.e., affective, behavioral, and cognitive), and had a particularly strong effect on employees' cognitive evaluation of the change (2006, p. 90).

Research by R. Ellonen et al. showed statistically significant negative relationships between vertical trust (between employees and a leader) and product and process innovativeness, and positive relationships between vertical trust and behavioral innovativeness (Table 3.5). Institutional trust is positively and significantly related to each dimension of organizational innovativeness, and the values of the regression coefficients are also relatively high, especially when it comes to product innovativeness (0.661) and process innovativeness (0.619) (Table 3.5). In contrast, lateral (horizontal) trust has no effect on any type of innovativeness (statistically insignificant results) (2008, p. 176).

Behavioral innovativeness and strategic innovativeness are noteworthy in this research, as these types of innovativeness are less frequently found in the literature, but they are relevant to hospitals. Behavioral innovativeness is defined as the behaviors exhibited by individuals, teams, and management that enable the formation of an innovative culture and overall internal openness to new ideas and innovations. Strategic innovativeness, on the other hand, encompasses an organization's ability to manage ambitious organizational goals and identify mismatches between those ambitions and existing

Table 3.5. Regression coefficients between trust and innovativeness variables

Type of trust	Product innovativeness	Behavioral innovativeness	Strategic innovativeness	Process innovativeness
Lateral trust (between employees)	−0.046	−0.007	−0.081	−0.025
Vertical trust (between employees and a leader)	−0.261[1]	0.407[1]	0.072	−0.282[1]
Institutional trust	0.661[1]	0.230[1]	0.337[1]	0.619[1]

[1] $p<0.05$

Source: Adapted from Ellonen et al., 2008, p. 175.

resources in order to creatively use or leverage scarce resources (2008, p. 164).

Previously, correlations between different types of trust (calculus-based trust, knowledge-based trust, identification-based trust) and innovation (technological, administrative, human resources, product-based) in hospitals were studied by S.R. Herting (2002, p. 301). In his study, all types of trust are positively correlated only with administrative innovations (Table 3.6), which the author defined as examples of innovations involving organizational management processes that involve organizational structures, organizational relationships and administrative policies. Innovations in this category included reorganizations, mergers, organizational restructuring, hospital partnerships, changes in hospital boards, personnel plans, strategic plans, etc. The classification criteria focused on various aspects of organizational infrastructure (2002, p. 300). The concept of different types of trust was adapted from the work of D. Shapiro et al. (1992). Calculus-based trust in Shapiro's work is called "deterrence-based trust." According to D. Shapiro et al., the primary motivation for keeping one's word is deterrence, which can be defined as the existence of means to prevent hostile action. Deterrence-based trust exists when the potential costs of breaking the relationship or the likelihood of retaliatory action outweigh the short-term benefits of distrust (1992, p. 366).

Knowledge-based trust can come from predictability of behavior. For example, if it is known that an employee will always choose to maximize his or her compensation at the expense of the company, it is simply necessary to align the employee's motivation with the company's interests. This type of trust is similar to trust based on a person's integrity (Mayer et al., 1995, p. 719). Identity-based trust refers to the assumption that one party has fully internalized the preferences of the other. In social psychology, it

Table 3.6. Correlation coefficients between trust and innovation variables

Innovation Types	Calculus-Based Trust	Knowledge-Based Trust	Identification-Based Trust
Technological	0.156	0.205	0.082
Administrative	0.457[1]	0.480[1]	0.385[2]
Human Resource	0.155	0.187	0.126
Product/ Service	−0.375[2]	−0.232	−0.220

[1] $p<0.01$, [2] $p<0.5$

Source: Adapted from Herting, 2002, p. 301.

has been shown that people in the same group behave in a more trusting manner toward each other than toward others outside that group. Corporate membership has a similar effect. Often the fact that someone is from the same company somehow makes them more trustworthy (Shapiro et al., 1992, p. 372). This type of trust can exist within professions, such as among physicians.

While the positive association of trust with administrative innovations was expected, the negative association of product innovations with calculus-based trust was not explained by the author of the study (Table 3.6). S.R. Herting defined product or service innovations as new services or functions that were made available to customers and end users (2002, p. 301). Examples of such services were social welfare programs, hospital events, transfer to outpatient care, treatment programs, marketing campaigns, care units, etc. One wonders whether a social welfare program or transfer to outpatient care can actually be considered innovation.

The studies presented above confirm the relationship between trust and innovativeness, although this relationship does not apply to all types of trust and innovativeness. On the one hand, the momentousness of innovativeness for the development of health care, especially hospital services, by their nature intended for the sickest patients, and on the other hand, the negligible number of studies of the relationship between trust and innovativeness in hospitals, confirms the need for research in this area.

In the context of the discussion at hand, it should also be made clear that trust, and in particular managers' trust in subordinates, is a key element supporting innovativeness in hospitals (Ellonen et al., 2008, p. 176; Herting, 2002, p. 292). S.R. Herting even notes that managers with a high level of trust in subordinates can expect to achieve the desired result, even on the basis of a verbal command. In his view, with high levels of trust, the need for control measures, such as supervision and auditing, may be negligible (2002, p. 303). In contrast, when managers have low confidence in the predictability of their subordinates' behavior, they are more likely to set restrictions and limitations to reduce the volatility of the environment, based on their perception that such an environment is more predictable, easier to manage, and more trustworthy. With that said, managers are the key to ingraining values and norms, such as trust and tolerance of risk-taking, associated with innovation (Williams, 2011, p. 215; Yang et al., 2017, p. 247). At the same time, a balanced atmosphere of trust and control among managers and organizational members can be an important factor in encouraging innovation in organizations. After all, perfect predictability equals perfect behavioral conformity, and, conversely, perfect unpredictability results in chaos and confusion, suggesting that innovativeness and conformity are, by definition, almost exact opposites. Where there is a high degree of conformity, innovativeness suffers, and vice versa. However, even with an optimal degree of organizational trust – a balance of rigor and freedom, predictability and randomness, empowerment and oversight, certainty and caution, risk and reward, vision and practicality – there can be maximum innovativeness while minimizing waste of resources (Herting, 2002, p. 293; Lill et al., 2020, p. 1). This means that innovation is as much a technical process as it is a cultural one, and, as such, it should be incumbent on managers to create a climate that encourages task orientation, and occasional mistakes should be accepted as inevitable.

3.6 Environmental Uncertainty

Uncertainty appears as the fundamental problem of complex organizations, and dealing with uncertainty as the essence of the administrative process (Thompson, 2003, p. 159). It is defined as the lack of information about the environmental factors involved in a given decision-making situation, or the ignorance of the outcome of a particular decision in terms of how much the organization would lose if the decision were wrong, as well as the inability to assign probabilities with any degree of certainty about how environmental factors will affect the success or failure of a decision-making entity (e.g., a manager) in performing its functions (Duncan, 1972, p. 318)320.

R.L. Daft et al. highlight two key features of the environment: dynamism and complexity. The concept of dynamism refers to the frequency of change and its predictability, expressed by the terms "stable" or "unstable." Complexity is defined as the number and dissimilarity of elements in an organization's environment and is described using the categories "simple" or "complex" (2010, p. 150). Thus, complexity and dynamism together create uncertainty. Uncertainty increases when complexity and dynamism increase, and a highly complex environment creates management challenges because a change in one element of the environment can cause unpredictable effects that are difficult to track (Begun & Kaissi, 2004, p. 32).

In this context, it should be noted that the way the uncertainty of the health-care environment is perceived and characterized is important for several reasons. First, an organization's performance depends on the level of fit between the perception of the environment and its objective state

(Bourgeois, 1985, p. 564). Thus, better results are obtained by health-care organizations that are able to perceive and manage uncertainty in their environment (Shortell et al., 2000). Second, organizations that are able to respond appropriately to different levels of environmental uncertainty are more effective (Ellis et al., 2002, p. 79).

The environment of hospitals can be considered at different levels of analysis. International forces such as the situation in the global and domestic economy, the demographic profile of the population, inflation, interest rates, and unemployment are part of the general environment of any organization; hence, the environment provides the context for health care and other sectors. The more specific, closer environment relates to areas that more directly affect an organization's ability to achieve its goals. With respect to hospitals, it includes, but is not limited to, competitors, patients, financial resources, human resources, suppliers, market conditions and regulators, and payers for health-care services. Significantly, the environment contains an infinite number of elements, but from an organization's point of view, only those that affect it and to the change of which it must respond in order to survive are relevant.

Hospitals as institutions of higher public utility are subject to public policy decision-making processes and often have to deal with political and economic actors with many divergent interests – although all are acting to achieve the public good. This causes hospital managers to operate in a context of uncertainty about what the problems are and how to counteract them, with no clear guidelines on what is moral (higher quality vs. lower costs, higher staff salaries vs. more staff and better care, etc.), constantly facing conflicting interests (Townley et al., 2003, p. 1066). However, an objective assessment of environmental uncertainty is virtually impossible because different people perceive environmental changes differently (Hatch, 2002, p. 100). Thus, uncertainty is rather a descriptor of the state of an individual who perceives himself as lacking relevant information about the environment, and should, therefore, be studied as a perceptual phenomenon (Milliken, 1987, p. 134), with perception fed by objective environmental conditions (Begun & Kaissi, 2004, p. 33). The perceptual understanding of uncertainty is influenced by the individual's conscious knowledge and intuitive judgments about the changing environment, which means that the environment and the experience of uncertainty are not completely objective or independent of the organization and its members. Uncertainty is a combination of objective and subjective reality, as all human perceptions have a subjective or interpretive aspect to the actual environment, and, for this reason, impressions of the experience can vary from person to person (Allred et al., 1994, p. 173).

As a result, it is particularly important to study the uncertainty of the hospital environment in the context of management control, since to date there has been no consensus among researchers on how to assess its volatility. Some researchers describe the health-care sector as turbulent, volatile, and characterized by high uncertainty, arguing that the health-care environment has moved from being reasonably predictable to unpredictable and highly unstable (Begun & Kaissi, 2004, p. 31; Yang et al., 2017, p. 246). Others, on the other hand, believe that the frequency of change in health care is low or even very low. I. Morrison even notes that "healthcare moves at glacial speed compared to most other industries," and that "hospitals and doctors have organizational time clocks geared more to geological speed than internet speed" (Morrison, 2000, pp. 199, 203). Perceived environmental uncertainty (PEU) is higher when the environment is changing faster. Moreover, the experience of uncertainty is perceptual only to the extent that there is an objective environment that limits the range of human capacity to cope with uncertainty (Allred et al., 1994, p. 173).

F.J. Milliken distinguished three types of PEU: state uncertainty, effect uncertainty, and response uncertainty. In state uncertainty, an individual does not understand how a component of the environment is changing and, therefore, lacks information about the predictability of the environment. Uncertainty of effect refers to an individual's inability to predict the impact of environmental changes on the organization. Uncertainty of response occurs when a decision must be made in response to an environmental threat, and manifests itself in a lack of knowledge about the available response options and the consequences of the choice – the utility of each possible course of action (1987, pp. 136–138). However, today, unlike at the time of F.J. Milliken's (1987) publication, there is a growing consensus that one of the best ways to assess environmental uncertainty in the organizational environment is to measure subjective perceptions of uncertainty by organizational leaders (Buchko, 1994, p. 411; Hameiri & Nir, 2016, p. 14; Nahavandi et al., 1992, p. 65; Sorrentino & Roney, 2013) focusing on the unpredictability of specific dimensions of the organization's environment (Begun & Kaissi, 2004, p. 33). Environmental uncertainty here refers to the degree to which managers find it difficult to accurately predict the future state of the environment (Yu et al., 2016, p. 22).

Compared to other industries, the health-care environment is more complex and contains different elements. The hospital environment is further complicated by the various institutional logics operating there (Lewandowski & Sułkowski, 2018, p. 152). In hospitals, individual internal units are less connected to each other, creating internal "silos" (e.g., hospital departments of different specialties) that limit interconnectedness, preventing the creation of an environment that is integrated and coordinated into a unified "system" (Begun & Kaissi, 2004, p. 34). As a result, hospital managers not only experience the uncertainty of the environment, but also face internal uncertainty regarding "production" as an "uncertain" technology or process, as the use of some treatment that worked for one patient does not mean success for the next patient. The sense of internal uncertainty can be reinforced for two reasons. First, health-care organizations deal with high-risk (life and death) situations, making the degree of uncertainty in the internal production process relatively higher than in other industries. Second, a key internal feature of health-care organizations is the high degree of uncertainty caused by complex interrelationships between a wide variety of organizational cells and entities (Begun & Kaissi, 2004, p. 35).

The results of a study by A.D. Meyer et al. indicate that the perception of uncertainty is influenced by both the personality traits of the person under study and the length of service in the health-care unit (1990, s. 98–101). Because of the events that occurred in the time frame that formed the context for the assessment, managers with experience may perceive uncertainty differently from those without experience (Begun & Kaissi, 2004, p. 35). Indeed, it was found that in the 1960s hospital executives perceived their environment as relatively calm and rich. In the 1970s, the environment was changing but in a way that managers could understand, while in the 1980s the changes were seen as an "industrial revolution" and perceived as discontinuous, restructuring the industry. The main impetus for these changes was a shortage of resources, and the primary goal was to accelerate diversification strategies. An example is the transformation of general hospitals into corporate-like organizations, when a regional holding company directly owned one hospital, while there was a formal affiliation with four other hospitals. This allowed the company to diversify its product and service offerings related to pre- and post-acute care. This example shows that the response to changing conditions and increased environmental uncertainty was to make innovative and radical changes. Also, the characteristics of the organization itself can affect its members' perception of uncertainty. For example, employees of organizations that have been efficient in the past may perceive the environment as less uncertain (Friedman et al., 2001).

To reduce the perceived uncertainty of the environment, organizations try to respond in various ways. One of these methods is to increase management control (Davila, 2000) and/or innovativeness (Lill et al., 2020, p. 9). This is because increasing environmental uncertainty, on the one hand, promotes continuous change in organizations, and, on the other hand, causes organizations to place more importance on management control. As a result, uncertainty directly affects innovativeness positively and additionally has a positive effect on innovativeness through strategic control (Yi et al., 2012, p. 701). However, while uncertainty positively affects financial control, financial control has a strong negative effect on innovativeness. Moreover, there is evidence that managers tend to use interactive control when they are exposed to high levels of market uncertainty (Davila et al., 2009, p. 340). Complementing the action of increasing management control in the context of a state of environmental uncertainty is also building information systems that enable information acquisition, analysis, and interpretation (Davila, 2000, p. 392), integrating knowledge (Bisbe & Sivabalan, 2017, p. 13), and innovating to better adapt to the changing environment (Kobrin, 1991; Lill et al., 2020, p. 8; Lisboa et al., 2011, p. 1157; Madhok & Osegowitsch, 2000; Meyer et al., 1990, p. 101; Tkotz et al., 2018, p. 4). Product development and innovation are critical to a company's survival and success, as they can meet customer needs and demands more effectively than existing offerings (Yalcinkaya et al., 2007, p. 74).

It should also be borne in mind that organizations, in order to adapt to changes in the environment, relatively often undertake various types of innovative changes, which intrinsically increase risk and uncertainty in the organization (Yoon et al., 2016, p. 413), but, on the other hand, organizations in response to the uncertainty of the environment, which can threaten their functioning, can respond by introducing various types of innovative solutions that adapt the organization to the environment (Atuahene-Gima, 2005, p. 78; Yang et al., 2017, p. 246). This means that innovations, on the one hand, can be a way to increase the organization's fit with the environment and reduce uncertainty, while, on the other hand, it increases uncertainty (Hameiri & Nir, 2016, p. 771). Hence, one of the essential ways for managers to deal with uncertainty is through trust, which can mitigate or reduce the effects of virtually any form of uncertainty (Bisbe & Sivabalan, 2017, p. 13; Colquitt et al., 2012, p. 2), while at the same time, in hospitals, it significantly supports the maintenance of harmonious relationships between doctors and managers (Yang et al., 2017, p. 247). It should also be remembered here that a systems perspective on innovation in the context of perceived uncertainty requires a multidisciplinary and interdisciplinary approach due to complex and non-linear policy interventions (OECD & Eurostat, 2019, p. 45). Hospitals that need to deliver products quickly to customers are required in this approach to develop efficient forecasting processes to manage the uncertainty of the environment (e.g., infection or virus) (Yoon et al., 2016, p. 419). Innovation creates a sense of uncertainty, so it is good when it operates in an environment covered by an effective information system, as the greater ability of managers to acquire information to reduce this uncertainty facilitates the adoption of innovation (Damanpour & Schneider, 2006, p. 221).

Note

1. Interpersonal support includes helpful, considerate, cooperative behaviors toward co-workers and work engagement behaviors involving persistence, taking initiative, attention to detail, effort, and self-discipline (Van Scotter, J., Motowidlo, S.J., Cross, T.C. (2000). Effects of task performance and contextual performance on systemic rewards. *Journal of Applied Psychology*, 85(4), 528, https://doi.org/10.1037/0021-9010.85.4.526. This construct has been studied with statements such as: "This subordinate supports or encourages a co-worker with a personal problem" and "This subordinate encourages others to overcome differences and get along."

Chapter 4

Research Methods

4.1 Mixed Methods Research Design

The research was conducted using a mixed methods research procedure, which is gaining recognition in the scientific world (Creswell & Plano Clark, 2017, p. 34). Mixed methods research is also referred to as the "third research paradigm" (Johnson & Onwuegbuzie, 2004, p. 14) or the "third methodological movement" (Morse, 2003, p. 14) and is an alternative to the quantitative-oriented and qualitative-oriented approaches previously considered the main methodological strategies. Research using both quantitative and qualitative methods has been conducted since the early 20th century, but it is only in the last 30 years that the mixed methods approach has been recognized as a distinct research strategy with its own paradigms and practices. In the management sciences, direct references to this particular research strategy have been appearing in scientific publications for more than a dozen years (Bazeley, 2018, p. 7). The primary reason for the choice made in this research is the difference between using two or more research methods and mixed methods. In the first approach, different methods are not combined, but treated as separate. In contrast, the second involves the use of complementary research strategies to collect and analyze data that in another procedure would not be possible using the main method (Morse, 2003, p. 191). Thus, in "mixed methods designs," two or more quantitative or qualitative strategies are combined within the same design in such a way that at many or all stages of the study, the research questions, methodology, data collection and analysis, and inference are logically linked and complementary.

DOI: 10.4324/9781003366553-4

At the same time, it has been noted that while using different methods of data collection, gathering and analysis requires more time, increases the cost of conducting a research project, and can lead to contrasting results for the same phenomenon, it provides many advantages. Combining research methods is helpful in minimizing the weaknesses of a single method, as long as the different methods are combined in a way that ensures that strengths are exploited and identified weaknesses are leveled (Khoo-Lattimore et al., 2017, p. 1533). Indeed, J. Brewer and A. Hunter point out that the diversity of methods implies rich opportunities for cross-validation and cross-fertilization of research procedures, findings, and theories (Brewer & Hunter, 2006, p. 1). This means that the use of mixed methods can be key to increasing the reliability of the data collected and providing stronger evidence, and thus it can lead to the generation of results that would not have been achievable if only a single method approach were used.

The three core mixed methods research designs can be distinguished: convergent design, exploratory sequential design, and exploratory sequential design (Creswell & Plano Clark, 2017, pp. 89–91). Convergent design occurs when a researcher compares or combines the results of quantitative and qualitative data analysis. The primary idea is to compare two types of results in order to gain a more complete understanding of the problem and to verify one set of results with the other. The sequential exploratory design involves two separate stages of research. In the first stage, quantitative data are collected and analyzed, and, in the second stage, qualitative data are collected and analyzed to explain or extend the quantitative results from the first stage. The next qualitative stage of the study is designed to follow from the results of the quantitative stage. Also, an exploratory sequential design consists of two consecutive research stages, except that an exploratory sequential design begins with the collection and analysis of qualitative data in the first stage and usually prioritizes it. Then, based on the results of the exploration, quantitative research is designed and conducted. Each of the presented mixed methods research designs is applicable to specific research situations. The characteristics presented above became the reason for choosing sequential exploratory mixed research design. The fundamental rationale for this is the fact that there is little recognition of management control in hospitals and no theory beyond the few qualitatively studied hospital cases. On the other hand, the research strategy adopted will allow the results obtained to be extended to a wider population of hospitals in Poland.

The choice made determined the course of the research process. The research began with the collection of qualitative data, the results of which became the starting point for quantitative research. The analysis of previous qualitative research conducted here showed that while management control research has been conducted in companies over the last century, inquiries in the area of control functions in public hospitals are still relatively rare and, in addition, some of them are of low quality. An example is the research related to the theory of levers of control in hospitals, which shows that, in many cases, researchers have trouble properly identifying diagnostic and interactive control (np.: (Kastberg & Siverbo, 2013, p. 264; Nyland & Pettersen, 2004, p. 77; Østergren, 2009, p. 185). In contrast, the qualitative research presented in the monograph made it possible to hear the views of hospital CEOs, who are the main creators of management control, and thus map the complexity of the issue. The field research conducted in this regard made it possible to identify the main variables of management control and the links between these variables, which provided the basis for proposing the author's conceptual model of management control in hospitals.

Quantitative research, on the other hand, serves to overcome the possible limitations of qualitative research, particularly those related to the small size of the research sample and the risk of personal interpretation by the researcher due to his experience and potential biases. At this stage of the research, the results of the qualitative research were used to build a measurement tool (survey questionnaire), which allowed us to collect quantitative data and analyze the model of management control in hospitals using a structural equation estimator. Thus, the quantitative research made it possible to generalize the results. However, what is important here is that the studied reality, although real and objective, is not possible to know in a perfect but probabilistic way, which is related to the difficulty of applying in management science the neo-positivist canon based on verifiable and certain knowledge. From this point of view, the role of modeling is seen as discovering mechanisms and structures, often not directly observable, rather than universal laws. In such modeling, the abduction method is recommended, in which hypothesis generation and evaluation are treated as inseparable elements of a single process (Veen, 2021, p. 1174).

The choice of qualitative and quantitative research used was, therefore, made with the intention of exploring different images and perspectives. Indeed, in this context, it should be recognized that although each of these studies has its limitations, the adoption of a mixed research strategy led to the achievement of an enhancement in the quality of the assessments undertaken, particularly caused by the fact that the strengths of one approach compensated for the possible weaknesses of the other. This combination, facilitating the combination of the in-depth and individualized approach of qualitative research and the generalizability of quantitative research, provided the opportunity to use both "words" and "numbers" in a single project and, in effect, combined inductive and deductive logics through abductive thinking. This is because the use of only one method would have resulted in the study of management control from a single angle, limiting a full understanding of the issue, and the combination made ensured that the research objective was fully realized.

4.2 Qualitative Research Strategy

The realization of the main objective of the monograph and the indicated specific objectives assigned to be achieved in qualitative research requires that, given the lack of a solid theoretical basis for management control in hospitals, the theoretical foundations underpinning this research should be developed through inductive qualitative research. Indeed, inductive research is particularly helpful in developing new and extending existing theoretical constructs. In addition, they provide clues for operationalizing the identified variables (Glinka & Czakon, 2021, p. 29) and enable the formulation of hypotheses on the basis of the collected empirical material (Babbie, 2013, p. 71; Czakon, 2020, p. 192; Glaser & Strauss, 2009; Glinka & Czakon, 2021, p. 28).

The need to fully understand how management control functions in hospitals led to the research being conducted as a naturalistic inquiry, during which coding and inductive inference were used to gain insight into the nature of the phenomenon under study (Czernek, 2020, p. 170; Glinka & Czakon, 2021, p. 26; Lincoln & Guba, 1985). In this procedure, the concepts used by the research participants were compared with the available literature in order to seek as faithful a match as possible between the conceptual apparatus used in the literature and the categories emerging from the field research. This approach implies a synthesis of apparent opposites: induction and deduction, which is characteristic of abductive reasoning (Klag & Langley, 2013, p. 153). In this research, the abductive approach involves generating hypotheses, selecting the most promising among them, and testing them.

Ensuring maximum heterogeneity of cases was achieved through the use of purposive selection (Czakon, 2020, p. 201; Eisenhardt, 1989b, p. 537; Eisenhardt & Graebner, 2007, p. 27; Glinka & Czakon, 2021, p. 82), on the basis of categories that are relatively significantly differentiating, e.g., the size of the budget, the degree of specialization, i.e., the type of hospital (monospecialty, general, specialized, university), the legal form (independent public health-care institution (IPHI), limited liability company (LLC)), the place of operation (different regions of Poland and hospitals from the United Kingdom, Ireland, and Lithuania), and the qualitative and financial results obtained. The last criterion for Polish hospitals was evaluated on the basis of the results of the European-funded project titled: "Portraits of hospitals – maps of possibilities, i.e., monitoring of the quality of public services and benchmarking of the scope of supervision of the operation of hospitals."[1] Under this project, hospitals were evaluated by means of a questionnaire they filled out, consisting of more than 500 questions in 13 areas, and then categorized in terms of qualitative and financial performance.

The final selection of interviewees was based on telephone interviews to ensure that the potential interviewee, i.e., the hospital director, was a valuable source of information (given the purpose of the research) and agreed to participate in the study. The essence of this approach was to ensure that the survey sample included a diverse set of hospitals with characteristics reflecting the general population of hospitals in Poland. Foreign hospitals provided a benchmark in the research sample.

In addition, providing anonymity to respondents (hospital directors) was intended to increase their freedom to speak about the management control solutions they use. Therefore, in the survey report, the names of the hospitals have been coded so that they cannot be identified (Table 4.1). The hospital codes are also the codes of the interviewees. At the same time, when more than one person was interviewed at a hospital (a British hospital), the job title was appended to the hospital code. Guaranteeing anonymity for respondents and the places where they work is a common practice in health-care research, as interviews conducted in this sector are particularly vulnerable to misrepresentations related to socially desirable responses (Kerpershoek et al., 2014, p. 424). The high exposure to the phenomenon of giving socially desirable answers stems from the need for external legitimacy, which is discussed in more detail in the body of the monograph.

4.2.1 Data Collection Procedure

During the field research, interviews were conducted, and various types of documents were collected from 16 hospitals, including 12 hospitals in Poland, 1 in the United Kingdom, 1 in Ireland, and 2 in Lithuania (Table 4.1). Expanded characteristics of each hospital can be found in Appendix 1. In the hospital in the United Kingdom, Ireland, and one hospital in Lithuania,

148 ■ *Management Control in Hospitals*

Table 4.1. Data of hospitals participating in qualitative research

No.	Hospital/ informant code	Legal form	Years of work as a director	Education	Number of hospital wards	Number of beds	Number of Nurses	Number of doctors, including residents	Total number of employees	Revenue (million)
1	SzS1	IPHI	26	Med.-doctor	23	460	580	330	1 100	223 PLN
2	SzO1	LLC	3	Non-med.	4	120	48	14	175	12 PLN
3	SzO2	LLC	9	Non-med.	12	302	184	109	504	83 PLN
4	SzO/S1	IPHI	4	Med.-other	10	250	250	110	550	92 PLN
5	SzS/U	IPHI	17	Med.-doctor	23	630	600	350	1 360	210 PLN
6	SzU	IPHI		Non-med.	18 clinics	980	1000	500	2 500	340 PLN
7	SzO/S2	LLC	11	Non-med.	19	540	450	170	980	127 PLN
8	SzO4	IPHI	16	Non-med.	11	313	250	100	540	88 PLN
9	SzO3	IPHI	9	Non-med.	11	165	98	53	290	46 PLN
10	SzM1	IPHI	6	Non-med.	6	220	56	18	230	27 PLN
11	SzS2	IPHI	8	Non-med.	19	420	530	290	930	190 PLN
12	SzM2	IPHI	19	Non-med.	4	219	48	14	210	21 PLN
13	SzGB	Trust	8	Non-med.	28	1 159	3 480	1400	13 180	870 GBP
14	SzUL	Public	6	Med.-doctor	35	2305	2500	1200	7 144	160 EUR
15	SzL	Public	12	Med.-doctor	17	812	750	440	1 940	35 EUR
16	SzI	Public	4	Non-med.	16	210	550	280	900	123 EUR

Legend: Sz – Hospital, SzO – General hospital, SzS – Specialty hospital, SzU – University hospital, SzM – Monospecialty hospital, SzGB – Great Britain hospital, SzL – Lithuanian hospital, SzI – Irish hospital (example: SzS/U – specialty hospital with formal scientific activity or cooperating with a medical university), Independent Public Health-Care Institution (IPHI), Limited Liability Company (LLC) interviews were conducted in English. In the other hospital in Lithuania, the CEO was interviewed in Russian. Due to the language barrier, additional materials from Lithuanian hospitals, such as orders, guidelines, strategies, reports, presentations, etc., were not analyzed. Field research in Poland was conducted in 2014–2019, in the United Kingdom and Ireland it was conducted in May and June 2017, and in Lithuania in October and November 2015. In some Polish hospitals, interviews were repeated when some ambiguities or inaccuracies were considered during the analysis of the collected material.

A total of 29 semi-structured interviews were conducted personally by the author, including 21 with directors of Polish hospitals and one interview each at foreign hospitals (Irish and Lithuanian), with the exception of a British hospital where the author conducted five interviews (with the chief executive officer (CEO), chief operating officer (COO), and managing directors of three clinical divisions with at least 300 beds). All of the British directors had non-medical backgrounds. The interviews, except in two cases where the directors did not consent to being recorded, were recorded as an audio file. In situations where the directors did not consent to recording, the author kept meticulous notes during the interview. After each interview, field notes were created to better understand the issues under investigation, as well as the context itself, which was specific to the interviewee and could have affected his perception. The field notes were a valuable supplement to the transcriptions of the interviews. The duration of each interview ranged from 60 to 150 minutes.

The data collection process was preceded by two pilot interviews, the purpose of which was, among other things, to reduce the number of possible misunderstandings in the data collection process and to evaluate the usefulness of the prepared, partially structured research scheme. These two pilot interviews were not included in the main research sample of 29 interviews, and the responses collected at this stage were not used in this dissertation. In preparation for the research, information about the hospital, the hospital's website, including documents on the Public Information Bulletin (PIB), was reviewed online before each interview.

The interviews used a set of questions on management control and hospital management. The questions were open-ended, allowing the interview to be tailored to each manager's knowledge, without losing the overall purpose of the study. The interviews generally began with questions about general hospital management, such as: What can you say about hospital management? In your opinion, how does hospital management differ from the management of other organizations, especially businesses? Do you use any management tools recognized in the literature? Do you feel that the goals adopted at the hospital are being achieved effectively and efficiently? How do you communicate the goals to hospital employees, especially medical professionals? What measures do you take to effectively and efficiently implement the planned goals? What influence do employees have in setting goals? To avoid having the questions suggest answers, the leading control questions were deliberately asked next. These were questions like: what do you think about control in general? What forms of control are most appropriate for a hospital? Do you see a difference between controlling doctors and other employees? What forms of control do you use in your hospital? The order of questions adopted allowed directors to narrate more freely and naturally, making it possible to identify phenomena that influenced the process of management control. Since a naturalistic study of social phenomena should be conducted in a natural setting, where contextual variables can be observed and taken into account in the search for an explanation of the phenomenon, the survey was conducted in a place chosen by the interviewees, so they felt comfortable and treated it as their own familiar environment (Czakon & Czernek-Marszałek, 2021, p. 8). Accordingly, most of the interviews were conducted in directors' offices, except for three that were conducted in restaurants.

During the interviews, a range of documents were identified that supplemented and expanded the information obtained from the directors. They were also asked to send by email or post documents that supported the theses discussed (e.g., orders, circulars, strategic plans, internal reports, restructuring plans, annual reports, and even PowerPoint presentations and newspaper articles when they related to the issues discussed). These were analyzed in detail and compared with the interviews. Relevant excerpts were added to the transcription of the interviews in MaxQDA12. If the director failed to mention an important fact or situation that was present in the archival materials and was important to the study, the situation was clarified by phone. In a few cases, the data were supplemented during subsequent in-person interviews.

4.2.2 *Phases of Data Analysis and Data Coding*

The research employed thematic analysis, which essentially consists of six steps (Braun & Clarke, 2006, p. 87; Glinka & Czakon, 2021, p. 137). The analysis of the transcribed materials collected in the field research began by familiarizing oneself with them through careful reading and rereading (Rice

& Ezzy, 1999, p. 258), in other words, becoming immersed in the data set as a whole to look for themes that appear important to the adopted research question. At this stage, a series of notes were also taken – a preliminary list of ideas about what is in the data and what is of interest. Initial coding of the data was conducted in an inductive and semantic manner, meaning that data extracts, ranging in length from one sentence to an entire paragraph that represent the most basic segment or element of the raw data or information that can be evaluated in a meaningful way in relation to the phenomenon (Boyatzis, 1998, p. 63), were identified and coded in a way that clearly reflected the content of the extracts being coded. They also did not look for hidden meanings in the coded passages, beyond what the participant explicitly said or what was written in the document. At this stage, 306 codes were assigned to 643 extracts of raw data. In order not to lose the context and meaning of the separated and coded extracts, and especially to allow readers to interpret them on their own, some surrounding data were left out. It is worth noting that some data extracts were coded multiple times, and some not at all. Efforts were made not to ignore or remove emerging tensions and inconsistencies within and between data elements. The overriding principle at this stage was to also preserve relationships that appeared to deviate from the accepted research objective related to management control. It was recognized that some fragments seemingly unrelated to control could be useful in further stages of analysis.

The third phase focused on sorting and assigning codes to potential first- and second-order themes (Fereday & Muir-Cochrane, 2006, p. 81). The analysis was performed using specialized MaxQDA12 software. In total, the codes were grouped into 96 first-order themes, which were combined into 14 preliminary second-order themes. As mentioned earlier, the codes were formed inductively, i.e., they were derived directly from the content of the coded extracts, while the themes were formed to correspond to existing theoretical constructs. Some of the codes were not assigned to any of the preliminary themes, considering them to be so-called candidate themes (Braun & Clarke, 2006, p. 91).

During the fourth phase of data analysis, it was verified that the content identified as theme candidates were not, in fact, themes. The verification was conducted by rereading the entire data set, which served two purposes. First, to determine which theme candidates operate in relation to the entire data set, i.e., the extent to which these phenomena are present in the majority of the hospitals studied. Second, to recode previously omitted extracts that appeared to be relevant to any of the themes, or possibly to refine earlier coding. During verification, additional attention was paid to three elements: (1) internal homogeneity within a theme, by considering whether the data within themes are meaningfully consistent with each other; (2) external heterogeneity, by looking for existing clear and identifiable differences between themes; (3) linking themes to the research objective and the adopted operational definition of management control. Individual theme candidates, particularly second-order themes, were also vetted for the sufficiency of the number of data supporting the topic.

Phase five of the study revisited the coded data extracts for each theme, organizing them into even more internally consistent sets and annotating them with notes suggesting a narrative for each set/theme, highlighting the most interesting themes. At this stage, with the help of the literature (Fereday & Muir-Cochrane, 2006, p. 82), eight second-order themes were defined and refined from 63 first-order themes. This made it possible to define the essence of each second-order theme, in terms of the latent variable (construct), and to name them. It should be noted that at this stage, not only were the constructs themselves considered, but also the meaning of each construct was explored in relation to other constructs, and the relationships between these constructs were identified. These relationships were identified on the basis of field research and, when possible, based on the literature, and then presented in the form of research hypotheses. As a result, on the basis of the analysis, a model of management control in hospitals was built, which in the following part of the research is estimated by quantitative methods using a path model estimator. Given the need, within the framework of the adopted research strategy, to apply statistical analysis, further theoretical refinement of the identified constructs was performed as part of their operationalization. Importantly, extracts that illustrate the institutional perspective were additionally marked in the study material. These have not been identified as separate themes, as they are intertwined with other themes that emerged in the research and only serve to deepen the interpretation of themes embedded in the organizational perspective.

The sixth and final phase of the qualitative research was "report writing" (Braun & Clarke, 2006, p. 93). This phase described the identified constructs and adopted hypotheses that speak to their interconnectedness. This allowed the construction of a conceptual model of management control in hospitals (Figure 5.1). In order to better understand the context of management control in hospitals, extensive quotations of statements made by hospital executives, even covering several excerpts, were quoted in many places in the research report.

4.3 Measurement Instruments for Latent Variables

The structural model developed in the qualitative research was built in such a way that each element of management control, including hospital performance, was treated as a separate variable (Figure 5.1). These variables are abstract and unobservable concepts (constructs). Their existence and the meanings attributed to them derive only from the underlying theory, and their content relevance in relation to the theoretical concept of the construct flows from the measurement model used. Thus, the problem of testing the model involves the need to find an adequate method to observe such variables within the framework of the developed model of management control in hospitals. Thus, it becomes important to distinguish the latent constructs under study, which are a combination of the level of theoretical concepts and the level of empirical and observable phenomena.

In this context, the primary task becomes the proper selection of observable variables (indicator) that best correlate with the given latent variable (construct) identified in the field research. The observable variables in this case are the individual questions in the survey. Linking the theoretical constructs, developed as part of the first stage of the research, with the corresponding indicators, i.e., questions to respondents, allows the variables to be operationalized. In the course of operationalizing the variables of the model of management control in hospitals identified in the qualitative research (Chapter 5), the aim was to achieve such a degree of construct content validity that, on the one hand, the full range of meanings identified during the qualitative research is covered as thoroughly as possible, and, on the other hand, phenomena that are not part of it are excluded. In this approach, measurement instruments were first sought from the scientific literature, validated in earlier studies, which highly covered the domain of the individual constructs of the management control model in hospitals. However, when the exact formulation of the original indicators did not adequately reflect a particular aspect of the construct being described, modifications were made. This was done taking into account the following assumptions: (1) when a review of the literature failed to identify previously developed measurement scales or indicator items designed to measure a given construct of the management control model, new measurement scales were developed based on the results of fieldwork and literature studies; (2) in operationalizing the variables, discriminant validity, that is, the degree to which the construct deviates from other variables to which it should theoretically not be similar, was also taken into account. This approach was considered crucial, as in each case decisions on how to measure a particular construct form the basis for referring to that variable in further theoretical analysis. The process and results of operationalization are presented in subsection 6.1.

However, it is important to pay attention not only to the content of indicators, but also to the way they are linked to the unobservable variable with which these indicators (observable variables) are associated. The linking of observable variables to a construct is called a measurement model. There are two basic measurement models: reflective and formative. The use of the appropriate measurement model is important not only for the correct description of the variable, which ensures that the model is consistent with the theoretical meaning of the variable (i.e., content validity), but also for the choice of the SEM estimator. Furthermore, two types of SEM estimators can be distinguished: covariance-based (CB-SEM) and variance-based (partial least squares – PLS-SEM) estimators, which analyze formative variables differently.

The explicit specification of the measurement model of individual latent variables is often omitted in the scientific literature, as most studies and some statistical methods (e.g., exploratory factor analysis) implicitly assume a reflective measurement model for all constructs, which is not always the appropriate choice. Incorrect specification of a construct's measurement model can negatively affect the quality of research. T. Coltman et al. claim that for decades scholars have blindly adhered to the procedure associated with exploratory factor analysis (Coltman et al., 2008, p. 1251). Some scholars have additionally questioned the usefulness of formative models as a means of measuring latent variables (Howell, 2013, p. 20; Lee & Cadogan, 2013; Lee et al., 2014), but, in recent years, mainly due to the rapid development and acceptance of PLS-SEM estimators (Bayonne et al., 2020; Benitez et al., 2020; Hair, 2020; Liengaard et al., 2021) as a full-fledged scientific method, such voices have become less frequent. Thus, to ensure high-quality research, it was assumed that operationalization, i.e., the adoption of specific measures of each construct and measurement model, should be carried out on the basis of the results of qualitative research, which resulted in a situation where the constructs identified in qualitative research have different measurement models: reflective or formative (Figure 4.1).

The operationalization of the constructs identified in the qualitative research, including the selection of the optimal measurement model for each construct, was described in subsection 6.1. The starting point for selecting the optimal measurement model was to understand the differences between the models. A reflective measurement model (also called Mode A

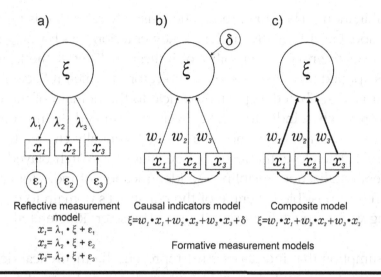

a) b) c)

Reflective measurement model

Causal indicators model
$\xi = w_1 \cdot x_1 + w_2 \cdot x_2 + w_3 \cdot x_3 + \delta$

Composite model
$\xi = w_1 \cdot x_1 + w_2 \cdot x_2 + w_3 \cdot x_3$

$x_1 = \lambda_1 \cdot \xi + \varepsilon_1$
$x_2 = \lambda_2 \cdot \xi + \varepsilon_2$
$x_3 = \lambda_3 \cdot \xi + \varepsilon_3$

Formative measurement models

Figure 4.1.   Types of measurement models

measurement in PLS-SEM) was assigned to the identified constructs when the effects (indicators) were a manifestation, an emanation of that latent variable (i.e., they came from the same domain), i.e., they were highly correlated with each other and could be used interchangeably (Figure 4.1a). That is, any single indicator could essentially be omitted without changing the meaning of the construct (Henseler, Ringle et al., 2016, p. 407). The fact that the correlation moves from the construct to its measures indicates that if the evaluation of the latent trait changes, all indicators will change simultaneously.

The basis for the indicated choice was the fact that reflective measurement models are based on the assumption of equality of the latent variable and the common factor underlying the set of observed indicators. Here, the relationship between the observed and unobserved variable (construct) is usually modeled according to the following equation:

$$x_i = \lambda_i \cdot \xi + \varepsilon_i$$

where x_i is the observed indicator variable; ξ is the latent variable, loading λ_i is the regression coefficient quantifying the strength of the relationship between x and ξ; and ε_i is the random error of measurement (Henseler, Ringle et al., 2016, p. 407; Henseler, 2017, p. 181).

The choice of a formative measurement model (also referred to as Mode B measurement in PLS-SEM) was based on the observation that these are solutions that rely on the assumption that indices form a construct using linear combinations. Therefore, researchers usually refer to this type of measurement model as a formative index. A key criterion for choosing a formative model was the non-convertibility of indicators. That is, the formative model was applied to constructs, each indicator of which reflected a specific aspect, that is, contributed a specific particle to the domain of the construct. In other words, when indicators collectively determined the meaning of a construct, the omission of an indicator could potentially change the meaning of a construct. Therefore, the results of qualitative research played a key role during operationalization, enabling the identification of indicators that provided the fullest possible coverage of the construct's domain to ensure that its meaning was adequately captured (por. (Henseler, Ringle et al., 2016, p. 408).

The assumption that indicators must represent the theoretical definition of the concept under study has important implications for modeling a latent variable, since it is highly unlikely that any set of causal indicators will be able to fully capture every aspect of the latent phenomenon. Therefore, latent variables measured by causal indicators have an error component (Figure 4.1b) that includes all other causes of the latent variable not included in the model. Formative causal variables are described according to the following equation:

$$\xi = \sum_{i=1}^{I} w_i \cdot x_i + \delta$$

Where w_i indicates the contribution of x_i ($i = 1,\ldots, I$) to the latent variable ξ, and δ is the error term (Henseler, Ringle et al., 2016, p. 408; Henseler, 2017, p. 182).

Unlike the reflective measurement method, which aims to maximize the overlap of interchangeable indicators in order to most accurately measure a predefined latent variable, in formative measurement there is no specific expectation of patterns or magnitude of intercorrelations between indicators. This is because there is no "common cause" for the elements of the construct, nor any requirement that the elements be correlated. Indicators of a formative variable can be completely independent. In fact, collinearity between formative indicators can create serious problems, as the weights linking formative indicators to the construct can become unstable and statistically insignificant (Coltman et al., 2008, p. 1254). In addition, formative indicators also do not have individual measurement errors, which has broad implications for the evaluation of formatively measured constructs, which are based on a set of criteria completely different from the evaluation of reflec- tively measured constructs. For example, a reliability analysis based on indi- cator correlations (internal consistency) can lead to the removal of important indicators and reduce the relevance of the index (Henseler, Ringle et al., 2016, p. 408). Therefore, as mentioned earlier, when operationalizing the constructs, great attention was paid to the content validity of the measures identified in the qualitative studies, and only secondarily referred to the scales used in earlier studies. This approach ensured the selection of indica- tors that adequately represented the domain (or at least the main aspects) of the second-order themes identified in the thematic analysis.

It is important to note the existence of two types of the formative mea- surement model: the causal model and the composite model. Causal vari- ables refer to the traditionally understood formative variable described above. Composite variables, on the other hand, also largely correspond to the definition of formative measurement models presented earlier, except that they do not have an error term (Figure 4.1c). Causal indicators assume that a given construct can be fully measured by a set of indicators and an error term (Figure 4.1b). Composite indicators make no such assumption, but treat the measurement as an approximation of some theoretical concept. A composite variable is described according to the following equation:

$$C = \sum_{i=1}^{I} w_i \cdot x_i$$

Where w_i indicates the contribution of the indicator x_i ($i = 1,..., I$) to the latent variable C (Henseler, Ringle et al., 2016, p. 408; Henseler, 2017, p. 181).

In practice, this means that the observable indicators in their entirety form a composite variable (i.e., the R^2 value of the composite variable is 1), although the indicators are not necessarily conceptually linked. This is important, since in the composite model the resulting variable is an accu- rate representation (proxy) of the latent variable (cf. (Hair et al., 2016, p. 47). Therefore, when operationalizing the variables, an effort was made to include all indicators identified in the qualitative research, since the omis- sion of any indicator is equivalent to missing part of the theoretical meaning of the composite variable (Aguirre-Urreta et al., 2016, p. 94). The solution adopted in the research takes into account the observation that there are several ways of interpreting models containing composite variables. They can be viewed as a useful tool for creating new entities to capture various arrangements and relationships or as a recipe for dimensional reduction, the purpose of which is to condense the data so that they adequately reflect the most important features of the concept. Some authors emphasize that the composite model perspective offers a more general and potentially more realistic approach to measurement (Henseler, Ringle et al., 2016, p. 408; Rigdon, 2014). In doing so, it should be noted that whether the formative variable is treated as causal or composite depends on the choice of path model estimator. The CB-SEM estimator takes into account the error component for the measured latent variable. In contrast, the PLS-SEM algorithm relies solely on the concept of composite indicators because of the way it estimates formative measurement models (Hair et al., 2016, p. 47).

In operationalizing the identified constructs and assigning them an appropriate measurement model, the principle was followed that the primary way to decide whether a measurement model for a particular latent variable should be formative or reflective is through theoretical reasoning (Hair et al., 2018, p. 89; Bollen & Diamantopoulos, 2017, p. 582). Thus, it was the theoretical and conceptual analysis of the relationship between indicators and the construct that influenced the choice of measurement model. In particular, theoretical consideration was given to whether indicators are manifestations of the construct or constitutive aspects of the construct. In many situations, deciding on the measurement model of a variable was complex, and theoretical analysis did not provide a clear answer to the question of choosing the optimal measurement model for a given construct. Therefore, in operationalizing the variables, in addition to the qualitative research data and theoretical conceptualization of the construct, the purpose of the study and guidance available in the literature were taken into account (Table 4.2). Previous research suggests that in the situation of testing well-established theory and operating on well-defined constructs, the reflective measurement model is preferable. On the other hand, in situations where it is necessary to know the indicators (observable variables) most strongly influencing a construct, the formative measurement model offers greater opportunities for more nuanced inference (Henseler, 2017).

In summary, it should be said that the basis for operationalizing the variables of the management control model in hospitals was the results of qualitative research juxtaposed with the scientific literature. On the other hand, the basis for the selection of the measurement model, i.e., the direction of the link between the observable variables and the latent variable (construct), were theoretical considerations. However, it is worth mentioning that during the statistical analysis of the measurement model, empirical methods of verifying the nature of constructs were also used, i.e., confirmatory tetrad

Table 4.2. Rules for determining the nature of a latent variable

Factor	Reflective Measurement	Formative Measurement	
		Causal Measurement	Composite Measurement
Relationship between construct and indicators	Indicators are an emanation of the construct.	The indicators affect the construct.	The indicators form the construct.
Expected correlational pattern among indicators	High correlations are expected.	Indicators do not have to be correlated. High correlation and associated collinearity are an obstacle in SEM estimation.	
Approach to measurement error	Takes measurement error into account at the item level.	Takes measurement error into account at the construct level.	Does not include measurement error.
Consequences of not including the indicator	Dropping an indicator does not alter the meaning of the construct.	Removing the indicator increases the measurement error at the construct level or may change its meaning.	Dropping an indicator alters the composite and changes its meaning.
Nomological net	The nomological network of indicators cannot differ. Indicators must have the same antecedents and consequences.	The nomological network of indicators may vary. Indicators do not have to have the same antecedents and consequences.	

Source: Adapted from Henseler, 2017 and Jarvis et al., 2003.

analysis (Bollen & Ting, 2000; Gudergan et al., 2008), as an auxiliary method in the theoretical specification of the measurement model (Table 6.17).

4.3.1 Procedure for Developing the Survey Questionnaire

The indicator variables adopted during the operationalization of the constructs (subsection 6.1.) were used to develop the survey questionnaire. Respondents rated the survey items (indicator variables) on a seven-point scale, as it is widely believed that a seven-point scale is the most appropriate for path model estimation.

To ensure the quality of the research, after the first version of the survey questionnaire was developed at subsequent stages, it was subjected to facial validation (cf. (Fayard et al., 2012, p. 176; Heinicke et al., 2016, p. 40; Morgan, 1990, p. 64; Shmueli et al., 2019, p. 2232). That is, it was pre-tested to verify that the entire questionnaire, as well as individual questions, were correctly understood by respondents, and, in particular, whether the measure was understood by the respondent according to the researcher's intentions. The pre-testing process took place in face-to-face meetings with four public hospital directors, alternating with remote consultation of insights with four experienced researchers. All the insights of practitioners and theorists were considered, enabling the final version of the survey questionnaire to be established.

Research on management control can address phenomena at different levels of analysis, the individual person, how he or she functions and reacts in a particular control environment, an organizational unit (e.g., a strategic business unit, a hospital department), and the organization as a whole. This survey refers to the level of the entire organization. When a survey uses a level of analysis beyond the individual level, consider whether to survey multiple respondents at each level (in this case, within the organization) or just one person, such as a unit manager. Although the use of a single respondent weakens the validity of the survey since a single individual may reflect to a lesser extent the situation of the organization as a whole. However, in practice, most surveys focusing on phenomena at the organizational level use only one respondent (por.: (Van der Stede et al., 2005, p. 666).

The same is true in this research. The choice of a single respondent, a hospital manager, is based on several considerations. First, as mentioned earlier, the basic assumption made during the research is that hospital directors are the most reliable source of information on the operation of management control. Second, because of the cost of surveying many respondents compared to the potential benefits gained. Surveying multiple individuals from a single organization in surveys of a large population of hospitals would have a beneficial effect only if the responses of individuals could be compared within a single hospital. However, in a situation where hospitals are assured of anonymity, it is impossible to identify the respondent's background and thus validate responses. In a similar vein, W.A. Van der Stede, S.M. Young, and C.X. Chen point out that: "In many cases, however, corroboration [of the information received] is impossible because the researcher has promised anonymity to respondents" (2005, p. 666). Third, if one were to assume that, in addition to the chief executive officer, members of senior management, such as deputy directors for treatment, nursing, technical, and financial affairs, are included in the research, this would generate further difficulties. Not all hospitals, especially smaller ones, have these positions established. Of course, one could refer to related positions, such as, for example, a nurse supervisor as a substitute for the director of nursing, or a chief accountant in place of the chief financial officer. However, while the perception of the supervisor of nurses may be similar to that of the deputy director of nursing, the responsibilities of the chief accountant, who is primarily responsible for the correctness of financial accounting, are already quite different from those of the deputy director of finance, who usually has a much broader area of responsibility. Thus, it would be difficult to assume that people with such divergent responsibilities present a similar perception of management control. Finally, it is worth noting that there is a certain level of "conflict" between medical professionals and managers in hospitals; this is mainly due to the different institutional logics used by the two groups (Lewandowski & Sułkowski, 2018, p. 152). In this situation, the approach to management control of both the medical director and possibly the nursing director is likely to be different from that of the chief executive officer. In most types of hospitals, the CEO bears the majority of responsibility, so they are the one who has the "last word," and thus creates, or at least should create, management control – in view of this, it seems that their perception is crucial.

Taking into account the above considerations, the pilot questionnaire was sent out to 35 directors of hospitals in Poland, purposely chosen to be as different from each other as possible. This number of questionnaires sent out meets the pilot sample size requirement of at least 5% of the future survey sample. Hospital directors, answering the questionnaire, coded their perception of the phenomena, that is, the constructs identified in the field research and then operationalized (cf. (de Harlez & Malagueño, 2016, p. 9). The results were used to further evaluate the questionnaire, including the identification of problematic items (cf. (Shmueli et al., 2019, p. 2232). In practice, verification looked as such: first, it was checked whether respondents answered all items for a given construct. If the number of responses was low, the item was considered incomprehensible, or that this phenomenon does not occur in some hospitals, and most often a decision was made to remove such an item. In addition, for the variable for which a reflective measurement model was adopted, the reliability of the scale was analyzed using Cronbach's alpha coefficient. Those items that lowered the value of this coefficient below 0.6 were removed. Admittedly, in many studies, research-ers do not use a preliminary test of the quality of questionnaires, with only 23% of publications reporting this step (Van der Stede et al., 2005, p. 670). However, it was thought that a preliminary verification of the questionnaire would, on the one hand, allow it to be shortened, which could translate into a higher return of completed questionnaires in the actual survey, and, on the other hand, a lower number of unfilled items in the questionnaires. The tables grouping the indicators of each variable indicate which ones were removed during the preliminary test of the questionnaire on a sample of 35 hospital directors.

4.4 Selection and Characteristics of the Sample in Quantitative Research

In Poland at the end of 2019, there were 592 hospitals included in the so-called hospital network that have guaranteed public financing. They were mostly public and not-for-profit general, specialized, and university hospitals. Together with monospecialty hospitals, such as rehabilitation, psychiatric, and other inpatient institutions, there were 747 public inpatient facilities, and 489 privately owned hospitals, including 25 for-profit and 464 not-for-profit hospitals, which altogether sum up to 1,236 hospitals. This population includes both very small entities, with only one inpatient ward, and large institutions, consisting of dozens of wards. Hospital structure in Poland, to a large extent, is similar to that of other OECD countries especially in the area of for-profit or not-for-profit orientation. In Poland, around 80% of beds are in public or not-for-profit hospitals, which is a similar share even to the United States, where according to AHA, 76% are not-for-profit, state, or local government owned. Generally, the analysis based on the OECD statistics for 27 countries that the data were available for shows that, on average, more than 80% are in not-for-profit and publicly owned hospitals (Table 1.1). However, on average, hospitals in Poland are smaller than in Germany or Austria, but larger than those in the United States or in the United Kingdom. This is mainly due to the overall different number of beds per 1,000 inhab-itants in Poland (6.17) than in Germany (7.91), Austria (7.19), or the United States (2.83) and the United Kingdom (2.42).[2] It is important to note that pub-licly owned and not-for-profit hospitals have, on average, more beds than the for-profit ones. Thus, it is fundamental to study these larger hospitals, which are the backbone of inpatient care in OECD countries. The relative similarity of Polish hospitals and hospitals in other OECD countries, which was also underlined in the first chapter, is important as it makes it possible, to some extent, to generalize the results obtained in this study.

Therefore, the study is focused on publicly owned and not-for-profit hospitals in Poland that are the largest and most important for the Polish healthcare system. These hospitals are financed by the government-owned single payer – National Health Fund (NHF). According to information contained in materials on hospitals that qualified for the hospital network, available on the National Health Fund's website and in the National Health Fund's directory of contracts concluded, only hospitals with a level of financing from the National Health Fund above PLN 10 million and had contracts for several medical specialties. In contrast, entities with lower budgets were relatively often characterized by a structure that differed quite significantly from that of the average hospital. Instead of having several inpatient wards and outpatient clinics, they had only day wards, same-day surgery, primary care, or several outpatient clinics with a small range of inpatient services. The complexity of the services provided in these facilities was also low, which may indicate that the needs for control and coordination in these entities were much less than in larger hospitals providing more advanced medical procedures.

Taking these arguments into account, general and monospecialty hospitals, such as rehabilitation, pediatrics, and psychiatry with a planned revenue volume of more than PLN 10 million from the National Health Fund in 2019, were qualified for the study (Table 4.3). Eliminating the smallest hospitals from the study population made it more homogeneous, i.e., achieving greater similarity in control and coordination needs between the smallest and largest hospitals. At the same time, it should be noted that further increasing the threshold for entry into the study population could result in the exclusion from the study of many county facilities, which are currently the backbone of the hospital system in Poland.

In the context of the assumptions presented, when proceeding to identify hospitals belonging to the study population (constructing a mailing list), after searching, based on information from the National Health Fund, among all providers, entities were selected that had a contract with the National Health Fund for an amount of not less than PLN 10 million in 2019. Subsequently, all providers that were not hospitals were eliminated from this list.[3] In particular, the following were removed: ambulance stations, sanatoriums, dedicated dialysis stations, and entities providing only outpatient services. As a result, a list of 601 hospitals from 16 provinces was obtained, which in

Table 4.3. Characteristics of the survey sample by hospital revenue size

Revenue range in millions	Number of hospitals	Mean value in the research sample					
		Number of wards	Number of outpatient clinics	Number of beds	Number of employees	Revenues in millions PLN	Profit
10–30	21	6.1	10.7	179.9	241.4	21.5	–0.9%
31–60	56	10.3	10.1	312.2	452.3	40.6	–3.3%
61–120	40	15.4	16.5	421.3	778.5	87.6	–3,2%
121–240	21	21.6	24.5	558.3	1369.2	198.8	–2,1%
Over 241	10	26.1	27.2	702.8	2067.3	398.6	–1,1%
No data	3						
Mean		**14.7**	**16.3**	**398.9**	**789.3**	**97.2**	**–2.6%**
Median		**14.0**	**14.0**	**380.0**	**600.0**	**52.4**	**–1.4%**
Min		**3.0**	**2.0**	**72.0**	**121.0**	**12.5**	**–22.5%**
Max		**53.0**	**62.0**	**1251.0**	**3500.0**	**672.1**	**9.0%**
Standard deviation		**8.7**	**12.1**	**224.7**	**577.1**	**104.9**	**5.1%**

further consideration will be referred to as the general population of hospitals in Poland.

Due to the relatively small size of the general population of hospitals, surveys were sent to all 601 identified hospitals. The survey was prepared as an anonymous Google Forms questionnaire and as a printable PDF file. The names of the directors (chief executives) and email addresses of the hospitals were identified before the questionnaire was sent out. Emails were sent to all hospitals, addressed by name to the CEOs, with a description of the survey, a letter of support from the Polish Federation of Hospitals, a link to the online, and printable PDF questionnaires.

The questionnaires were completed by 167 hospital directors (survey return rate of 27.8%). Before analyzing the data, the received questionnaires were examined in detail for completeness of answers and correct response patterns. All cases in which the percentage of completion was less than 95.0% were removed from the collected sample. There were 12 such questionnaires, with the majority being only marginally completed. Four questionnaires were removed because they mostly contained extreme responses, "7" alone or "1" alone, or middle responses of "4" alone. Response patterns, such as diagonal responses and alternating extreme polar responses, were not noticed. A total of 16 questionnaires were rejected due to low completion percentages or defective completion, so 151 questionnaires were qualified for quantitative research, which are referred to as the research sample in the following section.

The comparison of the survey sample, i.e., hospitals that completed the questionnaire with the general population in terms of revenue size, since this hospital characteristic was the main inclusion element in the general population, leads to the conclusion that despite the relatively small number of the smallest hospitals in the research sample, the sample well represents the group of hospitals most relevant to the health-care system in Poland.

A common test to verify the data is to compare the responses of early and late respondents. In this study, a total of four survey emails were sent (two were reminder emails). After the first two, 108 correctly completed surveys were collected; after the next two, 43 surveys were collected. To check whether the answers given earlier differed from those given later, the means of the individual indicators of the two parts of the research sample were compared. Comparison of averages using Student's t-test showed no significant differences ($p > 0.05$). For example, the average revenue of the hospitals in the first group was 102.7 million zlotys and that of the second group was 83.8 million zlotys, the standard deviation was 118.6 and 60.9, respectively, and the value of the t-statistic = 0.99 and $p = 0.32$, which means that the difference in the average revenue of the hospitals in the two groups is not statistically significant.

The survey sample (Table 4.3) includes hospitals that vary in terms of the number of beds, employees, departments, and outpatient clinics. The average number of employees is 789.3 (median – 600.0), with the largest hospital employing 3,500 people and the smallest employing 121 people. The annual revenue of hospitals in the study sample, on average, is 97.2 million zlotys (median – 52.4 million zlotys). The hospitals surveyed are also characterized by complex organizational structures, with an average of 14.7 departments and 16.3 outpatient clinics. Typically, each department deals with a separate field of medicine. However, they are supplemented by auxiliary medical units (e.g., laboratory, diagnostic imaging, pharmacy, pathomorphology, endoscopy labs, etc.) and non-medical departments (e.g., accounting and human resources, nutrition, cleaning, technical).

The majority of hospitals (68.8%) included in the survey sample reported a loss for 2018, with the loss amounting to an average of 2.6% of revenues, with the maximum value of the ratio reaching 22.5%. The data obtained from the analysis of the survey sample are in line with previous studies of the financial situation conducted on a sample of 321 public hospitals in Poland, which showed that the average net profitability ratio in 2016 and 2017, for example, was −1.29 and −1.12 (Miszczyńska & Antczak, 2020, pp. 139–140), respectively.

The smallest hospitals in the sample are monospecialty hospitals (Table 4.4), which are distinguished by their small number of wards and outpatient clinics (7.6 and 6.4 on average). Monospecialty hospitals, however, have departments with more beds on average than the other types of hospitals. Also of note is the comparison of specialty hospitals to university hospitals. While both types of hospitals have a similar average number of beds and employees, the average revenue of university hospitals is 66.9% higher. Such a significant difference in revenue is relatively most often due to the fact that university hospitals provide more complex and higher priced services. The characteristics of each type of hospital are shown in Appendix 1.

General and specialized hospitals are the most numerous in the survey sample. The former are usually county hospitals. The second are relatively more often located in larger urban centers, where they are referral hospitals, treating the most complex cases, such as those with complications that county hospitals are unable to treat.

In the surveyed population, 116 hospitals operated as independent public health-care facilities (IPHI) and 32 as limited liability companies (LLC). Three hospitals did not provide this information. For all companies, the operating bodies were public entities, most often counties, including urban counties, and provincial governments. The data collected show that, on average, hospitals converted to companies are smaller than hospitals remaining in the form of IPHIs (Table 4.5). There are significant differences in the number of wards, beds, and employees, while the number of outpatient clinics is similar or even higher in specialized hospitals operating in the form of a company. Also, the financial results do not change dramatically depending on the legal form. Entities included in both groups, on average, showed a loss in 2018. Similar results were revealed by a study conducted by the Polish Supreme Audit Office in 2014 (NIK, 2014, p. 33).

Most (60.3%) of the entities participating in the survey were managed by men. Male and female physicians as chief executives accounted for 20.5% of those surveyed (Table 4.6). It is worth noting that 70.9% of the directors did not have a medical degree, which means that after 1989, when people outside the medical profession also began to be appointed as directors, a significant management corps unrelated to medical education was built up in Poland.

Table 4.4. Characteristics of the survey sample by hospital type

Hospital type	Number of hospitals	Aggregate revenue	Mean value in the research sample					
			Number of wards	Number of outpatient clinics	Number of beds	Number of employees	Revenues in millions PLN	Profit
Monospecialty	21	897.7	7.6	6.4	237.4	377.2	42.7	–0.5%
General	78	4 164.0	11.4	13.1	302.6	525.0	53.4	–2.9%
Specialty	37	6 052.1	21.4	22.3	567.8	1261.6	163.6	–4.0%
University	12	3 276.9	22.4	35.2	638.0	1395.3	273.1	–0.7%
No data	3							
Sum/Mean	151	14 390.7	14.7	16.3	398.9	789.3	97.2	–2.6%

Table 4.5. **Characteristics of the research sample according to the legal form of the hospital**

Hospital type	Number of hospitals		Mean value in the research sample													
			Number of wards		Number of outpatient clinics		Number of beds		Number of employees		Revenues in millions PLN		Profit	
legal form	IPHI	LLC	IPHI	LLC	IPHI	LLC	IPHI	LLC	IPHI	LLC	IPHI	LLC	IPHI	LLC
General	15	6	8.1	6.3	6.5	6.0	238.4	235.0	406.4	304.3	48.2	29.0	−0.3%	−1.0%
Specialty	59	19	12.3	8.2	13.7	11.2	328.2	232.2	555.0	457.6	55.5	46.7	−2.9%	−2.7%
University	30	7	21.0	23.6	20.1	33.0	576.2	531.2	1266.5	1238.3	166.6	150.8	−4.4%	−2.0%
General	12		22.4		35.2		638.0		1395.3		273.1		−0.7%	
Sum/Mean	116	32	15.6	11.8	16.6	15.8	427.0	314.2	848.5	614.2	105.8	66.1	−2.7%	−2.2%

Note: Independent Public Health Care Institution (IPHI), Limited Liability Company (LLC).

Table 4.6. Characteristics of respondents in terms of gender and education

Education/Gender	Number of respondents			
	Medical – Physician	Medical – Other	Non-medical	Total (share)
Male	19	1	71	**91 (60.3%)**
Female	12	12	36	**60 (39.7%)**
Total (share)	**31 (20.5%)**	**13 (8.6%)**	**107 (70.9%)**	**151 (100.0%)**

Table 4.7. Average number of years as director and deputy director in hospitals

Education/Gender	Average number of years in the position of deputy director and director (director only)			
	Medical – Physician	Medical – Other	Non-medical	Total
Male	21.4 (15.4)	15.0 (12.0)	10.6 (5.3)	**12.9 (7.5)**
Female	18.8 (11.8)	6.5 (4.2)	11.9 (8.9)	**12.2 (8.5)**
Total	**20.4 (14.0)**	**7.1 (4.8)**	**11.0 (6.5)**	**12.6 (7.9)**

On average, the surveyed directors served in their position for 7.9 years. Those with medical degrees served as directors for significantly longer. In male physicians, more than 15 years (Table 4.7). Women with non-medical education other than a doctor served as directors for the shortest time. Directors with non-medical education averaged 6.5 years in their position, with women taking almost 8.9 years.

Counting the position of deputy director and director together, on average, the surveyed individuals have held these management positions for more than 12 years (Table 4.7). Thus, it can be concluded that the surveyed individuals have quite a lot of management experience and are, therefore, adequately versed in hospital management to provide answers to the survey questions on management control.

4.5 Justification for Choosing a Path Model Estimator

Another important element in the adopted exploratory sequential mixed methods research design is the selection of the optimal estimator of the management control model in hospitals. Indeed, two types of SEM estimators can be distinguished: covariance-based SEM (CB-SEM) and partial least squares SEM (PLS-SEM) estimators. Some researchers refer to PLS-SEMs as partial least squares path models (PLS-PMs) to distinguish between the two tools. For many years, covariance-based estimators led the way in structural equation modeling, but in the past decade, largely due to the introduction of new features, PLS-SEM has become a widely used, full-fledged research tool in many scientific disciplines (Benitez et al., 2020, p. 1), including management and quality sciences (Bayonne et al., 2020; Hair, Sarstedt et al., 2019, p. 567; Hair, Risher et al., 2019, p. 3; Johansson, 2018) and, in particular, in hospital research (Amos et al., 2021; Avkiran, 2018; Bastani et al., 2021; Gu et al., 2019; Valls Martínez & Ramírez-Orellana, 2019). Research using PLS-SEM has been successfully published for many years in the most prestigious journals, such as the Academy of Management Journal (Batjargal et al., 2013; Lioukas & Reuer, 2015).

Despite the widespread use of PLS-SEM, there are still researchers who believe that parameter estimation in this estimator is not optimal in terms of consistency. However, simulation studies have shown that the differences between PLS-SEM and CB-SEM estimates are negligible when the measurement models meet the minimum recommended standards for each method (e.g., the magnitudes of indicator loadings are greater than 0.70 (Reinartz et al., 2009)), making PLS-SEM deviation irrelevant for most applications (Astrachan et al., 2014). Moreover, the discrepancy in PLS-SEM parameter estimates should not be considered an error, but rather a difference resulting from the different treatment of latent variable measures in the two methods. It is also wrong to treat PLS-SEM deviations as erroneous on the grounds that covariance-based CB-SEM indicator loadings are implicitly considered a universal benchmark for PLS-SEM estimates. Indeed, many researchers caution against reflexively sticking to a reflexive (common factor) model (Schönemann & Wang, 1972, p. 88; Rigdon, 2016), and recent research suggests (Hair, Sarstedt et al., 2019, p. 572) that formative (composite) variables may actually capture the conceptual nature of a variable more accurately than a common factor.

Controversy over the use of particular estimators in structural equation modeling has arisen since H. Wold (1982) presented a composite-based (PLS-SEM) alternative to K.G. Jöreskog's common factor-based (CB-SEM) estimator (1970). In the last decade, in response to numerous publications comparing the two methods, and often even exaggerating the superiority of one method over the other, the dispute has intensified (Dijkstra, 2014; Henseler et al., 2014; Rigdon, 2012, 2014; Rönkkö & Evermann, 2013; Hair, Sarstedt et al., 2019). Proponents of one or the other estimation method, in order to demonstrate the superiority of the supported approach, are able to test models beyond the scope of the method (Rigdon, 2016, p. 603). An example is the work of M. Rönkkö and J. Evermann, *A Critical Examination of Common Beliefs about Partial Least Squares Path Modeling*, in which the known conditions of the PLS-SEM estimation algorithm were violated to demonstrate its ineffectiveness. The PLS-SEM algorithm requires that each composite variable be correlated with at least one other composite. In contrast, the aforementioned authors specified a model with two common factors with zero correlation, which they attempted to estimate using the PLS-SEM algorithm (2013). This algorithm alternately uses so-called internal proxies and external proxies. An internal proxy for a given composite is created from other composites that have a direct correlation with the composite in the statistical model. If a composite is not correlated with all other composites in the model, the algorithm fails (Rigdon, 2016, p. 603). This is why M. Rönkkö and J. Evermann's simulation model included two reflectively measured constructs with three observable indicators each (2013, p. 433). If the model had instead specified four indicators loaded on one variable and two on the other, then zero population correlation would have caused CB-SEM estimation to fail, just as PLS-SEM modeling failed in the previous model because the model would have been inadequately identified (Rigdon, 2016, p. 603). To sum up, it should be noted that every statistical method has its limitations, and breaking them can always demonstrate its ineffectiveness.

Since the multiplicity of publications praising or criticizing individual estimation methods makes the decision to choose the optimal estimator for the management control model in public hospitals vulnerable to criticism and difficult to prove objectively, to avoid the accusation of "methodological tribalism" (Saunders & Bezzina, 2015, p. 298), it is necessary to make documented arguments for choosing PLS-SEM as the optimal estimator in this study. Due to the different approaches to estimating the parameters of path models, the different estimators have partially different properties and, therefore, perform better in different applications. CB-SEM estimators can be used,, in particular when (Hair et al., 2011, p. 144):

■ the purpose is to test theories, confirm theories, or compare alternative theories;
■ the structural model has cyclic dependencies;
■ research requires a global matching criterion;
■ the invariability of the measurement model must be tested.

The PLS-SEM estimator, on the other hand, performs better in situations where(Hair, Risher et al., 2019, p. 4; Hair et al., 2011, p. 144):

- the goal of the research is to identify key constructs for a particular theory from an exploratory perspective;
- research focuses on theory development, and it is important not to dismiss constructs that may be candidates for further in-depth research;
- the structural model is complex and contains many constructs with a significant number of indicators and dependencies between constructs;
- the research goal is to better understand the growing complexity by exploring theoretical extensions of established theories (exploratory research for theory development);
- the structural model contains at least one latent variable measured formatively;
- small population limits sample size (e.g., limited number of hospitals); but PLS-SEM also works very well with large samples;
- data of individual indicators do not meet the conditions of non-normal distribution.

As mentioned, in most research situations, the results obtained from the PLS-SEM estimator differ slightly from those obtained from CB-SEM (Reinartz et al., 2009). Although usually in PLS-SEM modeling the strength of the relationship between constructs is underestimated, the parameters of the measurement models (loadings for reflective variables) (Model A) and weights for formative variables (Model B) are overestimated compared to CB-SEM results (Aguirre-Urreta & Marakas, 2014; Rigdon, 2016). However, it happens that CB-SEM results turn out to be extremely inaccurate, while PLS-SEM provides accurate estimates (Hair et al., 2016, p. 87; Sarstedt, Hair et al., 2016).

Based on the considerations presented here, it is, therefore, assumed that neither technique is generally better than the other, and neither is suitable for all applications (Hair et al., 2016, p. 21). In general, the strengths of PLS-SEM are the limitations of CB-SEM, and vice versa. The key here, thus, is to understand for which applications each SEM method was developed and to select it appropriately depending on the research objective, data characteristics, and model configuration. In this context, one of the primary rationales for selecting PLS-SEM as an estimator of the management control model in public hospitals is the use of formative measurement models for three variables: Information System Effectiveness, Uncertainty, and Performance (subsection 6.1.). The basis for this choice is the observation that PLS-SEM performs far better with formative and single-indicator based constructs, without creating model identification problems (Fornell & Larcker, 1981, p. 39; Smith & Langfield-Smith, 2004, p. 54).

Some researchers, to avoid using formative measurement models and thus be able to use the CB-SEM estimator, take theoretically formatively constructed latent variables as reflexive. An example is the frequently used construct "organizational performance," consisting of indicators such as sales growth or sales volume, profit growth or profit volume, market share, and return on investment. For example, in a study of the relationship among strategic, charismatic leadership, organizational performance, and environmental uncertainty among CEOs of major corporations in the United States, for four indicators – sales growth, profits, market share, and the company's return on investment (ROI) relative to its competitors – a factor analysis using principal components analysis placed these items in a single factor with respective loadings of 0.88, 0.89, 0.87, and 88 (Agle et al., 2006, p. 165). Similarly, in the diagnostic and interactive control studies, the organization's performance variable was operationalized by three indicators – sales volume, return on investment, and profits – and treated as a reflexive variable, for which Cronbach's alpha was 0.81 (Henri, 2006b, p. 542). Of course, in a particular data set, it may happen that these indicators are correlated in such a way that they form a one-dimensional scale, but one cannot assume a positive correlation between the aforementioned indicators at the theoretical level. This is because it may happen that in the population under study many companies will record high sales growth, but this does not necessarily mean high return on investment and profits. Such a situation will occur, in particular, when a company entering the market sacrifices high profits to gain market share. The opposite can also happen, when a company has declining sales but high profits (the "cash cow" of the BCG matrix). In the case of organizational performance, it is also difficult to consider that this idea of performance reflects the value of the indicators of this variable. While a dozen years ago such an approach could have been justified by the insufficient development of knowledge about the reliability of results obtained with PLS-SEM estimators, and thus the skeptical attitude of reviewers toward this method, today such a simplification seems unnecessary. Of course, it is subject to the confirmatory purpose of the study. A proposed way to overcome the problems of statistical model identification when incorporating formative measurement models with causal indicators into CB-SEM is to build a multiple indicator and multiple cause (MIMIC) model. Obtaining statistical identification of the model does not automatically provide information about the formative variance of the latent variable (Lee & Cadogan, 2013, p. 243) because the causal indicators in the MIMIC model under-represent the variance of the construct, which has adverse consequences for the accuracy of the results (Hair, Sarstedt et al., 2019, p. 569).

Note that distinguishing in PLS-SEM modeling between two types of measurement models "A" and "B," identified with "reflective measurement" and "formative measurement," respectively, is a simplification, which was also applied in the presented study of hospitals. This simplification is rooted in the transformation of both measurement models into composite variables during PLS-SEM estimation. The difference, however, is that during the estimation of the reflective variables (Model A), collinearity between indicators is ignored, while during the estimation of the formative measurement model (Model B), collinearity is a serious problem that must be overcome before validating the structural model. Disregarding collinearity in Measurement Model A means that researchers do not experience the results of estimating reflective measurement models with unexpected signs due to the effect of collinearity on the weights and, thus, are not misled, which could result in the removal of reflective indicators with high collinearity (Waller & Jones, 2010; Rigdon, 2012). Importantly, in practice, variables measured by Model A yield a slightly lower value of the R2 coefficient of determination in the sample than variables described by Model B (Rigdon, 2016, p. 602).

Other important arguments in favor of choosing the PLS-SEM estimator are the relatively high complexity of the model of management control in public hospitals, related to the inclusion of 8 constructs, 44 indicator variables, and 14 structural pathways, with a high risk of missing a normal distribution of data and a relatively small study sample. It is under these conditions that the PLS-SEM estimator performs better, providing a very robust model estimation (Hair, Risher et al., 2019, p. 2; Reinartz et al., 2009). Admittedly, the maximum likelihood (ML) estimator in CB-SEM is also robust to violations of normality (Olsson et al., 2000), but it requires a much larger sample size than PLS-SEM (Reinartz et al., 2009, p. 341). In certain situations, invalid data can also affect PLS-SEM results. For example, bootstrapping on data that deviate significantly from the normal distribution can result in slim (peaked) and skewed distributions. The use of Bias-Corrected and Accelerated (BCa) Bootstrap addresses this problem to some extent, as it adjusts the confidence intervals for skewness (Hair, Risher et al., 2019, p. 6).

The problem of obtaining multiple survey samples occurs in many areas of the social sciences, such as marketing (Hair, Sarstedt, Ringle et al., 2012), organization research (Sosik et al., 2009), strategic management (Hair,

Sarstedt, Pieper et al., 2012), management accounting (Nitzl, 2016), and psychology (Willaby et al., 2015), and it is often solved precisely by using the PLS-SEM estimator. Similarly, in this research, despite a relatively high survey return rate of 27.8%, due to the low size of the general population of hospitals in Poland, only 151 valid cases were collected, which is a relatively small sample size for estimating such a complex model using CB-SEM (Jackson, 2003, p. 139).

The ability to use small sampling in PLS-SEM, in principle, regardless of the complexity of the model, was described many years ago (Marcoulides & Saunders, 2006, pp. v–vi) and empirically confirmed in a number of simulation studies (Goodhue et al., 2012; Lu et al., 2011; Reinartz et al., 2009).[3] This property is due to the fact that the algorithm does not calculate all the relationships in the structural model simultaneously. Instead, it uses linear regression (the classic least squares method) to estimate partial relationships in the model (Hair et al., 2016, p. 23). However, this does not mean that sample size does not matter in PLS-SEM modeling. Nevertheless, PLS-SEM, compared to its covariance-based counterpart, has a higher level of statistical power in many situations when analyzing complex models with a smaller sample (Hair, Risher et al., 2019, p. 7; Reinartz et al., 2009, p. 340; Willaby et al., 2015, p. 76), meaning that PLS-SEM is more likely to make a given relationship significant in the estimation when, in fact, it will be significant in the population (Hair et al., 2016, p. 21) (more on this can be found in (Goodhue et al., 2017).

However, it should be remembered that, as with any other statistical method, the standard errors of estimates increase as the sample size decreases (Benitez et al., 2020, p. 4). Most sources indicate that the survey sample size should not be less than 100 cases (Hair et al., 2016, p. 22; Reinartz et al., 2009, p. 340), but the minimum sample size can be estimated more accurately using the guidelines developed by J. Cohen (1992). However, knowing the size of the research sample and the complexity of the model, expressed by the number of paths (arrows) indicating the construct combined with the largest number of exogenous variables, based on J. Cohen's research, one can estimate the accuracy of the estimation.

The values of the minimum requirements for the research sample used in the survey of hospitals are shown in Table 4.8. At the same time, for the model of management control in public hospitals, in which the maximum number of arrows indicating the construct in the path model is 6 for the variable Innovation (Figure 5.1), the size of the research sample is 151 cases. Thus, assuming a commonly used statistical power level of 80%, an R^2

Table 4.8. Minimum study sample size requirements necessary to detect the minimum level of the coefficient of determination R^2 of endogenous variables, for each level of significance, with an assumed statistical power of 80%.

The maximum number of arrows pointing to a variable in the model (Number of independent variables)	Significance level p											
	0.1				0.05				0.01			
	R^2				R^2				R^2			
	0.10	0.25	0.50	0.75	0.10	0.25	0.50	0.75	0.10	0.25	0.50	0.75
3	83	30	13	8	103	37	16	9	**145**	53	22	12
6	106	40	18	12	**130**	48	21	13	179	62	26	15

Source: Adapted from Cohen, 1992; Hair et al., 2016, p. 24.

coefficient of determination with a maximum value of 0.1 at a significance level of p = 0.5 can be detected (Table 4.8). On the other hand, for a modified management control model with a complexity level of "3 arrows" (Figure 6.6), the same coefficient of determination can be detected at p = 0.01.

The solution adopted in the study of management control in hospitals is also justified by the observation that PLS-SEM offers the possibility of not only explaining, but also predicting relationships (Cheah et al., 2020; Hair, 2020, p. 5). This is because it was recognized that predictive modeling would minimize the combination of bias and estimation variance. Although this sometimes results in sacrificing theoretical accuracy in favor of improving empirical precision, meaning that a "bad" model may predict better than a correct one (Shmueli, 2010, p. 293). By "wrong" model is meant a model that does not have a global fit index, as in CB-SEM. CB-SEM can achieve a slightly more accurate representation of the underlying theory by focusing only on minimizing bias, but this comes at the cost of less predictive power (Evermann & Tate, 2016, p. 4579). Even more critical, however, is that the indeterminacy of the latent variable results in CB-SEM makes any assessment of the predictive power of the structural model highly problematic (Hair, Sarstedt et al., 2019, p. 573). Additionally, unlike CB-SEM, which was designed solely for explanatory and confirmatory purposes (Hair, 2020, p. 5), PLS-SEM is an "exploratory-predictive" method and, as such, overcomes the apparent dichotomy between explanation and prediction (Sarstedt, Hair et al., 2016). Although PLS-SEM maximizes the explained variance of endogenous constructs embedded in a path model based on causal explanations,

PLS-SEM results are well suited to generating out-of-sample predictions (Shmueli et al., 2019, p. 2323). This approach assumes both an understanding of underlying causes and prediction as well as a description of theoretical constructs and the relationships between them (Gregor, 2006, p. 626).

In conclusion, it can be said that PLS-SEM provides a combination of explanation and prediction, providing a basis for practical use of causal explanations occurring in the management control model in public hospitals and predicting the behavior of the model also outside the studied sample of hospitals, which is an important objective of this work. Therefore, taking into account all the arguments presented in this subsection, the estimation of the management control model in public hospitals was carried out using the PLS-SEM estimator.

Notes

1. The data were obtained as a courtesy to the project's contractors, as it was not publicly available, but only provided to the local government units overseeing each hospital.
2. https://tradingeconomics.com/country-list/hospital-beds?continent=g20 (access: 07.01.2023).
3. It should be noted here that the definition of hospital adopted in this study from the Medical Activities Act is not the same as the category of "inpatient treatment" adopted by the National Health Fund. "Hospital treatment" as defined by the NHF as a "type of service" does not include inpatient psychiatry and rehabilitation, and such facilities were included in the study.

Chapter 5

Results of Qualitative Research on Management Control in Hospitals

5.1 Information Systems

The field research showed that information systems (IS) in place at each hospital differed in the scope and detail of data and the frequency of reporting. In the vast majority of the surveyed hospitals, IS was a tool for obtaining current information on hospital performance in various areas at the operational level. Some directors (e.g., SzO1, SzO4, SzM2) identified the information system mainly with treatment cost accounting (TCA), although hospitals also used information systems covering a wider range of data, including data related to treatment quality and patient safety (SzU, SzGB, SzI). In Poland, public hospitals were required to conduct medical cost accounting as early as 1998 by a decree of the Minister of Health on specific rules for cost accounting in public health-care institutions. In 2011, due to the enactment of the new law, the legal basis for the 1998 regulation expired, and thus it ceased to apply. It was not until January 2021 that the new decree of the Minister of Health, dated 26.10.2020, on recommendations for the standard of cost accounting at health-care providers became effective. Therefore, during the period of the study, hospitals were not obliged to conduct specific TCA guidelines.

The lack of uniform guidelines for TCA meant that hospitals approached the issue in different ways. In hospitals with the lowest level of TCA

DOI: 10.4324/9781003366553-5

development, measurement was based on data from financial accounting systems. Revenues were assigned to individual cost centers (ICC) of primary activities (hospital wards, outpatient clinics) on the basis of revenues for services rendered that were obtained from the National Health Fund or other sources. On the other hand, the cost values of the ICC of core activities were determined on the basis of direct costs and indirect costs calculated using simple allocation keys, such as the area occupied by each organizational unit or the number of employees, or simple performance measures, such as the number of patients or the number of days of treatment.

In contrast, in facilities with a high degree of TCA development, both revenue and costs, as well as the number of services performed, were measured at the level of individual procedures, the day of treatment, individual patients and physicians. However, such detailed measurement of hospital achievements required the construction of complex measurement systems. Sophisticated measurement systems were most often created by implementing a hospital information system containing a so-called white part, enabling electronic patient records, and a gray part, covering the financial aspect, including cost accounting. This type of system enabled the ongoing measurement of many aspects of the process of providing medical services, such as the number and type of diagnostic and therapeutic procedures ordered, as well as the consumption of materials per patient, thereby enabling the monitoring of costs and revenues generated per attending physician, in addition to the comparison of the costs of the same procedures performed by different physicians.

It should be noted that when analyzing costs at the level of, for example, a hospital department, a distinction should be made between the possibility of analyzing costs, revenues, and performance only at the level of that department based on financial accounting without the possibility of deeper analysis and the aggregation of information, that is, for example, summing up the costs and revenues of the department based on revenues received from the payer and costs resulting from the treatment applied to individual patients. In the first case, there is little opportunity for corrective action, since it is not known what the costs are due to or which patients are the most profitable. In the second case, the information is much more useful and enables analysis of both revenue and cost sources.

Hospital IT systems (HIS) in some hospitals (e.g., SzS1 and SzS2) were immediately implemented with the so-called gray part, i.e., an integrated medical cost accounting system. In others, TCA automation was achieved through a separate financial analysis module drawing data from two sources:

from the HIS, which includes the patient record and financial accounting (e.g., SzM2). The automation of the TCA made it possible to report and analyze data at different levels of aggregation, and to use this data to build more complex measures of the effectiveness and efficiency of hospital operations. In SzO4, management set the following tasks for the measurement system under development:

> I saw that it was time to look for places of losses strictly in the medical activity. That what depended on me, that is, in all these non-medical costs I did a lot, [...]. And now we are at the stage of describing treatment procedures, [...]. Why? For the fact that I want to know what the real cost of performing, for example, an arthroscopy procedure is, or an endoprosthesis procedure or an appendectomy procedure in order to just start steering the contract a little bit. I want to know how much it really costs us, how much the fund pays us, and this information I will pass on to the heads of medical departments.

In general, a large part of hospitals' measurement systems included information on costs, revenues, and performance of individual services, as well as the contract with the National Health Fund. In some hospitals (e.g., SzU, Sz S/U, Sz S1, Sz O/S1, SzO2, SzO4), measures also concerned the quality of services provided. These included, for example, the number of adverse events, the number of prolonged hospitalizations, and patient satisfaction or experience. In the hospitals surveyed, apart from patient satisfaction and, in part, adverse events, it was not possible to establish a common group of quality metrics that were measured by all hospitals. The issue of systematic monitoring and analysis of the number of complications came up sporadically in the interviews (SzU, SzS1, SzGB, SzI), although, according to information from hospital directors, they considered this indicator important. For example, the director of SzU declared that:

> It's not the level of reimbursement of the medical procedures that caused problems for hospitals. Because if someone says that medical procedures are badly priced, and he doesn't know such an answer, what is the percentage of complications in a particular group, he says so because it is more convenient for him. And here this percentage of complications has an absolute impact on the profitability. We observe that 95% of patients come out on

the profitable side, and three on the loss side, because there were complications. All these additional activities, medications, etc., are costly.

Detailed measurement of medical activity combined with costs and revenues enabled aggregation and analysis of data in various cross-sections.

> How the cost per patient is done, […] then, at the end, we count the cost per doctor. All of his patients, according to the services he provided and what the margins were on those services, we accumulate everything, and then in addition to that, […] what drugs, […] we link it all to the individual patient. At the very end, we have the doctor's metrics. We know exactly what revenue he generates, what real costs he generates, how many complications he has, etc.
>
> **(SzO2)**

The interviewees were aware that measurement, the information system, is an important tool for management control.

> "With the information system, then we acquire data, we identify problems, real ones, because really only with data in such a large hospital can you get to know about real phenomena. This tool can be given to people who can do something about it […] with this information, react with some changes, improve the results."
>
> **(SzU)**

The results of the qualitative research prove that an important element of the information systems in the hospitals studied was cost accounting, which, in addition to recording costs, included their accounting in various sections to determine unit cost and the preparation of various types of cost information in conjunction with clinical indicators. Measurement was carried out, in varying degrees of detail, most often in the following areas:

■ revenue and expenses by hospital department;
■ the level of contract performance, in terms of the amount of overperformance or non-performance of the contract signed with the National Health Fund;
■ bed occupancy;
■ average length of hospitalization;

- quality – patient satisfaction/experience, number of reoperations, quality of infrastructure, etc.;
- safety – nosocomial infections, adverse events (e.g., falls, administration of the wrong drug or the wrong dose, etc.).

The range of information collected was similar in Polish and Lithuanian hospitals. On the other hand, the British and Irish hospitals stood out positively, measuring a much larger number of indicators, including bacterial infections, patient safety indicators, avoidable bedsores, monitoring patient dementia, medical errors, staff absenteeism rates, and completion of mandatory staff training.

Measurement carried out at the surveyed hospitals mainly provided information on past events, their effects, and outcomes. Such reporting information is potentially useful for transparency, but it has limited utility for management decisions, which should mainly address current and future issues. All hospitals in Poland are required by law to anticipate future events to some extent. Forecasting and simulating alternative courses of action are among the most advanced functions of information systems. In the twelve-level maturity model of cost accounting, simulation to support optimization of decision making is in the 12th highest position (Raulinajtys-Grzybek et al., 2019, p. 137). This means that the process of forecasting and simulation may not be common in hospitals. However, the research showed that all of the hospitals surveyed projected various parameters of their operations to some extent, including the financial result in subsequent periods (in addition to the mandatory financial plan), although they varied considerably in the detail and scope of the projections. Some of the hospitals prepared detailed revenue and cost forecasts at the level of each department, based on the expected bed utilization rate, the average length of stay of patients, the number and type of procedures performed, and the number of patients billed in the relevant DRG.

Directors pointed out that there are significant seasonal fluctuations in some service areas, but also fluctuations between years. There were difficulties in predicting the number of patients, and thus revenues were mainly associated with pediatric departments. In the summer, there were usually fewer patients, their number increasing significantly in the fall with the increase in viral infections. The problem, however, as hospital director SzO2 pointed out,

> is that you have to monitor execution [of the contract with the NHF].[1] With a lump sum,[2] generating large overruns is unprofitable,

while underperformance results in a reduction of the contract the following year. And you never know what autumn will be like, whether there will be a lot of sickness. [...] You have to anticipate properly, well, and be flexible. That is, to have the kind of services [elective services] that can be done additionally, or cut back quickly.

Other hospitals did not forecast services as accurately, essentially limiting themselves to preparing a hospital-wide aggregate financial plan. The hospital director at SzM2 stated:

I always plan for an annual bonus [for employees]. This is a kind of [financial] buffer. If you manage to achieve a better result, there is a bigger annual bonus, and if not, it's hard, there is a smaller one. But planning in great detail, for each department, is not very accurate.

The study identified significant differences among hospitals in the form and frequency of reporting on hospital achievements to specific employee groups. The most frequent recipients of hospital achievement reports were chief executives. Some executives analyzed various indicators of hospital performance even on a daily basis, as long as the information system was fed with data on a daily basis. Others analyzed information once a week, and most often monthly or as needed. Different hospitals also differed in their approach to the groups of people to whom information on the hospital's achievements was provided, and the frequency with which information was delivered to each group. This variation in how information was analyzed and reported largely depended on how sophisticated the information system was. In hospitals where the information system was integrated with a comprehensive information system (HIS), including both the "white" part, i.e., data on the process of treating patients, and the "gray" part, i.e., financial and management accounting, including cost accounting, information was analyzed and reported at a much higher level. The level of analysis and reporting can be determined by a number of parameters. In addition to frequency and detail, the ability to aggregate and integrate information is of great importance. Aggregation means the ability to analyze the aggregated information in different cross-sections of time in relation to individual functional areas of the hospital (Ghasemi et al., 2019, p. 195), for example, information aggregated at the level of departments and other organizational units (laboratories, diagnostic laboratories) on a monthly or quarterly basis or even on individual physicians. Integration refers to data that crosses functional boundaries, helping to analyze different departments in the hospital to determine, among other things, whether a decision in one area affects other areas (Chenhall & Morris, 1986, p. 22; Hammad et al., 2013, p. 319).

The form of transmission of reports also varied. In some hospitals (e.g., SzS1, SzO2, SzO/S1, SzU), reports were distributed to hospital departments as hard copies, in several copies, so that every employee could become familiar with them. In other hospitals, data from the information system were presented at meetings with clinical ward managers, but they were not routinely distributed to other employees (e.g., SzM2). Of the surveyed units, only in the British hospital did employees have ongoing access to reporting information in the form of electronic dashboards. In Polish hospitals, some directors declared that an interested employee "can receive, and at any time, accurate data" (SzS2) on hospital performance. The approach to distributing information had a significant impact on the depth of penetration of information on goal achievement down the hospital's organizational structure. For example, the director of SzO/S1 reported:

> I issued orders regarding targets. At monthly meetings with head physicians, I show them how these goals are implemented. [...] I meet with lead nurses less frequently, well, maybe once a quarter. That's when I also show them how we function, how we achieve our goals. [...] Once every six months, or if there's a major change, I write such a circular to all employees. We photocopy it and give it to the departments. I write about our challenges, show how we achieve our goals, and of course thank them for their work. But do they read it? That's what I don't know. I think a large part reads it.

Some directors (e.g., SzU, SzS/U, Sz M1, SzM2) were very deliberate about communicating information to particular groups and hierarchical levels of employees. They were aware that information had to be propagated deep into the organizational structure, particularly to key individuals:

> In my opinion, out of these 1,360 employees, then you need to have, in order for the organization to be able to make changes, you need to have 10% of the people who constitute some kind of critical mass in the entity, that's 130 people for such a hospital. And that's where you have to have clinical managers, that's where you have to have the more active doctors and ward lead nurses,

who have a certain amount of competence and decision-making abilities. These people must be well informed. Such an establishment can't be based on a few people or 5 people at the level of the directorate, because then we can't control all the phenomena in the hospital. It must be this responsibility and appreciation of these people in terms of management functions distributed. They must have detailed information.

(SzS/U)

The above considerations indicate that IS is an important element of management control in hospitals. Confronting the results of the field research with the literature, a common set of IS characteristics affecting the effectiveness of IS in the service of management control was identified:

■ level of detail, referring to the system's ability to provide data on various objects, such as organizational units (e.g., hospital departments), individual products (DRG groups), and individual components (e.g., medical procedures, physicians) (Hammad et al., 2013, p. 319; Kaplan & Norton, 1996, p. 52);
■ the ability to disaggregate costs by behavior, such as fixed and variable costs (Feltham & Xie, 1994, p. 430);
■ the frequency of information reporting (Ghasemi et al., 2019, p. 195; Hammad et al., 2013, p. 319; Nguyen, 2018, p. 41; Simons, 1987b, p. 363), which is linked to its timeliness. It is assumed that the more often employees receive reports, the more up-to-date information they have and the greater the ability to solve problems (Chenhall & Morris, 1986, p. 20; Ghasemi et al., 2019, p. 195; Nguyen, 2018, p. 41; Mangaliso, 1995, p. 234);
■ performance forecasting capability determines the extent to which "what-if" forecasting data are included in reports (Ghasemi et al., 2019, p. 195; Hammad et al., 2013, p. 319; Simons, 1987b, p. 363);
■ scope refers to the purpose, quantification, and time horizon of the information. The scope can be narrow or expanded depending on whether the information is internal or external to the organization, financial or non-financial, and past or future oriented (Chenhall & Morris, 1986, p. 19; Ghasemi et al., 2019, p. 195; Nguyen, 2018, p. 41; Hammad et al., 2013, p. 319; Mangaliso, 1995, p. 234);
■ aggregation refers to the categorization of information by period or functional area. Data can be raw, unprocessed data or can be

aggregated for a period or functional area. Aggregated information also refers to aggregation in formats consistent with formal decision making (Chenhall & Morris, 1986, p. 21; Hammad et al., 2013, p. 319; Mangaliso, 1995, p. 235);

■ integration refers to data that crosses functional boundaries, which helps coordinate different segments within a subunit. Integrated data can help achieve organizational goals that depend on the interaction of multiple areas in an organization and when a decision in one area affects others (Chenhall & Morris, 1986, p. 22; Hammad et al., 2013, p. 319).

In summary, it should be emphasized that the primary task of the information system is to measure and provide information on the parameters of the hospital's processes to its employees at various levels of the organizational hierarchy. The overriding goal, however, is not to provide information per se, but to bring about improvements in the results achieved by hospitals.

5.2 Hospital Performance from the Perspective of Its Director

To exercise control, or even more generally to manage the hospital, directors constructed information systems, the main element of which was the measurement of various areas of hospital performance. However, it is important to distinguish between assessing the performance of individual processes and assessing the performance of the hospital as a whole. The analysis of the material obtained in the field research made it possible to identify the perception of hospital performance evaluation by chief executives. And, to be more precise, areas were identified that, in the opinion of hospital chief executives, say the most about how the hospital is managed, taking into account the effectiveness of management control. Identifying the areas that, in the opinion of the chief executives, say the most about how the hospital is performing and allow them to distinguish between a "well-performing" hospital and those that are "poorly performing" is a key element, as, to date, there is no consensus in the scientific world on methods to explicitly assess hospital performance.

The directors of the surveyed facilities agreed that evaluating hospital performance on the basis of objective financial data, such as profitability, liquidity, or return on investment ratios, is not appropriate. This approach is also presented by many researchers (Austen, 2010, p. 104; Hass-Symotiuk, 2011b, p. 67; Hensel, 2008, pp. 11–52; Kożuch & Kożuch, 2008, p. 34; Schwierz, 2016, p. 35). This is due, among other things, to the fact that directors take different approaches to the financial result of a hospital. Three approaches have been identified for understanding what is meant by a hospital's "positive financial result" (SzM1) "balancing the hospital finances" (SzM1). The first group (e.g., S zO4, SzS1, SzI) sought a maximum level of profit at the end of the year on the income statement that would "allow investment in hospital development" (SzO4). The second group (Sz O1, SzO3, SzM2, SzGB, SzUL and SzL) set the goal of getting "a few thousand in profit" (SzM2). This was precisely the approach of a British hospital that generated a loss of £15 million (1.7% of its budget) in the year preceding the survey. The director (CEO) of this hospital took a small profit as his goal, because, he said: "it would give us a certain greater level of independence from central control [from the NHS], it would give us a certain freedom, so we could do more [for patients] than we do now" (SzGB). The third group of directors (SzO/S1, SzO/S2, SzS/U) considered "a loss not exceeding depreciation expenses" (SzO/S2) to be an acceptable financial result. The reference of the threshold of the financial result to the level of depreciation was due to the provisions of the Law on Medical Activity, which at the time of the research in Article 59 said that the public owner of the hospital is obliged to "adopt a resolution on changing the organizational and legal form or on liquidation of the independent public health care institution – if the net loss for the fiscal year [...] after adding the depreciation costs has a negative value."

An example of this approach to the bottom line can be seen in a statement by the director of SzS/U:

> Our goal is to balance the hospital in such a way that we have the ability to use EU funds,[3] and this involves us having money for our own contribution. [...] The guiding principle of management is to be able to set aside these funds for our own contribution to those investments that we can make with EU funds.

This hospital was not making a profit. It had a loss only because of the large investments it was making. It also had high depreciation, which allowed it to generate cash for investments despite the book loss. This attitude was so widespread and well established that in the course of the survey, directors of public and not-for-profit hospitals had to be asked how they understood "positive financial result."

Previous studies show that many hospitals show losses at the end of the fiscal year (Miszczyńska & Antczak, 2020, p. 64); however, the picture emerging from interviews with directors suggests that some hospitals plan for these losses. This means that the financial loss of hospitals is not always due to internal or external circumstances but follows the adoption of a certain strategy. The different understanding of "good" financial performance means that comparing hospitals among themselves on the basis of, for example, the profit-to-income ratio says nothing about the effectiveness of achieving goals, since hospitals have different bottom line targets.

The exploratory research failed to identify a common set of quantifiable quality indicators that could serve as some uniform benchmark for measuring hospital performance that would enable reliable comparison among hospitals. Some directors (e.g., SzO/S2, SzO4) believed that having accreditation from the Ministry of Health (Quality Monitoring Center (QMC) in Krakow)[4] and ISO certificates were the best indicators of quality, in contrast to directors (e.g., SzU, SzS/U) who argued that only quantified metrics could give a picture of hospital quality. In this area, the indicators mentioned depended largely on the type of hospital. In specialized hospitals, directors made greater use of indicators, such as the number of complications, readmissions to the hospital for the same condition, or suggested indicators specific to particular specialties (SzS1, SzO/S1, SzS/U, SzU). More conservative hospitals pointed to patient or family satisfaction and experience as an adequate measure of the quality of services provided (SzM1, SzM2). Several directors said that there is a kind of dichotomy between financial performance and quality. That is, if a hospital wants to provide quality services, it will be very difficult for it to maintain a good financial position (e.g., SzO/S1). But opposite claims were also noted, that high quality, specifically the absence of complications, allows for a reduction in the cost of medical services (SzS1, SzU).

Scientific literature in the field of quality points to the use of performance measurement systems of hospitals based on objective indicators, such as hospital readmissions for the same condition (Craig et al., 2020, p. 4; Fonarow et al., 2017; Kim et al., 2019, p. 130; Po et al., 2019, p. 368; Shortell et al., 2021, p. 269; Tsai et al., 2013), hospital mortality rates (Jha et al., 2007; Krumholz et al., 2013; Po et al., 2019, p. 368; Salge & Vera, 2009, p. 59), mortality within 30 days after hospital discharge (Walkey et al., 2018), surgical site infections in surgical treatment (Yokoe et al., 2018), and the degree to which individual patient needs and capabilities are taken into account (Swedberg et al., 2021). But if one considers the diversity of hospitals, in terms of both the range of services provided (some hospitals provide only conservative services while others perform many acute complex procedures, including transplantation) and the type of these services (psychiatry, rehabilitation), the use of any of the above-mentioned indicators will not enable a uniform assessment of hospitals. Measurement models based on the opinions of patients (Anhang Price et al., 2014; Hoffer Gittell, 2002, p. 1415; Groene et al., 2015; Grigoroudis et al., 2012, p. 109; Isaac et al., 2010; Salge & Vera, 2009, p. 59; Wheat et al., 2018) and medical professionals (Ball et al., 2017; McHugh & Stimpfel, 2012) can also be found in the literature, but such a solution would require surveying a significant group of respondents for each hospital surveyed, which is not feasible for the present study.

The directors also raised the issue of a hospital's reputation as an overall indicator of its performance. While satisfaction and experience with the services provided relates to patients and their families, reputation relates to a much wider range of stakeholders, including, for example, the governing body, the National Health Fund, financing institutions, and the general perception of the hospital by the local community. In this dimension, the evaluation of the hospital's performance included the general perception of the hospital as "a well-organized place, providing quality medical services" (SzS1). Also in the scientific literature, reputation is treated as one of the dimensions of the quality of hospital performance (de Harlez & Malagueño, 2016, p. 9), also called public image (Abernethy & Stoelwinder, 1991, p. 110). However, this dimension of hospital evaluation was conceptually viewed differently in relation to the ability to attract key employees (de Harlez & Malagueño, 2016, p. 9). In their statements, executives pointed out that the overall reputation of the hospital helps, but it is not a determining factor in the ability to attract and retain key employees in the organization. In this area, top managers spoke of providing professionals with "development opportunities" (SzS1), "rich diagnostic and therapeutic facilities" (SzU), "a good, conflict-free work atmosphere" (SzM2) or significant "autonomy" (SzO3). General reputation is often based on media reports and possibly patient satisfaction and experience, while professionals' working conditions are most often discussed within professional groups inside and outside the hospital.

> It's colleagues in the same professions who pass on information about working conditions to each other. Ironically, I often found out that there are "not bad" working conditions for doctors in my hospital, although I had endless negotiations with doctors about it.
>
> **(SzU, SzO4)**

While it would seem that large hospitals in major urban centers, particularly university hospitals, are better positioned to provide training for professionals, research shows that smaller hospitals also have something to offer. The SzO1 director stated:

> It's true that large hospitals have better equipment and often treat more complex cases, but young doctors are also eager to come to us for specialization. Because, as a young resident told me: "there are so many doctors in Warsaw hospitals that it will take two or three years of specialization before they start allowing you to do some procedures, and so you stand and watch. And here, in a small hospital, there is a shortage of specialists and I operate right away. By the time they would let me operate in Warsaw, I'll have already gotten my hands pretty good here [gained experience]."

Another important element raised by directors in the context of evaluating hospitals was the ability to acquire resources. The operation of a hospital, and in particular the provision to patients of "health services that meet the requirements of current medical knowledge"[5] requires continuous investment. In Poland, hospitals obtain capital for investment from a number of sources, which set various criteria for accessing the grants offered. As an example, SzS/U has organized and synchronized a number of elements related to human resources and formal organizational structure in order to increase its ability to raise funds from those provided for science and research, such as those available to the National Center for Research and Development, for example:

> We built the hospital's development and fundraising strategy around scientific and research activities. First, we made efforts for the hospital to obtain the status of a research and development center, then we organized the research and development center in an institutionalized form, I created the position of attorney for clinical research. [...] We are not affiliated with any university. [...] We have earned the status of a national scientific leading center granted by the Ministry of Science and Higher Education. We benefit from NCR&D [National Center for Research and Development] funds, we have our own scientific grants that we implement. And this is a very important element. Not only does it provide opportunities for additional investment in the hospital in terms of modern

equipment, we have a scientific laboratory created here at the hospital on this basis, a number of molecular and other laboratories. This is in addition to such a dimension of creating human capital, which has certain competencies. People work not only in a way, in terms of crafting medical activity, but they work in a scientific way, and this element, the element of scientific activity is made visible even in the mission of the hospital. In the passage of the mission saying "hospital of the future for the region ..." We are trying to develop these procedures performed at the hospital, so that we are, as it were, ahead of this average standard in Poland. [...] This scientific activity affects the hospital's revenue.

(SzS/U)

University Hospital was similarly preparing to raise development funds. SzM2, on the other hand, was developing a wide range of international contacts to raise investment funds from international and cross-border programs. Other hospitals were developing competencies in certain specialties to raise capital from Ministry of Health sector programs. A review of previous studies shows that "Ability to attract resources" (Abernethy & Stoelwinder, 1991, p. 110) or resource-winning ability (Abernethy & Brownell, 1999, p. 202) has been used as a measure to assess hospital performance.

In the literature, studies can be found that based the evaluation of hospital outcomes on the average length of stay of patients (Hoffer Gittell, 2002, p. 1416; Grigoroudis et al., 2012, p. 109; Edwards et al., 2011, p. 5; Kroch et al., 2007, p. 23). Hospital executives, however, believed that this indicator was not appropriate for measuring hospital performance. In particular, they pointed to significant differences in the average length of hospital stay of patients depending on the specialty and the specific procedure. While arthroscopic treatment in orthopedics in many situations can be performed as a one-day procedure, that is, requiring a hospital stay of a few hours, large joint endoprosthesis or more serious spinal procedures require longer hospitalization. Similarly, it is difficult to compare the length of hospitalization in ophthalmology, where a significant number of procedures are performed as part of one-day surgery (e.g., cataract surgery), with neurosurgical hospitalizations requiring long stays.

It is still worth noting the relationship between the information system and hospital performance. On the one hand, the information system makes it possible to measure the hospital's performance, and, on the other hand, it exerts an influence on these results, as the measurement itself can influence the behavior of the organization's members (Flamholtz et al., 1985, p. 40; Neely et al., 1995, p. 95; Zábojník, 2014, p. 341). However, the forms of reporting operating in hospitals, which often juxtapose planned goals with their performance, generate feedback, which is an element of control. This means that the information system also performs the traditional control function to some extent. In addition, the relationship between the information system and hospital performance can be described in terms of a causal chain, in which a more functional IS generates more useful information that improves management decisions and thus leads to improved performance.

From the conducted exploratory studies, it is not possible to conclude unequivocally whether the effectiveness of IS directly affected the performance of hospitals. While it is true that surveys of the US and Egyptian hospital executives indicate that performance is improved by information systems that provide greater detail, better cost classification, and frequency of information delivery (Hammad et al., 2013, p. 326; Pizzini, 2006, p. 181), this study leaves some doubt in this regard. It can be assumed, also taking into account previous studies (Hammad et al., 2013, p. 326; A. Neely et al., 1995, p. 95; Pizzini, 2006, p. 181; Zábojník, 2014, p. 341), that an information system providing more detail and more up-to-date information and identifying and explaining more phenomena should have a stronger effect on hospital performance. Thus, it seems legitimate to pose the following hypothesis:

H1: Effectiveness of the information system has a positive impact on hospital performance.

The inclusion of this hypothesis in the management control model is also important for a certain completeness of the model, since the effectiveness of the information system and the performance of the hospital are key elements of management control, essentially setting its boundaries.

5.3 Diagnostic Use of Information System

The previous section described the information systems being developed in hospitals. This section focuses on the diagnostic use of these systems by hospital executives to exercise management control (Simons, 1995, p. 7). The diagnostic use of IS, or diagnostic control (DC), is the primary control system in organizations (Kastberg & Siverbo, 2013, p. 264). Diagnostic control is the backbone of traditional organizational control designed to ensure that planned objectives and predetermined standards are met and to detect deviations and trigger corrective actions (Bisbe et al., 2019, p. 130; Simons, 1995, p. 59). Thus, the key element enabling the exercise of DC is the setting of goals and standards.

In analyzing documentation on the goals and standards set by hospitals, it was noted that all hospitals adopted goals for the development of the hospital and improvement of the quality of services, which were implemented through investments, such as construction of an oncology block (SzS/U), modernization of the hospital emergency department (SzS1), and expansion of hematology (SzO/S1). However, it should be noted that the formalization of investment objectives is due to the obligation to create an investment plan imposed by the law. Hospitals paid little attention to formalizing the strategy they adopted. The need to develop and periodically, once every three years, update the strategy is included in the Polish medical quality accreditation standards. Hence, hospitals that were undergoing accreditation had and continually updated the strategy. When asked directly about the strategy, the majority of hospital directors responded that it was an important document, and they were able to provide such a document. However, further inquiries in this regard showed that directors were unlikely to be convinced of the strategy's usefulness in the area of management control and general management of the hospital. The SzS/U director commented as follows:

> There is a certain formal requirement for a strategy, if only in accreditation standards, while, I would say, this strategy does not change in such, in such three-year perspectives. So it is not useful for management. Here, here we have, as it were, such two strategic goals: the establishment of a center for innovative medicine, to transform this hospital into a center for innovative medicine, among other things, the construction of an oncology block serves this purpose, and the establishment of a center for regenerative medicine.

In contrast, non-investment goals (Table 5.1) were formalized to varying degrees. In some hospitals, these goals were written in director's orders, while in others they were only written in reports or presentations displayed at management meetings. Whether the goals were written in director's orders, documents with a high formal status, or only in reports or presentations, were mainly based on the management's assessment of the degree of usefulness of formalizing individual goals at each hospital.

In general, the degree of formalization of the goals ranged between two extreme approaches:

Table 5.1.   Areas in which directors formalized goals (excluding investment and long-term treatment capacity development goals)

1. Revenues and expenses, including a breakdown by organizational unit:
   a. Salaries;
   b. medicines and disposable materials;
   c. repair of medical equipment and apparatus;
2. Financial result;
3. Output of medical services by department;
4. Number of DRG procedures performed;
5. The degree of execution of the contract with the National Health Fund (example: Appendix 2. Formalization of performance indicators – limits on overruns);
6. Monitoring stock levels;
7. Efficiency and effectiveness of public procurement execution;
8. Rules for ordering diagnostics and admitting patients to the hospital (example: Appendix 3);
9. Quality of medical services;
10. Quality and completeness of medical records;
11. Principles of cooperation between departments (example: Appendix 4).

Source: documentation and interviews with hospital directors.

- formalization of most objectives in ordinances, reporting templates and electronic information systems;
- goals were set and presented at meetings with different groups of employees depending on current situations.

In the first case, directors entered goals, standards, and their expected values in ordinances or other documents (example: Appendixes 2–4), except that the number of goals and the detail of metrics varied from hospital to hospital. Some hospitals included only selected targets in their ordinances, such as the degree of fulfillment of the contract with the National Health Fund, while others referred to a wider range of indicators, including qualitative indicators. In the first group, the British hospital definitely stood out. There, the formalization of goals was structured according to the set of five strictly specified areas. Virtually every specialty or new initiative had to define goals and measures for achieving them in each of the five areas.

In the second approach, goals and optimal values for indicators were defined, not formally in documents, but they were agreed upon during management meetings with heads of organizational units. They were simply not written down in document form. The directors of these hospitals said that the lack of formalization of targets allowed them greater flexibility in managing the hospital. For example, with regard to the goal related to the implementation of the contract with the National Health Fund, the director of SzO1 stated:

> It is difficult at the beginning of the year to know what the level of contract [with NHF] overruns will be in each department. I tried to figure out what the political context is, what specialties might be prioritized by the National Health Fund and the government. Mostly I ask the heads of wards to perform more at the beginning of the year, so that if the HNF or the government "add" some money to the system, they will have some surplus to account for. If there is no chance of additional money, we put the brakes on in the last months, but mainly elective surgical procedures, where there is an expensive "input." The conservative ones, where variable costs are a small percentage, there is no point in cutting back. Anyway, we always get some money and it is beneficial for us. As if I formalized this [expected values of targets], wrote them into orders, I would have to change them many times afterwards, depending on what view we have of the possibility of paying overruns in a given period of the year. That would be a bit frivolous. Because, after all, formally, contract overruns are always due to an excess of patients to whom we cannot refuse treatment. [...] And often, several times during the year, we decide to increase or decrease the overruns, depending on whether there is some rumor that a particular scope [medical specialty] is to be subsidized. [...] And such situations do happen.

The director of SzS1 spoke similarly:

> I do not formalize how much in contract overruns will be done in each department, because it is a very complex matter, and it is not really possible to write it down formally. Because it's not a matter of how much the contract in a particular department can be exceeded by, or by what amount, but by what quality these overruns are. In some departments, where the procedures are well priced, it is enough for me that NHF pay half of the overruns, and I already get profitability. Trauma orthopedics, for example, is priced below cost, then the department has to perform four endoprostheses and two major spinal procedures every day, or

others that are very profitable to cover losses, such as carpal tun-
nel. Besides, when the overruns are in life-saving procedures, the
money can always be recovered in court, after a few years, but
still.[6] [...] How do we describe it with orders? If we don't understand each other and don't communicate with the prescribers, then
no orders will help either.

Some directors only held ad hoc meetings with different groups of employees and during these meetings set goals with reference to the current situation. And rather in the form of: "It would be great if you could increase the
number of elective procedures in hand surgery by 20%, and then there will
be a chance that all employees will receive an annual bonus" (SzM2). One
could say that they were trying to inspire employees rather than impose
rigid "targets" on them. Despite some "opportunities related to controlling
the patient stream" (SzS1), there was limited control in many areas.

> So what if I set targets..., for example, that the bed occupancy rate
> in pediatrics should be 80%. If children don't get sick, they won't
> be on the ward. If there's a flu, or rotavirus, it can be 110% occu-
> pancy, and if there's nothing going on – it's 40%. So what if I set a
> target?.
>
> **(SzO3)**

These directors declared in interviews that they "communicate targets to
employees [targets were present on the presentation slides], but I don't set
them formally, because it doesn't matter anyway" (SzO3). They referred to
this as "unnecessary work involving human resources" (SzO/S2). Similarly,
the director of SzM2 stated:

> I do not set goals and their measures in orders or other documents.
> On the other hand, I often analyze the situation in the hospital in
> terms of what is happening in the various departments and labo-
> ratories. What are the revenues, costs, performance of the contract
> with the National Health Fund, how many complications, adverse
> events, etc.? What critical situations have happened there? I pre-
> pare materials, presentations for monthly meetings and show this
> to clinical managers and lead nurses, and explain: "Listen, here the
> cost is too high, and here too little revenue. Think about what you
> can do there." We analyze the performance of the contract. Then I

meet in smaller groups with [key personnel of] individual departments. We look at what can be done.

The above discussion shows that the degree of formalization of goals and
metrics was largely due to the ambiguity and variability of goals in hospitals
in general (cf. Abernethy et al., 2006, p. 813). It should be emphasized, however, that the lack of formalization did not imply a lack of monitoring of the
achievement of goals and the level of indicators. Qualitative research identified many examples of information system use in this regard.

One of the main elements affecting the revenue-cost ratio and the quality
of treatment is the structure of the services provided. This is due to the fact
that the NHF's valuation of medical procedures and/or individual DRG is not
uniform. In other words, depending on the current valuation of the NHF,
the performance of some services is profitable (e.g., cataract surgery), i.e.,
it allows a financial surplus to be generated, while others are unprofitable
(e.g., orthopedic trauma procedures), i.e., the cost of performance is higher
than the payment from the NHF.[7] It should be remembered, however, that
despite the existence, to some extent, of objectively higher profitability for
some services, the profitability of individual services may depend, to a large
extent, on the individual circumstances of the department and hospital. The
research showed that directors with IS capture more accurate information on
the profitability of individual procedures and used it to implement controls
on the structure of services provided. The SzS1 director explained how the
information provided to the clinical managers is used by them:

> If he [the ward head physician] had a number of brain tumors or
> brain injuries that were unprofitable, for example, because there
> were serious complications with a patient treatment, the head of
> the ward knows that he has to perform a number of profitable
> procedures to balance the ward [its financial situation]. He gets
> monthly updates on his performance, or even more frequently if
> he wants.

The directors pointed out that often "the maladjustment between the 'cali-
ber' of procedures performed and the infrastructure in place leads to treatment quality and financial problems" (SzU). Because it's not the case that

> each department performs the same thing over and over again [a
> dozen major procedures], because "production" depends on the

skills of the doctors you hire and the facilities you have – these two determinants. There is no such thing that every procedure in a given field is performed in every department of a given profile. From the point of view of optimal use of the resources that a department and hospital have, the question is whether they are used optimally. That is, in a given department, specialists perform what they are able to perform with the highest quality and bring the highest possible revenue to the hospital. Because a completely different scope should be provided by the surgical department of a small district hospital and another by a specialized university hospital. For example, at my surgery [department], it was only simple procedures that they performed. But I brought in a good head physician, he trained the doctors, and it's better. But I am constantly monitoring this.

(SzS2)

Controlling the fit between the profile of services performed and the hospital's resources requires an effective IS that provides information on both the number of medical procedures performed and the cost of performing them, with the ability to aggregate and integrate the data accordingly. The SzU director said that

before the introduction of the system for monitoring and reporting clinical activities [medical costing], I was basically unaware of why the hospital was generating insufficient revenue. It wasn't until I saw that we were losing money on most procedures, and only the more complex ones were profitable, that I thought that indeed a university hospital couldn't make money on appendectomies and cholecystectomies. The infrastructure and staff are too expensive.

An effective IS also enables directors to monitor drug prescribing, which is basically under the exclusive jurisdiction of clinicians. One individual stated:

I'm talking to a head physician because suddenly drug costs have increased in his department in a given month. The head physician replies to me that there was a patient who required third-generation antibiotics, and so on. At the same time, I check whether they did any cultures at all, whether this antibiotic therapy was targeted or empirical. I understand that in the beginning for the first few days when you are waiting for the result from that culture it may be empirical, but the head physician no longer has any argument when it turns out that for 10 days this therapy was applied only empirically. What about the fact that I am not a medical professional? These are the basics. The wrong antibiotic not only destroys the health of the patient, but also unnecessarily generates costs. Because if the first one doesn't work, you have to give them another one.

(SzO4)

The research showed that even those directors who did not have medical training, as in the example above, given the right information, were able to conduct control in medical areas. Although they could not analyze medical records, diagnoses, and medical recommendations for accuracy, but, as the director of SzO3 pointed out, "By analyzing deviations compared to earlier periods, I am able to catch anomalies and consequently conduct some control of medical prescribing." The problem arises when, over a longer period of time, the practice of prescribing drugs or other activities in the department is abnormal, in that case the analysis of deviations does not allow for effective control. To counter this phenomenon, some hospitals (e.g., SzS/U) use external companies that benchmark hospitals with a high level of cost detail, including the cost of drugs used in individual medical procedures, so that prescribing practices can be compared. This allows directors to set ambitious but realistic goals, and thus implement more effective diagnostic control. Similarly, the quality of services provided, including, among other things, patient satisfaction, the number of adverse events, and so-called prolonged hospitalization, was controlled.

In some of the hospitals surveyed, directors completely commissioned subordinate employees (e.g., management attorneys, chief financial officers) or consulting firms to monitor deviations from set targets and standards. This consisted of having either designated hospital employees or employees of the consulting firm that conducted the analysis for that hospital meet directly with the heads physicians and managers of their organizational units and discuss the performance of their organizational units and any deviations. In this way, hospital directors did not have to spend much time on diagnostic control because it worked through three mechanisms. First, by regularly and routinely collecting information on the achievement of targets and key metrics, which were then analyzed and potential problems were thus diagnosed. The results of comparisons regarding the degree to which goals and standards were met formed the basis for corrective action by directors. Here, some management involvement was necessary, but not in the other two mechanisms. The second mechanism was that diagnostic control provided hospital employees with feedback on the basis of which they themselves could make corrections to their actions. In the third mechanism, the very fact that diagnostic control drew attention to an area of hospital performance caused people to modify their behavior.

The results of the field research presented so far allow us to accept the findings of hypothetical relationships for the model of organizational control in hospitals, the construction of which is the main objective of this work:

H2: Effectiveness of the information system positively affects its diagnostic use.

H3: Diagnostic use of the information system has a positive impact on hospital performance.

According to the hypotheses, it is expected that the effectiveness of the information system will have a positive effect on the use of diagnostic control, and that diagnostic control will have a positive effect on the performance of public hospitals. The adopted hypotheses will co-create the conceptual research model of management control, the other elements of which will be developed later in this chapter.

5.4 Rewarding Employees

Rewarding employees is an important element in management control, especially when it is linked to the evaluation of goal achievement and performance and/or the reliable observance of preferred behavior. Rewarding not only indicates to employees what is important to top management, but also strongly reinforces the intensity of rewarded activities (Ferreira & Otley, 2009, p. 272; Flamholtz et al., 1985, p. 43). Field research showed that some of the directors who had used employee rewards (SzO2, SzO3, SzO4, SzM1, SzM2, SzS/U) considered this mechanism a rather effective tool for improving hospital performance. The director of SzO4 reported:

> I used an incentive system based on paying performance bonuses.
> It was in a year when the fund [NHF] increased the contract for
> us quite significantly [the number of medical services with the

guarantee of payment], and I was worried that we might not manage to execute the contract, and then I introduced an incentive mechanism, that is, for carrying out the increased contract, there was 10% from the difference in the previous year's performance, and the money went to the entire doctors and nursing team, and 10% from the reduction in costs. Because I didn't want it to be the case that we would fly right away on costs. And this had, unexpectedly, quite a big effect. Head physicians began to search [...] "but these are not my costs, because this patient was not with me after all, he was transferred from another department."

"The cost of this blood, however, should be attributed to internal medicine, because this was an internal medicine patient, and we only consulted him." [...] such a greater identification with the department. I, unfortunately, later abandoned this, because the next year was already a reduced contract and I no longer had such a need." A comparable method of rewarding was used by the director of SzO2:

I used to reward with additional bonuses on profit or on cost savings regardless of the form of employment. That is, I allocated a budget to the ward and then the head of the ward distributed it. The ward [ward employees] had [a share] from the profit of the ward and [a share] from the profit of the whole hospital. That is to say, the bonus that the ward got consisted of two parts, how much the ward earned or from savings in costs. From the hospital, i.e., it depended on what was the performance of the hospital as a whole. For example, 9% from the department and 6% from the hospital. From the hospital's profit it was all employees who had 6%. But now I had to drop this bonus. With a lump sum,[2] the situation is a little different. I know that something should be introduced, some kind of system, but no, I don't see it happening.

Also in outpatient care within the hospital, the bonus system led to positive results in the number of services provided:

In the outpatient clinic, it's very simple to introduce an incentive system. When I had problems with the performance of the contract in the outpatient clinic, because it's on a full-time basis that "whether you do or lie down...,"[8] well, I introduced a points contract, then he [the doctor] has to make points to earn decent money. The first month he earned 5,500, the second month he earned 7,500, then 8,500, and now it's 11,000. So it works.

(SzO3)

The hospitals surveyed mostly had a mixed system of hiring medical staff. There was always some part of the medical staff employed under civil law contracts and some under employment contracts, but in different proportions in each hospital. Administrative employees were employed on the basis of employment contracts everywhere, while employees of auxiliary departments, such as cleaning and nutrition, were either employed on a full-time basis or these services were performed by specialized companies (outsourcing). Rewarding full-time employees, i.e., those with employment contracts, as required by labor law, should be described in the bonus regulations, which must be agreed on with the company's trade unions. The bonus criteria included in the regulations were usually relatively general, of the type: "a regulatory bonus may be awarded to an employee for showing initiative at work and improving productivity and quality" (SzM2), or "for efficiency and commitment to work (effective use of working time)" (SzO2), or "for accomplishing goals and tasks in a lawful, efficient, economical and timely manner" (SzO/S2). Such framework provisions allowed directors to reward employees in a relatively broad manner. Director SzM2 stated:

> The bonus regulations allow me to pay a maximum bonus of up to 60% of the base salary, which is a lot. I use these provisions in two ways. I award the bonus to employees individually or in groups; that is, to individual organizational units or to everyone in the hospital. Individually, employees receive a bonus mostly for performing tasks that were not in their scope. For example, a project needs to be developed, or additional duties come in and someone performs them until a new employee is hired. Individually, I did not reward for better performance, because it is mostly very difficult to assess. Group-wise, on the other hand, it's more common, such as for an increase in the number of procedures or patients treated.

Some directors also indicated that "they would like to motivate employees with bonuses, but in recent years, through legislative action,[9] the government has been successively taking over the authority of directors to compensate employees" (SzS2). Similarly, the director of SzO1 stated: "I lack funding for bonuses because the government has made it mandatory by law to increase employees' base salaries every year, and this has 'eaten up' the surplus I could have used for bonuses."

The director of SzM1 was convinced of the effectiveness of rewards as a tool for achieving desired employee performance or behavior. However, he stated:

> At the moment I don't have any incentive system, due to the fact that I abolished the bonus system, because it was some fraction of a percent of the hospital's revenue allocated to this bonus system, and it was on the principle that everyone got this fraction of a percent, and any attempt to regulate it, to take it away from someone ended in big arguments, so I included it in the basic salary and got rid of the problem. Well some good [incentive] system would certainly be useful. But to be honest, I don't have much of an idea how to do it. I used to work in a multinational corporation [on a managerial position], and there the bonus system was linked to targets, and there it worked.

From the interviews and document analysis of the hospitals surveyed, it appears that only some of the facilities had rewards in operation (SzO3, SzS2, SzM1, SzM2). In SzO4 and SzS/U hospitals, despite the claimed positive experience in earlier years, rewarding was stopped due to lack of funds. In more hospitals, bonuses were only planned for introduction for the same reason (e.g., SzO/S1). However, the vast majority of directors suggested that linking rewards to performance and achievement of goals was very important for improving the efficiency of hospital operations, and that they would try to introduce such arrangements in the future. Although the statements also included suggestions indicating mixed reactions from employees to the use of selective performance rewards. Some directors complained that, on the one hand, employees were reluctant to accept higher rewards in other organizational units, stating that: "This is one hospital, everyone works for its success, and why should there be such differences between departments" (SzO3), and, on the other hand, reacted unfavorably to attempts to set global, common indicators for all departments, such as "profit per department employee" (SzS2), claiming that the differences are so significant that it is impossible. The director of SzO2 said that "establishing acceptable performance measures for individual hospital departments, but in such a way that they do not raise questions in the other organizational units, is very difficult," because departments differ among themselves "in the technology of providing services, the structure of the staff employed, the level of consumption of hospital resources, and, above all, the level of valuation of the procedures they mainly perform" (SzU). The availability of accurate and reliable information on the performance of individual wards was also an important element. "You can't pay people extra money when the data on the basis of which these bonuses are to be allocated is questioned" (SzM2).

In the hospitals surveyed, rewards based on subjective evaluation of performance and behavior and informal rewards were of marginal importance. In a small number of situations, it involved individuals and was not presented at the hospital, so it was of little importance in management control. Similarly, the scale was small regarding punishment, although such situations were identified.

The situation is different in the case of employees employed under civil law contracts, the so-called contracts. These contracts are not as limited by the law because the employee appears in such a contract as a sole proprietor, which means that the contracts can contain many solutions linking the amount of remuneration to the employee's performance (output). Several arrangements for individual contracts between doctors and the hospital were identified in the hospitals surveyed:

1. The doctor's remuneration is calculated as the product of two indicators: the number of DRG points "earned" by the doctor, resulting from the number and type of patients treated, and a coefficient expressing the doctor's percentage share of the price of one DRG point. For example, the monthly total of DRG points worth 1 zloty that will be reported to the National Health Fund for patients treated by a given doctor is 400,000 and the doctor has a 15% share of the revenue (coefficient of 0.15), so in that month the doctor can bill the hospital for 60,000 zloty. The contracts also provide for larger operations involving several surgeons. Then, the coefficient is shared among a team of clinicians. The value of the coefficient is related to the position in the team (e.g., chief operator – 0.09 and assistant surgeon – 0.06), the scope of duties and responsibilities (e.g., for medical records). Which patient (with which condition, and thus with which DRG valuation) a given doctor treats is decided by the head of the department based on his own arbitrary assessment of the doctor's qualifications and skills.
2. The doctor's salary is not related to individual performance, but to the entire revenue of the department, a fixed percentage (coefficient). In

some hospitals, this coefficient is further increased in the case of a department's profit or decreased in the case of a loss. The head of the department distributes patients to doctors, but the amount of individual work does not affect the salary.

3. The doctor's salary is set in the form of a flat rate for each hour of work in the hospital. The flat rate per hour varies depending on the doctors' qualifications, such as medical education (specialization held), experience, and the time of day and day of the week. Most nurses working under civil law contracts are paid in the same way.

4. The salary of doctors is a fixed monthly amount for working in the department. The rate usually varies based on the level of qualification and scope of duties. This method of employment allows managers to avoid the legal necessity of strictly controlling doctors' working hours.

The types of civil law contracts analyzed contained other additional provisions for linking performance to physician compensation. An example was the inclusion of provisions in the contracts allowing for the payment of equal annual or monthly bonuses to contract and full-time employees (e.g., SzM2). Some directors (e.g., SzS1, SzO2, SzM2) spoke with some pride about the solutions used in the contracts, treating the incentive mechanisms written in there more as innovations in hospital management than as a regularly applied process for stimulating certain behaviors. Some contracts, especially those for outpatient services or same-day surgery, introduced complex algorithms for calculating compensation, making it dependent on a number of factors. For example, a doctor was granted a higher percentage of the National Health Fund revenue for patients, but the cost of materials and drugs used, and even other personnel (anesthesiologist, nurses) were deducted from this increased revenue. Such a solution introduces an incentive mechanism not only to save on materials and drugs, but also to optimize the scheduling of procedures in a way that makes maximum use of the team's time. The methods of payment for medical services described here are in line with agency theory, which considers remuneration as a method of reducing the divergence of interests and goals between the parties to the relationship (Eisenhardt, 1985, p. 137). By shaping an appropriate method of remuneration, an employee can be induced to behave as expected (Merchant & Otley, 2007, p. 786). The mechanisms identified in the hospitals surveyed for influencing employee behavior through rewards were in seven areas: the financial performance of the organizational units, their revenues and costs, the number of procedures performed, patient satisfaction, and other quality-related indicators.

In conclusion, it should be stated that the possibility of obtaining detailed and reliable information on the performance of the hospital at different hierarchical levels (hospital, department, employee) seems to be an important factor for the use of rewards. This finding, therefore, allows us to adopt the following hypothesis:

H4: The effectiveness of the information system has a positive effect on rewarding employees.

In addition, some directors consider performance rewards, despite various objections, to be an effective form of influencing hospital performance, so it was decided to put forward another hypothesis, saying:

H5: Rewarding employees has a positive impact on hospital performance.

Rewarding also seems to stimulate the search for innovative solutions, especially when the reward is based not on behavior, but achievement of certain goals or results. In that case, employees do not have to move along the beaten path, but they can creatively change their work environment and accomplish better results. For example, giving rewards for reducing costs at the SzO2 hospital led nurses to use new dressing and disposable materials. A comprehensive illustration of the link between rewards and innovation can be found in the various forms of civil law contracts used by hospitals with physicians. Paying doctors based on the number of DRG points performed enables them to change the way they organize their work. A representative example of such a solution observed in many hospitals, is the statement of the director of SzO1:

> I had a problem with one-day orthopedic surgeries. Despite the
> fact that there were 5–6 procedures planned per day, there were
> still some problems there. And it was the anesthesiologist who dis-
> qualified the patient, and it was the patient who gave up, or it was
> some patient who was left overnight and we had to pay for night
> nurse care, so the staff costs were high, and there was little rev-
> enue on such a surgical day. In the end, I talked to the operators
> and changed their contractual form of employment from hourly to

pay for DRG points performed. Theoretically, they were getting a larger share of the revenue from the National Health Fund, except that when calculating the orthopedists' salaries, I also subtracted staff costs from their salaries. At this point, they began to work completely differently. First, the orthopedists came to an agreement with the anesthesiologists, who now call patients two days before the procedure and conduct an initial telephone interview to reduce the risk of disqualifying the patient before the procedure, but also to find out whether the patient would arrive for the procedure. When the patient hesitates or declares that he or she will not come for the procedure after all, there is still time to call another patient. Also, the order of procedures is arranged so that a patient who may need some observation is operated on first, then often before the end of the treatment day such a patient can already be discharged home. […] All in all, almost all scheduled procedures take place, and for many months no patient has had to stay overnight.

In light of the results of the field study, it seems likely that linking hospital performance to rewards stimulates employees to seek innovative solutions. The impact of the mode of reward on innovation was also emphasized by M. Porter, who argued that rewarding for behavior, i.e., for following procedures and guidelines, can lead only to minor improvements in the processes that are implemented based on these guidelines, while rewarding for performance can lead to breakthrough innovations in the delivery of medical services (Porter, 2010a, p. 2478). Given these arguments, another hypothesis was proposed:

H6: Rewarding employees has a positive impact on hospital innovativeness.

5.5 Interactive Use of Information System

While the previous subsections discussed the information systems used in hospitals and their diagnostic use, this subsection focuses on the interactive use of the information system. Diagnostic use of the IS meant tracking the advancement of goals, monitoring the results achieved, and comparing them with established goals, standards, and plans. Interactive use of the information system, on the other hand, involves its use to initiate discussions and personal participation by directors in decisions made by subordinates, and to signal the desirability of focusing on strategic uncertainties (Bisbe et al., 2019, p. 130; Simons, 1995, p. 91). The director of SzS1 described the interactive use of IS as follows:

> Every Thursday, every week I have meetings with the heads, I have a briefing, I go and I don't always have specific topics, but I involve them in the problems of the hospital. I stimulate them all the time to analyze the situation of the hospital and their departments. I talk to them every week, every week. I don't give them time to turn their heads back somewhere, yes. I just focus their attention all the time and draw them, yes, to important problems. So that they also embrace the hospital holistically. [...] When I have such tasks, problems, special ones, there are so-called "coffees" with me. I invite one of the head physicians, whom I want to, em, individually inspire, then I invite him for coffee and then we talk individually, yes. I say, Mr. head physician, the following problem, we have such a situation in the hospital, what can we do here? We have such indicators here [...].

The above statement contains elements that clearly specify the interactive use of the information system. Namely, the data generated by the process are an important element that directors refer to and interpret and discuss during face-to-face meetings with subordinates, directing their attention to common problems of the hospital (Simons, 1987a, p. 351).

Also, the director of SzO3 stated: "If I have a problem, such as with patients staying too long in the hospital, I'm the one who meets [with head physicians]. I don't push my solution to them [head physicians, lead nurses], I just, just arouse them, arouse their curiosity. 'How is it please, [as much as] 6.5 days [of average time of hospitalization] we have.' It makes us have financial problems. And they response: 'and because they [patients] are on waiting lists, they should be operated on faster.' And I say, 'But maybe we should think about it, maybe prepare them differently?' It turned out that patients over 80 are in this group [the longest staying], 50 percent. So I keep pestering them: 'Well, think, well, maybe they need to be operated on differently, anesthetized differently? Maybe you don't have to do it that way right away? ... Well, because they bring an ambulance at night, maybe they need to be scheduled somehow, maybe internists should be hired? [...] Maybe think about it?'". Three important elements can be identified in this statement: (1)

the possibility of obtaining complex data from the information system (linking patient age to length of stay), which demonstrates the effectiveness of IS; (2) the personal participation of the director in the decision-making process of subordinates; (3) the search for a solution based on the involvement of the entire hospital, or at least some important parts of it.

The results of the field survey prompted attention to another aspect. In diagnostic control, directors set targets for the appropriate structure of medical procedures (e.g., profitable and unprofitable), and then monitored the performance of these targets. In interactive control, hospital directors did not formulate goals, but personally, together with their subordinates, they engaged in a review of changes that occurred in the environment and in the hospital itself that could invalidate the current strategy. Director of SzS2 stated:

> The head physicians know how many of each procedure they have to perform [profitable and unprofitable], every month they get, and even during the month they get data, […] we report to them all the time, they know it, at what stage they are. Sometimes there is an abundance [of patients] and they can't help but admit them to the hospital. Recently, nephrology did 145 percent [of my monthly contract], on average I have 103 [%] in the lump sum [for the whole hospital]. But I also told the finance division to now recalculate for me after the change [in funding], whether this nephrology, because now there is a lump sum [contract with the NHF], whether this nephrology is profitable for the hospital. I have a contract for nephrology [priced] at the level of fixed costs. It's like if the fund would pay me 100 percent of the contract overruns, I'll still have a loss. […] You have to change the current strategy. In the lump sum, I can shift [the budget between specialties], but before I shift, I have to know what I'm shifting. I have to talk it through with the head physicians. Because if it's not profitable for the hospital, I'll say no! 110 percent [maximal performance] and I'm not interested! […] How about waiting lists? […] But that's not how I want it. We meet with the head physicians, review the data, look at what can be accepted and what [what kind of patients] can be put on the waiting list. […] I participate in this personally. Because if the director doesn't get personally involved in such things, there is no effect.

(SzS2)

Thus, the SzS2 director did not stop at analyzing the ward's performance, but regularly used information from the SI to personally engage in the head of the department's decision making.

Hospitals are characterized by a functional organizational structure and high barriers between departments (Lega & DePietro, 2005, p. 264), which leads to coordination problems and causes negative effects in many areas. In addition to reducing the efficiency of resource utilization, it also causes "deterioration of the hospital's reputation" (SzS2), "staff frustration" (SzO4), and it "lowers [...] the ability to raise external funds" (SzO2). It also has a negative impact on the treatment of patients requiring multispecialty treatment. In hospitals, care for such patients is provided in the form of consultations given by doctors from multiple departments with different specialties. But

> the consultant system doesn't work, because the patient has to wait for consultations [from another department], and this prolongs the length of stay, because the same procedure when the patient lies down for 4 days is profitable, and when 8, it is not. [...] When there are a lot of consultants and a difficult patient, everyone tries to make such diagnostics to flip the patient to another department. He calls the consultants and says: "I think it would be better for the patient to put him to surgery, or maybe to gastroenterology." I'm trying to change that. But I have no idea. I tell the doctors, I meet with them, this is one hospital after all, let's think what we can do. We've been working here for so many years.
>
> **(SzO/S2)**

The lack of effective cooperation between departments reduces the hospital's revenue and increases the cost of treatment, because "when a patient waits a long time for a consultation, he often gets worse and then costs rise [of his treatment]. It also occupies the bed unnecessarily. I analyze this together with doctors. I try to convince them that better interdepartmental cooperation would benefit everyone" (SzS1).

As the above examples show, information systems are the basis not only for diagnostic control, but also for interactive control (cf. Martyn et al., 2016, p. 285). The distinction between the diagnostic approach and the interactive approach here concerns the way information is used, not the technical design features of the IS. There is a fundamental difference in using information in a diagnostic way to compare performance with set goals and to urge employees to meet those goals (Simons, 1995, p. 59) and using even the same information in an interactive way that enables an organization to learn from its experience, generate new strategies and plans (Simons, 1995, p. 7), and bring the organization together (Marginson et al., 2014, p. 66).

The primary variable that forces the introduction of interactive controls by top management to improve performance is uncertainty, both internal and external, related to various types of risks, among others. Such risks are a sleep factor for executives, and refer to "threats and contingencies that can invalidate the assumptions underlying strategy" (Simons, 2010, p. 158). As S.K. Widener points out, strategic risks that have the potential to harm an organization can arise from the environment as well as from the organization's core business, i.e., "malfunction in core internal operating procedures and the safety of those operations" (2007, p. 763). At the hospital, this type of risk is improperly maintained medical records, which makes it so that

> in the [lawsuits] we've had, the weakest element has always been medical records and patient consent" (SzO3), and failures in procedures to ensure patient safety. Defective documentation can bring far-reaching consequences, such as "failure to record a drug given on call led to a patient going into shock, and [other] doctors didn't know for what reason."
>
> **(SzS2)**

But loss of accreditation can also be a significant threat, affecting the hospital's reputation and impacting its contract with the National Health Fund. All of these consequences can affect the fundamentals of hospital operation. What medical records should cover is strictly defined in the Health Ministry's regulation. Despite this, virtually all directors reported problems with medical record keeping.

The SzO2 director stated:

> We're about to have an accreditation audit [QMC in Krakow Accreditation], it's terrible for me, because of the documentation I have [...] well my colleague [medical director] just said that since we won't get points on [patients' medical] documentation anyway, because they [the auditors] will always find something in the documentation. He didn't put any emphasis on it at all and focused on something else. We paid attention to documentation in order to mobilize doctors, but [...] I especially have such a problem with

orthopedists, where documentation is not kept at all. I have a lot of court cases because of them – such a dismissive attitude to medical documentation.

The director of SzO/S1 reported a similar problem:

> Doctors keep saying that this bureaucracy will kill them. Well, there is such a mundane problem, because we, in addition to being accredited, keep a close eye on medical records, and for six months there was an inspection of the medical records. Every piece of documentation, before it was handed over to the archive, went through such checks, such detailed checks with everything [...] 100%. Well, of course, they came back to be corrected and they [doctors] were terribly outraged, well, but trivial errors came out, yes. No signatures, no authorization, no date, sometimes in the documentation the result of the wrong patient [...] The worst thing is that these errors are repeated.

Diagnostic control requires limited involvement of top management. This type of control over documentation was carried out in the hospitals surveyed, for example, by a "medical records audit team" (SzO/S1), or there was "such a procedure used that it is the secretary in the ward who is supposed to check before handing over to the archives. She is supposed to tick off the various components of the documentation, and she is supposed to sign off who did the checking" (SzO/S1). However, in a significant number of hospitals (e.g.: SzO2, SzO/S1, SzS2), with the help of diagnostic control, the quality of medical records fails to improve. Interactive control, on the other hand, requires the personal involvement of the top management and can lead to renegotiation with subordinates of established goals and objectives and performance indicators (Simons, 1995, p. 104). The director of SzO4 stated:

> A few years ago, I introduced a perioperative control chart in the operating theaters. Now it is followed very strictly. But, well, I will tell you a story. I introduced it by order, but then it got to me, one of the head physicians told me that [...] this perioperative card is filled out, but it's like this, it's even referred to as the "hypocrite card." When this reached me, well, I invited all the head physicians who are also associated with the operating theaters. And I

tell them: "if it's supposed to be hypocritical, it's pointless, but I didn't introduce it for that. This is to protect you and the hospital." And what was the hypocrisy exactly? Well, that one person filled out, marked that everything was ok, [...] often without seeing the patient and after the procedure. [...] And then, when I told them that it's also about a sense of security for the doctors, that everything has been checked and there is no risk of some kind of error, such as the fact that the patient can't enter the block, as there is no marked surgical field, which limb to operate on, for example. [...] Well, one head physician told me: "Because it is too long. A lot of time is needed [...] and in our opinion not everything is necessary." Well, and during such a conversation with these people I'm talking about [...] the head of orthopedics suggested: "Well, then maybe let's shorten this card and then follow it perfectly." Of course, I was very happy that he himself suggested this, because if he hadn't said it, I would have said it myself. But there is a different reception, as I can cite: "we do as the head of this and that department proposed."

The interview excerpts presented above show how the directors of each hospital approached the problem of medical record control. In the first interview, the director of SzO2 took no action to improve performance in this area. In the SzO/S1 hospital, diagnostic control was applied by setting up a committee of lower-level employees. In this case, while it is true that the director drew attention to the problem of the completeness and quality of medical records, he did not become personally involved in the process, did not show a commitment that would alert employees that this area is important, that this is where they need to focus their efforts. The last example shows that, although the goals set were not fully achieved, thanks to the director's personal commitment, new goals were negotiated, the implementation of which consequently led to quality improvements. Thanks to the director's actions, employees were mobilized to commit to the set "new" goals.

The study found that the director's personal and continuous involvement in staff decision-making processes did not always yield positive results. In particular, when the solutions did not concern local problems related to the routine of work in a particular specialty, but cross-cutting issues uniting the hospital into a single whole, the implementation of some common strategy. Doctors did not come willingly to discuss hospital performance.

Doctors were irritated when we talked about the performance of their department or hospital. They were also not fond of discussing quality indicators, but I'm not discouraged. I meet regularly with the heads of departments and we analyze the results of the departments and the hospital. They would rather talk about new apparatus, some about doing research [...] They would most like to talk about what the hospital can give them, not about results, about what they can do.

(SzU)

Another example is an illustration of this. Many hospitals, especially the smaller ones, use their diagnostic facilities only during the daytime. At night, when fewer tests are ordered, they use outside facilities or arrange for on-call services, and when a technician (and possibly a doctor) is called in, they obtain extra pay. In many cases, companies providing diagnostics also offer different prices depending on the time of day. In such a situation, hospitals are looking for optimal ways to organize their work to reduce costs:

We don't have our own CT scanner. It's outsourced, but in place.[10] [...] We have an agreement signed with this company that when the tomography is performed until noon, it is 18% cheaper than in the on-call system. And I explain this to doctors, organize work differently, you have different options, think how to improve it. You can somehow get along between departments. After all, this is our common money. It is one who will listen and take some action, and ten who will not.

(SzO/S1)

The above analysis of the materials obtained from the field research and the literature shows that control of the same areas can be approached in both diagnostic and interactive ways. In some situations, the interactive approach appears to achieve better results than the diagnostic approach, and the opposite is true for solving other problems, with the diagnostic approach proving more effective. But there are also those in which neither control strategy positively affects the achievement of goals. In the last example, despite the director's apparent focus on the problem of inflated diagnostic costs, medical professionals do not implement organizational solutions that could improve the hospital's performance. Nevertheless, the field research shows that hospital directors use information systems interactively in addition to diagnostic use. Thus, taking into account the results of the field research and the existing literature covering issues related to interactive control (Bisbe et al., 2019; Bisbe & Otley, 2004; Henri, 2006a; Langfield-Smith, 2007; Martyn et al., 2016; Simons, 1995; Simons et al., 2000; Simons, 2010, 2014; Tessier & Otley, 2012; Tuomela, 2005; Widener, 2007), particularly those related to hospitals (Abernethy & Brownell, 1999; Da Silva et al., 2020; Demartini & Mella, 2014; Kastberg & Siverbo, 2013; Naranjo-Gil & Hartmann, 2007; Nyland & Pettersen, 2004; Østergren, 2009; Solstad & Petterson, 2020; Yu et al., 2018), a further research hypothesis can be made:

H7: The effectiveness of the information system positively affects its interactive use.

In the interviews and materials obtained at hospitals, many situations were identified in which directors used the information system interactively, getting personally involved in decisions made by subordinates and in discussing with subordinates strategic uncertainty and assumptions made, renegotiating established goals, and seeking common ground and coordination across the organization. On the other hand, however, only a few examples were recognized in which directors were able to unequivocally state the positive impact of interactive information system use on hospital performance. However, it seems likely that the personal and ongoing involvement of directors has a positive impact on hospital performance. Accordingly, the hypothesis was accepted stating that:

H8: Interactive use of the information system has a positive impact on hospital performance.

Previous quantitative studies suggest a positive impact of interactive control on organizational performance (Abernethy & Brownell, 1999, p. 199; de Harlez & Malagueño, 2016, p. 2; Naranjo-Gil & Hartmann, 2007, p. 751; Yu et al., 2018, p. 20), while qualitative studies conducted in hospitals do not clearly confirm the positive impact of this control on performance (Kastberg & Siverbo, 2013, p. 265; Østergren, 2009, p. 192). Therefore, further analysis of this relationship in quantitative studies conducted in hospitals will be an important contribution to the knowledge in this area.

5.6 The Role of Innovativeness in Management Control

Analyzing the materials collected in the field research, a second-order theme of innovation was identified. Innovations in hospitals were planned as part of hospital development and as a response to emerging problems. The first set included innovations enshrined in multi-year strategic plans, often adopted on the basis of provincial and even national strategies. These innovations were often a source of increased environmental uncertainty in hospitals. The second set identified innovations in response to environmental uncertainty and/or poor hospital performance recognized based on information system data. In reference to the second set of innovations, a telling response was that of the Chief Operating Officer (COO) of a British hospital (SzGB), who, when asked about the use of the information system, particularly various types of indicators to control clinical activities, stated:

> The chief executive told me that my role is not to tell people what to do, to hold them accountable for the performance of indicators, but to jointly seek innovative solutions to problems that appear to be the cause of poor performance. For example, we were not meeting the target set by the government for patients to wait in the ED [to be helped and sent home or admitted to a ward in less than four hours]. [...] It doesn't make sense to offer people some incentives or to go to the ED and tell them to work harder and faster, rather you have to look for the reasons for this state of affairs. [...] We saw that we had a problem with the space in the ED, that it was crowded, that there was a maladjusted skill mix of the people there. The staffing levels were mismatched with the peak hours of patient arrival. So, with the help of an information system, we looked at what is the pattern of conditions of people who come to the ED at particular hours. It turned out that most people with more serious problems would arrive between five in the afternoon and three in the morning, and this is not the most heavily staffed shift. There were less experienced doctors then. We had to change that.

In the British hospital, the *a priori* assumption of the management was that the response to the hospital's poor performance should not be to increase pressure to meet planned goals with existing methods, but to seek innovative solutions. This means that in this hospital innovativeness was consciously included in the area of management control. In a similar vein, the director of SzS1 said,

> I was recently reviewing old orders of previous directors, and I noticed one thing. The problems, the goals are generally the same, excessive costs, quality improvement, while the solutions change. It is practically impossible to permanently solve a problem – it will keep coming back. You just have to apply a different, new, creative solution each time.

A number of innovations were identified in the hospitals studied, which were reactive measures that corrected organizational processes in order to increase the likelihood of achieving intended results. And it is this corrective role of innovativeness carried out under the supervision of top management that makes it possible for innovation to be an element of management control. An example is the creation of a new division:

> Costs are killing us. But here I don't really see room for improvement. [...] We thought about how to increase revenues. Well, we came to the conclusion that we need to spin off a new ward. [...] We don't have a stroke ward, but now I have raised money and we will create a stroke ward. Because until now we'd been treating those stroke patients in neurology, but there it's priced lower than if [the patient] is treated in the stroke unit.

> **(SzS2)**

This type of innovation, which involves entering new areas of service delivery as a response to poor financial performance, was identified many times during the course of the study. It should be noted that in the present research, innovation was defined as any activity that is new to a hospital. This means that the establishment of a new stroke unit is not an innovation in the sense of a completely new and unknown to mankind, but it is an innovation in a particular hospital because there was no such unit in the hospital before.

One of the key tasks of hospital directors is to attract and retain professional staff, especially doctors. Overall, this element was rated by the directors as important to the evaluation of the overall hospital performance.

However, given the staff shortages that exist in Poland, this task is a major challenge. The director of SzM1 stated:

> I had a conflict with the doctors. They terminated their contracts and left the hospital, but somehow we came to an agreement. [...] I am clear about the financial situation of the hospital. [...] They are aware that there is simply no more money in this system, but I had to make some concessions. For example, I introduced a completely new on-call system, which is very beneficial. Because here I was able to give doctors more [money] without raising complaints from other staff, well, you know, here you can without conflicting with other staff. The issue of training leave, the issue of work discipline, working hours, coming off duty – things like that.
>
> **(SzM1)**

The impetus for innovation was not only the poor performance reported by hospital information systems, but also the need to obtain more accurate and reliable information to enable increased control:

> 99% of accountants count as an expense what comes out of a central depot, such as the hospital pharmacy, and there is no expense there. The expense is what is issued to the patient from that clinic depot. Because if what we issue from the [central] depot becomes a cost, then we don't control the in-process inventory. As we totaled it, we had a six-month supply [in handheld departmental depots]. Of course, this generated problems with payments. This caused a lack of control over the use of materials. [...] As the inventory was done once a year, as the regulations say, there was no control at all during the year. [...] We changed this. In our costing, we counted what the patient gets. With the information on the stock, we reduced costs.
>
> **(SzU)**

The innovative (at this hospital) assignment of drugs and supplies to a specific patient which was introduced by the management allowed for more detailed and reliable cost accounting and thus control. In-depth information on the hospital's achievements can only be obtained from combining financial and medical data.

Similarly, at SzS2, the response to years of debt resulting from overly expensive treatment was to invest in an innovative information system. The director was convinced that the cost of treatment in the wards was too high. However, the problem was how to prove to physicians that they were treating too expensively and how to convince them to treat more rationally. In this situation, the director of SzS2 and his appointed team applied

> similar principles as in financial controlling, except that the input was mostly based on medical data [...], ICD-9 and even more detailed elements of procedures. Then, we went down to ICD-10. This allowed us to compare costs with other departments that performed similar procedures, and then with facilities on the level of procedures, and patients with specific conditions. [...] Such detailed medical data, what procedures they use in our department, allowed us to compare medical practices, treatment patterns with other facilities, and even world recommendations. Because sometimes doctors use some more complicated or additional procedures that are altogether unnecessary, elsewhere they do it more simply and have better medical results and lower costs. But such analysis needs to be done at a high level of detail, not just for a given specialty, but rather for a given type of procedure.

The above solution has been successful because, on the one hand, it has allowed the adoption of good practices from other departments and hospitals, and, on the other hand, "the introduction of an extensive and reliable information system has strengthened trust between physicians and the director" (SzS2).

Other directors (e.g., SzU, SzS/U, SzS1 and SzO/S1) hired managers for hospital departments in response to poor hospital performance. The role of these managers "was not to control physicians, as this is basically impossible by non-medical staff" (SzO/S1), but to support the head physicians in patient billing processes [reports to NHF] and other administrative and management activities that distracted the head physicians from managing the medical activities of the ward. The process of introducing managers to the wards, where medical professionals had previously ruled indivisibly, was not easy.

> In the beginning, it was with a consulting company that we provided training for these people [managers], in this initial path of appointing them as business consultants. At the moment, there

are four such people in the hospital. It was an idea taken from a hospital in Bydgoszcz. [...] Initially, I would say, there was a little bit of fear on the part of the head physicians that this would be an element of supervision. On the other hand, this later evolved into advice on optimizing the work of the department. [...] The conditions for the operation of hospitals are quite variable. For the introduction of the new way of hospital financing or changes in the valuation of medical procedures, or ways of billing for services, it is necessary to have up-to-date knowledge of how to behave in this fluid situation. First of all, how to report and how to describe medical procedures to the National Health Fund, so that the department does not lose. Head physicians don't always have time to keep track of the ways in which patients are billed [to the NHF], and this can change.

(SzS/U)

In order to optimally adapt the role of these managers to the needs of the changing environment, they were assigned different responsibilities in each hospital.

The treatment process, it was the head of the clinic who was responsible, and resource management – the manager. And they had to get along. And at this point, there is no situation where someone comes back from medical congress and implements some purchases or methods for us, as was the case before. It's just that if someone came back from the congress, they had to prepare a certain business plan with the manager to convince them that it's worth it, because it's a known fact that in Poland all innovative things in hospitals are not financed from anything else but the hospital's resources. Either from the deficit or from surpluses, if the hospital has any. Innovativeness here, all these operations that we started from scratch, there were no grants. It was from our own resources. Well, here cost accounting and information was extremely important. But also there had to be trust in the doctors. Because you know, the head of the clinic could hide something from the manager and the business plan would come out positive.

(SzU)

As the interview excerpt above shows, innovations in the hospital were also introduced by clinicians, but they were evaluated and approved by the director. These were so-called semi-intentional innovations (Fuglsang, 2010, p. 76). However, directors pointed out that "it is not always possible to assess the effects of an innovation" (SzS/U), that is, its impact on the hospital's situation. Then, in deciding whether to accept the implementation of an innovation, "an important element was the trust [of the director] in the doctor" (SzU) who proposed such an innovation, since innovations "introduced by physicians were often associated with some improvement in the quality of treatment, but just as often had significant financial implications" (SzS2).

The hospitals surveyed also identified innovations that are direct employee initiatives, also known as *bricolage innovations* (Fuglsang, 2010, p. 76). Such innovations often emerge ad hoc as a response to specific practical problems or needs to improve daily operations, or to produce better results. Such bottom-up emergent innovations have also been made permanent in hospital operations. An adequate example of this type of innovation is the billing of patient treatment costs to the National Health Fund. The billing rate for homogeneous patient groups depends on several factors, including the type of ICD-9 diagnostic and treatment procedures performed, the ICD-10 diagnosis and the department in which the patient was treated. By directing patients with specific conditions to the appropriate departments from the emergency room, ED and specialized outpatient clinics, or by skillfully shifting patients between departments during hospitalization, hospitals can significantly increase their revenues without performing additional services. Since these situations are individual, the initiative of the doctors themselves in finding optimal solutions is particularly important in this case:

> This year I hired a new head of the dialysis department, who had worked for several years in a private health center, and there was a budgeting system there. [...] And he came to us with the habit of analyzing costs and looking for innovative solutions. And he discovered that the National Health Fund has priced procedures in such a way that, for example, it's better to do blood transfusion in internal medicine, because internal medicine will get, if it still does something there, it will get an additional few thousand zlotys [for the blood transfusion], so there will be revenue. And the costs will not unnecessarily burden the dialysis department, because whether I do him [the patient] transfusion or not, I will get the same amount [from the National Health Fund] for dialysis anyway. But this kind

of thinking is not common. The head physician himself made sure to get along with the head of internal medicine, how to transfer this patient, how to process him there, in terms of documentation, [...] Based on this example, I want to show others how it can work.

(SzO4)

Bottom-up innovations tend to be accepted by the management and perpetuated as routine both through dissemination by the management itself and through exchanges between employees. In the above example, the exact transfer of the solution to other departments was not possible, but it was possible to promote the search for new ways of providing and billing services that improve the hospital's financial situation.

Important external stakeholders of hospitals are suppliers. As public entities, hospitals must make all purchases based on the Public Procurement Law. Depending on the solutions adopted, hospitals can not only save or lose significant funds, but they can also increase or decrease the quality of medical services. A large part of hospitals' costs and a significant impact on the quality of services are drugs and disposable materials. The use of innovative solutions in the purchasing process can significantly increase the quality and reduce the price of purchased products, thus improving hospital performance. "Suppliers reduce the price of the products they offer usually in two situations, which are, by the way, related. When the volume of the order increases, but the number of line items does not, and when individual line items can be supplied by multiple manufacturers and multiple pharmaceutical wholesalers" (SzS2), i.e., competition increases. Similarly, the SzU director indicated that he also controlled pharmacotherapy costs with innovative solutions:

The issue of medicines was handled by framework agreements. At the time, these were probably the first such agreements in Poland. These are public contracts. We determined the assortment, put out a tender for that assortment, but also for the companies that will supply because the framework first determines the circle of suppliers. And then we did an online auction every quarter from these selected companies. Well, the prices dropped significantly for us.

(SzU)

Bringing in competition and maintaining quality supply is a complex process, "it's kind of a game with wholesalers" (SzS/U).

In the strategy for purchasing drugs, it is important not only to properly describe the drugs, select the optimal package size, dosage, so that unused ampules and other packages are not left open, but also to divide them into so-called packages.

> You really have to work a lot with each department to compose the specifications for the tender. […] Because it's not just medical considerations that a department wants a drug only from this company, here you need an innovative strategy. Here the medical department have to get along [to order similar drugs]. […] Wholesalers rarely have the entire assortment that a hospital needs, hence it is divided into packages that individual suppliers can offer. […] Dividing into too many packages provides [wholesalers] the opportunity to choose items with high volume and margin, and leave out unattractive packages. […] On the other hand, splitting into too few packages or inappropriately grouping [drugs into packages] can cause some of the smaller players [wholesalers] to be forced to order missing drugs from competitors, often competing in the same tender. Of course, this gives the larger companies the opportunity to lock out the smaller ones by inflating resale prices.

(SzS1)

A similar situation occurs in the process of purchasing medical equipment. Professionals, having worked for many years on a certain type of apparatus, master its operation, and changing to a device from another manufacturer requires extra effort from them. Hence, during the preparation of the terms of reference (ToR), "medics enter such parameter values that direct them to a particular manufacturer" (SzO2). Because the technical parameters of equipment are usually determined by users, and they want to reduce their efforts in the future, on the one hand. On the other hand, they are afraid that new equipment will turn out not to be as good as the already proven one. However, writing specifications for a specific company increases purchasing and service costs, so directors try to resist this: "Over and over again in purchasing [apparatus] the same companies would win. I said enough!" (SzS1). However, directors admit that "excessive openness to a wide range of equipment can lead to the purchase of equipment, admittedly cheap, but of low quality" (SzO2). Hence, a very important issue is to look for innovative solutions to construct equipment specifications that would simultaneously eliminate low-quality equipment, but introduce competition among reliable suppliers.

Often, however, "companies get the idea to come up with some new features and convince doctors that it's so terribly important" (SzS1). Thus, it is a mistake for a hospital to prepare specifications

> if only one company comes to the tender. Often the obstacle is some single parameter [which the specialists preparing the ToR consider crucial]. I am conducting technical dialogues [with my suppliers] at the moment, and it is a revelation. My people open their eyes, and suddenly they find out [during the dialogue] that I had a different idea about this, and I also had a different idea about this. I thought that this parameter that your company offers is more important for the quality of treatment.
>
> **(SzM2)**

But there is another reason for making specifications "under the manufacturer" (SzO4). Developing a specification that excludes low-quality products but allows some high-quality products is complex and time-consuming. It requires a huge commitment, studying the technical solutions used by individual manufacturers. That's why medical professionals often "make specifications under one company they know, of which they are sure, because it's so much easier and faster" (SzO2). This is not about corruption. It happens, which should not be the case, that "specifications are consulted and even prepared by representatives of companies, because they know the competitor's products very well and know how to prepare the specification in such a way that it looks 'good' but excludes the competition" (SzO3). To counteract this unfavorable phenomenon limiting competition, directors must resort to innovative solutions.

> With the purchase of medical equipment, this is a problem. Nobody wants to do specifications. Medics often say "a colleague from a university hospital told me that this and that arthroscopic set works superbly, so I would like one too." I say, "please prepare a specification, what functions it should have and we will buy one." But with that it's already a problem. So I hire external procurement experts. They are at the disposal of my medics, they help them develop the specification also from the technical side. The medics, when they have help, don't have to dawdle over technical

parameters themselves, which they often don't understand. They show much more initiative and courage in searching for equipment from different manufacturers. They are not afraid to make the mistake of buying something that they will later have a problem with. I recently demonstrated at a meeting: "See, this is the way we applied it. We aroused competition, but we bought good quality and the price was lower than last time." Because employees are afraid that we will undercut the quality, but I am also afraid. The hospital is specialized. I also want to have good products, but we have to prepare the ToR in such a way as to allow competition between, say, "Mercedes" and "Audi." Introducing external experts was a good idea because now the employees are already working with them themselves.

(SzS2)

As the directors point out, "new ways need to be constantly developed in tenders, of course, within the framework of the current law, as companies learn how to minimize competition" (SzS1). Developing specifications "that eliminate low-quality equipment and at the same time stimulate competition among the best requires a great deal of knowledge and innovativeness on the part of the medics preparing them" (SzO4). Directors can hire outside experts, but the equipment will be worked on by professionals from the hospital in question, and they are the ones who must approve it. The director of SzS2 commented on it this way: "There is no way for the director to be able to check all the specifications, the records that the medics introduce. This is where trust is needed."

In hospitals, the most costly resource is the time of medical professionals, so any method that "saves staff time" (SzS2) is very important. A British hospital, which has a low unit cost of tests due to its highly automated analytical laboratory, performing millions of tests per year, adopted such a principle that

in the case an external partner [e.g., a family doctor] sends, for example, blood for a test, and during this test a red blood cell level that is too low comes out, the system itself will automatically perform predefined additional tests, such as iron levels, without involving the time of the doctor and the diagnostician.

(SzGB, COO)

The director's rationale for adopting this type of innovation in external relations was that

> even if an external customer did not pay for an additional unordered test, the cost of deviating from this rule, i.e., contacting the ordering physician, waiting for additional orders, taking blood samples from the depot again and testing, is much higher than the cost of a small percentage of potentially unpaid tests.
>
> **(SzGB, COO)**

When considering the innovative activities of hospitals, not only cited in this section, but also when describing the other variables of the management control model, it is possible to identify the relationship between the effectiveness of information system (IS) and innovativeness, and between innovativeness and hospital performance. While the research of D. Naranjo-Gila and F. Hartmann (2007, p. 751) suggest that a wide range of IS is positively related to innovativeness, previous studies of the relationship between innovativeness and hospital performance are not conclusive (Chen et al., 2014; Cucciniello & Nasi, 2014, p. 96; Dias & Escoval, 2013; Hernandez et al., 2013; Leidner et al., 2010; Moreira et al., 2017; Salge & Vera, 2009; Tsai, 2013). However, a thematic analysis of the collected material indicates the important role of information system-induced innovations in shaping hospital performance. The accepted operational definition of management control speaks of all instruments, activities and systems used by top management that increase the likelihood of favorable adaptation of the hospital to the environment, and the measure of this adaptation is the results obtained by the hospital. Thus, in light of the accepted definition, the relationship of the information system to innovativeness and the relationship of innovativeness to performance is a vital element of management control. It seems highly likely that a more effective information system enables a more adequate response to emerging problems through innovative solutions that improve hospital performance. This means that hypotheses can be put forward stating that:

H9: The effectiveness of the information system has a positive impact on hospital innovativeness.

H10: Hospital innovativeness has a positive impact on hospital performance.

A picture of the relationship between the diagnostic use of IS and innovativeness is also emerging from the research described so far. On the one hand, the diagnostic use of IS can limit innovativeness, as it forces predictable achievement of set goals, but, on the other hand, when the goals are ambitious and cannot be achieved with existing measures, it can stimulate innovation.

> I introduced regular reporting of the financial situation of the departments at the hospital. I set financial targets, that is, what the level of costs and revenues should be, and controlled this. It's known that not everyone had to have a profit, but the level [set target] had to be kept. I generated pressure on the head physicians. I constantly reminded them of these goals. I constantly controlled this. And I have to admit that some really, really reorganized the work and improved the results.
>
> **(SzS1)**

R. Simons wrote that information and the management control system based on it play a key role in creating pressure that forces members of an organization to seek innovative solutions to achieve goals (Simons, 1995, p. 92).

A similar logic of events occurred at the SzO3 hospital, where the diagnostic use of IS "forced" the introduction of innovative solutions:

> I had the problem that they used very expensive disposable tools in electrosurgery, even in minor procedures. And there was a discussion that they could not use others because of quality, because of complications. But I asked the deputy [medical director] to check, to require a report every month, which tools and for which procedures were used. And in the end, they looked for other tools, got trained, and costs went down. And there are even fewer complications, I would say.

The impact of diagnostic control on innovativeness can also be seen in the example showing the introduction of control of ward depots in SzU and in the behavior of the head of the dialysis department in SzO4. It seems likely, therefore, that diagnostic control, i.e., monitoring the achievement of goals, can stimulate the search for innovative solutions, thus authorizing the following hypothesis:

H11: Diagnostic use of the information system has a positive impact on hospital innovativeness.

An analogous situation exists in the case of interactive use of IS. An analysis of the studies described in the subsection on interactive control also leads to the conclusion that directors' personal and ongoing involvement in subordinates' decision making based on IS information should have a positive impact on subordinates' innovation efforts. Such a relationship is suggested, for example, by the statements of directors describing the use of IS to link patient age to length of hospital stay (SzO3) and to analyze the profitability of overruns in the nephrology department (SzS2). Also, another example suggests such a link:

> Now it's starting to become a standard, but a few years ago, it wasn't. I had a situation that very many patients from elective procedures were "dropped" by anesthesiologists. And it was the patient's medical tests that weren't appropriate. He got sick, caught a cold, and they wouldn't allow the procedure. And the whole team was ready. By the time they found another patient, they had prepared it, how much time it takes? What losses! As I counted, the operating theaters had 10 percent downtime because of this. This I began to regularly discuss with the head physicians – how to fix it, how to improve it. And one doctor, I don't remember who, says, how about having an anesthesiologist look at this patient the day before? And I think, and why not! And I did. Like in an outpatient clinic. Now it's nothing new, but back then, we gained a lot from it. Well, and the patients.
>
> **(SzO/S2)**

Thus, it can be assumed that examples of interactive use of information obtained in field research indicate that:

H12: Interactive use of the information system has a positive impact on hospital innovativeness.

It is worth noting at this point an important difference between interactive control and innovativeness. Interactive control refers to the personal involvement of management in discussing with subordinates the assumptions made, strategic uncertainty, renegotiating established goals, and objectives and indicators, and seeking a common platform of action for the entire hospital. Innovativeness, on the other hand, involves initiating and implementing specific, often local, solutions that have not previously been applied in the hospital. Thus, it seems likely that interactive use of the information system can positively influence innovativeness.

5.7 Environmental Uncertainty

Extant research has not resolved the dilemma regarding the volatility of the hospital environment. Some academics characterize the health sector as turbulent, volatile, and highly uncertain (Begun & Kaissi, 2004, p. 31; Yang et al., 2017, p. 246), while others consider the sector stable (Morrison, 2000, pp. 199, 203). The picture emerging from the field research points to two elements. First, that the changes taking place significantly affect the operation of hospitals, and, second, that the perceived uncertainty is often the impetus for innovative solutions. This observation is well illustrated by the statement of the director of SzO/S1:

> After the recent changes in the region, unfortunately, the ambulance service [emergency] is in the structures of the other hospital, and they drive themselves as they please. They have come up with a philosophy that is convenient for them, that they deliver emergency patients to the nearest hospital. We are the hospital to which they have the closest 2/3 of the city and surrounding areas. They pick their own patients, in short. [...] This is a problem in cost and work organization. Because if they drive a lot [of emergency patients] to us, we have to drop elective patients, especially in orthopedics. The other such department that is clogged with elderly people is internal medicine. Discussions have leaned on the provincial governor, where I showed that we don't have an ED (Hospital Emergency Ward), but an emergency room,[11] and they drive more patients to us than to themselves in the ED. [...] The paramedics tell me they would rather bring people here than have problems with their employer. That is, they bring them as if we were a fully-fledged ED, even though we are an emergency room. And we have not enough power to change it. [...] It used to be that they brought us a patient, there was no room in the ICU (Intensive

Care Unit), and the doctor sent this patient to the other hospital, but this patient died. Well, they took the case to court, as a hospital, and our doctor was deprived of the right to practice. After that incident, doctors are afraid of trying to send back any patient. Well I have to invest, look for some solutions to deal with this problem. [...] The other hospital's handling of emergency medical services also causes other problems. For example, interventional cardiology [used to be a very profitable service in Poland]. Now that the pricing has dropped even more, they hardly bring these patients to us anymore. They made a second post (laboratory) at their place to make up for this reduced valuation with the increased numbers. I have to look for other solutions here as well. Well, it's electrocardiology that we're going into – putting in pacemakers and ablations because we've dropped a lot [interventional cardiology]. Like I said, this ambulance system brings profitable patients there, and not to us. Well, that and the stroke unit I still have to do.

The above excerpt from the interview shows that there is relatively strong competition between hospitals in Poland, although it is not felt in the same way by all directors. It depends mainly on the situation in particular specialties and in a given geographic area. However, it can be seen that hospitals are able to effectively use their advantages to improve their situation at the expense of their competitors, which prompts facilities that do not have such advantages to seek new market niches and innovative solutions in order to survive. A similar situation to that in the SzO/S1 hospital environment is occurring in the SzO2 hospital environment, which must respond with innovative solutions to intensifying competition with a much larger and rapidly growing provincial hospital operating in the same geographic market:

Well, that's the dilemma I have, whether the hospital can afford such development, so the hospital's going into highly specialized procedures. But our hospital, by virtue of its surroundings, because we have the Provincial Hospital here, which is now a huge investment and will develop, well, in a broader scope, we have to differ in something. Because if we repeat, implement these basic services, we will die. The point is not to swallow us. The provincial government have always wanted to absorb this hospital. To them, somehow, the salt in the eye is a hospital that is much smaller, but stands out for its specialty. That's why we continued to bet on the specialty. Luckily, our owner [local government of a city] is financing the purchase of specialized equipment. For now, it is the one who does the purchasing every year. But this is also difficult to predict in the future. This situation also forced me to change the remuneration system for the medics. Here we have, you could say, a task-based system now. We prefer it very much and it already functions in four departments. That is, doctors receive a percentage of the revenue from the National Health Fund. Of course, there are imposed limits on overruns. Well, and for us it is a secondary matter whether they will implement it with a team of five or eight. There is a pool of money allocated for all elements of doctors' salaries including on-call. [...] And this has greatly improved the performance.

(SzO2)

Public and many other, especially not-for-profit, hospitals are subject to political decision-making processes and have to deal with political actors with many divergent interests, although all are acting to achieve the public good. This causes hospital managers to operate in a context of uncertainty about what priorities to assign to particular problems and how to counter them. Nor do they have clear guidelines as to what is moral (higher quality or lower costs and better access, higher staff salaries, or more staff and better care) (cf. Townley et al., 2003, p. 1066).

The intense pressure is forcing hospitals to seek innovative solutions both in the field of new products, i.e., increasing the scope of health services provided, as well as organizational and management innovations. Uncertainty adds to the dynamism and complexity of the hospital environment, which intensifies the sense of uncertainty (Daft et al., 2010, p. 150) and poses further challenges to hospital directors. A change in one element of the environment can cause unpredictable effects in other areas:

A neighboring hospital expanded, increased its scope of operations, and started buying up doctors from me. [...] I had to react, give up the control of doctors' working hours. I know that [the doctors] still have some additional work in other places, but the big hospitals pay more money and doctors will get away from me. I know that one or the other [doctor] isn't there once or twice a week, but I don't react to that, I turn a blind eye. If I start pressing, they'll leave and I'll have a problem.

(SzO3)

However, the effects of such far-reaching autonomy for doctors can be dangerous for patients, as doctors under such conditions may bypass certain procedures. It can also be dangerous for the hospital, with the hospital having to pay high compensation due to medical errors caused by non-compliance with procedures. This means that hospital executives also experience internal uncertainty regarding "production" as an "uncertain" technology or process (Begun & Kaissi, 2004).

The director of SzO1, during the interview, complained about

> the instability of the environment in which we operate, in the sense of frequent changes in funding by the National Health Fund for certain services, but also the increase in the cost of treatment, because reviews of equipment are increasing, the cost of disposables, outsourcing, cleaning, security, not to mention professional unions and the picking up of doctors by other hospitals. This forces a lot of change. Something new has to be invented all the time. Here to combine something, there to separate something. Looking for new solutions all the time. I am already – frankly – very tired of this, because we are in constant change. It's also not good for the staff and, by the same token, for the patients, because people sometimes get lost.

There are also claims in the literature that managers exaggerate the uncertainty prevailing in health care (Begun & Kaissi, 2004, p. 37). However, it was difficult to determine in this study whether managers actually perceive the environment as highly uncertain, or whether by exaggerating the uncertainty of the environment they put more pressure on subordinate employees to make necessary changes or even to achieve their own goals.

> The previous legal solutions mandated that a hospital be converted into a company if it went into debt. I used this as a bogeyman [to scare people]. Because the rector told me, do everything to avoid being a company. [...] At meetings with the heads of the wards, I showed how much more we were missing [the increase in debt],

so that we wouldn't be a company. They didn't want a company either. This fear of transformation worked on them, and then they made various changes.

(SzU)

Directors may be inclined to exaggerate uncertainty in order to communicate threats more clearly and put pressure on medical professionals, if only to counter demands for salary increases. While in the case of doctors, such actions may not be very effective: "The unions surprised me. I didn't have money, because I didn't, but the doctors put me against the wall and I had to give in. They ruined the financial result for me because the cost of the increase in these salaries exceeded one million zlotys. What I saved on drugs, I had to give to the doctors" (SzO/S1). This is already the case with other medical workers, especially non-medical workers, that the exaggeration of threats is sometimes effective.

An analysis of the materials collected in the field survey shows that the main areas that were perceived as uncertain by the directors were not macroeconomic factors, but the so-called proximate environment, including competitors, human resources, suppliers, payment for health services, union activity on the hospital grounds, changes in revenue, and the unpredictability of costs associated with treating certain patients. In addition, it can be assumed that the perceived uncertainty of the environment was an important factor in the search for innovative solutions by both directors and medics. In view of the above, the following hypothesis can be formulated:

H13: Directors' perceived level of environmental uncertainty has a positive impact on hospital innovativeness.

This view is in line with previous studies that also pointed to the relationship between environmental uncertainty and innovativeness (Lill et al., 2020, p. 1; Tkotz et al., 2018, p. 4), suggesting that innovating can help an organization better adapt to a changing environment (Kobrin, 1991; Lill et al., 2020, p. 8; Lisboa et al., 2011, p. 1157; Madhok & Osegowitsch, 2000; Meyer et al., 1990, p. 101; Tkotz et al., 2018, p. 4). This means that innovation can be a method to increase an organization's alignment with the environment and consequently improve its performance (Atuahene-Gima, 2005, p. 78; Yang et al., 2017, p. 246).

5.8 Director's Trust in Physicians

In the course of thematic analysis of the material collected in the research, an area emerged related to the directors' trust in employees, particularly in physicians. The unique role of doctors is related to the fact that they occupy the main management positions at the operational level in the hospital (hospital departments) and thus "decide everything: which patient to admit to the ward and which to send away, what diagnostics and therapy to order, how many doctors are necessary for a given procedure, in which DRG group to bill the patient! That is, [they decide] on treatment effects, costs and – importantly – revenues" (SzO/S1). The study also identified the existence of a relationship between directors' trust in physicians and hospital innovativeness. As described earlier, innovations that do not require increased funding and significant organizational changes can be implemented outside the knowledge of hospital directors, while the more significant ones must be approved by directors. Even the acquisition by doctors of funds for medical apparatus or the apparatus itself in the form of donations must be approved by the directors, if only because of the current law on the management of fixed assets in hospitals. In addition, many local governments have placed restrictions on the ability of hospitals to accept donations, because in many cases such donations have proved disadvantageous to hospitals, especially when they were done by the producer of the equipment "because it's mostly the case that even when everything is paid for at the beginning [by the company that donates the equipment], then you have to do maintenance, buy special reagents and, to put it mildly, they are not always at market prices" (SzS2). Therefore, the SzO2 director stated:

> I don't always agree with raising funds for the purchase of equipment or accepting donations of medical equipment. Because mostly, after some time, there are additional costs that are not visible at the beginning. [...] When I trust a doctor, that he cares about the interests of the hospital, that he understands how important the costs are, that he is loyal, then I am much more willing to agree. Otherwise, I sometimes refuse.

The directors also pointed out that they do not support every scientific activity of doctors because "such scientific activity is not always synergistic with what is performed in the hospital" (SzU). And, second, it always generates some costs. This is not only about financial costs, but also about time, about the attention that doctors give during working hours.

> Sometimes a doctor or doctors come to me, that they want to intro-
> duce something new, about the grant they are applying for, that the
> money from outside will be [...] I think to myself – cool, we are
> developing. But I also always ask myself questions: Is this really
> going to benefit patients? Is this the direction we want to develop
> in? Are these additional capabilities that we will acquire, [...] are
> there patients who can benefit from this? I'm also thinking about
> money, of course. What happens when the grant money runs out?
> If it's some new therapy, and more expensive, will the National
> Health Fund pay for it? Won't the grant work pull doctors away
> from their current duties, and it will turn out after a while that an
> additional doctor will have to be hired, because there is no one to
> go to the clinic? [...] It's mostly a very difficult decision. You refuse,
> he [the doctor] will get demotivated, he may look for a job some-
> where else, where they will allow him to do it. You agree, then
> you can generate a lot of problems. It is known, everyone before-
> hand [before innovations are introduced] talks about what great
> benefits there will be for the hospital. And I have already been
> burned several times. But it's hard to judge beforehand, there's no
> rule here [...] If I trust a person, I care about that doctor, I know he
> cares about the hospital, then I agree, even if I feel it will generate
> some additional costs.
>
> **(SzO2)**

Organizational innovations proposed by doctors are sometimes seen by directors as "a way for doctors to take off some responsibilities or shift work to other staff, to reduce their own responsibility for patients. [...] Without trust in the doctor, it's hard to make a decision" (SzO1). Sometimes directors indicated that doctors tried to convince them to make some organizational changes, to hire additional specialists, and, according to the directors, in some cases this was not about improving the organization, treating patients, but was rather due to a lack of interest in improving their skills and trying to shift some activities to someone new. Here, too, the directors stressed the importance of trust due to the fact that it is very difficult to assess the effects of various actions.

Recently a department head came to me saying that he wanted
to hire an internist for his ward because it would, in his opinion,
reduce costs, that patients would stay on the ward for a shorter
period of time. I didn't agree because I had already hired a doctor for him in the past, there were supposed to be new treatments,
and all in all, something went wrong there. The new treatments
were not introduced, and the doctor still stayed.

(SzO4)

In the interviews, directors also emphasized the need to trust physicians
when introducing new therapies and treatments into the routine practices of
the wards. Directors' concerns in such cases mostly related to the possibility that innovative practices could have a negative impact on the financial
situation of the department, in the absence of significant improvement in
treatment outcomes. In such a case, directors paid attention to two aspects:
whether the doctor proposing the innovation was perceived as a person
who "actually has adequate medical knowledge" (SzO3), and whether he
or she had become known as a person who "seeks a compromise between
treatment quality and cost" (SzO1).

There is another key aspect of trust that directors pointed out. When
planning "large" innovations, directors often lacked the competence to
assess the impact of implementing such an innovation in a hospital. So they
often had to consult with their clinicians, from whom they expected information not only on how to implement such a project smoothly, but also on
whether to implement it at all. In addition, whether, by chance, the costs
and possible disruption to the hospital caused by implementation would outweigh the potential benefits. Directors were aware that people often oppose
change because change temporarily disrupts the routine of patient care. And
implementing a "major" innovation can be even more troublesome (Thakur
et al., 2012, p. 567). Therefore, the directors, in consideration of the criticism
from physicians about the new design, had to decide whether these comments were due to real weaknesses in the proposed design or whether they
were a manifestation of natural resistance to change. As they pointed out in
interviews, "the decision was often made based on trust in the head physician" (SzS2). The directors assessed "whether the doctors had been loyal to
the hospital in the past, and there was a high probability that they still were"
(SzS1), and whether they had so far "acted in accordance with the interests
of the hospital and have the necessary medical knowledge to evaluate a
project" (SzO/S1).

The above considerations lead to the conclusion that directors' trust in physicians has a significant impact on directors' decisions to initiate innovations, as it allows them to implement them with confidence, with the belief that physicians are competent and will not behave opportunistically, slowing down or even blocking new initiatives. If directors have trust in physicians, they will probably be more likely to accept and support innovations proposed and implemented by physicians, trusting that medics will behave loyally toward the hospital, and the implementation of innovations will consequently positively affect hospital performance. This approach is expressed in the form of the last research hypothesis in the model:

H14: Director's trust in physicians has a positive impact on hospital innovativeness.

Previous research also suggests that trust is important for the development of innovativeness in organizations (Shockley-Zalabak et al., 2000; Dovey, 2009; Shockley-Zalabak et al., 2010), and even that it is a key predictor of innovativeness (Spitzer, 2007, p. 228; Ellonen et al., 2008, p. 165; Dodgson et al., 2013, p. 209; Williams, 2011, p. 215). Studies among medical personnel testify that an atmosphere of trust encourages medics to propose new ideas and rally support to implement them (Afsar et al., 2018, p. 163).

5.9 Institutional Logics and Decoupling of Formal Structures from Day-to-Day Practices

Two more significant units of meaning were identified during the field research: institutional logics (cf. Ramsdal & Bjørkquist, 2019, p. 7; Reay & Hinings, 2009, p. 630) and the decoupling of formal structures from day-to-day practices (cf. Greenwood & Hinings, 1996; Meyer & Rowan, 1977, p. 341). These units were not extracted as separate second-order themes and directly incorporated into the model for two reasons. First, institutional logics and the decoupling of formal structures from actual practices are intertwined with the other themes that emerged in the research, so it is rather impossible to unambiguously isolate them. Second, the themes used to build the model are embedded in the organizational perspective, and institutional logics and the decoupling of formal structures from day-to-day practices are categories related to the institutional perspective. Thus, placing constructs from different research perspectives in one model raises legitimate questions. Accordingly, institutional logics and the decoupling of formal structures from actual practices provide additional ground for reference, interpretation, and deepening the understanding of management control in hospitals in this study. It seems that the lack of an institutional perspective in the hospitals' research is a significant reason for the inadequate understanding of the functioning of management control in these organizations.

The operation of two main institutional logics was identified in hospitals: the logic of medical professionals, represented by physicians, and the management logic, embodied by hospital directors. The research showed that in many situations management control is viewed from the perspective of institutional logics because:

> When you manage a hospital, you want to control the financial sphere or the quality sphere, but you have to keep in mind that doctors have a different perspective on many things. I, therefore, try to discuss a lot with doctors and, if possible, take their point of view into account.
>
> **(SzO/S2)**

This quote shows that hospital directors are aware of the difference in doctors' institutional logic and that this difference affects doctors' perception of reality. This means that there is a need to take a different approach to controlling the work of physicians than with other employees, especially non-medical ones. This is because physicians occupy a special position in the hospital compared to other employees, and this is due to a number of reasons, discussed in subsection 1.3.

Cost control was particularly challenging, as regardless of the actions of the directors,

> the decisions and actions of doctors at the bedside, but also in the various teams operating within the hospital, such as the teams for quality, hospital infections, antibiotic therapy, and at various meetings, were the main determinant of what services were provided to patients, and thus how money was spent. Although, in theory, I was largely responsible for the allocation of these funds in the hospital, if only by organizing tenders and approving invoices.
>
> **(SzO3)**

In view of the key role of physicians in generating costs, managers could not overlook medics in most initiatives related to this area. Some physicians even showed reluctance not only to adhere to set cost targets, but also to talk about the problem at all and seek solutions in this area. Some doctors repeated slogans like "we're for treating, not counting" (SzS2), or "ran off on a 'special mission' suggesting that they save lives, and I'm here about such mundane things, how much money went toward dressings or venflons" (SzO1), although "as time goes by, doctors get used to it and question less and less the need for, and in general the sense of, detailed cost control" (SzS2).

Directors admitted that they found it easier to talk "about increasing revenue, such as by controlling the length of hospitalization, than about reducing costs" (SzO1). This was due to differences in how physicians and directors perceived their role. This is because doctors "saw themselves as the main guarantor of treatment quality" (SzS/U) and "the patient's advocate for access to quality treatment" (SzO/S1), while directors had to care about "a positive financial result" (SzM1) and "balancing the hospital [costs with revenue]" (SzM1). Conflict between managers and professionals arose when "the medical director identified over-diagnosis, but also over-therapy" (SzO4). Directors were aware that "it is quite different to talk about the cost of unwarranted diagnostics without seeing the patient, and quite different to talk to a family who expects any action – not accepting the diagnosis that nothing more can be done" (SzS1). Therefore, in many situations, directors, together with physicians, sought other innovative solutions to preserve the quality of treatment and secure adequate revenues to cover its costs.

One area of seeking a balance between costs and revenues is the ability to control admissions of patients with "appropriate conditions" (SzS1). The decision to admit a patient to a ward is made by the ward's physicians, and, in doing so, they should take into account the patient's clinical condition, the waiting list and, if possible, also the impact of treating the patient in question on the financial situation of the ward. In fact, according to the directors' narratives, "doctors also take into account other factors related to, among other things, their individual preferences, skills, the degree of anticipated risk of complications, avoidance of 'difficult patients,' but also the goals set" (SzO3).

This greater "ease" of revenue talk was the result of doctors feeling that they were "guarantors of treatment quality" (SzS/U) and "patient advocates" (SzO/S1), but did not consider it their duty to reduce public spending on health. Thus, doctors readily accepted and initiated any innovative solutions when "it was clear that doctors would have a great deal of freedom to treat patients" (SzO/S1), and the only cost would be to sacrifice some of their autonomy to control the overruns of the contract with the NHF and structure of the services provided. The logic of medical professionals promoted autonomy on the one hand, but, on the other hand, an individualistic style of work, focused mostly on the problems of a particular specialty.

While an information system can provide more precise tools to control the profitability of procedures, costs and revenues generated not only by individual departments, but even by individual doctors, the final decision to perform a procedure or admit a patient still belongs to the clinician. However, managers and medical professionals use a different institutional logic, which leads to a discrepancy between the goals and interests of directors and physicians.

> After we introduced an advanced system of medical billing and quality monitoring, we began to control the costs, revenues and quality of work of individual doctors. We didn't punish anyone, we didn't say anything, we just started giving the head physicians lists of doctors in their departments, such rankings, which doctor is the most profitable, who has the most complications, the longest treatment period in each DRG group. In the beginning there were big differences [between doctors]. Then things started to even out, but the costs of the department were falling only slightly. We knew something was wrong. I took the head of the department for a manly conversation, and he tells me: "The most complex patients are usually treated by the most experienced doctors, and what, [...] then they, the best ones have the most complications. And the young [doctor], is what, the most profitable, because its the simple and uncomplicated cases he does? So, we, we assign the patients, if there's a complication, then we look at who hasn't had a complication recently, and then that one is the attending doctor. This system of measurement, [...] it's not possible, [...] medicine, everything by numbers." We stopped publishing these lists. Because what they were doing, [...] these assigning of patients to other doctors, it was kind of in a gray area. If there was a medical error, there would be a problem identifying [the attending doctor]. And also conflict with young doctors could arise. Now it's only when there's a big deviation, a cost, some problem, that the medical director talks.

(SzS2)

The above considerations support the idea that a hospital cannot be treated as a homogeneous organization, but as a collection of independent units (departments, clinics) centered around particular medical specialties. Medical professionals often opposed the directors, not because they behaved opportunistically and intended to pursue their own interests, but because they had a different perspective on certain issues, as they used a different institutional logic. This means that a hospital is a heterogeneous organization, and its management requires taking into account the impact of the institutional logics of the professionals working there. The heterogeneity described above further influenced the symptoms observed in hospitals of the separation of formal structures and narratives presented externally to maintain social legitimacy from actual practices, i.e., the internal work processes that ensured the hospitals' operational efficiency (cf. Greenwood & Hinings, 1996; Meyer & Rowan, 1977, p. 341).

Studies conducted show that one area where such "decoupling" occurred was in the combination of financing medical services based on payment fee-for-services mode and limiting the annual budget to a certain amount unless the medical service was immediately needed due to health or to save a life. This method of financing led hospitals to separate their practices related to qualifying patients for hospitalization from formal procedures related to reporting and billing of services to the National Health Service. A telling example is the statement of the director of SzO1: "Because, after all, formally, the excess of admitted patients was always due to excess patients to whom we could not refuse treatment."[12] The main motive for such behavior was competition among providers to obtain additional funds from the National Health Fund. This is because it happened that in the last months of the year or after the end of the year, additional funds appeared in the NHF to solve a designated medical problem (such as an increase in the number of arthroplasty). In such a situation, the hospital that "hit the jackpot with the overruns would win" (SzO4), i.e., receive more money in a given year and further increase the chance of an increased contract in the future, since the following year's budget was calculated most often based on the hospital's historical revenues from the National Health Fund. Playing this type of game between hospitals and the payer was possible because the need for urgent hospital admissions in many cases is ambiguous. Here, much depends on the individual decisions of doctors. The director of SzS1 presented this problem as follows:

> Emergency patients, such as those from an accident, should always be admitted. But urgent patients can already be managed. An

urgent patient is also subject to the waiting list and the timing of admission is determined by medical criteria, the stage of the disease and what the patient manifests today. [...] If there is space in the hospital and there is certainty or a high probability that the payer will pay – the patient can be admitted. Why not? But if there is certainty that the National Health Fund will not pay, then urgent patients must wait as well. [...] A patient can be pre-treated in the emergency room and it pays to give him some treatment, and not to admit him in the overruns – because you won't get that money back.

The decoupling of practical activities from the externally manifested mission of the public health service is due, among other things, to the pressure exerted by professionals and unions to increase salaries. Competition among health care providers for professional medical staff further intensifies this pressure, since a lack of sufficient medical professionals of a particular specialty can lead to the closure of a medical department and the loss of part of the contract with the NHF. For example, the director of the SzO4 hospital, in response to pressure from private providers, addressed the head physicians

with a clear recommendation to accept, if we have to put patients on waiting lists anyway, that we should rather shift the focus to procedures that are more profitable for us. I'll say this, I kind of have to start doing that because more and more for profit hospitals are being established which are doing exactly that. They are able – as they incur lower costs – to pay their medical staff more, which makes me less and less competitive, and I can't risk that specialists in whom we as a hospital have invested a lot will start leaving me. That's why I have this feeling that sometimes we are such suckers. Everyone can do business on medicine, and we are to follow the mission, right, we have to admit [patients]. And this is quite common. For example, I was talking to my head of the dialysis department and he said to me: "Madam director, but we are a public hospital department, we have to accept [all]. – But why are you admitting someone who was in a private dialysis department?' – Well, yes, but there is no doctor there. They don't have access to drugs there. They don't have access to the [operating] theatre to work on a fistula." As if we should bear the full responsibility. But when it comes to payment by the [National Health] Fund, both we

and that private dialysis department get the same price for hemo-
dialysis. Hence, I say "Enough!" We're going to steer this contract
a little bit, also choosing as much as we can, because of course
I won't take the risk and make such a decision, in the case even
when we've already exhausted the contract, not to accept a patient
from a private clinic in a life- or health-threatening condition.

To some extent, a similar example was presented by the director of an Irish
hospital: "In Ireland, many people have private insurance and, in principle,
can be treated in private facilities. But when private facilities do not have
space, for example in the emergency department, they refer patients to us,
to public hospitals, because we can't say no." (SzI).

The loss of specialists and the resulting closure of a department would
also have significant political repercussions at the local government level.
Often the retention of existing medical specialties and the development of
hospitals based on new scopes of services is an important element of local
government election campaigns. Directors signaled that the pressure from
constituent entities to maintain existing wards was significant in many cases,
despite the fact that it would be economically and practically advisable to
close a ward, particularly when a ward with the same specialty was located
in a hospital in a neighboring county.

The decoupling of external narrative and formal structures (e.g., financial plans, recovery plans) from day-to-day practices was also observed in
the area of directors' approach to the financial result at the end of the fiscal year. This consisted of public hospitals directors officially declaring that
they were making every possible effort to protect the hospital from a year-
end loss. In practice, on the other hand, they set the loss at a certain level
in advance, most often "a loss not exceeding depreciation write-offs" (SzO/
S2). This type of strategy allowed them, on the one hand, to accumulate
funds from a portion of depreciation and use them to contribute to ongoing projects with external funds (e.g., funds from the European Union or
the European Economic Area), and, on the other hand, to better finance
ongoing operations, including medical staff salaries. In addition, even those
hospitals that in the past had a situation in which they had overdue maturing liabilities received a "reward" in the form of additional funds for debt
relief (NIK, 2016, p. 72). A study of a group of 321 public hospitals in Poland
showed that between 2007 and 2018, the scale of Polish hospitals' liabilities
increased and affected as many as 80% of the surveyed units (Miszczyńska
& Antczak, 2020, p. 100), which could be related precisely to the deliberate

strategy of planning losses at the end of the fiscal year. As mentioned earlier, the provision in Polish law in effect for some time, obliging the owner of the public hospital to transform into a company or liquidate the hospital, actually gave some kind of permission to hospitals to have a negative financial result, setting its limits at a level not exceeding the amount of depreciation.

Unfortunately, previous studies on the financial situation of hospitals have completely ignored this key factor. The authors cited many reasons for the indebtedness of hospitals, such as the need to adapt to the changing local environment, regional disproportions between demand and supply for medical services, uneven allocation of funds to individual regions of the country compared to the concentration of facilities in a given region (Miszczyńska & Antczak, 2020, p. 99), insufficient public spending on health care, high specificity of the market for medical services leading to suboptimal allocation of benefits, the lack of reliable data on the health-care system, errors in the allocation of public funds, the monopolistic position of the payer (Szymańska, 2008), the takeover of profitable medical procedures by private entities and leaving not-for-profit entities with an ever-increasing portfolio of cost-intensive and undervalued procedures (Lenik, 2017, p. 43). Of course, all of the above-mentioned reasons for hospital indebtedness are important, but the field research reported here clearly indicates that some hospitals deliberately and consciously planned for a negative financial result. Similar behavior has been observed in earlier studies, such as that of a Norwegian hospital (Nyland & Pettersen, 2004, p. 77).

A decoupling has also been observed between formal billing rules for medical procedures and actual billing practices. Examples of such practices are when "patients are transferred between departments, when it turns out that a particular procedure can be billed more favorably in another department than in the original department – the one most related to his or her main condition" (SzO/S1), or the aforementioned transfer of patients from the dialysis department to internal medicine for more favorable billing of blood transfusion (SzO4). Another area where daily practice was decoupled from formal structures was the manipulation of patients' length of hospitalization.

> In rheumatology, we have a rule that either a patient stays one day and then he has a certain limited package of diagnostic tests and we don't pay for the hospitalization, or four days. Then he has a broader diagnostic and treatment package. Often the patient could stay for a shorter period of time, for example, two days, but then we would not recover the costs, what we have invested in the

patient. Because up to three days is half the amount of a four-day hospitalization.

(SzO/S2)

Decoupling of formal structures from daily practices did not occur only in Polish hospitals; such behavior was also identified in hospitals in other countries. However, in different countries this phenomenon affected different areas. It depended on the configuration of the environment in which the hospitals operated. A notable example was the British manager's approach to reducing the length of waiting lists and increasing physician productivity at the hospital, in a legal system where financial incentives tied to more services provided are prohibited. The hospital's official narrative was that when there was an urgent need to increase the number of scheduled procedures, additional operating time was arranged on weekends, for extra pay. In practice, however, so-called productivity agreements were made with doctors (SzGB, director of the surgery division). These agreements involved increasing the number of procedures on weekdays, with superbly remunerated weekend procedures. The director of a surgical division covering 320 beds in a British hospital described the mechanism as follows:

> This is some market negotiation. We have to enter into a so-called productivity contract for each treatment specialty. It is somehow not particularly formalized. This contract is negotiated collectively by teams of individual specialists. It does not directly address how many surgery procedures the team will perform each day, but by how much the waiting list for certain treatments will be reduced. Included in the overall settlement are the additional weekend sessions each team will receive. Such weekend sessions are very profitable. Of course, this contract has to be there, but what we do is show our team of clinicians all the information about the profitability of their services, costs, revenues, and operating room productivity. Most of the physicians have their own businesses, so they know very well what profits and losses are. We expect them to keep the hospital's finances in mind at all times as well.

> **(SzGB, director of the surgical division)**

Thus, legal restrictions on directly rewarding doctors for increased productivity have prompted managers and professionals to find another way to reward increased productivity. These actions, therefore, are an example of a certain workaround, the decoupling of formal procedures (legal prohibitions) from daily practices in hospitals. In this particular case, the workaround of directly rewarding surgeons for increased productivity by motivating them with lucrative weekend sessions. Officially, surgeons performed extra procedures in extra weekend sessions, as a safeguard against overly rushed procedures and reduced quality. But in practice, in exchange for significantly increased pay for weekend sessions, doctors agreed to perform more surgeries during the week as well. The basis for the "coming to terms" between managers and professionals and the control of contract performance was data from the hospital's information system.

The cited examples of the coexistence of the institutional logics of medical professionals and hospital managers show that hospitals cannot be considered as homogeneous organizations in which the main problems faced by management control are opportunism and the limited rationality of employees. Similarly, the examples presented of the decoupling of formal structures from daily practices highlight the complex and ambiguous response of hospitals to emerging problems. The presented field research report shows that the functioning of management control in hospitals is a complex issue, which is summarized holistically in Chapter 7, after discussing quantitative research based on structural equation modeling.

5.10 Conceptual Model of Management Control in Hospitals

The research consists of two main parts: exploratory and explanatory-predictive. The result of the exploratory research, which consists of thematic analysis of the material collected in the field research, is the identification of eight second-order themes: information system effectiveness, diagnostic use of information system, interactive use of information system, innovativeness, perceived environmental uncertainty, director's trust in physicians, rewarding employees and hospital performance as well as the determination of the relationships between these themes expressed in the form of 14 hypotheses, which together constitute a conceptual model of management control in hospitals (Figure 5.1).

As a result, the concept was adopted that the basis for the functioning of management control is an effective information system that can be used by hospital directors in an interactive and diagnostic manner. An effective

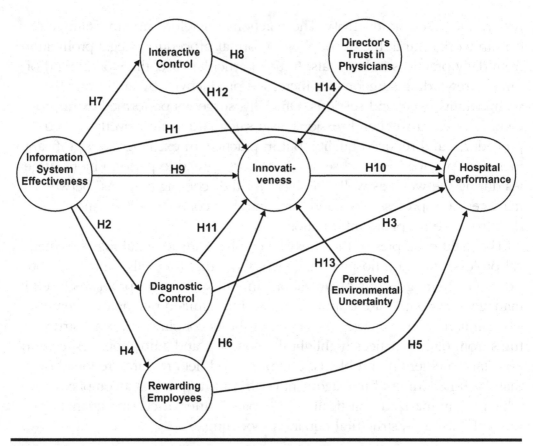

Figure 5.1: Conceptual model of management control in hospitals

IS can be used to reward employees based on the results they obtain. An important role in management control in hospitals is played by innovation, which depends on directors' trust in doctors and perception of the uncertainty of the environment. According to the analysis, all these elements have a positive impact on hospital performance.

The role of the proposed model is primarily seen in explaining and understanding the functioning of management control in hospitals. In addition, great emphasis is placed on prediction. The key to this is the discovery not of universal laws, but rather of mechanisms and structures that are often directly unobservable. The approach adopted in the work treats the model as a reflection of the fragment of reality of interest, with the omission of less important elements of that reality. In the process of building the model, the aim was to provide a simplified reflection of the reality under study, focusing on the most relevant elements and relationships, rather than reflecting the full complexity of management control in hospitals. Such models can play an important role in the development of theory of a general nature, more useful for practice.

The overarching goal of the second stage of the research is to confront the theoretical concept of management control in hospitals developed in the first stage on the basis of qualitative research with the perception of management control in the general population of hospitals. Structural models were used for explanatory-predictive research, facilitating analysis of the research hypotheses with high complexity of nomological networks. Path models consist of two components: the structural model (also called the internal model in the context of SEM), which in this research represents eight second-order themes, which will be treated as latent variables (constructs) with the following names: Information System Effectiveness or IS Effectiveness (ISE), Diagnostic Use of IS (Diagnostic Control – DC) and Interactive Use of IS (Interactive control – IC), Innovativeness (I), Perceived environmental uncertainty or Uncertainty (PEU), Directors' Trust in Doctors (Trust – T), Rewarding employees or Reward (R) and Hospital performance (HP). The second component of pathway models are measurement models (also called external models in SEM), which represent the relationship between constructs and indicator variables, also called indicators. In this model, the variables IS effectiveness, trust, and uncertainty are independent variables, or exogenous variables, in other words, explanatory variables. In contrast, the hospital performance variable is the dependent variable in this model, or endogenous variable (Figure 5.1).

The latent variables presented above and the relationships between them (paths), formulated in the form of research hypotheses, form a structural model of management control in hospitals (Figure 5.1), the analysis of which is presented in the next chapter. Estimation of the adopted conceptual model will enable its final formation based on quantitative research, which is based on a larger research sample than the qualitative research reported in this chapter.

Notes

1. In square brackets there are fragments of text added by the author, enabling better understanding of the interviewees' statements.
2. Hospitals in Poland sign an agreement with the NHF for a majority of their revenue, for the provision of a specified number of services for a specified amount of money (lump sum). Exceeding the number of contracted services means that the payment for consecutive services performed above the limit

is lower and lower (degressive rate). On the other hand, failure to provide the contracted number of services means that the contract with the NHF will be reduced in the following year.

3. Hospitals in Poland, to conduct investments, such as the purchase of medical equipment and construction of infrastructure, largely used EU funds, which usually covered the costs of such an investment at a rate of 85%. The remaining amount of the investment had to be donated by the hospital from its own resources.

4. This accreditation is similar to some extent to the Joint Commission on Accreditation of Healthcare Organizations (JCAHO).

5. The Act on Patient Rights and the Patient Rights Ombudsman.

6. Before the introduction of lump sum financing, this statement applied to situations where a particular medical procedure, usually an elective one, was not routinely considered life saving. In this case, it was necessary to prove in court that the patient had had to be treated at a given moment due to a threat to his or her health or life, and could not be put to a waiting list.

7. The Medical Technology Assessment Agency periodically changes its recommendations regarding the valuation of individual medical procedures. However, due to the relatively long period between individual revaluations, as well as local conditions in individual hospitals, some procedures may be profitable in a given period and others may not be.

8. Fragment of Polish idiom meaning pay regardless of effort.

9. Employees' salaries are increasingly regulated by legal acts, which have been continuously amended for many years.

10. This means that external company installed the CT scanner in hospital building. This is some type of outsourcing.

11. In Poland, there are two types of emergency departments (ED). The bigger ones with more staff and equipment called "hospital emergency ward" and smaller ones called "emergency room" or "admission room." There is a different level of financing of these facilities, but the criteria for patient admissions are blurred and rather depends on the number of patients a facility could admit than the patient's condition.

12. In Poland, hospitals treat both elective and acute patients within the annual budget negotiated with the NHF. If the budget is insufficient, the hospital should treat a fewer number of elective patients.

Chapter 6

Structural Modeling of Management Control in Hospitals

6.1 Operationalization of Variables

In order to analyze the conceptual model of management control developed in the qualitative research (Figure 5.1), the unobservable constructs identified in the qualitative research were linked to appropriately selected observable variables (indicators) based on the operationalization procedure presented in this section. The operationalization of the information system effectiveness (ISE) variable, on the one hand, is very important, since the information system is a central element of the management control model. On the other hand, it is problematic, as information systems researchers have been searching for an optimal model for measuring this construct for more than half a century, and so far have not agreed on a common position. It can even be said that the number of ISE measurement models matches the number of studies in this area (Floropoulos et al., 2010, p. 48). In addition, there is also the problem of defining the proper domain of the ISE measurement model, since it is very difficult to draw a clear line between models for measuring the information system, understood in the broader context of information provision, and measures relating to the evaluation of information technology as a component of the information system. In this work, the information system is understood in this broader context, in which information technology is only one component of the ISE, albeit a crucial

DOI: 10.4324/9781003366553-6

one. The operationalization of the ISE variable must be carried out from the perspective of the contribution that IS makes to the management control of hospitals. In this context, an approach oriented toward measuring the effectiveness (success) of the information system is adequate.

An analysis of the existing literature on measuring information system effectiveness (Ives et al., 1983; Chenhall & Morris, 1986, p. 17; Davila, 2000, pp. 395–396; Pizzini, 2006, pp. 183–184; Hammad et al., 2010, p. 766; Hammad et al., 2013, p. 319; Davis, 1989; Goodhue, 1998, p. 108; DeLone & McLean, 1992, p. 87; DeLone & McLean, 2016; Kludacz-Alessandri et al., 2019; Raulinajtys-Grzybek et al., 2019; Professional Accountants in Business Committee, 2013) did not identify a single model that adequately coincided with the results of the field research. Therefore, the variable of information system effectiveness (ISE) was operationalized by matching selected elements of the measurement models identified in the literature (Davila, 2000, p. 397; Chenhall & Morris, 1986, p. 17; Hammad et al., 2010, p. 766; Hammad et al., 2013, p. 319; Nguyen, 2018, p. 42; Ghasemi et al., 2019, p. 195; Pizzini, 2006, pp. 183–184) with the results of the field research (Table 6.1).

The scientific literature indicates that chief executives use information effectively to make decisions, but their role of disseminating and transmitting the information they have already filtered down the organizational structure is seen as ineffective (Laitinen, 2009, p. 564). Therefore, in the tool examining the effectiveness of IS, as many as three questions adopted the assessment of the frequency of transmission of reports to lower levels of the hierarchical organizational structure of the hospital (Table 6.1, items IS2, IS3 and IS5). This design is dictated by the assumption that lower-level managers, like chief executives, effectively use information to make decisions and implement innovative changes, but based on source information from the IS, rather than on information indirectly provided by the general director.

On the other hand, the performance indicator (Table 6.1, item IS4) was not related to the frequency of reporting, but only to the level of monitoring. The abandonment of questions on reporting frequency was influenced by two facts. First, qualitative studies showed that performance at the level of individual procedures, DRG, or individual physicians is rarely considered on a regular basis. Analyzing this indicator intensifies at different times depending on billing deadlines indicated by the National Health Fund or internal, rather exceptional, events at hospitals. Second, the question about the frequency of reporting would have to address each of the aforementioned scopes separately, which would mean that multiple questions would have to be introduced into the survey. This question, therefore, relates more

Table 6.1. **Operationalization of the information system effectiveness variable**

Indicator symbol	Indicator name	Indicator	Status	Source
SI1	Revenue and cost analysis	Please determine what the hospital's ability is to analyze revenues and costs at the levels indicated below: (IS11) entire hospital, (IS12) department, organizational unit, (IS13) individual physician, (IS14) individual patient?		(Chenhall & Morris, 1986, p. 19; Davila, 2000, pp. 395–396; Ghasemi et al., 2019, p. 195; Pizzini, 2006, p. 204)
SI2	Cost and revenue reporting	Please specify how often financial information (on costs and/or revenues) is reported to each of the following groups: (IS21) top management, (2) department and ward managers, (3) physicians, (4) lead nurses, (5) other employees?		(Davila, 2000, pp. 395–396; Ghasemi et al., 2019, p. 195; Nguyen, 2018, p. 41); (Pizzini, 2006, p. 205)
SI3	Quality	Please specify how often information on quality indicators is reported to each of the following groups: (1) top management, (2) department and ward managers, (3) physicians, (4) lead nurses, (5) other employees?		(Chenhall & Morris, 1986, p. 19; Ghasemi et al., 2019, p. 195; Nguyen, 2018, p. 41; Pizzini, 2006, p. 206)
IS4	Performance of services	Please indicate to what extent the performance of the planned number of services is monitored at the following levels: (1) hospital as a whole, (2) department/organizational unit, (3) individual physician, (4) individual procedures (DRG) and/or person–days?		(Chenhall & Morris, 1986, p. 19; Bloom & Van Reenen, 2007, p. 1393; Bloom & Van Reenen, 2010, p. 206)

(Continued)

Table 6.1 (Continued) Operationalization of the information system effectiveness variable

Indicator symbol	Indicator name	Indicator	Status	Source
IS5	Performance of the contract with the NHF	Please specify how often information on the progress of performance of the contract with the National Health Fund is reported to the following users: (1) top management, (2) department and ward managers, (3) physicians, (4) lead nurses, (5) other employees?		(Davila, 2000, pp. 395–396; Bloom & Van Reenen, 2007, p. 1393; Bloom & Van Reenen, 2010, p. 206)
IS6	Financial performance forecasts	Please indicate to what extent projections of the financial result are made (e.g., according to the bed utilization rate, average length of stay of patients, number and type of procedures performed, billing in the relevant DRG) at each level: (1) the entire hospital, (2) department/ organizational unit?		(Chenhall & Morris, 1986, p. 19; Hammad et al., 2013, p. 320; Ghasemi et al., 2019, p. 195; Raulinajtys-Grzybek et al., 2019, p. 137)
IS8	Cost classification	Please specify to what extent the information system enables differentiation and analysis of fixed and variable costs.	Dropped	(Pizzini, 2006, p. 205)
IS-Global	A single-indicator global component for verifying the convergent validity of a formative measurement model in redundancy analysis	Please specify to what extent the hospital's reported information on financial and quality indicators supports the effective achievement of planned results.		Indicator developed by the author based on (Hair i in., 2016, s. 140)

Note: During the survey, hospital directors referred to individual indicators using a seven-element scale, except that the elements of this scale differed for each indicator. For example, for indicator IS1: 1 meant "it is not possible to analyze at this level," 4 – "such analysis can be performed, upon request," 7 – "such analysis is routinely performed and presented." For indicators IS2, IS3, and IS5: 1 meant "Not reported," 2 – "once a year," 3 – "once every six months," 4 – "once a quarter," 5 – "once a month," 6 – "once a week," 7 – "daily."

to diagnosing whether the hospital monitors the performance of services on each scope at all, or whether it stoops to financial indicators, without getting into what services comprise revenues and costs. Another issue often raised by directors during the qualitative survey was the level of execution of the contract with the National Health Fund. This is in fact an important issue, since incomplete execution of the contract undoubtedly reduces the profitability of the hospital. This is due to the fact that most of the hospital's costs are fixed costs. The hospital's profitability also decreases in the case of excessive overruns, when they are not reimbursed by the NHF. Hence, a question about monitoring the performance of the contract with the National Health Fund was included in the survey tool (Table 6.1, item IS5).

The first stage of the survey of selected hospitals shows that hospitals do not have a standardized system for monitoring and reporting quality indicators. Virtually every hospital surveyed gave importance to different quality indicators. Of course, the vast majority of hospitals study patient satisfaction/experience and adverse events (especially when accredited), but this does not mean that information on these metrics is always used in management control. Since the field research failed to identify a common set of quality indicators that are relevant to management control in hospitals, a general approach was taken to the issue of quality. That is, only the question about the frequency of reporting on quality indicators (Table 6.1, item IS3) was included in the survey tool, assuming that each director decides on their own which quality indicators are important to their hospital. The question only on frequency of reporting was used for quality and performance of the contract with the National Health Fund. In practice, the frequency-only question also allows an assessment of whether such reports are performed and distributed at all. When reports were not performed, the respondent had the option to select the first item – "are not reported." On the other hand, selecting each subsequent item indicated that reports are performed and distributed to the various organizational levels at a certain frequency.

An element that often appeared in the statements of directors and in the scientific literature was the forecasting of the financial result (Table 6.1, item IS6). Although many hospitals plan for a loss as early as the beginning of the fiscal year, planning, simulating, and predicting such an important element as the financial result for the entire hospital and individual departments was considered essential. While planning the result for the entire hospital at the beginning of the year is required by law, it is not required for individual departments. The field research noted that some directors avoid planning the result of individual departments. This is related to the problem of adequate valuation of individual services by the National Health Fund and allocating overhead costs to individual departments and divisions. On the one hand, conflicts can arise in this area between the director and heads of departments and wards, while, on the other hand, analysis at this level enables better control of hospital finances. In addition, as the scientific literature indicates, the ability to simulate and plan the outcome indicates greater development of the information system. For example, in the 12-stage maturity model of cost accounting, planning is ranked among the four highest levels (Raulinajtys-Grzybek et al., 2019, p. 137).

A number of areas of IS effectiveness evaluation covered by other authors were not included in the measurement tool, mainly because qualitative studies have not shown them to be relevant to assessing IS effectiveness. Among other things, deviance analysis as a component of IS was not openly included. As mentioned earlier, it was implicitly assumed that reporting on indicators in a variety of settings would lead to their analysis. Qualitative research has shown that directors rarely plan execution and costs in greater detail than business units, but, rather, they look at the big picture to see if there are excessive cost increases and decreases in profitability during the year. While older studies, conducted in the days of the "reign" of budgets, indicated the usefulness of deviation analysis (Khandwalla, 1972, p. 277; Simons, 1987b, p. 368), more recent studies, especially those conducted in hospitals, have shown that deviation data are not particularly useful in management decision making (Pizzini, 2006, p. 186). The interdependence between deviations can cause measurement errors, as deviation analysis does not provide information on the causes of cost overruns, and deviations provide an incentive for short-term cost reductions rather than continuous improvement (Mak & Roush, 1996).

The next step toward optimal operationalization is to decide what type of variable IS effectiveness is – formative or reflective. In earlier studies, the variable expressing the effectiveness of the ISE was treated as a formative and multi-dimensional construct (Au et al., 2008, p. 53; Davila, 2000, p. 397; Ghasemi et al., 2019, p. 195; Hammad et al., 2013, p. 323; Nguyen, 2018, p. 41; Prajogo et al., 2018, p. 100). In the present study, the ISE variable was developed as an objective assessment of certain features of the information system (Table 6.1). On the one hand, the various features of IS effectiveness are independent of each other, which means that no correlation between these features can be assumed, and, on the other hand, the direction of dependence tends to be from the indicators toward the variable. For example, it can be assumed that increasing the frequency of reporting or expanding the scope of information reported to particular groups of employees can increase the effectiveness of IS. Conversely, decreasing the frequency or reducing the scope of information may decrease the effectiveness of IS. This means that the value of indicators determines the variable, as is the case with formative variables, and not the opposite, as is the case with reflective variables (Henseler, Ringle, et al., 2016, p. 408). Thus, it should be concluded that the optimal measurement model for the IS effectiveness variable is the formative model.

In formative measurement models, it is good practice to verify the relevance of the content covered by the construct. This step requires confirmation that the formative indicators include at least the main aspects of the latent variable. To verify the convergent validity of a formative measurement model, some authors suggest redundancy analysis, which involves correlating a formatively measured construct with a reflective measure of the same construct (Cheah et al., 2018, p. 3193; Hair et al., 2016, p. 140). Comparing a formative construct with a reflective construct is the most reliable solution. But a comparison with a single global indicator is also acceptable (Cheah et al., 2018, p. 3202). Since it was not possible to find a suitable reflective measure in the literature, it was decided to introduce a single global indicator into the research tool (Table 6.1, item IS-Global), which allowed us to build a model consisting of the formative variable as an exogenous latent variable predicting an endogenous latent variable operationalized by a single global indicator.

J.F. Hair, G.T.M. Hult, C. Ringle, and M. Sarstedt suggest using scales in the literature or expert opinions to formulate an appropriate global indicator (2016, p. 138). No appropriate global indicator has been found in the literature that can capture the main aspects of the construct. On the other hand, soliciting expert opinions in this case would be very difficult, as it would require familiarizing them with the extensive results of exploratory studies. Moreover, previous studies have shown that experts often fail to identify the best single global indicators (Sarstedt, Diamantopoulos, et al., 2016, p. 3165). In contrast, research by L. Bergkvist and J.R. Rossiter has proved that self-developed indicators are as predictively accurate as traditional reflective multi-indicator measures (2009, p. 618). Taking into account the above results of previous studies, the outcomes of responses to the following question were taken as a global indicator of ISE: Please specify to what extent the hospital's reported information on financial and quality indicators supports the effective achievement of planned results.

Originally, the IS effectiveness measurement tool was constructed based on seven global questions (Table 6.1). After conducting the previously

described preliminary revision of the survey questionnaire, the research ultimately used a tool consisting of six global questions covering 25 indicators.
During the initial verification process, indicators related to cost classification
were removed. In both cases, the reason for removing the indicator was the
high level of missing data during the pilot study, ranging from 30% to 60%.
It was felt that directors were unable to answer these questions due to a lack
of appropriate practices at the hospital.

In total, the ISE measurement tool consists of 25 indicators in six groups.
This is a large number if one considers the fact that these indicators describe
only one variable in a complex structural model. So, a solution must be
applied that makes it possible, on the one hand, to maximize the theoretical significance of the variable, but, on the other hand, to reduce the
number of indicators. Taking into account the fact that each group of indicators described in each row of Table 6.1 defines a different element of IS
effectiveness, and is not a manifestation, an effect of IS effectiveness, it can
be assumed that it forms a formative variable describing a single feature of
IS effectiveness, whereas, all observable variables create the IS effectiveness construct. This construction of a variable measurement model can be
handled in two ways. Either a higher-order measurement model could be
built, also known as a hierarchical component model (HCM) (Figure 6.1)
(Hair et al., 2016, p. 43; Hair et al., 2018, p. 38), or the scores for each group
of indicators could be summed up, describing each IS effectiveness element
(McNeish & Wolf, 2020; van der Ark, 2005).

The first approach, although methodologically more correct, was rejected
for five reasons. First, given the rule of thumb that the minimum sample
size in a PLS-SEM analysis should be at least 10 times the largest number of
formative indicators used to measure one of the variables (Hair et al., 2016,
p. 23), the developed model should be analyzed using a data set of at least
250 cases, which far exceeds the number of surveys collected in this study.
The number of 25 indicators is due to the fact that all indicators assigned
to lower-order constructs (LOCs) must be assigned to the higher-order constructs (HOCs) of the measurement model (Figure 6.1) (Hair et al., 2018, p.
48). Second, it is believed that in hierarchical models, the number of indicators at each lower-order construct (LOC) should be equal (Hair et al., 2018,
p. 54). In this case, there are LOC variables consisting of five, four, or even
two indicators (quality). Third, there is a high probability of high correlation
of answers to questions like "Please determine whether there is a hospital's
ability to analyze revenues and costs at the levels indicated below: (1) entire
hospital"; "Please specify how often financial information (on costs and/or

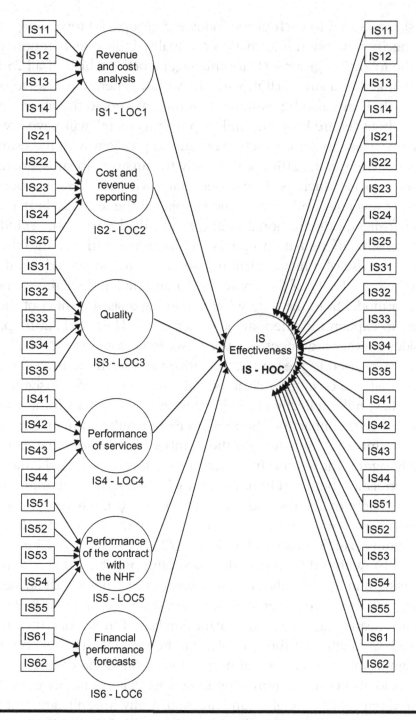

Figure 6.1.   Hierarchical measurement model of the information system effectiveness variable

revenues) is reported to each of the following groups: (1) top management?";
"Please specify how often information on quality indicators is reported to
each of the following groups: (1) top management?" – which, if all 25 indicators were linked to a single HOC variable, would generate excessive collinearity. Fourth, it can also be assumed that the answers to the above-quoted
questions about "entire hospital" and "top management" will have a very
low variance, close to zero, which may cause a problem with the estimation
of the model (Hair et al., 2016, p. 94). Only the answers to subsequent questions in each group, such as "Please determine whether there is a possibility
of analyzing revenues and costs at the hospital at the levels indicated below:
.... (2) department, organizational unit, (3) individual physician, (4) individual
patient?", mostly differentiate hospitals and introduce variance into the variable. Fifth, the use of a hierarchical measurement model would significantly
increase the complexity of the entire model and thus reduce the chances of
obtaining a model fit to the data without making a significant contribution to
the ability to explain the phenomena under study (Hair et al., 2018, p. 42).

Consider another argument in favor of six indicators instead of 25. With
more indicators used to measure a formative variable, there is an increased
likelihood that one or more indicators will have low or even insignificant
outer weight. Unlike reflective measurement models, in which the number of
indicators has little impact on the measurement results, formative measurement has an inherent limitation on the number of indicators that can retain
statistically significant weight. In formative measurement models, there may
be little correlation between indicators, in which case the maximum possible outer weight of a single indicator may be $1 / \sqrt{n}$, where n is the number of indicators. For example, with 2 (or 5 or 10) uncorrelated indicators,
the maximum possible outer weight is $1 / \sqrt{2} = 0.707$ (or $1 / \sqrt{5} = 0.447$ or
$1\sqrt{10} = 0.316$). With a decrease in the maximum possible outer weight with
an increasing number of indicators, it becomes more likely that subsequent
indicators will also have lower statistical significance (Cenfetelli & Bassellier,
2009). This means that with a significant number of indicators, they may not
only have low weights for the variable, but the weights may also be statistically insignificant for a substantial proportion of these indicators.

One could also consider removing indicators that are highly correlated,
have low variance, low weights, and are statistically insignificant, but it
seems that a better solution can be found than such far-reaching interference
with the measurement tool. The second method of dealing with the measurement model outlined above, which eliminates potentially high collinearity between indicators and reduces the number of indicators, is to sum up or

calculate the average of each group of indicators, so that the sum or average value of the indicators forms a single indicator of a higher-order variable – the HOC (Hair et al., 2016, p. 143). In the literature, such "summation" of indicators (sum scores) is relatively rarely used, because part of the scientific community believes that they reduce the quality of the results obtained with their help (Hair et al., 2016, p. 52). One has to agree with this view when using scales developed and validated without summing, and then used with summing of indicators and interpreted similarly to the original scale. Although here, too, research indicates that in certain situations the sum scoring can be safely used (McNeish & Wolf, 2020, p. 12; van der Ark, 2005, p. 300). The situation is different when the measurement tool is created from scratch, as in this case, and the information about the summation of indicators is then included in the inference process. The effect of summing indicators (responses from several items in the survey questionnaire) is to reduce the number of indicators representing the latent variable or, as in the case of this research, to reduce a second-order (two-layer) hierarchical variable to a "simple" latent variable with a single layer of abstraction (Hair et al., 2018, pp. 37–86).

The main difference between the use of individual indicators and the use of sum scores of indicators is that instead of explicitly estimating the weights of the relationship between the latent variable and its indicators, the result is equivalent to using the average value of the weights for the sums of the individual groups of indicators that define the latent variable. This means that summed indicators can be considered a special case in which all the weights of the summed indicators in the measurement model are equal (McNeish & Wolf, 2020, p. 3). As such, sum scores represent a simplification of PLS-SEM. In this context, the researcher does not find out which indicator has greater or lesser relative importance in the variable construct.

In the case of measuring the ISE variable (HOC variable) in this research, the lack of distinction between the impact of individual indicators of LOC variables is a welcome phenomenon. In hierarchical measurement models, the impact of the LOC variable on the HOC variable depends not only on the value of the indicators, but, as mentioned earlier, also on the number of indicators of the LOC variable (Hair et al., 2018, p. 50). This means that in a hierarchical measurement model, LOC variables that had more indicators would have a greater impact on the ISE variable. This would be an undesirable phenomenon, because, in reality, the number of indicators assigned to each component of the ISE variable does not depend on the predicted weight of the component, but only on the ability to measure it. For example, the two-indicator variable "Financial performance forecasts" would have the lowest impact on the variable simply because the qualitative research failed to identify more elements that would allow more accurate measurement of this area of the ISE. Therefore, in the described measurement model, it seems optimal to use average values of indicators describing the individual component areas of the ISE variable. This will ensure that the impact of individual areas does not depend on the number of indicators, but only on their average values.

Another argument supporting the sum scoring of indicators is that in this study the aggregation of indicators involved very detailed data and the resulting aggregated indicators (sum scores) sufficiently accurately describe the ISE. By using sum scoring, the results of the analysis will, on the one hand, be more comprehensible and, on the other hand, sufficiently detailed. The author's intention was not to study whether, for example, more frequent reporting of cost and revenue information specifically to lead nurses affected ISE more strongly than, for example, more frequent reporting of the performance of the contract with the NHF to physicians. While perhaps such considerations would be interesting, at this stage in the development of the theory of management control in hospitals and the design of this study, such detailed inquiries would be too far-reaching and subject to too much error. In an extreme case, one could also add up all 25 indicators of the ISE variable, resulting in a single global indicator; however, such a solution seems too far-fetched.

The logic behind using multiple elements, as opposed to single elements, to measure a construct is that a multi-element measure is more accurate. The expected better accuracy is based on the assumption that using multiple indicators to measure a single concept is more likely to represent all the different aspects of that concept (Hair et al., 2016, p. 106). Structural equation modeling often cites three indicators as the minimum number that facilitates good measurement, so six seems to be the optimal number of indicators for the SSI variable.

An analysis of the extant literature shows that an issue that remains unsolved in the scientific world is the problem of evaluating the performance of hospitals (Abernethy & Brownell, 1999, p. 202; Baird et al., 2017, p. 210; Grigoroudis et al., 2012, p. 109; de Harlez & Malagueño, 2016, p. 9; Eldenburg & Krishnan, 2007, p. 863; Kim et al., 2019, p. 139; Wang et al., 2018, p. 5). This is due to the fact that outcome indicators in health care are difficult to define. Instead, exploratory research has identified five areas that hospital executives believe are important in assessing hospital performance:

financial performance, quality of services, hospital reputation, ability to attract key employees, and ability to acquire financial resources.

The literature observes different approaches to assessing the financial performance of hospitals. Some researchers use objective indicators to measure the financial condition of hospitals, such as return on investment (Wang et al., 2018, p. 5), net profit margin, ratio of operating expenses to operating income (Grigoroudis et al., 2012, p. 109), profit before interest, tax, depreciation, and amortization in relation to total operating income (Po et al., 2019, p. 368). However, many researchers argue that actual financial ratios, especially profit, are not the primary focus of hospitals (Austen, 2010, p. 104; Hass-Symotiuk, 2011b, p. 67; Hensel, 2008, pp. 11–52), and, therefore, they are not an adequate measure of hospital performance either. Some authors even warn against the use of financial indicators, especially profit, as an indicator for measuring the performance of organizations of higher public interest (Kożuch & Kożuch, 2008, p. 34; Schwierz, 2016, p. 35).

Difficulties in objectively measuring the financial performance of hospitals, identified in the field research, are also due to the different ways hospital executives understand "good" financial performance. This is because comparing hospitals among themselves on the basis of, for example, the percentage ratio of profit to revenue says nothing about the effectiveness of achieving goals, since hospitals have different goals for their financial performance. The situation is similarly complex when evaluating the quality of services provided by hospitals. Here, too, the possibility of using objective indicators has not been found.

Thus, if one takes into account the difficulty of objectively assessing the financial situation and quality of services provided by hospitals, and the subjective nature of the other three performance measures (i.e., hospital reputation, ability to attract key personnel, and ability to acquire financial resources), the only possible solution is self-assessment of individual performance measures by hospital directors. A. Austen suggests that directors' subjective satisfaction with performance – both qualitative and financial – is a reliable method of evaluation for public health-care facilities (2010, p. 118). It should be noted that self-assessment of hospital performance, compared to similar facilities, by top management has been successfully used for decades (Abernethy & Stoelwinder, 1991, p. 110; Abernethy & Brownell, 1999, p. 202; Baird et al., 2017, p. 210; de Harlez & Malagueño, 2016, p. 9; Kim et al., 2019, p. 139). This method has even been used by some academics to study such quantifiable indicators as the efficiency of the patient admission/discharge process, average waiting time in the hospital emergency department, waiting time for surgery, and management of patient length of stay and management of patient complaints (Baird et al., 2017, p. 211). In addition, studies have proven the correspondence between the actual performance of organizations and the perception of the top management of these organizations (Dess & Robinson, 1984; Venkatraman & Ramanujam, 1987).

The use of subjective indicators based on self-assessment is also supported by past research practice. A review of 116 management accounting articles showed that in as many as 46 cases, organizational performance was measured using self-assessment, while only nine articles included objective performance measures (Van der Stede et al., 2005, p. 675). Admittedly, the magnitude of the average correlation between subjective (self-assessment) and objective performance measures is not substantial (0.39); however, significant arguments can be made in favor of using subjective measures of organizational performance (Van der Stede et al., 2005, p. 675). W.A. Van der Stede, S.M. Young, and C.X. Chen suggest that objective measures can also be a problem. This is because metrics such as profit or return on investment/capital are often chosen for their availability rather than their relevance. Thus, in many situations, subjective performance measures may provide a "better" kind of information, because they are based on those aspects of performance that are most relevant to the respondents, and therefore most likely to shape their behavior and guide their actions. Moreover, it is important to remember that both outcome measures contain some error (2005, p. 675). In light of the above statements, one should agree with the arguments of M.A. Abernethy and P. Brownell (1999, p. 197) that the performance of individual hospitals can be treated only as a relative measure, not an absolute one. This overcomes some of the measurement difficulties associated with a survey sample consisting of a very diverse set of hospitals. For example, teaching hospitals may have greater ability to attract staff and financial resources, but they may also have better reputations. Hospital executives' comparison of their facilities with similar units, providing a similar range of services and of similar size, indirectly controls for the impact of such factors on evaluation. Given the above considerations, a five-element scale (HP1-HP5) was adopted to measure the hospital performance variable (Table 6.2).

The multi-dimensional nature of the hospital performance measurement tool requires the direction of causality between indicators and the performance variable to be determined. In some of the studies on hospitals, the performance variable was treated as a reflective variable (Abernethy

Table 6.2. Operationalization of the hospital performance variable

Indicator symbol	Indicator	Source
HP1	Financial situation	(Abernethy & Brownell, 1999, p. 202; de Harlez & Malagueño, 2016, p. 9)
HP2	Ability to attract doctors, nurses, and other key personnel	(Abernethy & Brownell, 1999, p. 202; Abernethy & Stoelwinder, 1991, p. 110; de Harlez & Malagueño, 2016, p. 9)
HP3	Reputation of the hospital	(Abernethy & Brownell, 1999, p. 202; de Harlez & Malagueño, 2016, p. 9)
HP4	Quality of services provided	(Abernethy & Brownell, 1999, p. 202; Abernethy & Stoelwinder, 1991, p. 110; Baird et al., 2017, p. 211)
HP5	Ability to acquire financial resources	(Abernethy & Brownell, 1999, p. 202; Abernethy & Stoelwinder, 1991, p. 110)
HP-Global	General operation of the hospital	(Gong & Ferreira, 2014, p. 522; Schaefer & Guenther, 2016, p. 225; Widener, 2007, p. 773)

Note: Hospital directors referred to individual indicators using a seven-item scale, where 1 meant "well below average" and 7 meant "well above average."

& Brownell, 1999, p. 197; Baird et al., 2017, p. 211). Indeed, it is conceivable that good hospital performance manifests itself in high quality of services, ability to attract staff, and financial resources as well as good reputation and financial performance, which would indicate a reflective measurement model. On the other hand, however, it is difficult to make the theoretical assumption that all indicators are correlated. In particular, a certain dichotomy between service quality and financial position emerged in the exploratory research. Some executives claimed that providing quality services requires them to incur more costs, and thus negatively affects the bottom line. The above claim is supported by the results obtained in the "Portraits of Hospitals – Maps of Opportunity" project, in which some hospitals scored high in the area of quality of services and very low in the financial dimension. When considering the other indicators of the hospital performance variable, it should be noted that other competencies and qualities are needed to "attract staff" and others to "gain financial resources." This approach precludes the possibility of assuming a common cause creating the values of these indicators, i.e., a reflective measurement model. It, therefore, seems logical to make the alternative assumption that the results obtained in the various areas defined in indicators W1-W5 create "good" hospital performance rather than reflect it.

Also, many previous studies refer to summed indexes describing performance (Abernethy & Stoelwinder, 1991, p. 110; de Harlez & Malagueño, 2016; Kim et al., 2019, p. 130) or, in general, individual performance dimensions are treated as separate variables (Po et al., 2019, p. 372). If the above analysis is taken into account, it seems that the arguments for adopting a formative measurement model prevail. As mentioned earlier, for formative measurement models, the evaluation of convergent validity requires additional empirical evaluation through redundancy analysis (Cheah et al., 2018, p. 3193; Hair et al., 2016, p. 140), and for this purpose an additional indicator (W-Global) was added to the index, referring to the global assessment of hospital performance. This type of index has already been used in previous studies of organizational performance (Gong & Ferreira, 2014, p. 522; Schaefer & Guenther, 2016, p. 225; Widener, 2007, p. 773), and the use of a single index in redundancy analysis is widely justified in the literature (Cheah et al., 2018, p. 3193; Hair et al., 2016, p. 140).

The variable diagnostic use of IS, in other words, diagnostic control (DC), due to its fundamental nature in the control function, has been operationalized numerous times in earlier studies (Henri, 2006a, p. 551; Marginson et al., 2010, p. 368, 2014, p. 73; Widener, 2007, p. 785), including studies of hospitals (Abernethy & Brownell, 1999, p. 202; de Harlez & Malagueño, 2016, p. 10; Yu et al., 2018, p. 26), so five indicators were selected from those mentioned in earlier studies that best corresponded to the results of the field research. However, during the verification studies described earlier, two indicators did not qualify for further analysis (Table 6.3).

A theoretical analysis of the three indicators shown in Table 6.3 which qualified for further study leads to the conclusion that they are manifestations of directors' attitudes toward the use of information systems. In other words, directors' responses reflect the state of the latent (unobserved) construct, so changes in attitudes toward how IS is used cause changes in directors' responses. In addition, analyzing these questions, it can be assumed that they will be significantly correlated with each other, so given the experience of previous authors (de Harlez & Malagueño, 2016; Henri, 2006a, p. 551; Marginson et al., 2010, p. 368, 2014, p. 73; Widener, 2007, p. 785; Yu et al., 2018, p. 26), the assumption was made about the reflective nature of the diagnostic control variable.

No studies using scales on rewarding key medical personnel have been identified in the scientific literature. Accordingly, the model for measuring the

Table 6.3. Operationalization of the variable diagnostic control

Indicator symbol	Indicator	Status	Source
Please answer whether you agree that reports containing information on costs, revenues, and quality indicators serve to:			
DC1	• Track progress toward key goals		(de Harlez & Malagueño, 2016; Henri, 2006a, p. 551; Marginson et al., 2010, p. 368; Marginson et al., 2014, p. 73; Widener, 2007, p. 785; Yu et al., 2018, p. 26)
DC2	• Monitor results		(de Harlez & Malagueño, 2016; Henri, 2006a, p. 551; Marginson et al., 2010, p. 368; Marginson et al., 2014, p. 73; Widener, 2007, p. 785)
DC3	• Compare outcomes to expectations		(de Harlez & Malagueño, 2016; Henri, 2006a, p. 551; Marginson et al., 2010, p. 368; Marginson et al., 2014, p. 73; Widener, 2007, p. 785)
DC4	Data are reported to head physicians and managers through formal reporting procedures and top managers tend to be involved in the process infrequently and on an exceptions basis.	Dropped	(Abernethy & Brownell, 1999, p. 202)
DC5	Staff specialists (i.e., finance departments) play a pivotal role in preparing and interpreting the information produced	Dropped	(Abernethy & Brownell, 1999, p. 202)

rewarding variable (Table 6.4) was based on studies of management control systems in firms (Nguyen et al., 2017). The scale used there was developed on the basis of previous research (Chow et al., 1999, p. 459; Schulz et al., 2010, p. 25; Shields & Young, 1993, p. 272). This scale focuses on the strength of the formalization of the link between rewards and performance and consists of statements such as rewards are directly related to individual performance;

Table 6.4. Operationalization of the variable rewarding employees

Indicator symbol	Indicator	Source
R1	To what extent are rewards directly linked to individual employee performance?	(Chow et al., 1999, p. 459; Nguyen et al., 2017, p. 208; Schulz et al., 2010, p. 25; Shields & Young, 1993, p. 272)
R2	To what extent do employees' rewards increase as their productivity increases?	(Chow et al., 1999, p. 459; Nguyen et al., 2017, p. 208; Schulz et al., 2010, p. 25; Shields & Young, 1993, p. 272)
R3	To what extent are employees rewarded equally regardless of performance level? (reverse coding)	(Bloom & Van Reenen, 2010, p. 206)
R4	To what extent are rewards directly linked to performance measures?	(Chow et al., 1999, p. 459; Nguyen et al., 2017, p. 208; Schulz et al., 2010, p. 25; Shields & Young, 1993, p. 272)
R5	To what extent are individual employee rewards dependent on objective measurable indicators, such as the department's financial performance, revenue and/or cost levels, number of patients treated and/or procedures performed, patient satisfaction/ experience levels, and/or other indicators related to treatment quality?	Based on: (Chow et al., 1999, p. 459; Nguyen et al., 2017, p. 208; Schulz et al., 2010, p. 25; Shields & Young, 1993, p. 272)

Note: Hospital directors referred to individual indicators using a seven-item scale, where 1 meant "I do not use" and 7 meant "I use to a great extent."

rewards are directly related to performance measures; people's rewards increase as their performance increases. The survey of a sample of 152 managers yielded an overall reliability of 0.947 (Nguyen et al., 2017, p. 207).

Analyzing the measurement model of the rewarding employees variable (Table 6.4), it should be noted that all indicators cover a common domain, and a significant correlation between them can be expected, indicating a reflective measurement model. This conclusion is consistent with the approach to measurement models of rewarding employees in earlier studies, which also took this construct as reflective (Nguyen et al., 2017, p. 208; Schulz et al., 2010, p. 26).

Diagnostic control refers to the traditional use of information systems, that is, comparing assumptions with achieved results (Simons, 1995, p. 59). Interactive control, on the other hand, is a new element introduced into the discourse related to organizational control in the broadest sense by R. Simons (1987a, 1995). In some respects, interactive control (IC) may appear similar to innovativeness, so the following section cites a number of scales used in earlier studies to clearly separate the two constructs. Out of the vast literature on interactive control, one that stands out is the study by J. Bisbe et al. (2005, 2007), in which the authors argue that interactive control (interactive use of the management accounting system) consists of five elements: (1) intensive use by top management; (2) intensive use by operational managers; (3) face-to-face challenge and debate; (4) focus on strategic uncertainty; (5) non-intrusive, facilitating, and inspirational involvement (2007, p. 809).

A more recent study of the interactive use of a management accounting system by top management of Spanish hospitals used a six-item scale adapted from studies by M. Abernethy and P. Brownell and J. Bisbe and D. Otley (1999, p. 202) and (2004), consisting of six components (Naranjo-Gil & Hartmann, 2006, pp. 46, 48; Naranjo-Gil & Hartmann, 2007, p. 752): (1) setting and negotiating goals and objectives; (2) discussing data assumptions and action plans; (3) signaling key strategic areas for improvement; (4) challenging new ideas and ways of doing things; (5) engaging in ongoing discussion with subordinates; (6) organizational learning. In a study of a sample of 218 Spanish general hospitals, the Cronbach's alpha for this scale was 0.81 (Naranjo-Gil & Hartmann, 2006, p. 33); in a study of the management teams of 103 Spanish hospitals, the Cronbach's alpha was 0.82, and the composite reliability reached 0.86 (Naranjo-Gil & Hartmann, 2007, p. 745). The same scale was used in a study of 117 Belgian hospitals (de Harlez & Malagueño, 2016) in which the Cronbach's alpha was 0.86.

In a study conducted among executives of Australian hospitals (a total of 143 questionnaires completed by chief executive officers, chief financial officers, chief nursing officers and chief operating officers were collected), the authors independently developed a measurement scale based on R. Simons's theory (1995) that consisted of six statements (Yu et al., 2018, p. 26):

■ There are many ongoing interactions between operations managers and senior management in the process of using the performance management system;

- Performance measurement systems are regularly used in scheduled face-to-face meetings between operations managers and senior managers;
- Performance measurement systems are often used as a means to develop ongoing action plans;
- Performance measurement systems generate information that is an important and recurring agenda in discussions between operations managers and senior managers;
- Performance management systems are used by operational managers and senior managers to discuss the changes taking place;
- Performance measurement systems are often used as a means of identifying strategic uncertainties.

In this research, the reliability of the Cronbach's alpha scale was 0.90, the composite reliability reached 0.94, and the average variance extracted (AVE) = 0.68 (Yu et al., 2018, p. 14). On the other hand, a study conducted with 85 managers of Italian health-care organizations used a proprietary scale consisting of three items that speak to the use of a performance management system to: (1) detecting strategic uncertainty in the facility; (2) regularly reviewing assumptions and scenarios; (3) facilitating the sharing of goals between top management and their subordinates within the facility (Demartini & Mella, 2014, p. e10). The reliability of this scale (Cronbach's alpha) was 0.90 (Demartini & Mella, 2014, p. e29). It is still worth noting one of the more commonly used tools for measuring interactive information system use in business organizations. This scale in the first research achieved a Cronbach's alpha reliability of 0.87 (Henri, 2006a, p. 551) and is constructed of seven items. This scale highlighted two areas related to the use of the organization's performance measurement system, namely the constant questioning and debates about data, assumptions, and action plans and the holistic approach to the organization. The latter component was expressed in statements stating the use of the organization's performance measurement system to: presenting a common view of the organization, linking it together, and developing a common vocabulary within the organization.

The scales presented above cover diverse areas, so the measurement model for diagnostic control was based on the themes that emerged in the qualitative research and the elements of the scales cited (Table 6.5). Several themes can be found in the directors' statements that relate to the scales spoken of. They speak, for example, of analyzing the external environment and the internal environment in order to look for elements that may force

Table 6.5.   Operationalization of the variable interactive control

Indicator symbol	Indicator	Source
Please answer whether you agree that reports containing information on costs, revenues, and quality indicators serve to:		
IC1	• focus executives on common problems;	(Henri, 2006a, p. 551; Janke et al., 2014, pp. 257–258; Marginson et al., 2010, p. 368; Marginson et al., 2014, p. 73; Naranjo-Gil & Hartmann, 2007, p. 752)
IC2	• conduct a joint review with subordinates of potential changes that have occurred in the external environment and in the hospital itself that could invalidate the current strategy;	(Bisbe & Malagueño, 2009, p. 404; Janke et al., 2014, pp. 257–258; Marginson et al., 2010, p. 368; Marginson et al., 2014, p. 73; Naranjo-Gil & Hartmann, 2006, p. 46; Naranjo-Gil & Hartmann, 2007, p. 752; Yu et al., 2018, p. 26)
IC3	• renegotiate with subordinates the established goals and objectives and performance indicators;	(Janke et al., 2014, pp. 257–258; Marginson et al., 2010, p. 368; Marginson et al., 2014, p. 73; Naranjo-Gil & Hartmann, 2006, p. 46; Naranjo-Gil & Hartmann, 2007, p. 752)
IC4	• develop new goals and objectives and performance indicators;	(Janke et al., 2014, pp. 257–258; Naranjo-Gil & Hartmann, 2006, p. 46; Naranjo-Gil & Hartmann, 2007, p. 752)
IC5	• engage in continual discussions with subordinates the adopted goals and indicators and ways to accomplish tasks;	(Janke et al., 2014, pp. 257–258; Abernethy & Brownell, 1999, p. 202; Henri, 2006a, p. 551; Yu et al., 2018, p. 26)
IC6	• uniting the hospital as a whole, i.e., treating the hospital's main problems as common, rather than individual departments/ divisions or professional groups.	(Henri, 2006a, p. 551; Marginson et al., 2010, p. 368; Marginson et al., 2014, p. 73)

Note: Hospital directors referred to individual indicators using a seven-item scale, where 1 meant "disagree" and 7 meant "agree."

a change in the existing strategic assumptions. This is particularly evident in the statement of the SzO3 director, who, citing data from the information system, encourages the search not only internally, but also externally, of the hospital for solutions to reduce the average length of hospitalization. The statement by the director of SzS2 is an example of continuous and personal involvement in discussing with subordinates the adopted targets and indicators when discussing the level of execution of the contract with the National Health Fund. In the interviews, the issue of unifying the hospital into a single entity, i.e., treating the main problems of the hospital as common, rather than as problems of individual departments/divisions or professional groups, came up repeatedly. An example of this approach is the statement by the director of SzO/S1 regarding the use of the CT scanner in the afternoons, when this diagnosis is cheaper.

A theoretical analysis of the indicators shown in Table 6.5 leads to the conclusion that they are manifestations of directors' attitudes toward the use of information systems. In other words, directors' responses reflect the state of the latent (unobserved) construct, so changes in attitudes toward how IS is used cause changes in directors' responses. In addition, analyzing the adopted scale items (Table 6.6), it can be assumed that they will be significantly correlated with each other, so taking into account the experience of previous authors (de Harlez & Malagueño, 2016; Henri, 2006a, p. 551; Marginson et al., 2010, p. 368, 2014, p. 73; Widener, 2007, p. 785; Yu et al., 2018, p. 26), an assumption is made about the reflective nature of the interactive control variable.

Analyzing previous ways of operationalizing innovativeness in hospital research, two main approaches can be identified:

1. measuring objective indicators, e.g., B + R (Salge & Vera, 2009, p. 59) or implementation of specific technologies (e.g., MRI) and organizational solutions (e.g., pharmacy unit dose system) (Goes & Park, 1997, p. 682);
2. measuring subjective manifestations of innovativeness based on self-assessment, such as:
   a. employee involvement in innovativeness (Salge & Vera, 2009);
   b. process improvement (Demartini & Mella, 2014, pp. e10, e30);
   c. multiple domains of hospital operation (Lewis-Beck, 1977, p. 4; Moreira et al., 2017, p. 341).

An approach based on objective indicators may seem attractive because of its unambiguous and verifiable basis for comparison between hospitals.

Table 6.6. Operationalization of the innovativeness variable

Indicator symbol	Indicator	Source
I1	Our innovativeness as the hospital's overall propensity and ability to seek, implement and spread in practice technological, organizational, management, and service delivery and external relations innovations is ...	(Sankowska, 2011, p. 203)
I2	Our technological innovativeness as the implementation of new or significantly new pharmaceuticals, disposable materials, diagnostic and therapeutic equipment and treatment and diagnostic methods is ...	(Dias & Escoval, 2013, p. 270; Djellal & Gallouj, 2007, p. 188; Lewis-Beck, 1977, p. 4)
I3	Our organizational innovativeness as the implementation of new organizational methods in both non-medical and medical departments, involving the creation of new organizational units and positions to improve the delivery of medical services, the elimination of boundaries between organizational units, and changes in organizational structure is ...	(Goes & Park, 1997, p. 682; Djellal & Gallouj, 2007, p. 188; Moreira et al., 2017, p. 341; Sankowska, 2011, p. 203)
I4	Our management innovativeness as the implementation of new management methods, including costing, incentive systems, ways of hiring and rewarding employees, quality improvement techniques and patient safety is ...	(Djellal & Gallouj, 2007, p. 189; Lewis-Beck, 1977, p. 4; Madorrán García & de Val Pardo, 2004; Young et al., 2001)
I5	Our innovativeness in service delivery as the implementation of new ways to communicate with patients and their families, improve conditions for patients and their families, the hospital admission process, shorten waiting lists, etc., is ...	(Djellal & Gallouj, 2007, p. 189; Lewis-Beck, 1977, p. 4; Midttun & Martinussen, 2005; Sasaki, 2003)
I6	Our innovativeness in external relations as the implementation of new ways to establish relationships with suppliers, with medical facilities and other partners, such as the purchase and use of expensive equipment, support in the treatment of complex cases, coordinated transfer of patients between departments and to other hospitals, etc., is ...	(Djellal & Gallouj, 2007, p. 190)

Note: Hospital directors referred to individual indicators using a seven-element scale, where 1 means that innovativeness is "definitely lower" and 7 means that innovativeness is "definitely higher" compared to similar hospitals in Poland.

However, on the other hand, such an approach limits the scope of innovations evaluated mainly to those related to technology and capital expenditures, leaving out many other areas where quantified measurement is virtually impossible. Meanwhile, the field research shows that hospitals innovate in many areas. Confronting the results of the qualitative research with the scientific literature and previously used measurement models, five areas were identified, which were reflected in the adopted measurement scale of the innovativeness variable (Table 6.5).

The multi-domain approach to innovation is also in line with the general nature of the research reported here, which stems from two considerations. First, the definition of management control developed for this research includes all instruments, activities, and systems used by top management. Second, the theory of management control in hospitals has not been developed to date, so the search for the components of management control and the relationship between them must be done on a broad spectrum so as not to miss important aspects of this management function. Thus, it seems that an approach based on a subjective assessment of innovativeness compared to similar institutions in the region or possibly in Poland is the most adequate solution.

Also for the innovativeness variable, the configuration of the measurement model needs to be decided. On the one hand, the scale consists of separate innovativeness areas, which could suggest that they function independently of each other. In other words, an increase in innovativeness in the technological area does not necessarily mean an increase in innovative management and organizational solutions. Similarly, more innovative relationships with the environment do not necessarily correlate with innovations in quality. Such an approach would lead one to adopt a formative measurement model. However, qualitative research has shown that innovative activities are not planned in advance, and it is not known beforehand what field they will address. An example is a statement made by the chief operating officer of a British hospital: "my role is not to tell people what to do, [...] but to collectively find innovative solutions to problems that appear to be the cause of poor performance" (SzWB). Similarly, it is unclear in what area semi-intentional innovations and innovations arising ad hoc (bricolage) will be accepted and implemented. This is because it is not possible to plan for innovations arising from employees' needs to improve their work.

In conclusion, it should be emphasized that a more adequate way to view innovativeness in the context of field research and the adopted definition of operational management control seems to be a reflective approach. That is, innovativeness is a manifestation of the orientation of top management and employees. In other words, the level of innovativeness does not depend on planned innovations in specific areas, but on whether top management and employees have "open minds" to new ideas and solutions. This finding ultimately determines the adoption of a reflective measurement model of the innovativeness variable. However, it is also worth mentioning that later in the monograph the choices made regarding the specification of the measurement model will be empirically verified again using tetrad analysis (Bollen & Ting, 2000; Gudergan et al., 2008).

Qualitative research indicates that hospital directors, when referring to the uncertainty of the environment, focused on specific areas rather than the generally perceived speed of change and unpredictability of the effects of decisions. In this context, the basis for operationalizing the perceived environmental uncertainty (PEU) variable may be the scale developed by M.C. Burke (1984, p. 348) taking into account previous research (Duncan, 1972; Miles & Snow, 1978). Using this scale in a study of hospitals, 12 elements were included: suppliers of materials, suppliers of capital equipment, labor supply, labor unions, customers, competitors, government regulations, public opinion, technological advances, industry associations, financial markets, and the general economy (Lonial & Raju, 2001, p. 20). The scale was used in a study of hospitals. Considering the results of the qualitative research, nine elements were adopted regarding the uncertainty of the operating environment of public hospitals in Poland (Table 6.7).

In most studies, perceived environmental uncertainty is measured in a reflective model (Colquitt et al., 2012, p. 7; Meissner & Wulf, 2014, p. 628; Yu et al., 2016, p. 27; Bordia et al., 2004, p. 519; Kruis et al., 2016, p. 41; Hameiri & Nir, 2016, p. 776; Waldman et al., 2001, p. 137; Hoffer Gittell, 2002, p. 1414; Hammad et al., 2013, p. 321). However, given the results of the field research, it is difficult to find indications that hospital directors perceive all factors of environmental uncertainty in a similar way. In other words, general perceptions of uncertainty form its individual indicators. That is, perceptions of the uncertainty of legal requirements or the activities of competing providers, for example, derive from generally perceived uncertainty. While the first factor depends on the activity of state institutions, the second factor, the competitive activity of providers, depends on the local situation. Also, the resignation of key employees tends to be tied to the local labor market and independent of the other elements of environmental uncertainty. In this situation, it seems that it is the perception of each area of uncertainty that creates the variable. Thus, a formative

Table 6.7. **Operationalization of the variable perceived environmental uncertainty**

Indicator symbol	Indicator	Source
PEU1	Prices for drugs, disposable materials, medical equipment and apparatus	(Begun & Kaissi, 2004, p. 33; Burke, 1984, p. 348; Lonial & Raju, 2001, p. 16; Miles & Snow, 1978, p. 200; Price, 1997, p. 379)
PEU2	Hospital treatment costs	(Begun & Kaissi, 2004, p. 33; Hoffer Gittell, 2002, p. 1414; Kruis, 2008, p. 67)
PEU3	Trade union activities	(Begun & Kaissi, 2004, p. 33; Burke, 1984, p. 348; Lonial & Raju, 2001, p. 17; Price, 1997, p. 379)
PEU4	Repair and service costs of medical equipment	(Burke, 1984; Lonial & Raju, 2001, p. 17; Miles & Snow, 1978, p. 200; Price, 1997, p. 379)
PEU5	Actions of competing providers that may significantly affect the hospital's deterioration	(Burke, 1984, p. 348; Lonial & Raju, 2001, p. 17; Price, 1997, p. 379)
PEU6	Changes in the hospital's revenues, including those resulting from the demand for particular medical services, the ways in which patients qualify for DRG groups and the pricing of services, etc.	(Burke, 1984, p. 348; Hoffer Gittell, 2002, p. 1414; Kruis, 2008, p. 67)
PEU7	Resignation of key employees (e.g., doctors)	(Burke, 1984, p. 348; Lonial & Raju, 2001, p. 17)
PEU8	The possibility of long-term planning of investment and development of the hospital, in the sense of being able to plan to obtain external funds from EU programs, the founding authority or loans	(Begun & Kaissi, 2004, p. 33; Burke, 1984, p. 348; Lonial & Raju, 2001, p. 17; Price, 1997, p. 379)
PEU8	Changes in legal requirements including: staffing standards, infrastructure, salaries, etc.	(Begun & Kaissi, 2004, p. 33; Burke, 1984, p. 348; Lonial & Raju, 2001, p. 17; Price, 1997, p. 379)
PEU-Global	Please assess the extent to which: the prices of drugs, disposable materials, medical equipment and apparatus, the cost of treatment and service of medical equipment, labor union activities, changes in hospital revenues, the ability to raise capital and changes in legal norms are predictable or unpredictable	To some extent modeled on the definition of environmental turbulence (Khandwalla, 1977, pp. 641–643)

Note: Hospital directors referred to individual indicators using a seven-element scale, where 1 meant "completely predictable" and 7 meant "completely unpredictable."

measurement model seems more appropriate for measuring the perceived environmental uncertainty variable.

Unlike reflective measurement models, in which individual indicators are correlated and substitute for each other, giving greater confidence in the convergent validity of a given construct, in formative measurement models, the evaluation of convergent validity requires additional empirical assessment through redundancy analysis (Cheah et al., 2018, p. 3193; Hair et al., 2016, p. 140). In order to conduct redundancy analysis, an additional indicator relating to the global assessment of environmental uncertainty, the PEU-Global indicator, was added to the measurement tool (Table 6.8).

There is a rich body of literature on measuring organizational trust, including subordinates' trust in superiors and leaders (Adams & Sartori, 2006; Cummings & Bromiley, 1996; Fleig-Palmer et al., 2018; Engelbrecht et al., 2017; Shao, 2019; Håvold & Håvold, 2019; Yeşilbaş & Çetin, 2019; Brower et al., 2008; Kim et al., 2016), while superiors' trust in subordinates has been studied much less frequently. It should be noted, however, that even those few studies of superior-subordinate trust did not use scales specifically built for this purpose, but were based on modified earlier scales measuring subordinates' trust in superiors. For example, H.H. Brower et al. (2008, p. 338) used in their study a scale measuring superiors' trust in subordinates, developed by R.C. Mayer and J.H. Davis (1999, p. 136). Similarly, T.-Y. Kim et al. (2016) used the scale developed by D.J. McAllister (1995, p. 37) to measure superiors' trust in subordinates, adapting the content of statements accordingly to measure superiors' trust

Table 6.8. Operationalization of the trust variable

Indicator symbol	Indicator	Source
T1	I trust that the physicians in my hospital are loyal to the hospital.	(Colquitt et al., 2007, p. 913; Mayer et al., 1995, p. 723)
T2	I trust that physicians in my hospital always act in accordance with the interests (values) of the hospital.	
T3	I trust that the physicians at my hospital have the latest medical knowledge.	
T4	I generally trust the physicians at my hospital.	(Carmeli et al., 2010, p. 343)

Note: Hospital directors referred to individual indicators using a seven-item scale, where 1 meant "disagree", and 7 meant "agree."

in subordinates. The acceptability of adapting scales measuring subordinates' trust in superiors for measuring superiors' trust in subordinates
is not only due to the fact that trust has the characteristics of reciprocity
(Swärd, 2016, p. 1844), but it has also been confirmed by studies showing
a positive correlation between employees' trust in superiors and superiors'
trust in subordinates, as well as a positive correlation between employees'
mutual trust in superiors and superiors' trust in subordinates (Kim et al.,
2016, p. 952).

Based on the above considerations, managers' perceived benevolence,
honesty, and ability of their subordinate physicians were used to measure
the trust variable (Table 6.8). To increase the reliability of the scale, an
additional question about the general trust of the managers in the physicians working at the hospital was used: "I generally trust the physicians
at my facility." A similar statement was used in research on the impact of
innovative leadership on organizational performance (Carmeli et al., 2010,
p. 343).

The trust variable (T) is a manifestation of the perception of the chief
executives, and it would be rather difficult to consider the individual indicators separately and assume, at least theoretically, that there is no correlation
between them. Thus, it should be assumed that the indicators are the effect
of directors' trust in doctors, which means adopting a reflective measurement model.

In summary, it should be said that the eight constructs identified in the
qualitative research were operationalized in multi-dimensional measurement models using 44 indicator variables (Figure 6.2). All of the constructs
used in the model have counterparts in the theory; however, the theory
was of limited relevance to hospitals. No studies were found at all that
described the measurement of the constructs used in the model based on
Polish hospitals. Hence, in the process of operationalizing the variables,
single items of scales from tools validated in earlier studies of foreign hospitals and companies that were most consistent with the results of qualitative research were taken into account. In particular, the variables whose
measurement model was adopted as formative – information system effectiveness, perceived environmental uncertainty, and hospital performance –
are strongly based on the results of exploratory research, while in the case
of constructs, such as innovativeness, trust, rewarding employees, diagnostic use of IS, and interactive use of IS, their domain was more strongly
based on theory.

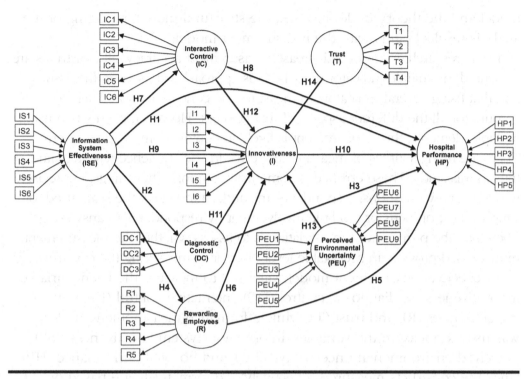

Figure 6.2: Internal (structural) model and external (measurement) model of organizational control in hospitals

6.2 Validation of the Measurement Model

The SmartPLS 3 estimator, v. 3.3.3 (Ringle et al., 2015), was used to analyze the management control model in hospitals. Before analyzing the proposed model, assumptions were made regarding the handling of missing data. As mentioned earlier, 12 cases with more than 5% missing data were removed from the data set. For the remaining cases, where the number of missing data did not exceed 5%, the mean value for the indicator (Hair et al., 2016, p. 56) was inserted in place of the missing data. Similarly, in accordance with practical recommendations, the "path" weighting option was selected in the SmartPLS estimator. This weighting scheme provides the highest value of the R^2 coefficient of determination for endogenous latent variables, and it is generally applied to all types of PLS path models (Hair et al., 2016, p. 89). The R^2 coefficient of determination represents the cumulative effect of exogenous variables on the endogenous variable, showing the amount of variance in the endogenous variable explained by all related exogenous constructs. Although structural modeling simultaneously evaluates the measurement model and the theory under test, i.e., the structural model, reporting of the analysis results begins with the measurement model.

In the research, in order to increase measurement accuracy, all constructs are measured in multiple-indicator models. This approach is based on the assumption that using several indicators to measure one concept is more likely to account for all the different aspects of that concept. However, even when using multiple elements, the measurement is likely to contain some degree of error. There are many sources of measurement error in social science research, and thus in this study. These errors can come from, among other things, imprecisely worded survey questions, respondents' misunderstanding of the scale used, or simply a lack of focus or too little involvement by respondents in answering. Therefore, the purpose of the validation is to assess whether the measurement models used provide an acceptable level of error in measuring the constructs.

A reflective measurement model was used to measure the latent variables' innovativeness (I), diagnostic control (DC), interactive control (IC), rewarding employees (R), and trust (T), while a formative measurement model was used to measure the variables' information system effectiveness (ISE), perceived environmental uncertainty (PEU), and hospital performance (HP). Since the constructs measured reflectively and formatively are based on different concepts, they require different evaluation. Reflective measurement models should be evaluated for their reliability of internal consistency and validity. Specific measures in this regard include composite reliability as a means of assessing internal consistency reliability, convergent validity, and discriminant validity. In the case of formative constructs, the content validity should be ensured already at the stage of theoretical work, during the design of the measurement model, even before data collection. To validate a formative measurement model, such metrics as convergent validity, statistical significance, and adequacy of indicator weights as well as the presence of collinearity between indicators are used (Hair et al., 2016, p. 107). It should be noted that model validation in PLS-SEM is based primarily on nonparametric evaluation criteria based on bootstrapping and blindfolding.

Before empirically evaluating the formative constructs, content validity was established, that is, it was ensured that the formative indicators covered at least the main aspects of the latent variable. To this end, redundancy analysis (Hair et al., 2016, p. 140) was conducted by building a model consisting of the formative variable under study as an exogenous latent variable predicting an endogenous latent variable operationalized with a single global indicator (Figure 6.3).

The results of the analysis indicated that the value of the path coefficient connecting the two ISE variables is 0.86, and the value of the explained variance

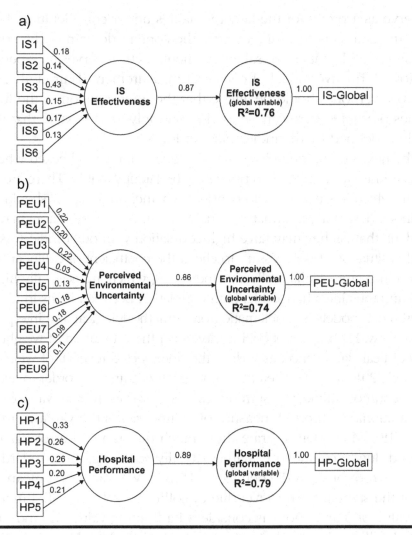

Figure 6.3: Analysis of variable redundancy: a) information system effectiveness, b) perceived environmental uncertainty and c) hospital performance

of the exogenous variable $R^2 = 0.76$ (Figure 6.3a). Such values indicate the validity of the adopted set of formative indicators IS1-IS6, as they exceed the threshold values of 0.80 for the value of the path coefficient and 0.50 for the explained variance of R^2 (Hair et al., 2016, p. 140). Similarly, for the variables uncertainty and hospital performance, the path coefficient values are 0.86 and 0.89, respectively, and the values of the coefficient of determination $R^2 = 0.75$ and $R^2 = 0.79$ (Figure 6.3b and 6.3c), and thus exceed the threshold value of 0.8. Therefore, all variables measured formatively can be considered valid.

In general, single indicator variables are not recommended in PLS-SEM; however, their role in redundancy analyses is different, as single indicators only serve as a proxy for the latent variables under consideration. In other words, the goal is not to fully capture the content domain of the construct, but only to validate its most salient elements, which serves as a benchmark for a formative model of construct measurement (Hair et al., 2016, p. 141). However, one should be aware that the interpretation of the formative variables presented here can be carried out only to the extent that the latent variable is defined by the indicators that form it.

In the next step of formative variable validation, it was checked whether each formative indicator actually contributes to the latent variable. There are two situations in which it is necessary to consider whether an indicator should remain in an index describing a formative variable. First, certain indicators may be redundant, that is, they may have high correlation with other indicators.

In this situation, it is necessary to check the coefficient of collinearity between indicators. Unlike reflective indicators, which are generally highly correlated and thus interchangeable, high correlation between items in formative measurement models is problematic from a methodological and interpretive point of view. High levels of collinearity affect the estimation of weights and their statistical significance, as well as the unexpected reversal of weight signs (Hair et al., 2016, p. 141). Therefore, among other things, in order to avoid the phenomenon of collinearity, sum scores were used for the ISE variable.

A traditionally reported measure of collinearity is the variance inflation factor (VIF), which demonstrates how much the standard error has been increased due to collinearity. Mathematically speaking, the standard error is the square root of the VIF coefficient. Thus, a VIF value of 4 means a doubling of the standard error level due to collinearity. In PLS-SEM modeling, a VIF value of 5 and above is considered a limiting value and indicates a potential collinearity problem (Hair et al., 2011, p. 145). More specifically, an indicator's VIF level of 5 indicates that 80% of its variance is accounted for by the other formative indicators associated with the same variable (Hair et al., 2016, p. 142). From the results of calculations with the SmartPLS estimator, the VIF values for the individual indicators of the formative variables uncertainty, IS effectiveness and performance did not exceed the cutoff value, indicating the absence of collinearity (Table 6.9).

Another parameter taken into account when deciding whether an indicator should be included in the index is the level of its contribution (outer weight) to the latent variable and whether this contribution is statistically significant at a preset confidence level (Hair et al., 2016, p. 141). In PLS-SEM, the values of the outer weights express the relative contribution of each indicator to the construct (Hair et al., 2016, p. 144), except that this contribution

Table 6.9. Results of estimation of indicators of formative variables

Variable name	Indicator symbol	Outer weights	t-Value	p-Value	Outer loadings	t-Value	p-Value	VIF
Perceived environmental uncertainty	PEU1	0.19	2.28	0.02	0.82	19.59	0.00	2.44
	PEU2	0.17	2.04	0.04	0.70	11.96	0.00	1.76
	PEU3	0.15	2.09	0.04	0.72	12.25	0.00	1.77
	PEU4	-0.11	1.72	0.09	0.13	1.35	0.18	1.16
	PEU5	0.25	3.29	0.00	0.80	18.68	0.00	1.94
	PEU6	0.19	2.07	0.04	0.82	18.80	0.00	2.53
	PEU7	0.22	2.46	0.01	0.82	18.84	0.00	2.38
	PEU8	-0.02	0.22	0.82	0.23	2.48	0.01	1.21
	PEU9	0.16	2.08	0.04	0.63	9.10	0.00	1.59
Information system effectiveness	IS1	0.22	3.07	0.00	0.80	16.12	0.00	2.16
	IS2	0.26	3.67	0.00	0.83	23.21	0.00	2.17
	IS3	0.15	1.92	0.06	0.84	21.42	0.00	3.07
	IS4	0.17	1.93	0.05	0.84	22.22	0.00	2.78
	IS5	0.16	1.93	0.05	0.82	19.24	0.00	2.84
	S6	0.27	3.68	0.00	0.78	19.19	0.00	1.92
Hospital performance	HP1	0.23	2.44	0.02	0.72	11.87	0.00	1.69
	HP2	0.42	5.58	0.00	0.82	20.33	0.00	1.87
	HP3	0.05	0.49	0.63	0.71	11.19	0.00	2.01
	HP4	0.30	3.52	0.00	0.78	15.24	0.00	1.81
	HP5	0.26	2.48	0.01	0.88	23.31	0.00	2.77

may not be statistically significant at a preset confidence level. To investigate this, a bootstrapping method was used, taking the recommended number of bootstrap random samples to be 5,000 (Hair et al., 2011, p. 145). The study sample is relatively small, so the SmartPLS estimator chose Bootstrap with bias-correction and accelerated correction (BCa), with two-tailed testing and a significance level of 0.05 (more in: (Gudergan et al., 2008)).

The results of the bootstrapping procedure show that the weights of indicators PEU4 and PEU8 are negative and statistically insignificant at the $p<0.05$ level (Table 6.9). From the practice of validating formative measurement models, it is known that statistically insignificant indicator weights should not be automatically interpreted as a suggestion to remove such an indicator from the measurement model. In such a situation, the absolute contribution (loading) of the indicator to the formatively measured latent variable should also be considered. The absolute loading of an indicator is the information that the indicator provides, without taking into account the contribution of other indicators. Unlike external weights, internal loadings result from simple regressions of each indicator against its corresponding construct, which is equivalent to a two-dimensional correlation between each indicator and construct (Benitez et al., 2020, p. 9).

In the studied formative measurement model of the perceived environmental uncertainty variable, the weights of indicators PEU4 and PEU 8 are statistically insignificant and have relatively small loadings. The weight of indicator PEU4 is -0.11, which can still be considered a borderline value (Hair et al., 2016, p. 147), while the weight of indicator PEU8 is only -0.02. In addition, the absolute loadings of both indicators are relatively low – PEU4 (0.13), PEU8 (0.23) (Table 6.9), (less than 0.50) – meaning that the indicators have low absolute validity, which argues for their removal from the measurement model. In addition, the loading of the PEU4 indicator is statistically insignificant at the assumed level of $p<0.05$, so there is no certainty that in reality this indicator has any effect on the variable. In such a situation, only the extremely important theoretical significance of these indicators could support their retention in the model. In the measurement model of the uncertainty variable, the PEU4 indicator relates to the cost of servicing medical equipment, and the PEU8 indicator relates to the possibility of long-term planning of investment and development of the hospital, in the sense of the possibility of planning to obtain external funds from EU programs, the hospital owner, or loans. Thus, it does not seem that these indicators are key to this variable.

Indicators IS3 and HP3 are also statistically insignificant at the assumed level, and their weights are small, but nevertheless their loadings are significant (0.84 and 0.71, respectively) and statistically significant, indicating the high absolute value of these indicators for estimating related variables. In addition, indicators IS3, IS4, IS5, and HP3 have significant theoretical relevance to the content validity of their constructs. Indicator IS3 is the only component of the measurement model that relates to the quality of medical services. Similarly, indicator HP3, which relates to hospital reputation. Thus, eliminating these indicators would result in missing an important part of the content of each construct.

An additional argument for removing indicators PEU4 and PEU8 is that the construct perceived environmental uncertainty consisted of as many as nine indicators. And the variables information system effectiveness and hospital performance have six and five indicators, respectively. Unlike reflective measurement models, in which the number of indicators has little impact on measurement results, formative measurement has an inherent limitation on the number of indicators that can retain statistically significant weight (Cenfetelli & Bassellier, 2009, p. 692; Hair et al., 2016, p. 145). The model estimation results show that the elimination of two formative indicators that did not meet threshold levels in terms of their contribution to the latent variable did not significantly affect the parameter values after model re-estimation. Additionally, the statistical significance of the IS3 indicator improved, which now only slightly exceeds the threshold of p = 0.05 (Table 6.10).

After removing the two indicators from the formative measurement model of the uncertainty variable, the content validity of this construct was again tested through redundancy analysis, which shows that still the value of the path coefficient connecting the two variables – the uncertainty measured formatively and the uncertainty described by the global indicator – shows satisfactory values: path coefficient = 0.86 and R^2 = 0.73 (Figure 6.4). This means that the elimination of the PEU4 and PEU8 indicator practically did not reduce the content validity of this construct.

Table 6.10. Outer weights and outer loadings of formative variable indicators obtained from bootstrapping after removing variables PEU4 and PEU8 from the measurement model

Variable name	Indicator symbol	Outer weights (loadings)	t-Value	p-Value	BCa confidence interval (95%)	Significance (p<0.05)
Perceived environmental uncertainty	PEU1	0.18 (0.83)	2.26 (20.01)	0.02 (0.00)	0.03-0.35; (0.73-0.89)	Yes
	PEU2	0.16 (0.70)	1.95 (11.91)	0.05 (0.00)	0.00-0.32; (0.57-0.80)	Borderline
	PEU3	0.15 (0.72)	2.01 (12.48)	0.04 (0.00)	0.00-0.30; (0.59-0.82)	Yes
	PEU5	0.26 (0.80)	3.32 (19.49)	0.00 (0.00)	0.10-0.40; (0.70-0.87)	Yes
	PEU6	0.18 (0.83)	2.10 (19.21)	0.04 (0.00)	0.01-0.35; (0.72-0.89)	Yes
	PEU7	0.20 (0.83)	2.13 (19.73)	0.03 (0.00)	0.01-0.37; (0.73-0.89)	Yes
	PEU9	0.17 (0.63)	2.28 (9.27)	0.02 (0.00)	0.02-0.31; (0.48-0.74)	Yes
Information system effectiveness	IS1	0.22 (0.80)	3.03 (15.8)	0.00 (0.00)	0.07-0.35; (0.67-0.87)	Yes
	IS2	0.26 (0.82)	3.62 (22.96)	0.00 (0.00)	0.13-0.41; (0.74-0.88)	Yes
	IS3	0.15 (0.84)	1.94 (21.08)	0.05 (0.00)	0.00-0.30; (0.74-0.90)	Borderline
	IS4	0.17 (0.84)	1.92 (21.91)	0.05 (0.00)	-0.02-0.32; (0.75-0.90)	Borderline
	IS5	0.16 (0.82)	1.91 (19.34)	0.06 (0.00)	-0.01-0.33; (0.72-0.88)	No
	S6	0.27 (0.78)	3.74 (19.06)	0.00 (0.00)	0.14-0.42; (0.69-0.84)	Yes
Hospital performance	HP1	0.23 (0.72)	2.51 (12.29)	0.01 (0.00)	0.05-0.40; (0.59-0.81)	Yes
	HP2	0.41 (0.82)	5.68 (20.38)	0.00 (0.00)	0.27-0.55; (0.72-0.88)	Yes
	HP3	0.05 (0.71)	0.48 (11.07)	0.63 (0.00)	-0.15-0.23; (0.56-0.81)	No
	HP4	0.30 (0.78)	3.44 (14.79)	0.00 (0.00)	0.12-0.47; (0.65-0.86)	Yes
	HP5	0.26 (0.88)	2.50 (23.45)	0.01 (0.00)	0.06-0.47; (0.79-0.93)	Yes

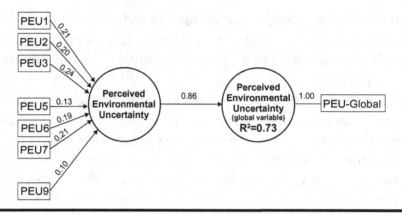

Figure 6.4. Redundancy analysis of the perceived environmental uncertainty variable after removal of indicators PEU4 and PEU8

A basic element in the evaluation of reflexive measurement models is the size of the outer loadings of individual indicators. Their high values suggested that the related indicators have much in common with the construct they emanate. The size of indicator loadings is also commonly referred to as indicator reliability. It is generally believed that the loadings of all indicators should be at least statistically significant, and it is desirable that the latent variable explain a significant portion of the variance of each indicator by at least 50%. This then means that the variance shared between the construct and its indicator is greater than the variance of the measurement error. From this condition, it follows that the value of the loading of each indicator should be no less than 0.71, since this number squared (more precisely: 0.7082^2) gives a value of 0.50, which explains 50% of the variance of the construct.

The results of the estimation of reflective measurement models show that the values of the loadings of individual indicators of latent variables in all cases exceed the value of 0.71 and are statistically significant at the level of $p < 0.000$ (cf. Table 6.13, values at the intersection of indicator symbols with the name of the construct). The estimated model includes the uncertainty variable already after eliminating the indicators PEU4 and PEU8.

Internal consistency reliability was initially estimated using the Cronbach's alpha coefficient, which exceeded 0.81 for all formative constructs (Table 6.11), indicating their high internal consistency and reliability. Cronbach's alpha, however, has some limitations. It assumes that all indicators have equal reliability, that is, that they have equal outer loadings in relation to the construct. This is problematic for the PLS-SEM estimator, which prioritizes indicators according to their individual reliability (Hair et al.,

Table 6.11. Reliability and validity of reflective variables

Variable name	Cronbach's alpha	ρ_A	Composite reliability	Average variance extracted (AVE)
Innovativeness	0.86	0.86	0.89	0.58
Diagnostic control	0.81	0.81	0.89	0.72
Interactive control	0.89	0.89	0.91	0.64
Rewarding	0.88	0.89	0.91	0.68
Trust	0.90	0.90	0.93	0.76

2016, p. 111). In addition, Cronbach's alpha is sensitive to the number of items on the scale and tends to underestimate internal consistency reliability. Therefore, another measure of internal consistency reliability was used, referred to as composite reliability, also known as total or composite reliability. Composite reliability can range from 0 to 1, with higher values indicating a higher level of reliability. According to J.F. Haira et al., (2016, p. 111) in exploratory research, composite reliability values of 0.60 to 0.70 are acceptable, while in more advanced stages of research the values should exceed 0.70. However, it should be noted that values above 0.95 are inappropriate, as they indicate that all indicator variables are measuring the same phenomenon (Hair, Risher, et al., 2019, p. 8). This may indicate item redundancy, for example, by using the same question in a slightly altered form in the survey tool. In the estimated model of management control in hospitals, the overall reliability oscillates between 0.89 and 0.93 (Table 6.11), indicating good reliability and internal consistency of the measurement models.

The average variance extracted (AVE) was used to assess convergent validity at the construct level. This criterion is defined as the average value of the squares of the indicator loadings associated with the latent variable (i.e., the sum of the squares of the loadings divided by the number of indicators). As with indicator loadings, an AVE value of 0.50 or higher indicates that, on average, a construct explains more than half of the variance in its indicators. Conversely, an AVE of less than 0.50 indicates that, on average, more variance remains in the item error than in the variance explained by the construct (Hair et al., 2011, p. 145). The estimation results show that the trust variable explains the most variance of its indicators (AVE = 0.76), while the innovativeness variable explains the least (AVE = 0.58). But even for the innovativeness variable, the value of the explained variance is well above the minimum threshold of 50% (Table 6.11). Thus, also the AVE for the latent variables of the proposed managerial control model in hospitals indicates high joint convergence of the measurement models.

While Cronbach's alpha underestimates the internal consistency reliability of latent variables and composite reliability overestimates this parameter, the reliability coefficient ρ_A accurately reproduces the true reliability of the construct scores. This is partly because, unlike composite reliability, ρ_A assesses the weights of the variables rather than their loadings (Dijkstra & Henseler, 2015a, pp. 300, 302). The recommendation for the minimum value of the ρ_A indicator is 0.71 (Benitez et al., 2020, p. 8; Henseler, 2017, p. 185), which means that more than 50% of the variance in construct scores can be explained by a latent variable. Thus, also this indicator, which ranges from 0.81 to 0.90 for all study variables (Table 6.11), supports the claim of internal consistency reliability of the study constructs.

The heterotrait-monotrait (HTMT) index was used to test discriminant validity, i.e., to determine how far the constructs in the model differ from each other. HTMT was assessed in two ways: (1) by comparing the calculated HTMT value with a threshold value and (2) by constructing a confidence interval using bootstrapping to test the statistical significance of the HTMT result (Benitez et al., 2020, p. 6; Franke & Sarstedt, 2019; Henseler et al., 2015). The exact threshold level of HTMT is debatable and, in principle, the latent variables included in the structural model can be assumed to be distinct constructs when the HTMT value is less than 1. However, simulation studies suggest a high reliability for detecting discriminant validity problems with a threshold value below 0.90 – if the path model contains constructs that are conceptually very similar, and below 0.85 when the constructs in the path model are conceptually more distinct (Franke & Sarstedt, 2019, p. 9; Henseler et al., 2015, p. 124). In other words, a HTMT value above 0.90 suggests a lack of discriminant validity. In contrast, the lower the value, the more distinct the constructs are, i.e., they are indeed different theoretical concepts. In the model under study, all HTMT values are not only below the value of 0.9, but also do not exceed the more conservatively defined threshold value of 0.85 (Table 6.12), which means that the latent variables proposed in the model are distinct constructs.

However, it should be noted that PLS-SEM makes no assumptions about the normality of the distribution, so standard parametric significance tests could not be used. Therefore, to test whether the HTMT statistic is significantly different from 1, bootstrapping was used to determine the confidence interval which the true HTMT value belongs to, assuming a certain confidence level (e.g., 95%). A confidence interval containing a value of 1

Table 6.12. Values of the Heterotrait-Monotrait (HTMT) ratio

Variable name	HTMT values from the sample	HTMT values from the bootstrapping	Confidence Interval (95%)
Diagnostic control <-> Innovativeness	0.69	0.70	0.56-0.80
Interactive control <-> Innovativeness	0.52	0.52	0.38-0.66
Interactive control <-> Diagnostic control	0.50	0.50	0.30-0.66
Rewarding <-> Innovativeness	0.51	0.51	0.33-0.69
Rewarding <-> Diagnostic control	0.57	0.57	0.39-0.72
Rewarding <-> Interactive control	0.33	0.33	0.15-0.51
Trust <-> Innovativeness	0.83	0.83	0.75-0.89
Trust <-> Diagnostic control	0.41	0.41	0.25-0.54
Trust <-> Interactive control	0.41	0.41	0.25-0.56
Trust <-> Rewarding	0.26	0.26	0.11-0.44

Note: In the bootstrap method, calculations were made based on 5,000 random samples with returns.

indicates a lack of discriminant validity (Hair et al., 2016, p. 118). The results of the bootstrap procedure indicate that in the measurement model under study, a value of 1 is not within the confidence interval for any variable (Table 6.12). For example, the highest value of HTMT occurs for the correlation of the variables trust <-> innovativeness and is (0.83), but also in this case the upper value of the confidence interval is below 1, suggesting that the tested constructs are empirically different.

Traditionally, cross-loadings and the Fornell-Larcker criterion (1981) have been used to test discriminant validity, but recent research has shown that these methods do not reliably detect discriminant validity problems (Henseler et al., 2015; Voorhees et al., 2016). Cross-loadings do not indicate a lack of discriminant validity when two constructs are perfectly correlated, which limits the use of this criterion in empirical studies (Hair et al., 2016, p. 116). Similarly, the Fornell-Larcker criterion performs poorly when the indicator loadings of latent variables differ only slightly (e.g., all indicator loadings vary between 0.60 and 0.80) (Voorhees et al., 2016). However, since cross-loadings and the Fornell-Larcker criterion have long been recommended for assessing the discriminant validity of latent variables, this analysis was also conducted. The analysis of the cross-loadings indicates that the loadings of the indicators reflecting each construct are higher than those for the other indicators (Table 6.13), indicating the discriminant

Table 6.13.   Values of outer loadings of reflective measurement models and cross loadings

Variable name	Indicator symbol	Innovative-ness	Diagnostic control	Interactive control	Rewarding	Trust
Innovativeness	I1	**0.76**	0.50	0.34	0.40	0.47
	I2	**0.79**	0.48	0.30	0.35	0.54
	I3	**0.77**	0.40	0.38	0.31	0.64
	I4	**0.73**	0.40	0.33	0.41	0.52
	I5	**0.80**	0.49	0.36	0.43	0.61
	I6	**0.71**	0.38	0.37	0.20	0.55
Diagnostic control	DC1	0.55	**0.85**	0.33	0.41	0.38
	DC2	0.49	**0.86**	0.41	0.44	0.25
	DC3	0.44	**0.84**	0.36	0.40	0.25
Interactive control	IC1	0.33	0.30	**0.78**	0.22	0.19
	IC2	0.35	0.35	**0.77**	0.25	0.30
	IC3	0.39	0.38	**0.85**	0.27	0.36
	IC4	0.40	0.36	**0.86**	0.22	0.33
	IC5	0.35	0.35	**0.76**	0.17	0.29
	IC6	0.35	0.30	**0.77**	0.26	0.29
Rewarding	R1	0.38	0.37	0.19	**0.78**	0.21
	R2	0.27	0.39	0.25	**0.82**	0.15
	R3	0.35	0.36	0.26	**0.79**	0.22
	R4	0.41	0.39	0.25	**0.89**	0.20
	R5	0.47	0.49	0.26	**0.83**	0.17
Trust	T1	0.65	0.32	0.36	0.23	**0.88**
	T2	0.63	0.33	0.32	0.24	**0.88**
	T3	0.64	0.26	0.33	0.17	**0.85**
	T4	0.62	0.31	0.28	0.18	**0.88**

Note: The values of the outer loadings of the reflective measurement models are underlined and are statistically significant at the $p<0.00$ level.

validity of the reflectively measured constructs of the management control model of hospitals.

According to the Fornell-Larcker criterion, the square root of each construct's AVE should be higher than the construct's highest correlation with any other latent variable measured reflectively in the model. In other words, the values on the diagonals should be greater than those in the other boxes in the table (Table 6.14). The results of evaluating the Fornell-Larcker criterion with

Table 6.14. Fornell-Larcker criterion

Variable name	Innovativeness	Diagnostic control	Interactive control	Rewarding	Trust
Innovativeness	**0.76**				
Diagnostic control	0.58	**0.85**			
Interactive control	0.45	0.43	**0.80**		
Rewarding	0.46	0.49	0.29	**0.82**	
Trust	0.73	0.35	0.37	0.23	**0.87**

the square root AVE of the reflective constructs in the management control model indicate that there are higher values on the diagonal than with correlations between constructs in off-diagonal positions. For example, the reflective construct interactive control has a value of 0.80 for the square root of its AVE value, which is higher than other row and column values for this variable (Table 6.14). Similarly, the square roots of the AVE values for all the reflective latent variables innovativeness (0.76), diagnostic control (0.85), rewarding (0.82), and trust (0.87) are greater than the correlations of these constructs with the other latent variables in the path model, indicating that all the latent variables are valid measures of unique constructs.

In summary, it should be concluded that the HTMT measure should be used as the main criterion for assessing discriminant validity in the PLS-SEM estimator, in light of the limitations presented in this regard by methods based on cross-loading and the Fornell-Larcker criterion. However, the latter two measures should still be used as supporting means of assessing discriminant validity.

6.3 Evaluating the Structural Model of Management Control in Hospitals

This part of the book presents the results of the estimation of a structural model based on the conceptual model of management control in hospitals, and on this basis a preliminary assessment of the hypotheses was made. The path model, shown in Figure 6.5, was analyzed in terms of predictive ability and relationships between constructs. The key criteria for evaluating the structural model in PLS-SEM were the significance of the path coefficients, the effect size f^2, the level of the R^2 value, the predictive relevance of Q^2, and the effect size q^2 (Hair et al., 2016, p. 191).

Given the frequent perception that structural modeling is synonymous with CB-SEM type estimation, it is worth recalling that PLS-SEM estimates parameters so as to maximize the explained variance of endogenous variables, while CB-SEM estimates parameters so as to minimize the differences between the covariances from the sample and those predicted by the theoretical model. Therefore, the concept of goodness-of-fit in PLS-SEM has slightly different mathematical foundations. Rather than assessing the goodness-of-fit, the structural model in PLS-SEM is evaluated primarily on heuristic criteria, in terms of how well it predicts endogenous latent variables. However, despite these limitations, the scientific literature proposes several measures of model fit based on PLS-SEM, which will be presented later in this book (Sarstedt et al., 2014).

First, we analyzed the **path coefficients of the preliminary structural model (PCoPSM)**, i.e., the strength of the relationships between the variables that represent the research hypotheses previously stated about the relationship between the constructs (Table 6.15). What is important, however, is not only the size of the PCoPSMs, but also their statistical significance. Given the lack of assumptions about the normality of the data distribution, the Bias-Corrected and Accelerated (BCa) Bootstrap option for 5,000 samples with two-tailed testing was used to estimate the statistical significance of the PCoPSM.

Path coefficient estimates are essentially normalized regression coefficients, which are interpreted as the change in the dependent construct as measured by standard deviations. If the independent construct is increased by one standard deviation, while holding constant the parameters of all other explanatory constructs, the dependent construct changes by the product of the PCoPSM and the standard deviation (Benitez et al., 2020, p. 11). For example, increasing innovativeness by one standard deviation will improve hospital performance by 0.74 standard deviations (Figure 6.5) if all other variables remain constant.

However, there are significant problems in the analyzed model. Assuming a significance level of 5%, it can be concluded that such path indicators as diagnostic control → innovativeness, interactive control → innovativeness, rewarding → innovativeness, rewarding → hospital performance, and IS effectiveness → hospital performance not only have small values in absolute terms, but are also statistically insignificant (Table 6.15). This means that it is difficult to conclude that there is a relationship between the variables connected by these paths. Therefore, one should consider whether to include paths with small and statistically

Table 6.15. **Results of estimating path coefficients in the preliminary structural model using the bootstrap method**

Path description	Path coefficients	t-Value	p-Value	Confidence Interval (95%)
Innovativeness -> Hospital performance	0.74	8.93	0.00	0.59-0.91
Diagnostic control-> Innovativeness	0.04	0.75	0.45	-0.06-0.12
Diagnostic control-> Hospital performance	0.30	3.54	0.00	0.14-0.47
Interactive control-> Innovativeness	-0.06	1.27	0.20	-0.16-0.03
Interactive control-> Hospital performance	-0.30	4.04	0.00	-0.46--0.17
Rewarding -> Innovativeness	0.01	0.40	0.69	-0.06-0.09
Rewarding -> Hospital performance	0.04	0.51	0.61	-0.10-0.17
Uncertainty -> Innovativeness	0.41	9.55	0.00	0.33-0.50
IS Effectiveness -> Innovativeness	0.41	6.18	0.00	0.29-0.55
IS Effectiveness -> Diagnostic control	0.73	14.70	0.00	0.62-0.81
IS Effectiveness -> Interactive control	0.66	11.37	0.00	0.53-0.76
IS Effectiveness -> Rewarding	0.56	7.91	0.00	0.41-0.69
IS Effectiveness -> Hospital performance	-0.05	0.43	0.67	-0.32-0.18
Trust -> Innovativeness	0.26	6.06	0.00	0.17-0.34

insignificant coefficients in further analysis. This is because it should be remembered that adding irrelevant exogenous variables to the structural model, which are even slightly correlated with the endogenous variable, increases the value of R^2, the coefficient of determination (Hair et al., 2016, p. 198).

Therefore, before deciding to remove paths with small and statistically insignificant coefficients, the magnitude of the effect of each variable was analyzed using an effect size (Hair et al., 2016, p. 201). The effect size index,

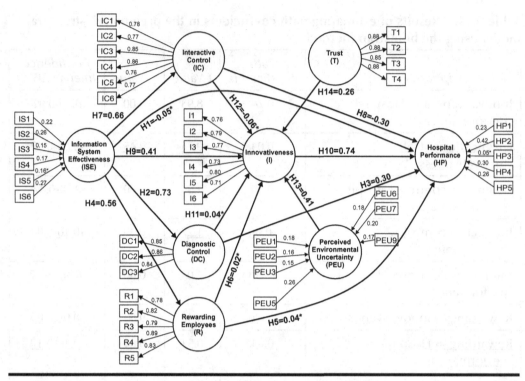

Figure 6.5. Estimation results of the preliminary structural model of management control in hospitals Note: * Statistically insignificant (p>0.05).

denoted by f^2, shows the changes in R^2 values when a specific exogenous construct is omitted from the model. It is calculated from the quotient of the difference of the coefficient of determination R^2 for the endogenous variable in the presence (full model) and after removing the specified exogenous variable, and the complement to unity of the coefficient of determination R^2 of the endogenous variable (full model):

$$f^2 = (R^2(\text{full model}) - R^2(\text{removed exogenous variable})) / (1 - R^2(\text{full model}))$$

Where: R^2(full model) and R^2(exogenous variable removed) are the values of the coefficient of determination R^2 of the endogenous latent variable when the selected exogenous latent variable is included in or removed from the model. Technically, the change in R^2 value is calculated by estimating the model twice. The first time as a full model with the exogenous latent variable included R^2(full model), and the second time with the exogenous latent variable removed – giving R^2 (exogenous variable removed). Thus, the above calculations allow us to assess whether the omitted exogenous construct has a significant effect on endogenous constructs (Table 6.16).

Table 6.16. **Results of bootstrap estimation of the effect size f^2 on individual variables in the structural model**

Path description	Effect size f^{2*}	t-Value	p-Value	Confidence Interval (95%)
Innovativeness -> Hospital performance	0.64	3.47	0.00	0.39-1.11
Diagnostic control-> Innovativeness	0.00	0.28	0.78	0.00-0.05
Diagnostic control-> Hospital performance	0.12	1.58	0.11	0.03-0.32
Interactive control-> Innovativeness	0.01	0.54	0.59	0.00-0.08
Interactive control-> Hospital performance	0.15	2.02	0.04	0.05-0.34
Rewarding -> Innovativeness	0.00	0.10	0.92	0.00-0.03
Rewarding -> Hospital performance	0.00	0.14	0.89	0.00-0.06
Uncertainty -> Innovativeness	0.51	3.50	0.00	0.30-0.87
IS Effectiveness -> Innovativeness	0.25	2.83	0.00	0.12-0.47
IS Effectiveness -> Diagnostic control	1.13	3.30	0.00	0.63-1.97
IS Effectiveness -> Interactive control	0.76	3.07	0.00	0.40-1.37
IS Effectiveness -> Rewarding	0.45	2.50	0.01	0.21-0.90
IS Effectiveness -> Hospital performance	0.00	0.11	0.91	0.00-0.05
Trust -> Innovativeness	0.24	2.49	0.01	0.09-0.46

Note: * Estimated with the Bias-Corrected and Accelerated (BCa) Bootstrap option for 5,000 samples with two-tailed testing

Guidelines for interpreting the effect size f^2 are that values of 0.02, 0.15, and 0.35 represent small, medium, and large effects of the exogenous latent variable on the endogenous variable, respectively. Effect size values of less than 0.02 indicate that there is no effect of the exogenous variable on the endogenous variable (Cohen, 1988, pp. 413–414). A large or medium effect size indicates that these constructs are significant and important elements of the structural model.

Analyzing the f^2 results obtained from the SmartPLS estimator (Table 6.16), it can be seen that the same exogenous variables in a given relationship (diagnostic control, rewarding, and IS effectiveness) have a non-significant value ($f^2 < 0.02$) and statistical significance ($p > 0.05$) of the effect size on the corresponding endogenous variable (innovativeness and performance), and the lower limit of the confidence interval is 0.00. In addition, the analysis showed that the effect size of the diagnostic control variable on the performance variable is, admittedly, at the average level ($f^2 = 0.12$), but it is statistically insignificant at the assumed confidence level, although the lower limit of the confidence interval is greater than zero. This means that with the assumed 95% confidence interval, the value of the effect size f^2 does not reach zero.

Comparing the results obtained in the analysis of the path coefficients of the structural model and the f^2 effect size, it was decided to remove from the original model of management control in hospitals the paths' diagnostic control → innovativeness, interactive control → innovativeness, rewarding → innovativeness, rewarding → performance and IS effectiveness → hospital performance. However, the diagnostic control → hospital performance path was retained, because in this case the path coefficient is relatively high (0.30) and the lower limit of the confidence interval is also relatively substantial (0.14) (Table 6.15). In addition, the lower limit of the confidence interval for f^2 is 0.03 (Table 6.16), which means that the value of this coefficient is greater than zero with an assumed confidence interval of 95%. The removal of both paths starting from the rewarding variable (i.e.: rewarding → innovativeness and rewarding → hospital performance) renders the retention of this variable in the model not theoretically justified in light of the research problem addressed here, since the effect of the IS effectiveness variable on the rewarding variable is irrelevant when rewarding does not affect any other variable.

Removal of the aforementioned paths and variable leads to a significant modification of the model. Of the eight variables and 14 paths from the original model, seven variables and eight paths remain. Therefore, continuing its analysis is pointless. The rest of the paper presents a full analysis of the modified model of management control in hospitals (Figure 6.6).

6.4 Evaluation of the Modified Management Control Model in Hospitals

Before reporting the results of the estimation analysis of the modified structural model, which is referred to as the management control model in hospitals in the remainder of this book, the data on the estimation of formative measurement models are presented again. The need to re-evaluate these measurement models is due to the fact that when analyzing formative variables, the values of the weights of formative indicators are affected by other relationships in the path model analyzed with the PLS-SEM estimator. Such a problem does not occur in the case of reflective variables, and therefore the re-reporting of these data was omitted.

As with the preliminary structural model, the analysis began with all variable indicators, that is, the variable perceived environmental uncertainty was restored to the previously removed indicators PEU4 and PEU8. In the results of the analysis, no collinearity was observed either between the indicators of the formative variables uncertainty, IS effectiveness, and hospital performance or between the constructs. The variance inflation factor (VIF) did not exceed the threshold values (Shmueli et al., 2019, p. 2334). From the re-estimation of the formative measurement models, the weights of the indicator variables PEU4 and PEU8 were negative and statistically insignificant at the p<0.05 level, so they were removed from the measurement model. The final results of the estimation of the measurement models of the formatively measured constructs are shown in Table 6.17.

As mentioned earlier, the primary way to decide whether a measurement model for a particular latent variable should be formative or reflective is through reasoning and theoretical underpinnings (Table 4.2). However, a potentially flawed measurement model specification is a threat to the validity of SEM (Jarvis et al., 2003) results. For example, modeling a construct in a reflective way, when the conceptualization of the measurement model, and thus the way questions are formulated in the survey questionnaire, is consistent with the formative measurement model, can result in biased survey results. This is because the observable variables in the formative model of the latent variable may not be highly correlated with each other, which means that their loadings in the reflective measurement model may be low, for example, below 0.50. Such a low value of the outer loadings of an indicator will result in its removal from the reflective measurement model of the unobservable variable (Hair, Risher, et al., 2019, p. 16), while, in fact, due to the theoretical conceptualization of the construct, it should remain. Any attempt to clean up actually formative measurement models based on the guidelines for reflective measurement models may have adverse consequences for the validity of the construct content and, as a result, may have a significant impact on the estimation results of the structural model.

In order to confirm the theoretically selected measurement model specification, the tetrad analysis introduced by Bollen and Ting (Bollen & Ting, 2000) and adapted to PLS-SEM by (Gudergan et al., 2008) was used (Table 6.18). The Confirmatory Tetrad Analysis (CTA) function in Smart-PLS v.3.3.3 was used for this purpose. The tetrad analysis can confirm whether the relationship between indicators and the latent variable is reflective. CTA is based on the concept of tetrads (τ), which describe the relationship between pairs of covariances of indicators of a latent variable. In reflective measurement models, each tetrad is expected to be zero and thus disappear

Table 6.17.   Results of formative variable analysis after removal of indicators PEU4 and PEU8

Variable name	Indicator symbol	Outer weights (loadings)	t-Value	p-Value	Confidence Interval (95%)	Significance (p<0.05)
Perceived environmental uncertainty	PEU1	0.18 (0.83)	2.21 (20.16)	0.03 (0.00)	0.02-0.35; (0.73-0.89)	Yes
	PEU2	0.16 (0.70)	1.97 (12.07)	0.05 (0.00)	0.00-0.32; (0.57-0.80)	Yes
	PEU3	0.15 (0.72)	2.03 (12.49)	0.04 (0.00)	0.01-0.30; (0.59-0.82)	Yes
	PEU5	0.26 (0.80)	3.32 (19.24)	0.00 (0.00)	0.10-0.41; (0.71-0.87)	Yes
	PEU6	0.18 (0.83)	2.10 (19.14)	0.04 (0.00)	0.01-0.36; (0.73-0.89)	Yes
	PEU7	0.20 (0.83)	2.12 (19.66)	0.03 (0.00)	0.01-0.37; (0.73-0.89)	Yes
	PEU9	0.17 (0.63)	2.22 (9.18)	0.03 (0.00)	0.02-0.32; (0.48-0.75)	Yes
Information system effectiveness	IS1	0.23 (0.81)	3.29 (16.55)	0.00 (0.00)	0.09-0.37; (0.69-0.88)	Yes
	IS2	0.23 (0.81)	3.47 (21.33)	0.00 (0.00)	0.09-0.36; (0.72-0.87)	Yes
	IS3	0.13 (0.83)	1.78 (22.07)	0.08 (0.00)	-0.01-0.27; (0.74-0.89)	No
	IS4	0.23 (0.86)	3.33 (26.64)	0.00 (0.00)	0.08-0.35; (0.79-0.91)	Yes
	IS5	0.15 (0.81)	1.93 (19.55)	0.05 (0.00)	0.00-0.30; (0.72-0.88)	Borderline
	S6	0.26 (0.78)	3.94 (21.32)	0.00 (0.00)	0.14-0.39; (0.70-0.84)	Yes
Hospital performance	HP1	0.21 (0.71)	2.48 (12.23)	0.01 (0.00)	0.04-0.38; (0.58-0.81)	Yes
	HP2	0.41 (0.82)	5.53 (20.86)	0.00 (0.00)	0.26-0.55; (0.73-0.89)	Yes
	HP3	0.05 (0.71)	0.58 (11.00)	0.56 (0.00)	-0.14-0.23; (0.56-0.81)	No
	HP4	0.3 (0.78)	3.59 (15.69)	0.00 (0.00)	0.12-0.46; (0.66-0.86)	Yes
	HP5	0.27 (0.88)	2.53 (23.64)	0.01 (0.00)	0.07-0.48; (0.79-0.94)	Yes

(Gudergan et al., 2008, p. 1239). The reason for this is that reflective indicators similarly represent one specific concept or characteristic. Therefore, the differences between pairs of covariance indicators that equally represent a construct should be zero. If even just one value of the tetrad in the measurement model is significantly different from zero (it does not disappear), the reflective measurement model should be rejected and an alternative formative specification adopted instead. Technically, CTA is a statistical test that takes into account the hypothesis H0: $\tau = 0$, saying that the tetrad equals zero, and the alternative hypothesis H1: $\tau \neq 0$, indicating a tetrad value different from zero. Thus, rejecting the null hypothesis stating that the measurement model is reflective means accepting the alternative hypothesis H1, suggesting that the measurement model is formative.

Before proceeding with the confirmatory tetrad analysis, the presence of statistically significant correlations between the indicators of each construct was confirmed using Statistica 13.3. This step is important because a necessary requirement of CTA-PLS analysis is that the items be correlated to at

Table 6.18. Results of CTA-PLS tetrad analysis

Variable name	Tetrad number and indicator symbol	The lower threshold of the Confidence Interval for p=0.1	The upper threshold of the Confidence Interval for p=0.1
Innovativeness	1: I1,I2,I3,I4	-0.39	0.55
	2: I1,I2,I4,I3	-0.32	0.62
	4: I1,I2,I3,I5	-0.23	0.82
	6: I1,I3,I5,I2	-0.23	0.63
	7: I1,I2,I3,I6	-0.40	0.49
	10: I1,I2,I4,I5	-0.30	0.70
	16: I1,I2,I5,I6	-0.36	0.66
	22: I1,I3,I4,I6	-0.69	0.14
	26: I1,I3,I6,I5	-0.34	0.55
IS Effectiveness	1: S1,S2,S3,S4	-0.07	0.04
	2: S1,S2,S4,S3	-0.12	0.01
	4: S1,S2,S3,S5	-0.05	0.04
	6: S1,S3,S5,S2	-0.05	0.03
	7: S1,S2,S3,S6	-0.10	0.02
	10: S1,S2,S4,S5	-0.15	0.02
	16: S1,S2,S5,S6	-0.17	0.03
	<u>22: S1,S3,S4,S6</u>	<u>0.01</u>	<u>0.16</u>
	26: S1,S3,S6,S5	-0.12	0.04
Interactive control	1: KI1,KI2,KI3,KI4	-0.17	0.37
	2: KI1,KI2,KI4,KI3	-0.16	0.31
	4: KI1,KI2,KI3,KI5	-0.13	0.46
	6: KI1,KI3,KI5,KI2	-0.24	0.24
	7: KI1,KI2,KI3,KI6	-0.23	0.31
	10: KI1,KI2,KI4,KI5	-0.07	0.45
	16: KI1,KI2,KI5,KI6	-0.11	0.34
	22: KI1,KI3,KI4,KI6	-0.05	0.35
	26: KI1,KI3,KI6,KI5	-0.47	0.13

(Continued)

Table 6.18 (Continued) Results of CTA-PLS tetrad analysis

Variable name	Tetrad number and indicator symbol	The lower threshold of the Confidence Interval for p=0.1	The upper threshold of the Confidence Interval for p=0.1
Perceived environmental uncertainty	1: N1,N2,N3,N5	-0.18	0.15
	2: N1,N2,N5,N3	-0.20	0.15
	4: N1,N2,N3,N6	-0.11	0.18
	6: N1,N3,N6,N2	-0.26	0.12
	10: N1,N2,N3,N9	-0.04	0.30
	13: N1,N2,N5,N6	-0.11	0.20
	19: N1,N2,N5,N9	-0.09	0.21
	25: N1,N2,N6,N9	0.05	0.43
	30: N1,N7,N9,N2	-0.20	0.06
	34: N1,N3,N5,N7	-0.12	0.23
	38: N1,N3,N9,N5	-0.16	0.15
	40: N1,N3,N6,N7	-0.16	0.27
	50: N1,N5,N7,N6	-0.11	0.21
	55: N1,N5,N7,N9	-0.06	0.22
Hospital performance	1: W1,W2,W3,W4	-0.26	0.04
	2: W1,W2,W4,W3	-0.51	-0.03
	4: W1,W2,W3,W5	-0.30	0.01
	6: W1,W3,W5,W2	-0.19	0.20
	10: W1,W3,W4,W5	-0.17	0.23
Trust	1: Z1,Z2,Z3,Z4	-0.17	0.02
	2: Z1,Z2,Z4,Z3	-0.05	0.16

least some degree. If they were uncorrelated, all tetrads would be zero by definition, making the CTA-PLS analysis meaningless (Gudergan et al., 2008, p. 1243). Table 6.18 shows the results of the CTA-PLS analysis, performed for 5,000 bootstrap subsamples with a two-tailed test and a recommended significance level of p = 0.10 (Hair et al., 2018, p. 98). The number of tetrads considered for each latent variable in the analysis increases exponentially with the number of indicators per measurement model. The variable with four indicators includes only two non-redundant tetrads, since two unique pairs of indicators can be compared. The diagnostic control variable is missing from Table 6.18 because it has only three indicators, and therefore not a single case can be constructed in which covariances of indicator pairs are compared. For the IS effectiveness variable with five indicators, 5 tetrads can be distinguished, and for the uncertainty variable with seven indicators, there are already 14 tetrads.

An analysis of the lower and upper confidence intervals ($p = 0.1$) adjusted for bias and Bonferroni correction indicates whether or not the non-redundant tetrads are significantly different from zero. If zero falls within the confidence interval, the tetrad is not significantly different from zero, which means it is a vanishing tetrad. Otherwise, if zero is not within the confidence interval corrected for bias and adjusted for Bonferroni correction, then the non-redundant tetrad is significantly different from zero. The latter situation occurs when the signs of the lower and upper limits of the corrected confidence interval are identical, that is, both are negative or both are positive. This is the case for the 22nd tetrad of the IS effectiveness variable, the 25th tetrad of the uncertainty variable, and the 2nd tetrad of the performance variable (Table 6.18). This means that for these variables, the null hypothesis of null tetrads should be rejected, and the alternative hypothesis should be accepted that the measurement models of the IS effectiveness, uncertainty, and hospital performance variables are indeed formative, providing support for the adopted measurement models at the stage of operationalization of the variables. If the CTA analysis did not provide support for the adopted measurement models, however, this would not automatically mean a change in modeling specifications.

Estimation of the modified model of management control in hospitals showed that all **path coefficients of the modified structural model (PCoMSM)** are statistically significant and have significant absolute values, ranging from 0.25 to 0.73. The effect size f^2 are also at medium to high levels (Table 6.19). Several estimated paths have changed slightly from the initial structural model, but this has not fundamentally altered their significance. There is a noteworthy increase in the f^2 effect size for all variables, except for the effect size of the trust variable on the innovativeness variable. In this case, there was a slight decrease in this parameter. In favor of the modified model, however, is not only the increase in the f^2 effect size of the diagnostic control variable on the performance construct, but, above all, the increase in the statistical significance of f^2 to a p-value below the threshold of 0.1.

Table 6.19. Path coefficient values and effect size ƒ² for the modified management control model in hospitals

Path description	Path coefficients (effect size ƒ²)	t-Value	p-Value	Confidence Interval (95%)
Innovativeness -> Hospital performance	0.72 (0.97)	11.71 (3.65)	0.00 (0.00)	0.61-0.85; (0.63-1.65)
Diagnostic control -> Hospital performance	0.29 (0.16)	4.46 (1.74)	0.00 (0.08)	0.16-0.42; (0.04-0.41)
Interactive control -> Hospital performance	-0.32 (0.23)	4.56 (2.60)	0.00 (0.01)	-0.46-0.19; (0.10-0.44)
Uncertainty -> Innovativeness	0.43 (0.56)	10.54 (3.59)	0.00 (0.00)	0.35-0.51; (0.34-0.94)
IS Effectiveness -> Innovativeness	0.39 (0.58)	9.62 (3.98)	0.00 (0.00)	0.31-0.46; (0.34-0.90)
IS Effectiveness -> Diagnostic control	0.73 (1.15)	15.13 (3.30)	0.00 (0.00)	0.63-0.82; (0.65-1.99)
IS Effectiveness -> Interactive control	0.67 (0.80)	11.89 (3.08)	0.00 (0.00)	0.55-0.77; (0.43-1.44)
Trust -> Innovativeness	0.25 (0.22)	6.04 (2.58)	0.00 (0.01)	0.16-0.33; (0.09-0.42)

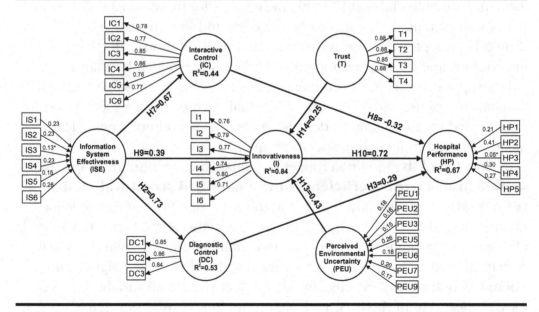

Figure 6.6. Modified model of management control in hospitals (the final model)

The estimation results of the modified model show that the R² coefficients of determination representing the combined effect of the exogenous latent

Table 6.20. Results of estimating coefficients of determination (R²) for endogenous variables of the modified model of management control in hospitals

Variable name	Coefficients of determination – R²	t-Value	p-Value	Confidence Interval (95%)
Innovativeness	0.84	34.98	0.00	0.79-0.88
Diagnostic control	0.53	7.65	0.00	0.39-0.67
Interactive control	0.44	6.00	0.00	0.30-0.59
Hospital performance	0.67	14.65	0.00	0.59-0.77

variables on the endogenous latent variable are relatively high and statistically significant (Table 6.20). This shows that the variables and relationships in the model explain a significant portion of the variance in the data. In analyzing the results of the model estimation, it can be seen that the exogenous variables IS effectiveness, uncertainty, and trust explain as much as 84% of the variance of the innovativeness variable. Similarly, the variables innovativeness, diagnostic control, and interactive control explain 67% of the variance of the variable performance. Also, a relatively large amount of the variance of the variables diagnostic control ($R^2 = 0.534$) and interactive control ($R^2 = 0.44$) is explained by the variable IS effectiveness (Figure 6.6). This means that in light of commonly accepted evaluation criteria indicating that R^2 values of 0.75, 0.5, and 0.25 are significant, moderate, and weak, respectively (Hair et al., 2011, p. 145), the proposed model has significant to moderate predictive power in the study sample.

6.5 Analysis of the Predictive Power of the Model

The R^2 value only assesses the explanatory power of the model, but does not indicate its predictive power, out-of-sample in the sense of its ability to predict the value of new cases not included in the estimation process. Assessing the predictive power of a model out-of-sample involves estimating the model on a learning (analytical) sample and evaluating its predictive performance on data other than the learning sample (Shmueli et al., 2016). Evaluating the predictive power of a statistical model is a key component of the study, as it enables assessment of the ability of the adopted model to make falsifiable predictions on new observations. In other words, it makes it possible to estimate the model's behavior in the general population.

In addition to assessing the R^2 determination coefficient as a criterion for predictive accuracy, the Q^2 value estimate developed by M. Stone and S. Geisser was also used as an assessment measure for the cross-validated predictive accuracy of the PLS path model (1974, 1974). Cross-redundancy of the Q^2 construct is a type of R^2 cross-validation between indicators of an endogenous latent variable and all indicators associated with constructs explaining that endogenous variable, using the estimated structural model (Tenenhaus et al., 2005, p. 174). Technically, the Q^2 indicator is calculated using a blindfolding procedure (more in: Hair et al., 2016, pp. 202–206). Given the blindfolding procedure used, it can be assumed that the Q^2 value is an indicator of the model's predictive power for a specific endogenous variable for data other than those used for model estimation (Hair et al., 2016, p. 202). In order to calculate Q^2 values for individual dependent variables of the management control model of hospitals, a blindfolding procedure was run in the SmartPLS estimator. A default omission distance of 7 was assumed, which is not a divisor of the number of cases in the research sample equal to 151.

In Table 6.21, SSO shows the sum of the squared observations, SSE the sum of the squared prediction errors, and the last column (1 - SSE / SSO) the final Q^2 value, which determines the predictive accuracy of the model with respect to each endogenous variable. As can be seen, the Q^2 values of all four endogenous constructs are well above zero, indicating the predictive power of the model with respect to the endogenous latent variables.

Q^2 values estimated using the blindfolding procedure provide a measure of how well a path model can predict the originally observed values. Similar to the f^2 effect size method, the relative impact of a specific exogenous variable on an endogenous variable can be estimated in terms of the

Table 6.21. Q^2 values calculated by blindfolding procedure

Variable	SSO	SSE	$Q^2 = (1\text{-}SSE/SSO)$
Innovativeness	906	478	0.47
Diagnostic control	453	284	0.37
Interactive control	906	659	0.27
Uncertainty	1057	1057	
IS Effectiveness	906	906	
Hospital performance	755	454	0.40
Trust	604	604	

R^2 determination index – the relative impact of predictive accuracy can be compared using the q^2 effect size measure (Hair et al., 2016, p. 207). The q^2 effect size is calculated similarly to the f^2 effect size, except that instead of the change in R^2, the change in Q^2 values is included in the calculations.

$$q^2 = (Q^2(\text{full model}) - Q^2(\text{removed exogenous variable})) / (1 - Q^2(\text{full model}))$$

Where: Q^2 (full model) and Q^2(exogenous variable removed) are the Q^2 values of the endogenous latent variable when the selected exogenous latent variable is included in or removed from the model. Technically, the change in Q^2 values is calculated by estimating the model twice using the blindfolding option. The first time as a full model with the exogenous latent variable included, then we get Q^2(full model), and the second time with the exogenous variable removed, which gives Q^2(exogenous variable removed). Interpretation of the effect size q^2 is similar to the effect size f^2, meaning that values of 0.02, 0.15, and 0.35 indicate low, medium, or high predictive relevance of a given exogenous construct for a given endogenous construct, respectively.

Calculated in an Excel spreadsheet, the q^2 effect size, based on repeatedly running the blindfolding procedure in SmartPLS, indicate relatively low predictive relevance of the variables trust (0.04) and close to average predictive relevance of the variables IS effectiveness (0.10) and uncertainty (0.09) for the innovativeness variable (Table 6.22). Similarly, the predictive relevance is close to the average of the variables diagnostic control (0.07) and interactive control (0.08) for the variable performance. On the other hand, innovativeness (0.47) has a high predictive relevance for the performance variable, and

Table 6.22. Q^2 effect size values for modified management control model in hospitals

Variable	Innovativeness	Diagnostic control	Interactive control	Hospital performance
Innovativeness				0.47
Diagnostic control				0.07
Interactive control				0.08
Uncertainty	0.09			
IS Effectiveness	0.10	0.60	0.38	
Trust	0.04			

the variables diagnostic control and interactive control for the IS effectiveness, 0.60 and 0.38, respectively. The relatively low predictive relevance of the variables IS effectiveness, uncertainty, and trust for innovativeness may be due to the fact that this significance is spread across three variables. In contrast, it is worth noting that innovativeness has a much higher predictive relevance for hospital performance than both types of controls.

The value of Q^2, and consequently q^2, is calculated using a blindfolding procedure. Blindfolding omits individual data points, but not entire cases. For example, it assigns mean values to the omitted data points and estimates a path model. Since the Q^2 value is not based on unused records, but on individual omitted and imputed data points, this indicator is a combination of in-sample and out-of-sample prediction without explicitly indicating whether the model has a good explanatory fit (in terms of R^2 value) or shows predictive power (Shmueli et al., 2019, p. 2324). Thus, the Q^2 metric is a quasi-test of the model's predictive power outside the research sample. The Q^2 metric has two main limitations: it does not make a clear distinction between training and holdout samples (i.e., it is not a "true" out-of-sample measure), and it is an ad hoc measure that does not provide clear boundaries for model comparisons (Liengaard et al., 2021, p. 366). Focusing on metrics for assessing a model's explanatory power is problematic because the optimal predictive model may differ from that obtained in the context of explanatory modeling. In other words, a well-fitting model designed in an explanatory context may perform poorly in terms of out-of-sample forecasting, thus limiting its practical utility (Shmueli, 2010).

These limitations are overcome by the PLSpredict procedure, developed by G. Shmueli et al. (2016), which generates case- or construct-level predictions based on holdout samples to take full advantage of the predictive properties in PLS-SEM. That is, unlike standard structural model evaluation using R^2 and Q^2 measures, PLSpredict offers methods to assess the predictive power of a model out-of-sample, essentially to predict outcome values for new cases. PLSpredict is based on the extraction of separate training and holdout samples during the estimation of model parameters, and then used to assess the predictive power of the model. The training sample is the portion of the entire data set used to estimate model parameters (e.g., path coefficients, indicator weights, and loadings), and the remainder of the data set that was not used to estimate the model is referred to as the holdout sample. When calculations are conducted on training cases, then these are in-sample predictions. In contrast, calculations conducted on the holdout sample are out-of-sample forecasts. A small discrepancy between actual and out-of-sample predictions suggests that the model has high predictive power. In contrast, a marked discrepancy between actual and predicted values indicates low predictive power. To estimate the predictive power of the modified management control model, the PLSpredict option in SmartPLS was used. According to the recommendations of its developers, the number of samples was set to ten and one repetition was selected (2019, p. 2330).

The data obtained from the calculations show that all indicators of endogenous constructs outperform the most naive benchmark, that is, the average indicator from the training sample, as the $Q^2_{predict}$ values of all indicators are well above zero (Table 6.23, col. 4). This means that the model

Table 6.23.   Estimation of indicators in the PLSpredict procedure

Indicator name	PLS-SEM			LM		PLS-SEM – LM	
	RMSE	MAE	$Q^2_{predict}$	RMSE	MAE	RMSE	MAE
Col. No.	2	3	4	5	6	7=2-5	8=3-6
I1	1.061	0.863	0.472	1.139	0.924	-0.078	-0.061
I2	1.082	0.854	0.474	1.131	0.925	-0.049	-0.071
I3	1.008	0.820	0.537	1.062	0.834	-0.054	-0.014
I4	1.048	0.878	0.452	1.063	0.868	-0.015	0.010
I5	0.978	0.836	0.553	1.033	0.849	-0.055	-0.013
I6	1.064	0.859	0.340	1.096	0.881	-0.032	-0.022
DC1	0.835	0.686	0.358	0.924	0.736	-0.089	-0.050
DC2	0.984	0.797	0.363	1.080	0.876	-0.096	-0.079
DC3	1.028	0.863	0.386	1.127	0.954	-0.099	-0.091
IC1	1.041	0.811	0.223	1.131	0.894	-0.090	-0.083
IC2	1.070	0.816	0.280	1.145	0.892	-0.075	-0.076
IC3	1.040	0.876	0.353	1.049	0.876	-0.009	0.000
IC4	0.989	0.806	0.301	1.071	0.839	-0.082	-0.033
IC5	1.060	0.857	0.215	1.166	0.964	-0.106	-0.107
IC6	1.257	1.068	0.218	1.354	1.142	-0.097	-0.074
HP1	0.999	0.855	0.233	1.063	0.905	-0.064	-0.050
HP2	1.077	0.908	0.230	1.139	0.938	-0.062	-0.030
HP3	1.021	0.797	0.144	1.151	0.925	-0.130	-0.128
HP4	1.122	0.928	0.222	1.186	1.010	-0.064	-0.082
HP5	0.838	0.663	0.361	0.859	0.672	-0.021	-0.009

has predictive capabilities beyond the study sample. However, the $Q^2_{predict}$ criterion is very simplistic, as it ignores any input information that the PLS path model provides. An alternative way to estimate predictive power, which takes into account the input layer of the PLS path model while ignoring its specific structure (e.g., interdependencies between constructs), is to use a linear regression model (LM) to generate predictions for indicator variables by running a linear regression of each indicator of the dependent construct on indicators of exogenous latent variables in the PLS path model (Evermann & Tate, 2016; Shmueli et al., 2016). This analysis (LM) ignores any specific model structure based on measurement and structural theory, so PLS-SEM-based forecasts that take into account the entire model structure (i.e., measurement models and structural model) can be expected to outperform the naive LM benchmark. This means that the predictive power of the PLS path model should be at least equal to that of LM (Shmueli et al., 2019, p. 2328).

To test whether the predictive power of the path model is greater than that of the LM benchmark, prediction errors were compared for both methods: PLS-SEM and LM (Table 6.23, col. 2, 3, 5, and 6). Two metrics are useful in this regard – mean absolute error (MAE) and root mean square error (RMSE). MAE measures the average magnitude of errors in a set of forecasts without regard to their direction (above or below). These are the average absolute differences between predictions and actual observations, with all individual differences given equal weight. The RMSE is the square root of the average differences between predictions and actual observations squared (Shmueli et al., 2019, p. 2327).

Error comparisons (Table 6.23, columns 7 and 8) show that for all indicator variables, PLS-SEM analysis yields smaller prediction errors of RMSE and MAE compared to LM, as manifested by the negative value of the error difference. The exception is the I4 indicator of the innovativeness variable, for which the error of the MEA from a naive benchmark derived from linear regression (LM) is smaller than from predictions based on PLS-SEM modeling. Given that in the crushing majority of indicators the prediction errors of the RMSE and MAE derived from the PLS-SEM estimation are smaller compared to the LM, the high predictive power of the proposed model of management control in hospitals should be recognized.

The PLSpredict procedure also provides an opportunity to compare the predictive power of models at the construct level. Admittedly, the original path model of management control of hospitals was modified due to low-valued and statistically insignificant path coefficients (Table 6.15) and effect sizes f^2 (Table 6.16), but it is worth testing whether the modified model

Table 6.24. **Comparison of preliminary and modified management control model in hospitals based on PLSpredict results**

Variable name	Modified model (MM)			Preliminary model (PM)			MM – PM		
	RMSE	MAE	$Q^2_{predict}$	RMSE	MAE	$Q^2_{predict}$	RMSE	MAE	$Q^2_{predict}$
Innovative-ness	0.430	0.340	0.820	0.431	0.336	0.819	-0.001	0.004	0.001
Diagnostic control	0.707	0.553	0.518	0.712	0.553	0.514	-0.005	-0.001	0.004
Interactive control	0.771	0.624	0.427	0.776	0.629	0.418	-0.005	-0.005	0.009
Hospital performance	0.800	0.631	0.376	0.801	0.629	0.376	-0.001	0.002	0.000
Uncertainty				0.857	0.664	0.291			

will also have higher predictive power. To conduct the test, the SmartPLS program was run and, as recommended by its developers, the number of samples was set to ten and ten replicates were selected to obtain the mean estimation value (Shmueli et al., 2019, p. 2330).

The results of the analysis show that, both based on the $Q^2_{predict}$ value analysis and based on the prediction error analysis, the two models differ slightly (Table 6.24). However, it should be noted that the scales tilt toward the modified model, which, although to a small extent, nevertheless shows better predictive properties.

6.5.1 Mediating Effects in the Structural Model

Mediation occurs when a third variable (mediator) intervenes between two other constructs. More specifically, an exogenous construct causes a change in the mediator construct, which, in turn, results in a change in the endogenous construct in the PLS path model. Thus, the mediator variable determines the relationship between the two constructs. However, it is important to note that one cannot only rely on the calculations of the PLS-SEM estimator, but strong theoretical and conceptual support is also required to study mediation effects (Hair et al., 2016, p. 228).

The results of the model estimation show that the total effect of the IS effectiveness variable on hospital performance variable mediated by interactive control variable is -0.21, the total effect of the IS effectiveness on

Table 6.25. Total and indirect effects of mediation (path coefficients)

Variables name	Effect	t-Value	p-Value	Confidence Interval (95%)
IS Effectiveness -> Interactive control -> Hospital performance	-0.21	3.51	0.00	-0.35-0.11
IS Effectiveness -> Innovativeness -> Hospital performance	0.28	7.47	0.00	0.21-0.36
IS Effectiveness -> Diagnostic control -> Hospital performance	0.21	4.24	0.00	0.12-0.32
IS Effectiveness -> Hospital performance	0.28	4.09	0.00	0.14-0.41
Uncertainty -> Innovativeness -> Hospital performance	0.31	7.73	0.00	0.24-0.40
Trust -> Innovativeness -> Hospital performance	0.18	5.33	0.00	0.12-0.25

performance mediated by diagnostic control is 0.21, and the total effect of the IS effectiveness on hospital performance mediated by innovativeness is 0.28, ultimately resulting in a total effect of the IS effectiveness on hospital performance of 0.28 (Table 6.25). This shows that interactive control weakens the effect of innovativeness and diagnostic control on hospital performance. On the other hand, it can be seen that the total effect of trust and uncertainty on hospital performance mediated by innovativeness is positive at 0.18 and 0.31, respectively. Considering the direct path values, it can be seen that innovativeness has the greatest effect on hospital performance (0.72) (Table 6.19). However, innovativeness acts as a mediator for three exogenous variables: IS effectiveness, uncertainty, and trust. In this context, directors' perception of the uncertainty of the environment has the greatest impact on hospital performance (0.31) (Table 6.25).

6.5.2 Goodness of the Model Fit

PLS-SEM is considered suitable mainly for predictive applications, predicting causal relationships to provide causal explanations in less developed or still developing theories (Cheah et al., 2020). J.F. Hair, J.J. Risher and others believe that some researchers have come to the erroneous conclusion that PLS-SEM is not useful for testing and confirming theories (2019, p. 7). According to some researchers, this approach was due to the fact that for many years a global measure of goodness-of-fit had not been developed for PLS-SEM, which limited the applicability of this estimator for confirmation purposes, i.e., testing previously developed theories. In recent years, there have been several publications supporting the use goodness-of-fit measures within the PLS-SEM framework, expanding the possibilities of using this method (Bentler & Huang, 2014; Henseler, Hubona, et al., 2016). Note, however, that the term "fit" has different meanings in CB-SEM and PLS-SEM contexts. Goodness-of-fit statistics for CB-SEM are derived from the discrepancy between the empirical covariance matrix and that implied from the model (theoretical), while PLS-SEM focuses on the discrepancy between the observed (in the case of indicator variables) or approximated (in the case of latent variables) value of the dependent variables and the value predicted by the model in question (Hair et al., 2016, p. 86).

PLS-SEM provides some global measures of goodness-of-fit, for example, the standardized root mean square residual (SRMR) (Henseler et al., 2014) and metrics such as the Euclidean distance (d_{ULS}) and the geodesic distance (d_G) (Benitez et al., 2020, p. 5), but one should be cautious in using these measures to reject or modify the model, since PLS-SEM estimates parameters in such a way that it does not focus on minimizing these discrepancies. Nevertheless, there has been quite a bit of work that argues that the use of global measures of model fit in PLS-SEM is reasonable (Hair et al., 2016, p. 208; Henseler et al., 2014, p. 193). For example, J. Henseler (2017, p. 185) believes that an SRMR value of less than 0.08 usually indicates that the degree of lack of fit is not significant. SRMR is defined as the difference between the observed correlation and the implied correlation matrix from the model. Thus, it enables assessment of the average magnitude of the discrepancy between observed and expected correlations as an absolute measure of the model's fit criterion. For the modified model of management control in hospitals, the SRMR value is 0.06, which may indicate a high goodness-of-fit of the model to the data (Table 6.26).

The goodness-of-fit was also tested using squared Euclidean distance (d_{ULS}) and geodesic distance (d_G), which represent two different ways of calculating the quantitative discrepancy between the empirical correlation matrix and the correlation matrix implied from the model (Dijkstra & Henseler, 2015b, p. 20; Hair, Sarstedt, et al., 2019, p. 574). Note that there are no threshold values for d_{ULS} and d_G, only by performing a bootstrap procedure can these goodness-of-fit metrics be interpreted. Parameters for these goodness-of-fit metrics are calculated for two models: saturated and estimated. The estimated model assesses correlation, taking into account the model structure predicted by the researcher, while the saturated model

Table 6.26. Goodness-of-fit measures of the preliminary and modified management control model in hospitals

Goodness-of-fit measures	Model type	Modified model (MM)		Preliminary model (PM)	
		Original value	Upper limit of the confidence interval (95%)	Original value	Upper limit of the confidence interval (95%)
SRMR	Saturated	0.055	0.056	0.058	0.056
	Estimated	0.060	0.062	0.062	0.063
d_{ULS}	Saturated	2.154	2.168	2.992	2.822
	Estimated	2.516	2.663	3.481	3.582
d_G	Saturated	1.132	1.285	1.694	1.770
	Estimated	1.167	1.314	1.734	1.796

assesses correlation between all constructs. It is, therefore, a more elaborate and conservative version of the fit measure. The scientific literature does not specify which model to use in reporting goodness-of-fit criteria, although it seems that the estimated model, that is, including the structure proposed by the researcher, is a sufficient choice.

Because the calculations were performed with an adapted bootstrap procedure (Bollen & Stine, 1992), their interpretation is different. For the exact fit criteria of d_{ULS} and d_G, their original value is compared with the confidence interval formed from the sampling distribution. A model is a good fit if the difference between the correlation matrix implied by the model and the empirical correlation matrix is so small that it can be attributed solely to sampling error. Hence, the difference between the correlation matrix implied by the model under study and the empirical correlation matrix should be insignificant ($p>0.05$). Otherwise, if the discrepancy is significant ($p<0.05$), goodness of the model fit has not been confirmed. This means that the confidence interval should contain the "original value" (Table 6.26), that is, the upper limit of the confidence interval should be greater than the original value of the d_{ULS} and d_G fit criteria to indicate that the model has a good fit.

The results of the calculations show that the modified model of management control in hospitals has a good fit, as the null hypothesis that the correlation matrix implied by the model and the empirical correlation matrix are consistent cannot be rejected, since the values of the d_{ULS} and d_G discrepancy measure are below the 95% percentile. It is worth noting that the preliminary management control model also has a good fit.

A recommended indicator for assessing the goodness-of-fit of a model is also RMS$_{\text{theta}}$, (root mean squared residual covariance matrix), which assesses the degree of correlation of external model residuals. RMS$_{\text{theta}}$ is based on the external model residuals, which are the differences between predicted indicator values and observed indicator values, and is the root mean squared residual covariance matrix of the external model (Lohmöller, 1989, p. 53). The RMS$_{\text{theta}}$ value for the modified (final) model of management control in hospitals is 0.1199, while for the preliminary model it is 0.1219. RMS$_{\text{theta}}$ values below 0.12 indicate a good fit of the model, while higher values indicate a lack of fit (Hair et al., 2016, p. 208; Henseler et al., 2014, p. 193). But it is important to keep in mind that this measure of goodness-of-fit is useful only for evaluating reflective models, since the residuals of the outer model for formative measurement models are irrelevant.

Taking into account the measures of goodness-of-fit of the model mentioned above, it can be concluded that the model of management control in hospitals has a good fit. However, it should be remembered that PLS-SEM focuses on predicting rather than explanatory modeling, and therefore requires a different type of validation. Rather, the evaluation of PLS-SEM results should be concerned with generalizability, i.e., the model's ability to predict out-of-sample data or, better yet, outside the sample data, as in the PLSpredict procedure. In this context, fit (as implemented by SRMR), RMS$_{\text{theta}}$, and the d$_{\text{ULS}}$ and d$_{\text{G}}$ exact fit test are of secondary importance. However, the motive for citing these measures in this publication is to inform readers of the degree of model fit based on contemporaneous measures, although the inference of model value is based on the previously mentioned prediction measures.

6.6 Non-Linear Relationships between Constructs and Data Heterogeneity

In general, structural equation modeling assumes linear causal relationships in path models between constructs. However, in some cases, this assumption is not justified because the relationships may be non-linear. When the relationship between two constructs is non-linear, the size of the effect between two constructs depends not only on the magnitude of the change in the exogenous variable, but also on its value. Non-linear relationships can involve all kinds of curves. In principle, all relationships are non-linear to some extent, but linear relationships often approximate non-linear relationships well enough that simplification to a linear relationship is satisfactory.

In this context, the key challenge becomes whether the observed non-linearity is statistically significant for the analyzed model of management control in hospitals and for the interpretation of the results. A two-step procedure was used to verify potential non-linearity in the structural model's relationships, in which the quadratic effect (a polynomial of degree 2) is viewed as a special case of moderation of an endogenous variable (Hair et al., 2018, p. 72). Theoretically, one can consider the existence of a cubic effect or the existence of another function in the relationship, but due to the increasing complexity of the analysis, considering simpler quadratic effects is usually a sufficient approximation when modeling and testing non-linear effects, especially since quadratic effects are more common in social science models than other types of non-linear effects (Hair et al., 2018, p. 68).

Technically, the analysis of the impact of the non-linear effect on the model estimation results was calculated using the "Add quadratic effect" option of SmartPLS v. 3.3.3. The results of the analysis based on the boot-strap procedure indicate that the relationships between the variables diag-nostic control → hospital performance, IS effectiveness → innovativeness and IS effectiveness → diagnostic control show non-linearity at a signifi-cance level of $p < 0.05$ (Table 6.27). Also, the values of the t-statistic for the two-tailed test exceed 1.96, which means that the non-linear effect of these variables is significant.

Note that when the quadratic effects are added, the path coefficients in the structural model also change (Table 6.27). For example, the relation-ship between the variables diagnostic control and hospital performance under the assumption of a linear function can be written as: $HP = 0.29 \cdot DC$ (Table 6.19). And with the introduction of a quadratic effect, the relationship between these variables can be expressed by a polynomial of degree 2: $HP = 0.41 \cdot DC + 0.12 \cdot DC^2$, where the parameter 0.29 denotes the value of the path coefficient after structural model estimation assuming a linear relation-ship, and the coefficients 0.41 and 0.12, respectively, denote the path coef-ficient between the diagnostic control and hospital performance variables and the quadratic effect assuming a polynomial relationship of 2nd degree. Similarly, the equations can be written for the variables IS effectiveness and diagnostic control: $DC = 0.73 \cdot ISE$, and taking into account the non-linear effect: $DC = 0.67 \cdot ISE - 0.07 \cdot ISE^2$. Taking into account the non-linear effect in the case of the relationship of the variables IS effectiveness and diagnostic control not only reduces the path coefficient by 8.6%, but also diminishes

Table 6.27.   Evaluation of non-linear relationships in the structural model

Path description	Evaluation of non-linear effects				Path coeff.*	Path coeff. change (%)	Effect size f^2
	Quadratic effect	t-Value	p-Value	Confidence interval (95%)	Path coefficients including Quadratic effect			
[1]	[2]	[3]	[4]	[5]	[6]	[7]	[6]/([7]-1)	[8]
I -> HP	0.08	1.88	0.06	-0.01-0.17	0.73	0.72	0.8%	0.015
DC -> HP	0.12	2.88	0.00	0.04-0.20	0.41	0.29	41.8%	0.039
IC -> HP	0.08	1.51	0.13	-0.06-0.15	-0.29	-0.32	-10.0%	0.016
ISE -> I	0.06	3.82	0.00	0.03-0.10	0.46	0.39	16.9%	0.011
ISE -> DC	-0.07	2.13	0.03	-0.15--0.01	0.67	0.73	-8.6%	0.026
ISE -> IC	0.01	0.18	0.85	-0.07-0.11	0.67	0.67	1.1%	0.001
T -> I	-0.02	0.74	0.46	-0.07-0.03	0.25	0.25	-0.6%	0.000
PEU -> I	-0.01	0.02	0.51	-0.05-0.03	0.43	0.43	-0.6%	0.000

* Path coefficients of the structural model assuming linear relationships between variables.

the effect of IS effectiveness on the diagnostic control of this system (Table 6.27). The above equations show that depending on the sign of the quadratic effect, the strength of the relationship calculated assuming a linear function is strengthened or weakened.

When analyzing the statistical significance of a quadratic effect, it is important to keep in mind that statistical significance does not imply a real effect on the model estimation results. Especially with larger test sample sizes, very small effects can become statistically significant. Therefore, to confirm the real impact of the non-linear effect on the model estimation results, the strength of the non-linear effect was calculated using the effect size f^2. The effect size f^2 indicates the extent to which the quadratic effect contributes to the explanation of the endogenous unobservable variable. This indicator was calculated as the change in the value of the coefficient of determination R^2 of the endogenous latent variables when the exogenous quadratic component was omitted from the model. Technically, the value of the effect size f^2 was calculated from the following equation (Hair et al., 2018, p. 73):

$$f^2 = (R^2(\text{model with quadratic effect}) - R^2(\text{model without quadratic effect})) / (1 - R^2(\text{model with quadratic effect}))$$

Guidelines for interpreting the f^2 effect size for structural model analysis are that values of 0.02, 0.15 and 0.35, respectively, represent small, medium and large effects of the exogenous latent variable on the endogenous variable. Effect size values of less than 0.02 indicate no effect (Cohen, 1988, pp. 413–414). However, it should be taken into account that the quadratic effect in PLS-SEM (SmartPLS 3.3.3) is calculated using a method designed for moderating effect analysis, similar to the interaction effects in standard moderator analysis, except that regarding the calculation of the quadratic effect, the variable interacts with itself (Rigdon et al., 2010, p. 262). In this situation, the effect size f^2 should be related to the possible values of moderating effects rather than to the generally accepted values of the effect size f^2 of the coefficient of determination in path models. H. Aguinis et al. (2005, p. 97), on the basis of 261 analyses of studies over 30 years, came to the understanding that the average observed value of the effect size f^2 with moderation ranges from 0.0089-0.0091 (CI 95%). Considering the median (due to the high skewness of the collected studies), the value of the effect size f^2 is 0.002. In this situation, it seems that the generally accepted threshold values for f^2 are far too high. Perhaps a more realistic standard for effect size f^2 is 0.005, 0.01 and 0.025 for small, medium, and large effect sizes, respectively (Hair et al., 2018, p. 73; Kenny, 2018).

Given the statistical significance, the change in the value of path coefficients with quadratic effects compared to the path coefficients with a linear relationship between the variables, and the mean and even significant effect size f^2 (Table 6.27), it can be concluded, with a high degree of probability, that the relationships between the variables diagnostic control → hospital performance, IS effectiveness → innovativeness and IS effectiveness → diagnostic control are non-linear.

The value of the quadratic effect of the variables IS effectiveness → innovativeness and IS effectiveness → diagnostic control is well below 0.1, and the effect sizes f^2 are at an average level. The change in the value of path coefficients compared to the estimation with the assumption of linearity of the relationship between these variables is also relatively small, at 16.9% and -8.6%, respectively (Table 6.27). Thus, in these cases, it appears that the omission of the non-linear effect does not affect the interpretation of the relationship of these variables in the model of management control in hospitals. On the other hand, the quadratic effect of the variable diagnostic control → hospital performance above 0.12 and the change in the value of the path coefficient compared to the estimation with the assumption of linearity of the relationship between the variables by 41.8% must provoke reflection. Admittedly, even changes in the parameters obtained from the estimation of the relationship of the variables diagnostic control → hospital performance taking into account non-linearity do not critically affect the change in the relationship in the model, since the directions and strength of the relationship still remain similar, but it is worth analyzing these results from a theoretical perspective.

It would seem natural that as the level of diagnostic control increases, its effect on hospital performance should remain positive, but nevertheless diminishing, as in research on the effect of satisfaction on loyalty (Eisenbeiss et al., 2014, p. 257). However, the results indicate the opposite. An increase in diagnostic control results in increasingly rapid improvements in hospital performance. This nature of the relationship seems counterintuitive, as it would imply that continually increasing control would lead to infinitely better results. Reaching far back in control theory, however, one can find studies that to some extent confirm the results obtained in these studies. A.S. Tannenbaum (1962, p. 256) pointed out that more intensive control does not necessarily mean blocking the creative invention and commitment of employees; on the contrary, high intensity of control leads to a more integrated social system, improves its performance, and causes an increase in employee commitment, motivation, and productivity (Likert, 1960; McMahon

& Perritt, 1973, p. 627). More recent studies have shown that organizations with higher levels of control are more willing to undergo further increases in control (Tessier & Otley, 2012, p. 175).

In conclusion, it should be noted that the inclusion of non-linearity of relationships in the model of management control in hospitals enriches the theoretical interpretation, while – as a rule – unless the deviations from linearity are extreme, which they are not, the assumptions of linearity of relationships offer a reasonable approximation of the relationship between variables in the model of management control in hospitals.

Structural modeling assumptions suggest that exogenous variables explain endogenous variables without the systematic influence of other variables. However, in many cases, this assumption is not met. A number of factors are involved. First of all, respondents answering the survey questions may be heterogeneous in their perceptions of the constructs and thus in their assessments of the indicators, which may result, for example, in significant differences in path coefficients among different groups of respondents (e.g.: women – men, values held, membership in socioeconomic groups). Failure to take into account the existence of different groups of respondents in the data, i.e., data heterogeneity, can pose a serious threat to the accuracy of the results of structural equation modeling using the PLS-SEM method (Becker et al., 2013, p. 672). The heterogeneity of the data can lead to a situation where, for different subsets of the data (groups of respondents), the path coefficients can differ significantly and even have different signs.

Many authors do not examine the homogeneity of the data, implicitly assuming the absence of heterogeneity; however, out of concern for high quality research, the FIMIX-PLS (finite mixture partial least squares) procedure, which assumes that the entire population is a mixture of group-specific density functions, was used to identify potential heterogeneity in the data. The purpose of FIMIX-PLS is to extract each group's distributions from the overall mixture in a regression and estimate the model parameters for that group (Becker et al., 2015, p. 644). "Mixture of distributions" regressions facilitate simultaneous probabilistic classification of observations into groups and estimation of group-specific path coefficients. Simulation studies show that FIMIX-PLS effectively reveals the existence of heterogeneity in PLS path models and correctly indicates the appropriate number of segments in the data (Hair et al., 2018, p. 177).

The FIMIX-PLS procedure itself does not determine the number of segments (subgroups) in the data, but it calculates probability-based model selection criteria to estimate the number of heterogeneous data segments in the survey sample. Technically, the analysis looks as such: separately, you have to repeat the FIMIX-PLS procedure for an increasing number of segments, and then compare the model selection criteria, looking for the best segmentation. An upper limit on the number of segments to be considered was adopted based on the required minimum number of cases necessary for model estimation. With the maximum number of three arrowheads pointing to any construct in the model (innovativeness and hospital performance variables) and assuming a 5% significance level, as well as a minimum R^2 of 0.25, the minimum number of observations is 37 to reliably estimate the model (Table 4.8). The largest total number obtained from dividing the study sample of 151 cases by the minimum sample size of 37 cases yields a theoretical upper limit of 4.08 = 4. However, given that some segments could be very small and omitted, for the sake of due diligence, the maximum number of segments, and thus runs of the "Finite Mixture (FIMIX) Segmentation" option in SmartPLS 3.3.3, was taken to be 5, saving the results report for each run.

Table 6.28 shows the breakdown of the survey sample into homogeneous segments in percentage and numerical terms. This summary shows that there is a core group of homogeneous data (86.5%, 131 cases in a two-segment situation), which is broken into smaller and smaller groups as the number of segments increases. It should be noted that the segment sizes are not derived from hard clustering of observations based on maximum segment

Table 6.28. Segment sizes according to the number of segments separated

Number of segments	Relative segment sizes (%)				
	Group 1	Group 2	Group 3	Group 4	Group 5
2	86.5%	13.5%			
3	56.1%	38.5%	5.4%		
4	55.6%	28.2%	10.4%	5.8%	
5	51.1%	25.5%	11.8%	6.9%	4.7%
Segment sizes (number of cases)					
2	131	20			
3	85	58	8		
4	84	43	16	8	
5	78	39	17	10	7

Table 6.29. Fit indices obtained from the FIMIX-PLS procedure

Criteria	Number of segments				
	1	*2*	*3*	*4*	*5*
AIC (Akaike's Information Criterion)	958.7	943.3	921.6	921.0	**900.8**
AIC3 (Modified AIC with Factor 3)	970.7	968.3	**959.6**	972.0	964.8
AIC4 (Modified AIC with Factor 4)	**982.7**	993.3	997.6	1023.0	1028.8
BIC (Bayesian Information Criteria)	**993.5**	1015.7	1031.7	1068.8	1086.2
CAIC (Consistent AIC)	**1005.5**	1040.7	1069.7	1119.8	1150.2
HQ (Hannan Quinn Criterion)	972.9	972.7	**966.3**	981.1	976.1
MDL5 (Minimum Description Length with Factor 5)	**1228.6**	1505.5	1776.2	2068.0	2340.1
EN (Entropy Statistic (Normed))		**0.765**	0.650	0.742	0.760
NFI (Non-Fuzzy Index)		0.789	**0.628**	0.705	0.715
NEC (Normalized Entropy Criterion)		**31.5**	46.9	34.6	32.2

membership probabilities, but from weighted least squares regressions in which these probabilities are inputs (Hair et al., 2018, p. 197).

The FIMIX-PLS analysis indicators (Table 6.29) are interpreted to mean that the smaller the value of a given information criterion in a given row, the better the segmentation fit. The exception is the EN index, whose higher values indicate better segmentation (Sarstedt et al., 2011). The results of the analysis show (Table 6.29) that the largest number of indices, as many as 4 (AIC4, BIC, CAIC, MDL5), suggests a single-segment split. It should be taken into account that the EN, NFI, and NEC indices are not calculated for a single-segment split, which means that the single-segment split had no chance to gain an additional advantage. Summarizing the results presented, it can be concluded that heterogeneity is not a problem with the data analyzed here. The fit indices give an indication of a one-segment solution.

Chapter 7

Discussion of Research Results

7.1 Quantitative Research Findings in the Context of Qualitative Research and Implications for Theory and Practice

This research, based on a sequential exploratory mixed-methods design, suggests that management control consists of six interrelated variables that together affect hospital performance. The first stage of qualitative research conducted on a sample of 16 public European hospitals identified eight second-order themes (latent variables) and 14 hypotheses about the relationships between the identified unobservable variables, which together formed a preliminary conceptual model of management control in hospitals (Figure 5.1). During the second stage of quantitative research, the identified unobservable variables were operationalized, and based on structural equation modeling using the PLS-SEM method, the strength of the relationships between the constructs and between the constructs and their indicators was estimated. As a result of statistical analysis, five hypotheses (Table 7.1), one construct and two indicator variables were rejected, yielding a modified model of management control in hospitals, which was accepted as the final result of the study (Figure 6.6). It is noteworthy that while the second-order themes that emerged from the qualitative research were adopted as unobservable variables (constructs) of the model, the first-order themes became an important source of knowledge about the functioning of management control in hospitals, allowing an in-depth interpretation of the obtained results of the quantitative research.

DOI: 10.4324/9781003366553-7

Table 7.1. Evaluation of research hypotheses based on estimation of the preliminary and the modified (final) structural model of management control in hospitals

Hypothesis	Hypothesis testing result	Statistical significance p=0.05	Preliminary model (PCoPSM; p)	Modified model (final) (PCoMSM; p)
H1: Effectiveness of the information system (ISE) has a positive impact on hospital performance (HP).	Rejected	Not	-0.05; 0.67	–
H2: Effectiveness of the information system (ISE) positively affects its diagnostic use (DC).	Confirmed	Yes	0.73; 0.00	0.73; 0.00
H3: Diagnostic use (DC) of the information system has a positive impact on hospital performance (HP).	Confirmed	Yes	0.30; 0.00	0.29; 0.00
H4: Effectiveness of the information system (ISE) has a positive effect on rewarding employees (R).	Confirmed	Yes	0.56; 0.00	–
H5: Rewarding employees (R) has a positive impact on hospital performance (HP).	Rejected	Not	0.04; 0.51	–
H6: Rewarding employees (R) has a positive impact on hospital innovativeness (I).	Rejected	Not	0.01; 0.69	–
H7: Effectiveness of the information system (ISE) positively affects its interactive use (IC).	Confirmed	Yes	0.66; 0.00	0.67; 0.00
H8: Interactive use of the information system (IC) has a positive impact on hospital performance (HP).	Partially confirmed*	Yes	-0.30; 0.00	-0.32; 0.00

(Continued)

Table 7.1 (Continued) Evaluation of research hypotheses based on estimation of the preliminary and the modified (final) structural model of management control in hospitals

Hypothesis	Hypothesis testing result	Statistical significance $p=0.05$	Preliminary model (PCoPSM; p)	Modified model (final) (PCoMSM; p)
H9: Effectiveness of the information system (ISE) has a positive impact on hospital innovativeness (I).	Confirmed	Yes	0.41; 0.00	0.39; 0.00
H10: Hospital innovativeness (I) has a positive impact on hospital performance (HP).	Confirmed	Yes	0.74; 0.00	0.72; 0.00
H11: Diagnostic use of the information system (DC) has a positive impact on hospital innovativeness (I).	Rejected	Not	0.04; 0.75	–
H12: Interactive use of the information system (IC) has a positive impact on hospital innovativeness (I).	Rejected	Not	-0.06; 0.20	–
H13: Directors' perceived level of environmental uncertainty (PEU) has a positive impact on hospital innovativeness (I).	Confirmed	Yes	0.41; 0.00	0.43; 0.00
H14: Director's trust in physicians (T) has a positive impact on hospital innovativeness (I).	Confirmed	Yes	0.26; 0.00	0.25; 0.00

* The estimation showed a negative relationship, assuming a positive relationship in the hypothesis.

Note: PCoPSM – path coefficients of the preliminary structural model (Table 6.15); PCoMSM – path coefficients of the modified (final) structural model (Table 6.19).

An unexpected result of the estimation of the conceptual model is that there is no effect of IS effectiveness (ISE) on hospital performance (HP), (H1: PCoPSM: ISE → HP = -0.05, p = 0.67; f^2 = 0.00) (Table 6.15, Table 6.16). This means that measurement alone is ineffective in the service of management control in hospitals. This finding contradicts previous research, which suggests that the very act of measurement elicits a response from employees and focuses their actions in the right direction, allowing them to assess the effects of their work, and thus enabling them to correct their actions (Flamholtz, 1979, p. 79, 1996, p. 601; Neely et al., 1995, p. 95; Zábojník, 2014, p. 341). In contrast, the present research shows that the measurement function does not work if employees do not receive specific guidance on organizational goals. This means that information itself, without managers setting appropriate goals and levels of targets, does not affect performance. The model developed indicates that the impact of IS effectiveness on hospital performance is mediated (in the context of the path model) by three variables: diagnostic control (DC), interactive control (IC), and innovativeness (I) (Figure 6.6). The mediating effect of this relationship is, respectively: 0.21 (p<0.00), -0.21 (p<0.00), and 0.28 (p<0.00), and the total indirect effect of IS effectiveness on hospital performance is 0.28 (p<0.00) (Table 6.25). However, given the ambiguity of hospitals' goals, expressed through a deficit of clear and understandable priorities read by all employees at the organizational level, the lack of a relationship between the measurement itself and performance is reasonable and characteristic of the organizations studied.

The study strongly confirmed the robust positive relationship (H2) between the effectiveness of the information system and diagnostic control: PCoMSM: ISE → DC = 0.73, p<0.00; f^2 = 1.15, p<0.00 (Table 6.19). Thus, the more effective an information system is, the greater the scope, level of detail, and frequency of reporting deep into the organizational structure of a hospital, the greater its diagnostic use. This also gives rise to the observation that, having the right characteristics, feedback can be used for single loop organizational learning, i.e., for taking corrective action in response to deviations from the planned course of action. This includes controlling the behavior of employees in the organization, both by providing performance information for taking corrective action and by motivating specific behaviors and actions. The presented findings are also in line with the conclusions of the publications discussed in the theoretical part, which emphasized the support of the evaluation and decision-making processes of internal stakeholders by information systems that provide appropriately detailed data. At the same time, these systems support primary control processes.

It should also be noted that the diagnostic use of the information system helps improve hospital performance (H3). Although if one uses the observations presented in the theoretical part of the book, this relationship can be considered confirmed. In the present study, such an assessment based on the analysis of the relationship between the diagnostic control variable and the performance variable in the linear model (Table 6.19) indicates a rather moderate level of relationship: the path coefficient in the final model (0.29, p<0.00), the effect value ($f^2 = 0.16$) is statistically insignificant at the 5% level (p = 0.08) (Table 6.19). It can be concluded that taking into account the non-linear nature of the relationship between diagnostic control and hospital performance significantly changes the strength of the observed relationship (Table 6.27). The non-linearity of the relationship (quadratic effect) between the variables in question increases the path coefficient by 41.8% – from 0.29 to 0.41 and further increases the results by the quadratic effect (Table 6.27). This means that intensifying the diagnostic use of the information system causes a disproportionately greater improvement in performance according to the following equation:

$$HP = 0.41 \cdot DC + 0.12 \cdot DC^2$$

Interpreting the estimation results taking into account the quadratic effect, therefore, allows us to conclude that increasing the diagnostic use of the information system serves to improve hospital performance. At the same time, as extant studies show (Tannenbaum, 1962, p. 256; Likert, 1960, 1958; McMahon & Perritt, 1973, p. 627; Tessier & Otley, 2012, p. 175), intensive control can make employees more submissive to control and cause an increase in their commitment, motivation, and productivity, and it seems that under conditions of ambiguity and variability of goals, more frequent and intensive tracking of the progress of goals and objectives is a condition for improving the performance of a hospital.

Estimation of the model confirmed strong support for hypothesis 4, that is, that hospital directors believe that an effective information system is an important element in rewarding employees (R) for performance (H4, PCoPSM: ISE → R = 0.56, p<0.00). The high value of the path coefficient indicates the directors' strong belief in the need to tie measurable indicators of goal and task achievement to rewards. Note that the rewarding employees variable is operationalized as linking performance to rewards, i.e., it does not refer to the amount of remuneration guaranteed in an employment contract or in a civil law contract based on an hourly rate, since in these types of contracts higher remuneration is generated by more hours of work, not efficiency. In contrast, civil law contracts, which are tied to the number of procedures performed, largely fulfill the definition of rewarding performance. However, this type of contract is usually only in a portion of treatment departments.

Importantly, while the model analysis showed a strong relationship between the variables IS effectiveness and rewarding, the effect of the variable rewarding on the variable hospital performance was already found to be very weak and not statistically significant (PCoPSM: R → HP = 0.036, p = 0.61). Thus, hypothesis 5 was not confirmed. This result stands in strong opposition to the high value of the path index of the impact of IS effectiveness on rewarding. This means that although the link between rewarding and ISE is perceived and considered important, there is no conviction among hospital directors that such a link has an impact on hospital performance. As a result, it should be noted that the lack of impact of rewarding on hospital performance in the model is the result of at least three beliefs among directors. First, managers believe, as was indicated in interviews, that the government is increasingly taking over employee compensation for them, and they do not expect to be able to use rewards to improve hospital performance in the near future. Second, the goals of hospitals are so complex, contradictory, and variable that the impact of linking employee rewards to a relatively severely limited number of indicators does not have a comprehensive effect on improving hospital performance. In addition, the directors suggested that it is almost impossible to establish fair performance measures, as perceived by most employees, for individual organizational units in such a complex organization as a hospital, where organizational units are highly differentiated. And in a situation where some employees questioned the fairness of the rewards, the impact of these arrangements on hospital performance could be detrimental.

It is also worth noting that if the directors believed in the effectiveness of linking rewards to the achievement of goals, particularly financial ones, they would introduce such mechanisms since better financial performance should provide the means for rewards. On the other hand, one relatively important reason for not openly criticizing the use of performance reward systems may be the fear of losing the legitimacy of the director as an enlightened manager, since tying rewards to performance is quite widely regarded as an important sign of good management (Franco-Santos et al., 2012, p. 81; Jaworzyńska, 2015; Lachmann et al., 2013; Kaplan & Norton, 1996; Rahimi et al., 2017; Ritchie et al., 2019). Thus, directors' declarations of the need to link employee performance in a causal chain to compensation or plans to implement complex systems for measuring and evaluating performance may be a manifestation of institutional isomorphism (Andreasson et al., 2018, p. 26; DiMaggio & Powell, 1983, pp. 148–149). This phenomenon is well known in the literature and mainly affects public and not-for-profit entities. This is because, as already noted, public organizations absorb "off-the-shelf" solutions from business; however, the effectiveness of applying these solutions in hospitals is often only a socially accepted myth. Business companies, operating in an environment dominated by economic and technological demands, ensure their survival and growth by using resources efficiently to deliver value to the customer. Otherwise, the customer will not purchase the goods or services offered. Hospitals, on the other hand, being paid by a third-party payer (public or private) rather than directly by their "customers," and operating in an environment dominated by legal, political, and social requirements, must obtain legitimacy for their actions. Thus, in order to secure their development and survival, they must comply with legal norms and yield to political pressures and social expectations (Andreasson et al., 2018, p. 26). This means that in many cases it is more advantageous for them to make decisions in accordance with external expectations (e.g., implementing incompatible management concepts) rather than with rational benefits for the organization.

The results also failed to confirm the existence of a relationship between rewards and hospital innovation (H6). This contradicts the observation that employees who are additionally motivated to achieve specific results are more determined to seek innovative solutions, which is indicated, among others, by M. Porter, who noted that rewarding for results, as opposed to rewarding for behavior, can lead to breakthrough innovations in the delivery of medical services (Porter, 2010a, p. 2478). The value of the path coefficient for the relationship between the variables rewarding and innovativeness is close to zero (PCoPSM: R $\rightarrow$ I= 0.02, p = 0.69) and not statistically significant. It is possible to explain the result of the study in an analogous way due to the lack of impact of performance-based rewards on hospital performance, i.e., by the relatively low possibility of using diverse and time-varying indicators in relation to the variability and ambiguity of the goals for the achievement of which employees were to be rewarded.

In the context of the subject matter addressed in this monograph, it is significant that, as in the case of diagnostic control, there is also a positive interaction between the effectiveness of the information system and interactive control (H7, PCoMSM: ISE $\rightarrow$ IC = 0.67, p<0.00; f^2 = 0.80, p<0.00).

However, it is important to remember that interactive use of the information system, unlike in diagnostic control, can be applied to double loop learning of the hospital (Ferreira & Otley, 2009, p. 273). In this case, deviation from the accepted standard can also be treated as an opportunity to question the initially adopted goals or strategies, particularly when the reason is precisely the incorrectly adopted goals and strategies (Kaplan & Norton, 1996, p. 251; Simons, 2014, p. 234).

Model estimation also revealed the presence of a statistically significant but negative interaction between interactive control and hospital performance (H8). That is, the personal and ongoing involvement of managers in employee decision-making processes and ensuring that information was shared throughout the organization and allowing top management concerns to be communicated had a negative impact on hospital performance. Admittedly, while directors spoke of situations resembling interactive use of the information system, as in the case of medical records (SzO3), nephrology overbooking (SzS2), or the use of the CT scanner at appropriate times (SzO/S1), the results of this involvement were no longer so obvious. This observation, therefore, provided a basis for predicting a weak relationship, although the negative direction of the effect of interactive control on hospital performance was unexpected (PCoMSM: IC → HP = -0.32, p<0.00; f^2 = 0.23, p = 0.01). Indeed, as noted earlier, studies conducted in hospitals tended to report a positive effect or possibly no effect of interactive control on hospital performance (Abernethy & Brownell, 1999, p. 199; de Harlez & Malagueño, 2016, p. 2; Naranjo-Gil & Hartmann, 2007, p. 751; Yu et al., 2018, p. 20). The authors of earlier qualitative studies also tended to confirm the positive effect of this control on performance (Kastberg & Siverbo, 2013, p. 265; Østergren, 2009, p. 192). However, these studies seem to misidentify interactive control, confusing it with diagnostic control and, in particular, with high-intensity bureaucratic control (Tannenbaum, 1962, p. 256; Ouchi, 1980) and with social (clan) control (Ouchi, 1980), triggered by the need to cover each other's deficits in the wards. In the case of K. Ostergren's study (2009, p. 185), it was the fear of colleagues' criticism that a ward had failed and would require help from others, rather than questioning assumptions and seeking other solutions, that led to budget balancing. Therefore, clinical managers, even when they did not feel the pressure of losing their jobs, felt peer pressure related to social control. This mechanism can also be compared to concertive control, which is implemented through peer pressure in situations of self-managed teams (Kohli & Kettinger, 2004, p. 377; Larson & Tompkins, 2005, p. 3).

Analyzing the results of the study, it is important to pay attention first of all to the operationalization of the construct, which shows that managers' focus on common problems and constant discussion with subordinates about the adopted goals and indicators and ways to implement tasks negatively affect the performance of a hospital. As already mentioned, interactive control implies frequent and regular involvement of top management in dialogue with subordinates and discussion of their decisions. At the same time, the strong participation and involvement of directors in the activities and decisions of subordinate employees can take various forms. On the one hand, top manager participation and involvement may evolve into greater centralization of authority and decision making, and, thus, through regular and frequent interventions, directors may violate the autonomy of professionals, replace consensus-building, and team decision-making with hierarchical directives, and impose their own decisions at critical junctures and even change the decisions of subordinates. On the other hand, the participation of directors can involve a facilitating and integrating role that acts as a catalyst that encourages, facilitates, and inspires. Importantly, the hallmark of interactive control should be the latter, non-invasive, facilitating, and inspiring type of involvement. However, given the divergence of the institutional logics of directors and medical professionals in middle management roles in hospitals, as described in the literature and identified during qualitative research, the involvement of directors may be perceived as intrusive and seeking to persuade professionals to follow a management logic. As a result, it seems fair to recognize that ensuring the interactivity of control systems requires that the personal involvement of a senior manager reinforce decision-making processes at lower levels, rather than relying on open intervention and leading to the appropriation of subordinates' decision-making rights.

When evaluating the phenomenon in question, it should be emphasized that the management control model was estimated based on data collected from hospital directors, which means that the respondents themselves perceived the opposite of the desired effect of personal involvement. Diagnostic control, based on monitoring the achievement of goals, gives some autonomy to subordinates, as it does not indicate how goals will be achieved. In interactive control, on the other hand, the director's personal involvement can be regarded as micromanagement. This observation requires the resolution of the problem of why interactive control is considered micromanagement to the detriment of the organization. This problem involves assessing whether it depends on the skills and behavior of the top management, or on conditions related to different institutional logics and related beliefs of managers and doctors. In doing so, it is important to highlight that positive and negative impressions of control-related interactions depend on perceptions of control rather than on control itself. This statement can be understood to mean that while the intent of interactive control was not to micromanage, in practice it can be perceived as such. An example of this would be pointing out to physicians that they should use the CT scanner at appropriate times. The intention of the SzO/S1 director was merely to draw attention to a common cost issue, and could be perceived as limiting physicians' autonomy to order diagnostics when they are most necessary.

Some indication of the negative impact of interactive information system use on performance can be found in earlier studies. These studies showed that the implementation of such information systems caused potential resistance from medical personnel (Carroll & Lord, 2016, p. 177). Interactive control initiating discussions about strategic uncertainties revealed more information about the actions of subordinates and colleagues compared to diagnostic control. This likely exacerbated resistance to change. In addition, the introduction of new non-financial measures also disrupted power structures in the organization (Tuomela, 2005, p. 314).

The research also shows that innovation, whether implemented top-down by directors, semi-intentional, or ad hoc (*bricolage*), requires information to not only identify areas of poor performance where innovation is necessary, but also to subsequently assess the effectiveness of the introduction of these innovations. Hence, there is a positive relationship between the variables of IS effectiveness and innovativeness (H9, PCoMSM: ISE → I = 0.39, p<0.00, f^2 = 0.58, p<0.00). At the same time, the analysis of the model of management control in hospitals by means of the PLS-SEM estimator shows that the main element influencing organizational performance is innovativeness (H10). The value of the path coefficient in the final model between the innovativeness and hospital performance variables is 0.72 (effect size f^2 = 0.97), which is much higher compared to the positive effect of diagnostic control on hospital performance (PCoMSM: DC → HP = 0.29 and f^2 = 0.16), even when considering the non-linear nature of the relationship (HP = 0.41 DC + 0.12 · DC^2) and the negative effect of interactive control (PCoMSM: IC → HP = -0.32 and f^2 = 0.23). This means that neither diagnostic control, based on the traditional feedback mechanism, nor interactive control, but precisely innovativeness is the main driver of hospital performance. This issue is important because, while at the health system level innovation is associated with increased costs (Bodenheimer, 2005, p. 932; Rye & Kimberly, 2007, p. 236) that result, among other things, from safer, more accessible health services being provided to more people, at the level of the individual hospital, innovation in health-care delivery can provide more effective and, in some cases, less expensive treatments (Afsar et al., 2018, p. 2).

Estimation of the model did not confirm the hypotheses (H11 and H12) regarding the impact of the variables diagnostic control (PCoPSM: DC → I = 0.04, p = 0.45) and interactive control (PCoPSM: IC → I = 0.06, p = 0.21) on the innovativeness variable. In both cases, the effect on innovativeness is inconsiderable and not statistically significant. This is an unexpected result given previous research (Bisbe & Otley, 2004, p. 729; Simons, 1987b, p. 370), including studies in hospitals (Abernethy & Brownell, 1999, p. 199). Although a survey of CEOs of Spanish manufacturing companies found that interactive use of information systems promotes product innovation, but only in low-innovation companies, while the effect appears to be the opposite for high-innovation companies (Bisbe & Otley, 2004, p. 729). In the context of these inconclusive results, it is important to note the problem of operationalizing variables. Rather, both interactive control and diagnostic control refer to strategies and goals common to the entire hospital. The organizational level of interactive control is particularly prominent in the IC1 and IC6 indicators (Table 6.5), which refer to "focus executives on common problems" and "uniting the hospital as a whole, i.e., treating the hospital's main problems as common, rather than individual departments/divisions or professional groups." In contrast, the innovativeness variable refers to individual areas of operation, such as technological, organizational, management and service delivery and external relations innovations, while in hospitals each medical specialty usually has a very strong element of individualized technology, specific organization of service delivery processes and relations with the environment.

Thus, it seems that the barrier limiting the impact of diagnostic and interactive control on innovativeness is the low possibility of establishing a common strategy for the entire hospital, since, as the studies discussed in the theoretical section show, hospitals are highly decentralized and have a significant share of the bottom-up method of decision making. The problem of the lack of a unified hospital strategy and the limited ability of directors to build broad professional support for such a common strategy was also identified in the field research. If the above observation is taken into account, the negative impact of interactive control on performance seems justified.

Testing of the structural model also made it possible to confirm (H13) that there is a positive interaction between perceived environmental uncertainty and innovativeness (PCoMSM: PEU → I = 0.43, p<0.00; f^2 = 0.56, p<0.00), whereby the value of the uncertainty variable cannot be related to the overall variability of the environment, but should be considered within the specific areas (indicators) that make up this variable. This assumption stems from the need to take into account the relationship between the variables and how each construct is measured in the analysis. Indeed, the variable uncertainty, with its composite nature, is a linear combination of seven specific elements of the hospital environment (Table 6.7). At the same time, as the qualitative research shows, although hospitals experience environmental uncertainty, this uncertainty usually does not threaten their existence, is rather at a medium level, has a local character, and positively influences innovation. These observations support the findings on diagnostic and interactive control. Because, as the research described in the theoretical section shows, managers tend to use interactive control when they are exposed to high levels of uncertainty or when innovation is driven by external factors. By contrast, in situations with less change, companies rely more on diagnostic control.

Complementing the insights of hypothesis 13, it also appears to confirm the existence of a positive relationship (H14) between directors' trust in physicians (T) and hospital innovativeness (PCoMSM: T → I = 0.25, p<0.00; f^2 0.22, p<0.00) and, importantly, a positive total effect on the hospital performance variable (PCoMSM: T → I → HP = 0.18, p<0.00). This confirms the results of already well-known studies indicating that trust and an atmosphere of trust are key to the development of innovativeness in organizations.

Summarizing the results obtained, it can be concluded that most of the bilateral relationships between the variables identified in the qualitative research have already been recognized to some extent in the literature. Nevertheless, to date, no comprehensive model has been built to illustrate how these individual relationships interact in the complex process of management control in hospitals. Previous studies have suggested a positive impact of information system effectiveness on hospital performance, but they have not explained how this impact occurs. The proposed model shows that the information system does not directly affect performance but is mediated through its diagnostic and interactive use and innovativeness, which, in turn, is supported by directors' trust in physicians and induced by environmental uncertainty.

Taking into account the previous considerations, it should be noted that the implementation of the specific objectives in the theoretical, methodological, and empirical areas made it possible to identify the key elements of management control and the links between them and to develop a coherent model of management control in hospitals (Figure 7.1). The use of exploratory, sequential mixed-methods research design in this study allowed us to capture a more complete, more holistic, and more firmly situated model of management control in hospitals that, if used alone, might have omitted important variables or included variables and relationships that, in reality, are of marginal importance.

The analysis of the proposed model of management control in hospitals points to the key role of the information system, while emphasizing that the effectiveness of performance improvement efforts requires investment in the information system, which should provide a wide range of information on hospital performance and carry it down the organizational structure. However, it should be noted that in hospitals, the information system does not directly affect hospital performance, and its impact in this regard is related to the way it is used. This means that the measurement does not function if employees are not given specific guidance and standards for organizational goals, and their performance measures are ineffective when they are not equipped with information from top management. One reason for this phenomenon is the ambiguity, variability, and often local scope of goals in hospitals. This ambiguity is due, among other things, to a lack of consensus on the priorities to be assigned to the goals to be pursued and even on the nature of the goals. In an environment where goals are

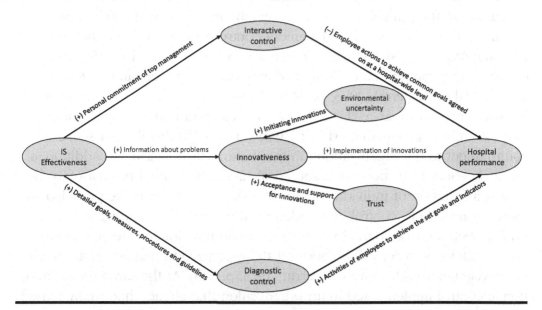

Figure 7.1.   The interaction pattern of the management control model in hospitals

ambiguous, medical professionals use their own rules and norms of conduct, set within collegial institutions outside their workplace (universities, scientific societies, professional associations).

The analysis of the proposed model also indicates that when the direct influence of the information system on hospital performance is observed to be lacking, it is mediated by diagnostic control, interactive control, and innovativeness. All three require top management involvement. Innovativeness is further influenced by perceptions of environmental uncertainty and managers' trust in physicians.

The solutions presented make it possible to consider the observation that diagnostic control is used to motivate, control, and evaluate employees to be correct (Bisbe et al., 2019, p. 130; Simons, 1995, p. 59). In this view, it is a formal control system used by managers to regularly review "exceptions," correct deviations from plans and established performance standards, and thus monitor hospital performance. Such an approach determines the coverage of control of all critical components of the organization. The quality of such a system depends on the ability to set goals and standards, measure their achievement, and be able to proactively intervene when deviations are observed. As a result, which is also confirmed by the identified non-linear relationship between diagnostic control and performance, more intensive diagnostic control amplifies its positive impact on hospital performance.

At the same time, it should be made clear that the observations rendered within the framework of this research are in line with both early and more recent results of management control studies. Indeed, they indicate that more intensive control does not necessarily mean blocking the creative invention and commitment of employees (Tannenbaum, 1962, p. 256; McMahon & Perritt, 1973, p. 627). Greater control in an organization improves its performance (Likert, 1960), increases employee engagement, motivation, and productivity (Likert, 1958), and helps distribute a sense of commitment to the organization (Tannenbaum, 1962, p. 256). In addition, a focus on control can become a source of satisfaction and a basis for psychological integration of individuals into the system, and can make participants more submissive to control, since identification with the organization and loyalty resulting from participation can lead an individual to respond favorably to attempts to act for the good of the organization that he or she might otherwise ignore (McMahon & Perritt, 1973, p. 626). At the same time, "[additional] control implemented in an organization that already had many [other] procedural controls was generally perceived more positively than control implemented in an organization that had [previously] fewer controls"(Tessier & Otley, 2012, p. 175).

It should also be remembered that diagnostic control, unlike interactive control, does not require the frequent and personal involvement of top management. Two main reasons for using diagnostic control can be seen: effective implementation of strategy and saving management attention. In this view, the low involvement of management in the exercise of diagnostic control gives subordinate employees more autonomy. They are not constantly monitored, but only held accountable for the eventual achievement of set goals, with the ambiguity of goals already mentioned so that hospital executives cannot rely on key employees' long-term understanding of the hospital's goals but must define goals and standards on an ongoing basis, depending on the current context, thereby framing the actions taken.

The solutions proposed in the study serve, in the long term, given the volatility and vagueness of goals, to increase the scope of ex ante information provided to employees, particularly information about the goals to be achieved and the ways to achieve them, reducing the number of decisions based on ad hoc judgments. Indeed, information systems must be able to create a platform for reaching consensus on the importance of goals and the best way to achieve them. This reduces the number of conflicting or ambiguous goals, creating a decision-making context in hospitals governed by constant negotiation and compromise between professionals and managers. In theory, effective decision making should be based on communication that allows debates and consideration of alternative perspectives in order to reach some level of agreement on priorities to be pursued. Under these circumstances, interactive control should be a key tool, allowing for the creation and deepening of dialogue among organizational members (Simons, 2014, p. 233). However, a prerequisite for this solution, which stems from the identified negative impact of interactive use of the information system on performance, is to limit the number and extent of directors' personal involvement in debates with subordinates that challenge existing assumptions, focusing on strategic uncertainty and common problems.

The research conducted gave rise to the identification of at least five reasons for the negative impact of interactive information system use on hospital performance. The first relates to the link between the highly functional organizational structure of hospitals, centered around individual medical specialties, and the high autonomy of professionals who exercise control over their own work and the external origin of medical practice standards. Physicians' work standards and the institutional guidelines or norms that medical professionals must adhere to come from outside the organization, such as from local government associations or universities, or are defined by other authorities, and are, therefore, non-negotiable at the hospital level. In addition, each medical specialty has its own guidelines, national and provincial consultants, and sectoral scientific societies focused on practitioners in the field. The methods, tools, and processes of an internist's work are very different from those of a surgeon. Divergent work environments make it difficult to agree on common strategies, goals, and work standards. A solution that will benefit surgical departments may be unfavorable for conservative departments.

The second reason is the perception that managers' frequent and personal involvement in interactive control is an offensive form of micromanagement. This is because, as the practice of hospital operations shows, the director's knowledge of the work processes in a particular department, even when he or she is a physician, is mostly insufficient to engage in an equal discussion of the strategic uncertainties and goals of the department. As a result, this personal involvement can be counterproductive. The third reason is the simultaneous operation of the hospital in two bureaucratic orders. On the one hand, the hospital functions as a traditional Weberian bureaucracy headed by a director, and, on the other, as a decentralized organization dominated by medical professionals, that is, as a professional bureaucracy. Within the latter order, a bottom-up method of decision making dominates, in which managers must accept proposed solutions, leading to the emergence of two parallel administrative hierarchies: a bottom-up, democratic one for professionals and a second top-down, hierarchical one for other employees. Professionals do not expect the director to be involved in their decisions, but rather to protect their autonomy and "buffer" them from external pressures. But on the other hand, they expect managers to solicit external support for the organization, in terms of both gaining external legitimacy and raising funds for treatment.

The fourth reason for problems with interactive use of the information system is related to the hybrid nature of the hospital, that is, the operation of different institutional logics within a single organization: a professional logic, focused on treatment quality and autonomy, and a management logic, focused on efficiency and financial stability of the hospital. As highlighted earlier, due to the differences in goals, norms, and values, dialogue between people operating under different logics is very difficult, if only for the reason that managers tend to focus the discussion around financial issues, while medical professionals tend to focus the discussion around quality issues (Kuhlmann et al., 2013).

The problems identified also call for attention to the fact that control carries two fundamental consequences: pragmatically and symbolically, which is the fifth reason for the problems with interactive control. Pragmatically, control means something that a person must do or cannot do, the constraints to which he or she is subject, and defines areas of choice and freedom. In the symbolic area, on the other hand, control determines a person's place in the organizational hierarchy, that is, it determines who controls whom and who is controlled by whom, and, as a result, suggests a kind of superiority or inferiority, dominance or submissiveness, and exposure to criticism. Thus, control also has special psychological significance for those involved and is emotionally charged. In the specific conditions of hospitals, the indicated characteristics of control stand in obvious contrast to the attributes of the medical profession, characterized by high autonomy, special social status, exclusive jurisdiction over diagnosis and treatment and evaluation of the process and outcome of treatment, self-regulation, and self-control.

The above discussion leads us to accept the interpretation that hospital directors, in an effort to bind the hospital together through frequent and personal discussions with subordinates about strategic uncertainty, adopted goals, indicators, and ways to accomplish tasks, have succumbed to temptation, perhaps not entirely consciously, and reached for material and symbolic means of pressure and display of power to control the behavior of professionals. In addition, the higher position in the organizational hierarchy is associated with some kind of power, which means that the director's discussion with professionals rarely takes place without some manifestation of power relations and subordination. This type of discussion atmosphere can provoke opposition from professionals, which directors perceive as a negative impact of their interactive control activities on hospital performance.

Interaction initiating and implementing innovative solutions are completely different. Interactive control focuses on management's personal involvement in discussions with subordinates, while innovative control involves initiating and implementing new solutions to specific, often local, problems of individual departments, clinics, and processes in response to information system data and environmental uncertainty. These innovations, as the accepted definition of control suggests, serve to increase the likelihood of favorable adaptation of the hospital to the environment.

According to the identified model of management control in hospitals, innovativeness is influenced by three variables: IS effectiveness, uncertainty and trust. Ensuring the highest value of these variables allows for high innovativeness, and performance. On the other hand, a decrease in the value of these three variables results in a decrease in innovativeness and performance. These relationships lead to the conclusion that innovativeness has the greatest positive impact on hospital performance when the director and employees, activated by the uncertainty of the environment to seek innovative solutions, have the right information and show trust in each other. This trust ensures that professionals do not oppose innovative actions taken by directors, and, similarly, directors do not torpedo the innovative actions of subordinates (Figure 7.1). When an effective information system is not in place, it is impossible for organizational actors to make the right decisions and take effective actions, despite the perceived uncertainty of the environment and high trust. Of course, some decisions may be accurate despite the lack of information; however, the probability of making accurate decisions when there is insufficient information is lower. Conversely, when there is both a high level of uncertainty and adequate information, and the level of trust is low, then actions taken by directors and professionals may be mutually unsupported or even possibly sabotaged. In this context, however, it should be noted that a hospital is an organization in which the top management cannot improve the main organizational processes, i.e., those related to the provision of medical services, without the support of professionals. This is due to the professionals themselves exercising jurisdiction over their operations and their high degree of autonomy. In turn, the introduction of innovations often requires not only organizational and financial support, but also the assistance of external stakeholders. In such a situation, introducing innovations without the support and approval of top management may not be very effective.

The three ways of generating innovations in hospitals based on information system data identified in the research are supported by trust and environmental uncertainty. In turn, uncertainty itself positively affects innovativeness and indirectly affects hospital performance for two reasons. First, uncertainty stimulates professionals and directors to seek innovative solutions to better adapt the organization to the environment. And, second, it is used by directors as an argument for introducing their own initiatives. In this context, managers' trust in physicians plays an important role. This is because innovativeness, on the one hand, can be a response to uncertainty, but, on the other hand, innovation carries the risk of failure. This risk is feared both by directors, responsible for the operation of hospitals, and by employees, who do not want to suffer the negative consequences of possible failures. Therefore, directors are more likely to decide to innovate when they trust their subordinates to be knowledgeable and loyal to the hospital. In other words, when directors believe that the professionals have sufficient capacity (competence) to meet the challenges posed, they will not behave opportunistically, using their knowledge and autonomy to sabotage new solutions, and they will be honest, that is, they will work and act in such a way as to improve the hospital even against their own interests. After all, if it were known in advance that the outcome of the innovation would be positive, there would be no need for trust. Trust is important for any way of creating and implementing innovations.

Taking into account the properties of trust to induce trust feedback and the proven positive correlation between employees' trust in superiors and superiors' trust in subordinates, one can accept the explanation of professionals' greater propensity to innovate (semi-intentional innovation) when directors' trust in physicians increases. More precisely, thanks to trust, employees believe that their superior will reward their attempts to innovate, even if such attempts fail (cf: Afsar et al., 2018, p. 163; Weinert, 2013, p. 42). For this pathway of innovation, the effect of trust on hospital innovativeness can occur in several ways. When directors trust in physicians, then they accept the ideas they present with greater openness and support their implementation more strongly. Trust expands the freedom that top management gives professionals to innovate on their own, and it also supports professionals' inclination to develop and implement innovations, because to some extent it frees them from the fear of a negative reaction from their superiors. When employees trust that their ideas will be listened to and supported, then they tend to exhibit high levels of innovative behavior at work (Afsar et al., 2015, p. 108).

The research showed that innovations often responded to local problems, leading to the separation of formal structures and external pressures from daily work processes. The introduction of innovations that included an element of "decoupling" was also fostered by trust. Directors with trust in physicians were more likely to report innovations that bypassed formal structures to increase efficiency or hospital revenue. Professionals, on the other hand, were more likely to accept directors' innovations and to report such innovations themselves when they trusted them to maintain autonomy and obtain additional resources for treatment. After all, greater hospital revenues enable doctors to practice medicine more effectively and achieve better health outcomes for individual patients, and thus sustain the legitimacy of the profession. In addition, this "decoupling" allows for easier compromise and mitigation of conflicts between managers and physicians that would undoubtedly arise in the course of achieving cost-cutting goals.

The research conducted thus shows that management control is an effective way to improve hospital performance. However, this observation applies to control understood in a broader than traditional way, which also includes innovative solutions that respond to the uncertainty of the environment and support the achievement of set goals. Noteworthy is the negative impact on hospital performance of the frequent and personal use of the information system by chief executives in discussions with subordinates and the search for common solutions for the entire hospital. In the context of the different institutional logics of medical professionals and directors, such intense personal involvement of directors can be read as micromanagement and an attempt to limit the autonomy and jurisdiction of clinicians. Trust also plays an important role in this model, stimulating innovation in the service of management control.

Adopting an additional research perspective, institutional theory, allowed for a deeper understanding of management control. This is because it turned out that some of the goals and innovative solutions developed and implemented in response to the environmental uncertainty led to the decoupling of formal structures from daily work processes. This was often due to the already mentioned varied institutional logics of managers and professionals. While there was agreement between managers and professionals about the desired outcomes of patient care, there was uncertainty about how to achieve them. Under such circumstances, decisions could be made only by professionals, based on their knowledge and experience, to which managers did not have access. To avoid relying on ineffective ceremonial or ritualistic control that would prevent any reduction in uncertainty, managers sought agreement with professionals and sectoral innovative solutions that provided some level of efficiency at the expense of separating structures and formal control from practice.

It also seems that in light of the institutional perspective, a more robust explanation can be offered for such a significant gap between the negative impact of interactive control on hospital performance and the significant positive impact of innovativeness. This is because directors using interactive control sought common solutions for the entire organization, imposing a unified perception of organizational goals. Professionals, "coerced" by the directors' continuous and personal commitment to a unified perception of the hospital's goals, ostensibly implemented practices prescribed by management logic, while they actually performed actions derived from their professional logic, thus separating their normative structure and operational activities in the hospital from formal structures. Overcoming such inefficiency, resulting in negative hospital performance, requires developing local innovative solutions at the level of specialties, departments, and clinics that reconcile the goals and interests of competing institutional logics. Importantly, this is easier when there is a separation of the daily working practices of professionals from formal structures.

7.2 Conclusions

Theoretical considerations presented, supported by research and verification of research hypotheses, have become the basis for understanding and explaining the way management control functions in hospitals and its impact on these organizations' performance. They made it possible to provide a number of insights and conclusions:

■ The identified peculiarity of hospitals poses significant challenges to management control in hospitals compared to organizations operating in a less heterogeneous environment and with more specified goals and criteria for evaluating their performance. Among other things, the peculiarity of hospitals is due to the interconnectedness of (1) two bureaucratic orders of professional and Weberian bureaucracy, (2) the dominance of medical professionals with a high degree of autonomy, (3) the difficulty – being the result of relative ambiguity – in determining the performance of hospitals and the expectations of major interest groups manifested by strong uncoordinated pressures from the external environment, which makes it very difficult to set long-term goals and consistently implement them.
■ Hybridization of hospitals, manifested by the presence of different institutional logics (management, focused on efficiency, and professional, focused on quality and autonomy), exacerbates the problem of goal ambiguity in these organizations.
■ Hospitals operate in a politicized environment in which health-care preferences, particularly issues of economic efficiency, are contested and debated. This is mainly due to the ambiguity of goals occurring on at least two levels: (1) at the national level, the government often modify priorities regarding the direction of changes in health care, and (2) at the local level, the owner of the hospital, which is often a political or collegiate body, such as a foundation, religious organization, or local government sets conflicting expectations for the hospital to meet multiple social goals while reducing operating costs.

■ The ambiguity of the goals of hospitals, where different institutional logics meet, makes it necessary for managers to constantly interpret information coming from the external and internal environment in order to set goals and standards of operation at both the strategic and the operational levels often enough. In particular, this applies to the issue of efficiency considered, respectively, in economic terms (management logic) or more in medical terms (professional logic). For, as has been seen, top management cognitively and emotionally supports directing human and capital resources of hospitals to areas of highest social utility. However, when cost pressures are strong, they direct resources to areas of highest economic value to ensure the organization's survival.

■ Conducting research on management control in hospitals must take into account not only the organizational perspective, but also the institutional perspective. After all, as has been shown, the factor that differentiates the functioning of companies and hospitals is a more complex institutional environment, consisting of both a variety of internal actors (e.g., different groups of professionals characterized by different institutional logics) and a number of external stakeholders (e.g., public and private payers/insurers, national government, local governments, health professions councils, patient associations), whose actions relatively often complicate the application of management control.

■ Theory, economic practice, and empirical research on the performance of hospitals help to define three main pathways from the information system to hospital performance. In this view, the impact of information system effectiveness on hospital performance is mediated by three elements: (1) interactive use of IS, i.e., interactive control, (2) diagnostic use of IS, i.e,. diagnostic control, and (3) innovativeness, which depends on the perceived environmental uncertainty and managers' trust in physicians.

■ The model estimation results showing the lack of direct impact of IS on hospital performance suggest that measurement itself, which involves assigning numbers to activities and processes according to specific rules, cannot be used for management control in hospitals. This finding contradicts previous studies, which suggest that the act of measurement itself influences employees' behavior, allowing them to determine the effects of their work and thus enable them to correct their actions. The main reason for the lack of influence of the information (measurement) system on hospital performance is the ambiguity of hospital goals. This is due to the fact that managers cannot assume in their decisions a long-term understanding of the hospital's goals by key employees, but must define ad hoc goals and standards on an ongoing basis, depending on the current context, which frame the actions taken.

■ The measurement function does not work if employees are not given specific guidance and standards for organizational goals. So information by itself, without managers setting appropriate goals and levels of metrics, does not affect performance. It is the use of diagnostic control, related to goal setting, regular review of "exceptions," and monitoring to ensure that critical elements of the business are within the control focus that helps to strengthen and guide employees' actions and motivation to achieve the goals set. In other words, hospital performance is positively affected by the diagnostic use of the information system, i.e., the ongoing monitoring of hospital performance and correction of deviations from plans and established performance standards. The strength of diagnostic control depends on the ability to link the results obtained to service delivery processes, to the availability of measurements of current activity, and to evaluation standards as well as to the capability to proactively intervene when deviations between current performance and standards are observed.

■ Under conditions of ambiguity and variability of goals, more frequent and intensive tracking of the progress of goals and objectives and their ongoing updating is a prerequisite for improving hospital performance. As shown, there is a non-linear relationship between diagnostic control and hospital performance, which can be expressed by the equation: $HP = 0.41 \cdot DC + 0.12 \cdot DC^2$. This means that intensifying the diagnostic use of the information system results in a disproportionately greater improvement in performance. Such a relationship in hospitals, described in the literature (Tannenbaum, 1962, p. 256; Likert, 1960, 1958; McMahon & Perritt, 1973, p. 627; Tessier & Otley, 2012, p. 175), may be due to the fact that intensive control makes employees more submissive to control and increases their commitment, motivation, and productivity.

■ Interactive control requires the use of an information system for organizational learning and fostering dialogue to identify, prioritize, and develop ways to achieve goals, but given the ambiguity and sectoral nature of goals in hospitals, it is virtually impossible to agree on a common strategy, goals, and work standards for the entire hospital.

■ The negative impact of interactive control on hospital performance, identified during the study, means that attempts to conduct dialogues at the hospital through frequent and personal involvement of the chief executive in decisions made by professionals is counterproductive. In other words, not only do such dialogues not improve performance, but in the perception of the directors they lead to a deterioration of hospital performance.

■ The performance of a hospital is most strongly influenced by innovativeness. This is because innovativeness allows organizational processes to be better adapted to the environment in which the hospital operates. This aspect seems to be overlooked in the literature in the context of control. This is because in the literature, control is relatively most often associated with setting goals and monitoring their implementation, which should lead to improved organizational performance. On the other hand, the research shows that the introduction of local innovations, tailored to the specific functioning of individual hospital departments, has the strongest impact on hospital performance.

■ The relatively weak impact of the information system's effectiveness on innovativeness compared to its impact on diagnostic and interactive control is due to the fact that in the course of agreeing on and developing innovative solutions that reconcile the goals and interests of competing institutional logics, there is often a decoupling between work practices and formal structures, and therefore between official performance measures derived from the information system. On the whole, innovative solutions at the local level, such as individual hospital departments or medical specialties, are more effective because they facilitate local consensus between conflicting goals.

■ A key element in enabling a hospital to achieve good results is the introduction of innovations, both by directors and by medical professionals. Innovations are induced by two factors: (1) planned activities that support the achievement of key organizational goals, and as (2) part of a response to environmental uncertainty. On the other hand, the level of innovation absorption is related to the trust of directors in medical professionals and, in general, to the trust between subordinates and superiors. It is worth considering here the property of reciprocity of trust described in the literature (Swärd, 2016, p. 15), as well as the positive correlation between the trust of superiors in subordinates and the mutual trust between employees and superiors (Kim i in., 2016, s. 952).

■ The level of directors' trust in medical professionals translates into the level of innovativeness in the hospital in two ways. First, when directors trust medical professionals, they accept the ideas they present with much greater openness and support the implementation of those ideas with greater commitment. Second, trust increases the amount of freedom that top management gives to professionals to innovate on their own, with acquiescence to innovation applying both to day-to-day day decisions and to larger "strategic" changes within technology, organization, management, relationships with other hospital units and external stakeholders. Professionals' trust in the director, meanwhile, helps them to take more innovative actions, reducing fears of negative consequences in the case of unsuccessful innovation results.

■ For complex and unprogrammable work processes in hospitals, neither outcome control nor behavioral control are sufficiently effective, and ceremonial or ritualistic forms of control may take their place. This is because, by definition, there is agreement between managers and professionals on the desired outcomes of patient care, but differences arise from perceptions of how to achieve those outcomes. In such circumstances, decisions can be made only by professionals, based on their knowledge and experience, to which managers do not have access. Therefore, directors cannot fully participate in these decisions even in the form of interactive control. To avoid ceremonial or ritualistic control, managers seek agreements with professionals and sectoral innovative solutions to ensure some level of efficiency, often leading to the separation of daily practices from formal structures.

■ The positive impact of perceived environmental uncertainty on innovation stems from the stimulating and initiating role of uncertainty in finding innovative ways to achieve goals in response to emerging risks. Managers, in response to environmental uncertainty, are more likely to cooperate and negotiate with professionals in the search for joint solutions. In this context, managers' trust in professionals also plays an important role, allowing the parties to communicate more openly and thus foster solutions that take into account the separation of daily practices from formal structures.

■ The model of management control in hospitals shows that innovativeness has the greatest positive impact on hospital performance when organizational actors, compelled by the environmental uncertainty, seek innovative solutions and have the right information and show trust in each other. When an effective information system is not in place, it is not possible for organizational actors to make the right decisions or take effective action, despite the perceived environmental uncertainty and high trust. Of course, some decisions may be accurate despite the lack of information; however, the probability of making accurate decisions when information is scarce is lower. It is also worth noting that in the absence of information, identification of problems and uncertainties may be impaired.

■ From an institutional perspective, trust is necessary because decoupling of daily work processes from formal structures in a way that benefits the organization requires far-reaching cooperation. In line with the expectations of the government and health-care payers, managers should reduce medical costs and ensure the financial stability of their facilities by challenging doctors' autonomy and urging them to be more efficient and treat less expensively. However, the only way managers can achieve these government goals is by cooperating with doctors, since only physicians can actually perform medical services and decide about their costs, but also, to some extent, the amount of payment for those services, i.e., the hospital's revenue.

■ Physicians, being interested in good treatment outcomes, which, in many situations, require significant financial resources, agree to seek local innovative solutions aimed at increased hospital revenues. To generate more revenue, hospital directors and physicians can cooperate in at least three areas: regulating the number and type of patients admitted to the hospital, providing more profitable services, and modifying parameters such as length of stay and the number and scope of medical procedures performed for increased revenue (more favorable billing) with the payer for health services.

■ Medical professionals also have an interest in sustaining the decoupling of daily practice from formal structures. On the one hand, this enables them to practice medicine more effectively and achieve better health outcomes for individual patients, and, on the other hand, it sustains the social legitimacy of the profession, based on an ethos of social service. In addition, this decoupling allows for easier compromise and mitigation of conflicts between managers and physicians that would undoubtedly arise in the course of achieving organizational goals, particularly those aimed at reducing costs.

■ The research showed that the formal structures and methods of management control, reflecting patterns of efficiency established and recognized in the broader social system, identified in the documentation of hospitals during the qualitative research, were not entirely "freely chosen" by directors, but they were at least partially drawn from the environment or even imposed by the environment in order for the hospital to gain external legitimacy as a "rational" and "efficient" organization.

The above-mentioned key findings resulting from the research show that the proposed model of management control in hospitals is an approach that encompasses many areas, relationships, and specific conditions of hospital operations. Admittedly, the constructs found in the proposed model are well known and some of them have been widely described in the literature, but the previously identified connections between these constructs and the theoretical explanations of these connections make it possible to consider that the model as a whole is a new and unique proposal for understanding management control in hospitals. In this context, it also seems important that the scientific community has not yet developed a comprehensive concept of control in hospitals, and, at the same time, the model presented in the monograph significantly differs from previously proposed general control models (Flamholtz et al., 1985, 1996; Haustein et al., 2014; Kruis, 2008; Malmi & Brown, 2008; Merchant & Van der Stede, 2017; Ouchi, 1979; Simons, 1995, 2014), which means that as a new theory it requires further research, which should be carried out by representatives of various scientific disciplines.

7.3 Limitations of the Model and Directions for Further Research

The research presented in the book paves the way for further research in the area of management control in hospitals. Focusing on the possibility of considering management control also from an institutional perspective, rather than only an organizational one, allows for a deeper understanding of the issues of the initiation, development, operation, and implications of management control in hospitals. However, it is also important to note the limitations associated with both the model itself and the research process. This is because despite the exercise of due diligence to ensure the objectivity and rigor of the research, the model is characterized by limitations related to the complexity and multifaceted nature of management science. This is due to the impossibility of identifying a complete list of factors and the interrelationships between them that determine the various phenomena in the model of management control in hospitals. Therefore, the improvement of management control on the basis of the proposed model should be regarded as a key activity, but at the same time as a certain part of the broader whole, prejudging the possibility of using the proposed theory in the processes of improving the organizations in question. For this reason, the proposed model makes it possible to identify a number of important areas of further research that will serve to deepen the knowledge of management control in hospitals.

The observation made finds specific expression in the need to deepen research on the relationship detected in empirical studies between the hospital information system and its interactive use negatively affecting hospital performance. While the research identifies a few reasons for the negative impact of interactive control on performance, the possibility that there are more reasons for this phenomenon should be recognized, not least because the scientific literature also insufficiently recognizes the relationship between innovativeness from different sources (intentional, semi-intentional, and *bricolage*) and hospital performance. The relationship between environmental uncertainty and innovativeness also requires deeper analysis. Significant added value in this area can be developed through a discussion of the impact of perceived uncertainty not only on hospital directors, but also on employees, particularly physicians. Similarly, the relationship between trust and innovativeness also needs further examination. Indeed, while there are numerous studies of subordinates' trust in superiors, the reverse of trust is virtually unexplored. The literature on trust lacks studies related to this issue. Thus, conducting research related to organizational trust, in general, and interpersonal trust, in particular, can be an interesting field of inquiry, as it is impossible to analyze management control when the mechanisms of trust are not understood. Adopting such a perspective in further research in hospitals will allow us to grasp the effects of management control both from the perspective of the organization and from the perspective of the individual.

The research provides insight into the important mediating role of interactive and diagnostic control and innovativeness between the information system and hospital performance. Thus, in the course of further research, it seems reasonable to consider other aspects of the hospital management system and/or their mediating role in improving the effectiveness of achieving organizational goals. It should also be noted that management control is a very complex issue, and the research presented in this monograph covered only areas of management control related to formal control mechanisms, while areas related to the role of organizational culture, ideology, clan control, characteristic of medical professionals, and trust as direct control mechanisms were omitted by design.

Estimation of the original (conceptual) model (Figure 5.1) eliminated the variable employee rewards due to the lack of statistically significant relationships with the other constructs. However, this does not exclude connections with other constructs that were not identified – although they occur in business practice – within the framework of the adopted research method. Indeed, this thread appears to be important and should continue to be studied. Thus, further attention of researchers should be directed to developing a model that also takes into account these additional dimensions of control.

A fundamental and, it seems, with the current state of science in this area, an unwavering problem of conducting research in the field of hospital management is also the significant limitations on the ability to evaluate hospital performance and the results obtained. A large part of the scientific community agrees on one thing – that it is impossible to evaluate a hospital solely on the basis of financial indicators. In the context of the research presented and the current state of knowledge, the model for assessing hospital performance adopted in the book seems optimal. However, it is essential to remember that in the measurement model used, the directors, in assessing the performance of the hospital, were basically assessing the performance of their own activity. Despite the obvious weaknesses, the model of self-assessment of performance is widely used not only in the field of hospitals, but also in enterprises. However, it would be necessary to intensify research on the search for more objective methods of measuring and evaluating hospital performance and, in this context, verify the solutions of the model presented here.

An important limitation of the methodology adopted in this research is that the survey was conducted only among hospital chief executives. Expanding the scope and verifying the model in further research should allow the hypotheses posed here to be strengthened by addressing alternative respondents, such as organizational unit (clinical) managers or even all physicians. Of course, surveys can also be undertaken among other personnel (e.g., among randomly selected employees at all levels of the organizational structure), but the results of such surveys would have to be interpreted taking into account the fact that a significant number of employees function under the direction of physicians, carrying out their orders and supporting their work as the main decision-makers in the healing processes of hospitals.

Undertaking further research should also address other resolutions that, in the solution adopted here, may be methodological limitations, but at the same time may determine the possibility of multidirectional verification of the model. In particular, this concerns the measurement of variables. This is because all the constructs used in this study required the development of measurement instruments. Thus, although the properties of the instruments were carefully developed and evaluated, their further testing in other studies will add significant value to the knowledge of management control in hospitals. The use of formative (composite) measurement models, on the one hand, allows them to be more accurately reflected in a given context, such as the Polish health-care system, but, on the other hand, this context-dependence makes it difficult to transfer this type of operationalization to other settings. A glaring example of this is the variable environmental uncertainty, which relates to problems observed in Polish hospitals, but its international generalizability should still be studied. Importantly, reflective constructs are also not free from problems of definition and operationalization. For example, the negative impact of interactive control on hospital performance may also result from the way this variable is operationalized, that is, from the definition of its domain of meaning. The problem with a clear definition of this construct is pointed out in the body of the book.

Replication of quantitative studies in hospitals in other countries, in other health systems, is also an important factor in extending the research presented in the book, providing increased generalizability. While limiting the study to a single health system allows for indirect control of potentially disruptive local factors, research in other health systems would increase the potential of the proposed model. Replication of this study in other countries would help determine whether the hypothesized relationships hold across health systems and cultural contexts.

The non-linear relationships between the variables diagnostic control and hospital performance, IS effectiveness and innovativeness, and IS effectiveness and diagnostic control also require in-depth analysis. In the described research, the theoretical analysis on the basis of previous studies has only analyzed the non-linear relationship between the variables diagnostic control and hospital performance as a relationship with by far the largest square coefficient and effect size f^2. However, given that an increase in diagnostic control leads to an exponential improvement in hospital performance, questions arise as to where the limit of this increase lies and what the negative effects of continuously strengthening diagnostic control may be. Further research should also confirm the quadratic increase in innovativeness with increasing SI effectiveness ($I = 0.46 \cdot ISE + 0.06 \cdot ISE^2$) and the non-linear decrease in diagnostic control with increasing SI effectiveness suggested in this study (Table 6.27). What is important in this case is not only the confirmation of the non-linearity, but also the theoretical interpretation. For example: whether an increase in SI effectiveness causes some excess information (information noise) that leads to a decrease in diagnostic control.

In conclusion, it should be said that despite the potential difficulties in building a model of management control in hospitals, the study has attempted to develop a comprehensive model of this issue. Concerns about the difficulty of measuring variables and model construction in this study are somewhat mitigated by the theoretically consistent results obtained. However, this is a post hoc rationalization, and validation of the measurement instruments and structural model requires further work that will verify the limitations identified here and facilitate the generalization of the proposed model to hospitals operating under different external and internal environmental conditions, ensuring the efficiency of the management control system and its translation into the success of these organizations.

Chapter 8

Ending/Summary

This book is a voice in what is widely considered to be an important discussion on improving the efficiency of hospitals and the quality of the services they provide. This is an intriguing topic, and, at the same time, an important one also from the perspective of the theory and practice of management of public and not-for-profit organizations. Indeed, the issue of management control in hospitals is a broad field of research at the intersection of many fields and scientific disciplines, particularly management and medicine, as well as economics and finance. The demand for this type of research is the result of the needs drawn in the conditions of a permanent increase in public spending on hospital services and the small effects of previous activities related to the introduction of new solutions, both of a practical and of a theoretical nature, into economic practice. The challenges identified in this way became the main reason for identifying the main objective of the book, which was realized in three areas: theoretical, methodological, and empirical.

On the basis of the literature research, the specific characteristics of hospitals as organizations were recognized and characterized, which made it possible to achieve the goal of identifying the specific characteristics of hospitals and their environment. The ambiguity of goals, a highly politicized operating environment, and a health-care market characterized by the separation of the consumer of services from the payer were identified as the primary distinguishing features of the hospital environment. The unique characteristics of hospitals themselves included the affiliation of hospitals with units of higher public utility, the immense complexity of basic operational processes, a highly functional organizational structure, the presence of two bureaucratic orders (Weberian bureaucracy and professional bureaucracy), hybridization, i.e. the functioning within the hospital of at least two distinct institutional logics (professional and management), and the extensive autonomy of medical professionals, who simultaneously constitute the main workforce and control the primary operational processes. All of the indicated characteristics were considered to be the causes of problems in evaluating the performance of both individual professionals and the hospital as a whole, which greatly complicates management control.

In an effort to systematize theories on control in the management science literature, a review of the more important theories and definitions related to control and a synthesis of theories that may be applicable to management control in hospitals was made. The interrelationships and common elements of these theories, both in the area of operational control and in the area of strategic control, are also indicated. An analysis of management control from an institutional perspective is also made here. Given the broad nature of the operational definition of management control, encompassing all instruments, activities and systems used by top management to increase the likelihood of a hospital's favorable adaptation to the environment, in the process of formulating a systematic basis for interpreting the interrelationships between elements of management control in hospitals, a critical analysis of the literature related to specific elements of management control, such as information systems, employee evaluation and reward, innovativeness, trust, and perceived environmental uncertainty, was conducted. Particular attention was paid to previous research related to the evaluation of hospital performance. This is because, to date, the scientific community has not reached a consensus on criteria for measuring hospital performance.

Before embarking on the empirical objectives, an exploratory sequential mixed-methods research procedure was chosen as a strategy for achieving the adopted goals. In this study design, the quantitative phase of data collection and analysis follows the qualitative phase of data collection and analysis. In the qualitative research phase, based on thematic analysis, the coding of practices and elements of management control was conducted in inductive logic; however, the grouping of codes into first-order themes and first-order themes into second-order themes was conducted in parallel with the literature analysis. This procedure identified eight second-order themes, assumed in the study as latent variables (constructs), related to management control, and proposed 14 hypotheses about the relationship between these constructs, which constituted a preliminary model of management control in hospitals (Figure 5.1).

In the quantitative research phase, an initial element was the elaboration of the measurement models of constructs identified in the qualitative phase. The measurement models of identified constructs were based on actual control practices in hospitals, but, at the same time, they are embedded in existing theory and are abstract in nature. Thus, a key challenge was to find the right rules for correspondence of unobservable variables with directly measurable variables, since observable events, including human feelings, are secondary to the real latent phenomena sought. Therefore, in operationalizing the variables, where possible, previously used scales or single indicators were used to maximize the fidelity of reflection of latent structures. Three variables: information system effectiveness, perceived environmental uncertainty, and hospital performance were operationalized as formative variables, which had implications for the selection of the path model estimator. In addition to the formative nature of the three variables, the choice of an estimator based on the partial least squares method (PLS-SEM) was influenced by the novelty of the proposed theory, the high complexity of the model, the inability to collect a large research sample, and the predictive properties of the PLS-SEM estimator. The book describes in detail the criteria for selecting the measurement model of latent variables, the path model estimator, and the modeling procedure itself, including the evaluation of measurement models using PLS-SEM.

Based on the measurement models of the constructs (operationalization), a survey questionnaire was developed. The data collected by the survey questionnaire formed the basis for further statistical research. During the estimation of the preliminary model (Figure 6.5), paths with low impact value and statistically insignificant were identified. Due to the overstatement of the explained variance of variables targeted by more paths, paths with negligible impact and statistically insignificant were dropped, which reduced the number of constructs to seven and paths to eight (Figure 6.6) and constituted the modified (final) model of management control in hospitals. This model explains as much as 67% of the variation in hospital performance.

The essential result of the presented research, which adds significant value to management science, is an action-oriented theory of management control in hospitals. The research process adopted seems to ensure the consistency and universality of this theory. As a result, the proposed model is a proposal that fills an important gap in knowledge regarding the control function in hospitals. This is because the knowledge contained in the literature, to date, provides little systematic guidance on strategic and operational control in these organizations, which operate in a specific and politicized environment that is simultaneously required to meet multiple, often conflicting, objectives. However, even clarified goals cannot be achieved without adequate knowledge to ensure effectiveness and economic efficiency in operations. The concepts and solutions presented here, therefore, fill the gap in this knowledge, particularly by proposing a new concept of management control that can be used by theoreticians and practitioners of management in hospitals to bridge the tensions between economic and social goals and to transform the innovative solutions thus obtained into increasingly better hospital performance.

Filling the identified research gaps should at the same time provide an impetus for a wide range of researchers to address the issue of management control, particularly when it has not been a popular research area in recent decades. It also seems necessary to enable management practitioners in hospitals to analyze more deeply the practical aspects of this control, which forms the basis for many improvements in this area.

References

Abbott, A. (1988). *The system of professions: An essay on the division of expert labor.* University of Chicago Press.

Abernethy, M. A., & Brownell, P. (1999). The role of budgets in organizations facing strategic change: An exploratory study. *Accounting, Organizations and Society,* *24*(3), 189–204.

Abernethy, M. A., & Chua, W. F. (1996). A field study of control system "redesign": The impact of institutional processes on strategic choice. *Contemporary Accounting Research,* *13*(2), 569–606.

Abernethy, M. A., Chua, W. F., Grafton, J., & Mahama, H. (2006). Accounting and control in health care: Behavioural, organisational, sociological and critical perspectives. In C. S. Chapman, A. G. Hopwood, & M. D. Shields (Eds.), *Handbooks of management accounting research* (Vol. 2, pp. 805–829). Elsevier.

Abernethy, M. A., & Stoelwinder, J. U. (1990). The relationship between organisation structure and management control in hospitals: An elaboration and test of Mintzberg's professional bureaucracy model. *Accounting, Auditing and Accountability Journal,* *3*(3), 18–33. https://doi.org/10.1108/09513579010142616

Abernethy, M. A., & Stoelwinder, J. U. (1991). Budget use, task uncertainty, system goal orientation and subunit performance: A test of the 'fit' hypothesis in not-for-profit hospitals. *Accounting, Organizations and Society,* *16*(2), 105–120.

Adams, B. D., & Sartori, J. A. (2006). *Validating the trust in teams and trust in leaders scales.* Humansystems Inc.

Afsar, B., Badir, Y., & Khan, M. M. (2015). Person–job fit, person–organization fit and innovative work behavior: The mediating role of innovation trust. *The Journal of High Technology Management Research,* *26*(2), 105–116. https://doi.org/10.1016/j.hitech.2015.09.001

Afsar, B., Cheema, S., & Bin Saeed, B. (2018). Do nurses display innovative work behavior when their values match with hospitals' values? *European Journal of Innovation Management,* *21*(1), 157–171. https://doi.org/10.1108/EJIM-01-2017-0007

Agle, B. R., Nagarajan, N. J., Sonnenfeld, J. A., & Srinivasan, D. (2006). Does ceo charisma matter? An empirical analysis of the relationships among organizational performance, environmental uncertainty, and top management team perceptions of Ceo Charisma. *Academy of Management Journal, 49*(1), 161–174. https://doi.org/10.5465/amj.2006.20785800

Aguinis, H., Beaty, J. C., Boik, R. J., & Pierce, C. A. (2005). Effect size and power in assessing moderating effects of categorical variables using multiple regression: A 30-year review. *Journal of Applied Psychology, 90*(1), 94–107. https://doi.org/10.1037/0021-9010.90.1.94

Aguirre-Urreta, M. I., & Marakas, G. M. (2014). Research note—Partial least squares and models with formatively specified endogenous constructs: A cautionary note. *Information Systems Research, 25*(4), 761–778. https://doi.org/10.1287/isre.2013.0493

Aguirre-Urreta, M. I., Rönkkö, M., & Marakas, G. M. (2016). Omission of causal indicators: Consequences and implications for measurement. *Measurement: Interdisciplinary Research and Perspectives, 14*(3), 75–97. https://doi.org/10.1080/15366367.2016.1205935

Ahgren, B. (2008). Is it better to be big? The reconfiguration of 21st century hospitals: Responses to a hospital merger in Sweden. *Health Policy, 87*(1), 92–99. https://doi.org/10.1016/j.healthpol.2008.02.001

Ahrens, T., & Khalifa, R. (2015). The impact of regulation on management control: Compliance as a strategic response to institutional logics of university accreditation. *Qualitative Research in Accounting and Management, 12*(2), 106–126.

Aidemark, L.-G., & Funck, E. K. (2009). Measurement and health care management. *Financial Accountability and Management, 25*(2), 253–276. https://doi.org/10.1111/j.1468-0408.2009.00476.x

Allred, C. A., Hoffman, S. E., Fox, D. H., & Michel, Y. (1994). A measure of perceived environmental uncertainty in hospitals. *Western Journal of Nursing Research, 16*(2), 169–182. https://doi.org/10.1177/019394599401600204

Alvesson, M., & Willmott, H. (2002). Identity regulation as organizational control: Producing the appropriate individual. *Journal of Management Studies, 39*(5), 619–644. https://doi.org/10.1111/1467-6486.00305

Amarantou, V., Kazakopoulou, S., Chatzoudes, D., & Chatzoglou, P. (2018). Resistance to change: An empirical investigation of its antecedents. *Journal of Organizational Change Management, 31*(2), 426–450. https://doi.org/10.1108/JOCM-05-2017-0196

Amos, D., Au-Yong, C. P., & Musa, Z. N. (2021). The mediating effects of finance on the performance of hospital facilities management services. *Journal of Building Engineering, 34*, 101899.

Ancelin-Bourguignon, A., Saulpic, O., & Zarlowski, P. (2013). Subjectivities and micro-processes of change in accounting practices: A case study. *Journal of Accounting and Organizational Change, 9*(2), 206–236.

Andersen, O. J. (2008). A bottom-up perspective on innovations: Mobilizing knowledge and social capital through innovative processes of Bricolage. *Administration and Society, 40*(1), 54–78. https://doi.org/10.1177/0095399707311775

Andersson, T., & Liff, R. (2018). Co-optation as a response to competing institutional logics: Professionals and managers in healthcare. *Journal of Professions and Organization, 5*(2), 71–87. https://doi.org/10.1093/jpo/joy001

Andreasson, J., Ljungar, E., Ahlstrom, L., Hermansson, J., & Dellve, L. (2018). Professional bureaucracy and health care managers' planned change strategies: Governance in Swedish Health Care. *Nordic Journal of Working Life Studies, 8*(1), 23–41.

Anhang Price, R., Elliott, M. N., Zaslavsky, A. M., Hays, R. D., Lehrman, W. G., Rybowski, L., Edgman-Levitan, S., & Cleary, P. D. (2014). Examining the role of patient experience surveys in measuring health care quality. *Medical Care Research and Review, 71*(5), 522–554.

Ansari, S. L. (1977). An integrated approach to control system design. *Accounting, Organizations and Society, 2*(2), 101–112.

Anthony, R. N. (1965a). *Management accounting principles.* Richard D. Irwin, Inc.

Anthony, R. N. (1965b). *Planning and control systems: A framework for analysis.* Division of Research, Graduate School of Business Administration, Harvard University.

Anthony, R. N. (1988). *The management control function.* The Harvard Business School Press.

Anthony, R. N., Govindarajan, V., Hartmann, F. G., Kraus, K., & Nilsson, G. (2014). *Management control systems: European edition* (Kindle Edition). McGraw-Hill Higher Education.

Appelbaum, S. H., Cameron, A., Ensink, F., Hazarika, J., Attir, R., Ezzedine, R., & Shekhar, V. (2017). Factors that impact the success of an organizational change: A case study analysis. *Industrial and Commercial Training, 49*(5), 213–230. https://doi.org/10.1108/ICT-02-2017-0006

Archer, S., & Otley, D. (1991). Strategy, structure, planning and control systems and performance evaluation—Rumenco Ltd. *Management Accounting Research, 2*(4), 263–303. https://doi.org/10.1016/S1044-5005(91)70038-3

Ashenfelter, O., Hosken, D., Vita, M., & Weinberg, M. (2011). Retrospective analysis of hospital mergers. *International Journal of the Economics of Business, 18*(1), 5–16.

Ashford, S. J., & Cummings, L. L. (1983). Feedback as an individual resource: Personal strategies of creating information. *Organizational Behavior and Human Performance, 32*(3), 370–398. https://doi.org/10.1016/0030-5073(83)90156-3

Astrachan, C. B., Patel, V. K., & Wanzenried, G. (2014). A comparative study of CB-SEM and PLS-SEM for theory development in family firm research. *Journal of Family Business Strategy, 5*(1), 116–128.

Atuahene-Gima, K. (2005). Resolving the capability–rigidity paradox in new product innovation. *Journal of Marketing, 69*(4), 61–83. https://doi.org/10.1509/jmkg.2005.69.4.61

Au, N., Ngai, E. W. T., & Cheng, T. C. E. (2008). Extending the understanding of end user information systems satisfaction formation: An equitable needs fulfillment model approach. *MIS Quarterly, 32*(1), 43–66. JSTOR. https://doi.org /10.2307/25148828

Austen, A. (2010). Pomiar efektywności w organizacjach ochrony zdrowia. In A. Frączkiewicz-Wronka (Ed.), *Pomiar efektywności organizacji publicznych na przykładzie sektora ochrony zdrowia* (pp. 100–131). Wydawnictwo Uniwersytetu Ekonomicznego w Katowicach.

Avkiran, N. K. (2018). An in-depth discussion and illustration of partial least squares structural equation modeling in health care. *Health Care Management Science, 21*(3), 401–408. https://doi.org/10.1007/s10729-017-9393-7

Babbie, E. (2013). *Podstawy badań społecznych.* Wydawnictwo Naukowe PWN.

Bach, S. (1994). Managing a pluralist health system: The case of health care reform in France. *International Journal of Health Services, 24*(4), 593–606. https://doi .org/10.2190/915A-FTXV-ATQR-KCGY

Bachmann, R., & Zaheer, A. (Eds.). (2006). *Handbook of trust research.* Edward Elgar Publishing.

Baiman, S., & Evans, J. H. (1983). Pre-decision information and participative management control systems. *Journal of Accounting Research,* Autumn, 1983, Vol. 21, No. 2 (Autumn, 1983), pp. 371–395.

Baines, A., & Langfield-Smith, K. (2003). Antecedents to management accounting change: A structural equation approach. *Accounting, Organizations and Society, 28*(7–8), 675–698. https://doi.org/10.1016/S0361-3682(02)00102-2

Baird, K. M., Tung, A., & Yu, Y. (2017). Employee organizational commitment and hospital performance. *Health Care Management Review, 44*(3), 206–215. https://doi.org/10.1097/HMR.0000000000000181

Baker, G., Gibbons, R., & Murphy, K. J. (1994). Subjective performance measures in optimal incentive contracts. *The Quarterly Journal of Economics, 109*(4), 1125–1156.

Ball, J., Day, T., Murrells, T., Dall'Ora, C., Rafferty, A. M., Griffiths, P., & Maben, J. (2017). Cross-sectional examination of the association between shift length and hospital nurses job satisfaction and nurse reported quality measures. *BMC Nursing, 16*(1), 1–7.

Barker, J. R. (1993). Tightening the iron cage: Concertive control in self-managing teams. *Administrative Science Quarterly, 38*(3), 408–437.

Bastani, P., Alipoori, S., Imani-Nasab, M.-H., Jamalabadi, S., & Kavosi, Z. (2021). Evidence-based decision making among healthcare managers: Evidence from a developing country. *International Journal of Healthcare Management, 14*(1), 197–202.

Batjargal, B., Hitt, M. A., Tsui, A. S., Arregle, J.-L., Webb, J. W., & Miller, T. L. (2013). Institutional polycentrism, entrepreneurs' social networks, and new venture growth. *Academy of Management Journal, 56*(4), 1024–1049. https://doi.org/10 .5465/amj.2010.0095

Bayonne, E., Marin-Garcia, J. A., & Alfalla-Luque, R. (2020). Partial least squares (PLS) in Operations Management research: Insights from a systematic literature review. *Journal of Industrial Engineering and Management, 13*(3), Article 3. https://doi.org/10.3926/jiem.3416

Bazeley, P. (2018). *A practical introduction to mixed methods for business and management*. Sage.

Becker, J.-M., Rai, A., Ringle, C. M., & Völckner, F. (2013). Discovering unobserved heterogeneity in structural equation models to avert validity threats. *MIS Quarterly*, *37*(3), 665–694.

Becker, J.-M., Ringle, C. M., Sarstedt, M., & Völckner, F. (2015). How collinearity affects mixture regression results. *Marketing Letters*, *26*(4), 643–659. https://doi.org/10.1007/s11002-014-9299-9

Begun, J. W., & Kaissi, A. A. (2004). Uncertainty in health care environments: Myth or reality? *Health Care Management Review*, *29*(1), 31–39.

Benabou, R., & Tirole, J. (2003). Intrinsic and extrinsic motivation. *Review of Economic Studies*, *70*(3), 489–520.

Benitez, J., Henseler, J., Castillo, A., & Schuberth, F. (2020). How to perform and report an impactful analysis using partial least squares: Guidelines for confirmatory and explanatory IS research. *Information and Management*, *57*(2), 103168. https://doi.org/10.1016/j.im.2019.05.003

Bentler, P. M., & Huang, W. (2014). On components, latent variables, PLS and simple methods: Reactions to Rigdon's rethinking of PLS. *Long Range Planning*, *47*(3), 138–145. https://doi.org/10.1016/j.lrp.2014.02.005

Bergkvist, L., & Rossiter, J. R. (2009). Tailor-made single-item measures of doubly concrete constructs. *International Journal of Advertising*, *28*(4), 607–621. https://doi.org/10.2501/S0265048709200783

Berlant, J. L. (1975). *Profession and monopoly: A study of medicine in the United States and Great Britain*. University of California Press.

Berwick, D. M., & Hackbarth, A. D. (2012). Eliminating waste in US health care. *JAMA*, *307*(14), 1513–1516.

Bijlsma-Frankema, K., & Costa, A. C. (2005). Understanding the trust-control nexus. *International Sociology*, *20*(3), 259–282. https://doi.org/10.1177/0268580905055477

Bisbe, J., Batista-Foguet, J.-M., & Chenhall, R. (2007). Defining management accounting constructs: A methodological note on the risks of conceptual misspecification. *Accounting, Organizations and Society*, *32*(7–8), 789–820.

Bisbe, J., Foguet, J. M. B., & Chenhall, R. (2005). *What do we really mean by interactive control systems? The risks of theoretical misspecification*. 6th International Management Control Systems Research Conference (Edinburgh Business School). https://www.semanticscholar.org/paper/What-Do-We-Really-Mean-by-Interactive-Control-The-%2B-Bisbe-Batista-Foguet/04daf2764dd34f1e80818f07be9d8183b4350079#extracted

Bisbe, J., Kruis, A.-M., & Madini, P. (2019). Coercive, enabling, diagnostic, and interactive control: Untangling the threads of their connections. *Journal of Accounting Literature*, *43*, 124–144. https://doi.org/10.1016/j.acclit.2019.10.001

Bisbe, J., & Malagueño, R. (2009). The choice of interactive control systems under different innovation management modes. *European Accounting Review*, *18*(2), 371–405. https://doi.org/10.1080/09638180902863803

Bisbe, J., & Otley, D. (2004). The effects of the interactive use of management control systems on product innovation. *Accounting, Organizations and Society,* *29*(8), 709–737. https://doi.org/10.1016/j.aos.2003.10.010

Bisbe, J., & Sivabalan, P. (2017). Management control and trust in virtual settings: A case study of a virtual new product development team. *Management Accounting Research,* *37,* 12–29. https://doi.org/10.1016/j.mar.2017.02.001

Bloom, N., & Van Reenen, J. (2007). Measuring and explaining management practices across firms and countries. *The Quarterly Journal of Economics,* *122*(4), 1351–1408. https://doi.org/10.1162/qjec.2007.122.4.1351

Bloom, N., & Van Reenen, J. (2010). Why do management practices differ across firms and countries? *Journal of Economic Perspectives,* *24*(1), 203–224. https://doi.org/10.1257/jep.24.1.203

Bodenheimer, T. (2005). High and rising health care costs. Part 2: Technologic innovation. *Annals of Internal Medicine,* *142*(11), 932. https://doi.org/10.7326/0003-4819-142-11-200506070-00012

Bollen, K. A., & Diamantopoulos, A. (2017). In defense of causal-formative indicators: A minority report. *Psychological Methods,* *22*(3), 581–596. https://doi.org/10.1037/met0000056

Bollen, K. A., & Stine, R. A. (1992). Bootstrapping goodness-of-fit measures in structural equation models. *Sociological Methods and Research,* *21*(2), 205–229. https://doi.org/10.1177/0049124192021002004

Bollen, K. A., & Ting, K. (2000). A tetrad test for causal indicators. *Psychological Methods,* *5*(1), 3–22. https://doi.org/10.1037/1082-989X.5.1.3

Bordia, P., Hobman, E., Jones, E., Gallois, C., & Callan, V. J. (2004). Uncertainty during organizational change: Types, consequences, and management strategies. *Journal of Business and Psychology,* *18*(4), 507–532. https://doi.org/10.1023/B:JOBU.0000028449.99127.f7

Bourgeois, L. J. (1985). Strategic goals, perceived uncertainty, and economic performance in volatile environments. *Academy of Management Journal,* *28*(3), 548–573. https://doi.org/10.5465/256113

Boyatzis, R. E. (1998). *Transforming qualitative information: Thematic analysis and code development.* Sage.

Braun, V., & Clarke, V. (2006). Using thematic analysis in psychology. *Qualitative Research in Psychology,* *3*(2), 77–101.

Brennan, N., Barnes, R., Calnan, M., Corrigan, O., Dieppe, P., & Entwistle, V. (2013). Trust in the health-care provider–patient relationship: A systematic mapping review of the evidence base. *International Journal for Quality in Health Care,* *25*(6), 682–688.

Brewer, J., & Hunter, A. (2006). *Foundations of multimethod research: Synthesizing styles.* Sage.

Brower, H. H., Lester, S. W., Korsgaard, M. A., & Dineen, B. R. (2008). A closer look at trust between managers and subordinates: Understanding the effects of both trusting and being trusted on subordinate outcomes. *Journal of Management,* *35*(2), 327–347. https://doi.org/10.1177/0149206307312511

Brower, H. H., Schoorman, F. D., & Tan, H. H. (2000). A model of relational leadership: The integration of trust and leader–member exchange.
The Leadership Quarterly, *11*(2), 227–250. https://doi.org/10.1016/S1048
-9843(00)00040-0

Buchko, A. A. (1994). Conceptualization and measurement of environmental uncertainty: An assessment of the Miles and Snow perceived environmental uncertainty scale. *Academy of Management Journal*, *37*(2), 410–425. https://doi.org
/10.5465/256836

Burke, M. C. (1984). Strategic choice and marketing managers: An examination
of business-level marketing objectives. *Journal of Marketing Research*, *21*(4),
345–359.

Carabalí, J. V. J. (2017). *The Dynamics of Cost Management Practices in Portuguese
Hospitals* [Universidade do Minho]. http://repositorium.sdum.uminho.pt/

Carlsson-Wall, M., Kraus, K., & Messner, M. (2016). Performance measurement systems and the enactment of different institutional logics: Insights from a foot-
ball organization. *Management Accounting Research*, *32*, 45–61.

Carmeli, A., Gelbard, R., & Gefen, D. (2010). The importance of innovation leadership in cultivating strategic fit and enhancing firm performance. *The
Leadership Quarterly*, *21*(3), 339–349. https://doi.org/10.1016/j.leaqua.2010.03
.001

Carroll, N., & Lord, J. C. (2016). The growing importance of cost accounting for
hospitals. *Journal of Health Care Finance*, *43*(2), 172–185.

Cave, E. (2020). Selecting treatment options and choosing between them:
Delineating patient and professional autonomy in shared decision-making.
Health Care Analysis, *28*(1), 4–24. https://doi.org/10.1007/s10728-019-00384-8

Cenfetelli, R. T., & Bassellier, G. (2009). Interpretation of formative measurement in
information systems research. *MIS Quarterly*, *33*(4), 689. https://doi.org/10.2307
/20650323

Cerasoli, C. P., Nicklin, J. M., & Ford, M. T. (2014). Intrinsic motivation and extrinsic
incentives jointly predict performance: A 40-year meta-analysis. *Psychological
Bulletin*, *140*(4), 980–1008. https://doi.org/10.1037/a0035661

Cheah, J.-H., Roldán, J. L., Ciavolino, E., Ting, H., & Ramayah, T. (2020). Sampling
weight adjustments in partial least squares structural equation modeling: Guidelines and illustrations. *Total Quality Management and Business
Excellence*, *0*(0), 1–20. https://doi.org/10.1080/14783363.2020.1754125

Cheah, J.-H., Sarstedt, M., Ringle, C. M., Ramayah, T., & Ting, H. (2018). Convergent
validity assessment of formatively measured constructs in PLS-SEM: On using
single-item versus multi-item measures in redundancy analyses. *International
Journal of Contemporary Hospitality Management*, *30*(11), 3192–3210. https://
doi.org/10.1108/IJCHM-10-2017-0649

Chen, I.-H., Yun-Ping Lee, A., Parboteeah, K. P., Lai, C.-S., & Chung, A. (2014).
The effects of physicians' personal characteristics on innovation readiness in
Taiwan's hospitals. *Innovation*, *16*(1), 158–169. https://doi.org/10.5172/impp
.2014.16.1.158

Chenhall, R. H. (2003). Management control systems design within its organizational context: Findings from contingency-based research and directions for the future. *Accounting, Organizations and Society, 28*(2–3), 127–168.

Chenhall, R. H., & Langfield-Smith, K. (2003). Performance measurement and reward systems, trust, and strategic change. *Journal of Management Accounting Research, 15*(1), 117–143.

Chenhall, R. H., & Morris, D. (1986). The impact of structure, environment, and interdependence on the perceived usefulness of management accounting systems. *The Accounting Review, 61*(1), 16–35. JSTOR.

Chow, C. W., Shields, M. D., & Wu, A. (1999). The importance of national culture in the design of and preference for management controls for multi-national operations. *Accounting, Organizations and Society, 24*(5), 441–461. https://doi.org/10.1016/S0361-3682(99)00047-1

Christensen, T., Lægreid, P., & Stigen, I. M. (2006). Performance management and public sector reform: The Norwegian hospital reform. *International Public Management Journal, 9*(2), 113–139. https://doi.org/10.1080/10967490600766987

Cockerham, W. C. (2015). Max Weber: Bureaucracy, formal rationality and the modern hospital. In F. Collyer (Ed.), *The Palgrave handbook of social theory in health, illness and medicine* (pp. 124–138). Springer.

Cohen, J. (1988). *Statistical power analysis for the behavioral sciences* (2nd ed.). Lawrence Erlbaum Associates.

Cohen, J. (1992). A power primer. *Psychological Bulletin, 112*(1), 155–159.

Collier, P. M. (2005). Entrepreneurial control and the construction of a relevant accounting. *Management Accounting Research, 16*(3), 321–339. https://doi.org/10.1016/j.mar.2005.06.007

Colquitt, J. A., LePine, J. A., Piccolo, R. F., Zapata, C. P., & Rich, B. L. (2012). Explaining the justice–performance relationship: Trust as exchange deepener or trust as uncertainty reducer? *Journal of Applied Psychology, 97*(1), 1–15. https://doi.org/10.1037/a0025208

Colquitt, J. A., Scott, B. A., & LePine, J. A. (2007). Trust, trustworthiness, and trust propensity: A meta-analytic test of their unique relationships with risk taking and job performance. *Journal of Applied Psychology, 92*(4), 909–927. https://doi.org/10.1037/0021-9010.92.4.909

Coltman, T., Devinney, T. M., Midgley, D. F., & Venaik, S. (2008). Formative versus reflective measurement models: Two applications of formative measurement. *Journal of Business Research, 61*(12), 1250–1262. https://doi.org/10.1016/j.jbusres.2008.01.013

Covaleski, M. A., Dirsmith, M. W., & Michelman, J. E. (1993). An institutional theory perspective on the DRG framework, case-mix accounting systems and health-care organizations. *Accounting, Organizations and Society, 18*(1), 65–80. https://doi.org/10.1016/0361-3682(93)90025-2

Craig, T. K. J., McKillop, M. M., Huang, H. T., George, J., Punwani, E. S., & Rhee, K. B. (2020). U.S. hospital performance methodologies: A scoping review to identify opportunities for crossing the quality chasm. *BMC Health Services Research, 20*(1), 640. https://doi.org/10.1186/s12913-020-05503-z

Cranfield, S., Hendy, J., Reeves, B., Hutchings, A., Collin, S., & Fulop, N. (2015). Investigating healthcare IT innovations: A "conceptual blending" approach. *Journal of Health Organization and Management, 29*(7), 1131–1148. https://doi .org/10.1108/JHOM-08-2015-0121

Creswell, J. W., & Plano Clark, V. L. (2017). *Designing and conducting mixed methods research* (Adobe Digital Edition). Sage publications.

Cucciniello, M., & Nasi, G. (2014). Evaluation of the impacts of innovation in the health care sector: A comparative analysis. *Public Management Review, 16*(1), 90–116. https://doi.org/10.1080/14719037.2013.798026

Cummings, L. L., & Bromiley, P. (1996). The organizational trust inventory (OTI). *Trust in Organizations: Frontiers of Theory and Research, 302*(330), 39–52.

Cutler, D. M., & Zeckhauser, R. J. (2000). The anatomy of health insurance. In *Handbook of health economics* (Vol. 1, pp. 563–643). Elsevier.

Cygańska, M. (2018). *Integracja informacji finansowych i klinicznych na potrzeby zarządzania operacyjnego szpitalem.* Wydawnictwo Uniwersytetu Warmińsko-Mazurskiego.

Czakon, W. (2020). Zastosowanie studiów przypadków w badaniach nauk o zarządzaniu. In W. Czakon (Ed.), *Podstawy metodologii badań w naukach o zarządzaniu* (Wydanie III, pp. 189–210). Wydawnictwo Nieoczywiste.

Czakon, W., & Czernek-Marszałek, K. (2021). Competitor perceptions in tourism coopetition. *Journal of Travel Research, 60*(2), 1–24. https://doi.org/10.1177 /0047287519896011

Czernek, K. (2020). Wprowadzenie do badań jakościowych w naukach o zarządzaniu. In W. Czakon (Ed.), *Podstawy metodologii badań w naukach o zarządzaniu* (Wydanie III, pp. 167–188). Wydawnictwo Nieoczywiste.

Da Silva, M.-Z., Lunardi, M.-A., Serpa-Ganz, A.-C., & Da Silva-Zonatto, V.-C. (2020). Management control levers in hospitals: The influence of accreditation on other management control systems. *Estudios Gerenciales,* 239–247. https://doi .org/10.18046/j.estger.2020.155.3562

Daft, R. L., Murphy, J., & Willmott, H. (2010). *Organization theory and design.* Cengage Learning EMEA.

Damanpour, F., & Evan, W. M. (1984). Organizational innovation and performance: The problem of "organizational lag." *Administrative Science Quarterly, 29*(3), 392. https://doi.org/10.2307/2393031

Damanpour, F., & Schneider, M. (2006). Phases of the adoption of innovation in organizations: Effects of environment, organization and top managers. *British Journal of Management, 17*(3), 215–236. https://doi.org/10.1111/j.1467-8551.2006 .00498.x

Damayanthi, S., & Gooneratne, T. (2017). Institutional logics perspective in management control research. A review of extant literature and directions for future research. *Journal of Accounting and Organizational Change, 13*(4), 520–547.

Das, T. K., & Teng, B.-S. (2001). Trust, control, and risk in strategic alliances: An integrated framework. *Organization Studies, 22*(2), 251–283. https://doi.org/10 .1177/0170840601222004

Davies, H. T. O. (2000). Organisational culture and quality of health care. *Quality in Health Care, 9*(2), 111–119. https://doi.org/10.1136/qhc.9.2.111

Davies, H. T., & Harrison, S. (2003). Trends in doctor-manager relationships. *British Medical Journal, 326*(7390), 646–649.

Davila, A., Foster, G., & Li, M. (2009). Reasons for management control systems adoption: Insights from product development systems choice by early-stage entrepreneurial companies. *Accounting, Organizations and Society, 34*(3), 322–347. https://doi.org/10.1016/j.aos.2008.08.002

Davila, T. (2000). An empirical study on the drivers of management control systems' design in new product development. *Accounting, Organizations and Society, 25*(4–5), 383–409. https://doi.org/10.1016/S0361-3682(99)00034-3

Davis, F. D. (1989). Perceived usefulness, perceived ease of use, and user acceptance of information technology. *MIS Quarterly, 13*(3), 319. https://doi.org/10.2307/249008

Dawes, S. S., Cresswell, A. M., & Pardo, T. A. (2009). From "need to know" to "need to share": Tangled problems, information boundaries, and the building of public sector knowledge networks. *Public Administration Review, 69*(3), 392–402. https://doi.org/10.1111/j.1540-6210.2009.01987_2.x

de Campos, C. M. P., Rodrigues, L. L., & Jorge, S. M. F. (2017). The role of management accounting systems in public hospitals and the construction of budgets: A literature review. In Information Resources Management Association (Ed.), *Public health and welfare: Concepts, methodologies, tools, and applications* (pp. 289–312). IGI Global.

de Harlez, Y., & Malagueño, R. (2016). Examining the joint effects of strategic priorities, use of management control systems, and personal background on hospital performance. *Management Accounting Research, 30*, 2–17.

de Waal, A., & Kourtit, K. (2013). Performance measurement and management in practice: Advantages, disadvantages and reasons for use. *International Journal of Productivity and Performance Management, 62*(5), 446–473.

DeLone, W. H., & McLean, E. R. (1992). Information systems success: The quest for the dependent variable. *Information Systems Research, 3*(1), 60–95. https://doi.org/10.1287/isre.3.1.60

DeLone, W. H., & McLean, E. R. (2016). Information systems success measurement. *Foundations and Trends® in Information Systems, 2*(1), 1–116. https://doi.org/10.1561/2900000005

Demartini, C., & Mella, P. (2014). Beyond feedback control: The interactive use of performance management systems: Implications for process innovation in Italian healthcare organizations. *The International Journal of Health Planning and Management, 29*(1), e1–e30. https://doi.org/10.1002/hpm.2177

Dent, M. (2005). Post-New Public Management in public sector hospitals? The UK, Germany and Italy. *Policy and Politics, 33*(4), 623–636. https://doi.org/10.1332/030557305774329208

Dess, G. G., & Robinson Jr., R. B. (1984). Measuring organizational performance in the absence of objective measures: The case of the privately-held firm and conglomerate business unit. *Strategic Management Journal, 5*(3), 265–273.

Deverell, C. S. (1967). *Management planning and control*. Gee & Company.

Dias, C., & Escoval, A. (2013). Improvement of hospital performance through innovation: Toward the value of hospital care. *The Health Care Manager, 32*(2), 129–140. https://doi.org/10.1097/HCM.0b013e31828ef60a

Dick, R. S., Steen, E. B., & Detmer, D. E. (1997). *The computer-based patient record: An essential technology for health care*. National Academies Press.

Dijkstra, T. K. (2014). PLS' Janus face – Response to Professor Rigdon's 'rethinking partial least squares modeling: In praise of simple methods'. *Long Range Planning, 47*(3), 146–153. https://doi.org/10.1016/j.lrp.2014.02.004

Dijkstra, T. K., & Henseler, J. (2015a). Consistent partial least squares path modeling. *MIS Quarterly, 39*(2), 297–316.

Dijkstra, T. K., & Henseler, J. (2015b). Consistent and asymptotically normal PLS estimators for linear structural equations. *Computational Statistics and Data Analysis, 81*, 10–23. https://doi.org/10.1016/j.csda.2014.07.008

DiMaggio, P., & Powell, W. W. (1983). The iron cage revisited: Collective rationality and institutional isomorphism in organizational fields. *American Sociological Review, 48*(2), 147–160.

Dirks, K. T. (2006). Three fundamental questions regarding trust in leaders. In R. Bachmann & A. Zaheer (Eds.), *Handbook of trust research* (pp. 15–28). Edward Elgar Publishing.

Dirks, K. T., & Ferrin, D. L. (2002). Trust in leadership: Meta-analytic findings and implications for research and practice. *Journal of Applied Psychology, 87*(4), 611–628. https://doi.org/10.1037/0021-9010.87.4.611

Dixon-Woods, M., Yeung, K., & Bosk, C. L. (2011). Why is UK medicine no longer a self-regulating profession? The role of scandals involving "bad apple" doctors. *Social Science and Medicine, 73*(10), 1452–1459.

Djellal, F., & Gallouj, F. (2005). Mapping innovation dynamics in hospitals. *Research Policy, 34*(6), 817–835. https://doi.org/10.1016/j.respol.2005.04.007

Djellal, F., & Gallouj, F. (2007). Innovation in hospitals: A survey of the literature. *The European Journal of Health Economics, 8*(3), 181–193. https://doi.org/10.1007/s10198-006-0016-3

Dodgson, M., Gann, D. M., & Phillips, N. (2013). *The Oxford handbook of innovation management*. OUP.

Doolin, B. (2002). Enterprise discourse, professional identity and the organizational control of hospital clinicians. *Organization Studies, 23*(3), 369–390. https://doi.org/10.1177/0170840602233003

Dornbusch, S. M., & Scott, W. R. (1975). *Evaluation and the exercise of authority*. Jossey-Bass.

Dovey, K. (2009). The role of trust in innovation. *The Learning Organization, 16*(4), 311–325. https://doi.org/10.1108/09696470910960400

du Gay, P., & Pedersen, K. Z. (2020). Discretion and bureaucracy. In T. Evans & P. Hupe (Eds.), *Discretion and the quest for controlled freedom* (pp. 221–236). Springer International Publishing. https://doi.org/10.1007/978-3-030-19566-3_15

DuBose, B. M., & Mayo, A. M. (2020). Resistance to change: A concept analysis. *Nursing Forum*. https://doi.org/10.1111/nuf.12479

Duncan, R. B. (1972). Characteristics of organizational environments and perceived environmental uncertainty. *Administrative Science Quarterly, 17*(3), 313–327. https://doi.org/10.2307/2392145

Durán, A., Dubois, H. F., & Saltman, R. B. (2011). The evolving role of hospitals and recent concepts of public sector governance. In R. B. Saltman, A. Durán, & H. F. Dubois (Eds.), *Governing public hospitals: Reform strategies and the movement towards institutional autonomy* (pp. 15–33). European Observatory on Health Systems and Policies.

Durkheim, E. (1960). *The division of labor in society* (Fourth printing). The Free Press. https://archive.org/stream/in.ernet.dli.2015.233884/2015.233884.The -Division#page/n0/mode/2up

Edwards, J. N., Silow-Carroll, S., & Lashbrook, A. (2011). Achieving efficiency: Lessons from four top-performing hospitals. *Commonwealth Fund, 15*, 1–22.

Eicher, B. (2017). Transaction cost economics and trust in the hospital sector: An empirical examination using the example of Germany. *International Journal of Healthcare Management, 11*(4), 341–350. https://doi.org/10.1080/20479700 .2017.1333295

Eilon, S. (1961). Problems in studying management control. *International Journal of Production Research, 1*(4), 13–20.

Eisenbeiss, M., Cornelißen, M., Backhaus, K., & Hoyer, W. D. (2014). Nonlinear and asymmetric returns on customer satisfaction: Do they vary across situations and consumers? *Journal of the Academy of Marketing Science, 42*(3), 242–263.

Eisenhardt, K. M. (1985). Control: Organizational and economic approaches. *Management Science, 31*(2), 134–149.

Eisenhardt, K. M. (1989a). Agency theory: An assessment and review. *Academy of Management Review, 14*(1), 57–74. https://doi.org/10.5465/AMR.1989.4279003

Eisenhardt, K. M. (1989b). Building theories from case study research. *Academy of Management Review, 14*(4), 532–550. https://doi.org/10.5465/AMR.1989 .4308385

Eisenhardt, K. M., & Graebner, M. E. (2007). Theory building from cases: Opportunities and challenges. *Academy of Management Journal, 50*(1), 25–32. https://doi.org/10.5465/AMJ.2007.24160888

Ekman, I., Swedberg, K., Taft, C., Lindseth, A., Norberg, A., Brink, E., Carlsson, J., Dahlin-Ivanoff, S., Johansson, I.-L., Kjellgren, K., Lidén, E., Öhlén, J., Olsson, L.-E., Rosén, H., Rydmark, M., & Sunnerhagen, K. S. (2011). Person-centered care—Ready for prime time. *European Journal of Cardiovascular Nursing, 10*(4), 248–251. https://doi.org/10.1016/j.ejcnurse.2011.06.008

Eldenburg, L. G., Krishnan, H. A., & Krishnan, R. (2017). Management accounting and control in the hospital industry: A review. *Journal of Governmental & Nonprofit Accounting, 6*(1), 52–91. https://doi.org/10.2308/ogna-51922

Eldenburg, L., & Krishnan, R. (2007). Management accounting and control in health care: An economics perspective. In C. S. Chapman A. G. Hopwood, & M. D. Shields (Eds.), *Handbooks of management accounting research* (Vol. 2, pp. 859–883). Elsevier.

Ellis, S., Almor, T., & Shenkar, O. (2002). Structural contingency revisited: Toward a dynamic system model. *Emergence, 4*(4), 51–85. https://doi.org/10.1207/S15327000EM0404_6

Ellonen, R., Blomqvist, K., & Puumalainen, K. (2008). The role of trust in organisational innovativeness. *European Journal of Innovation Management, 11*(2), 160–181. https://doi.org/10.1108/14601060810869848

Emsley, D., & Kidon, F. (2007). The relationship between trust and control in international joint ventures: Evidence from the airline industry. *Contemporary Accounting Research, 24*(3), 829–858. https://doi.org/10.1506/car.24.3.7

Engelbrecht, A. S., Heine, G., & Mahembe, B. (2017). Integrity, ethical leadership, trust and work engagement. *Leadership and Organization Development Journal, 38*(3), 368–379. https://doi.org/10.1108/LODJ-11-2015-0237

Engin, M., & Gürses, F. (2019). Adoption of hospital information systems in public hospitals in Turkey: An analysis with the unified theory of acceptance and use of technology model. *International Journal of Innovation and Technology Management, 17*(1), 1950043. https://doi.org/10.1142/S0219877019500433

England, I., Stewart, D., & Walker, S. (2000). Information technology adoption in health care: When organisations and technology collide. *Australian Health Review, 23*(3), 176. https://doi.org/10.1071/AH000176

Epstein, M., & Manzoni, J.-F. (1998). Implementing corporate strategy: From Tableaux de Bord to balanced scorecards. *European Management Journal, 16*(2), 190–203. https://doi.org/10.1016/S0263-2373(97)00087-X

Etzioni, A. (1965). Organizational control structure. In J. G. March (Ed.), *Organizational control structure, handbook of organizations* (pp. 650–677). Rand McNally. http://www.gwu.edu/~ccps/etzioni/A38.pdf

Evermann, J., & Tate, M. (2016). Assessing the predictive performance of structural equation model estimators. *Journal of Business Research, 69*(10), 4565–4582.

Expert Panel On Effective Ways Of Investing In Health. (2015). *Report on investigating policy options regarding competition among providers of health care services in EU member states.* European Commission.

Ezzamel, M., & Bourn, M. (1990). The roles of accounting information systems in an organization experiencing financial crisis. *Accounting, Organizations and Society, 15*(5), 399–424. https://doi.org/10.1016/0361-3682(90)90025-P

Ezzamel, M., Robson, K., & Stapleton, P. (2012). The logics of budgeting: Theorization and practice variation in the educational field. *Accounting, Organizations and Society, 37*(5), 281–303.

Fayard, D., Lee, L. S., Leitch, R. A., & Kettinger, W. J. (2012). Effect of internal cost management, information systems integration, and absorptive capacity on inter-organizational cost management in supply chains. *Accounting, Organizations and Society, 37*(3), 168–187.

Feltham, G. A., & Xie, J. (1994). Performance measure congruity and diversity in multi-task principal/agent relations. *The Accounting Review, 69*(3), 429–453. JSTOR.

Fereday, J., & Muir-Cochrane, E. (2006). Demonstrating rigor using thematic analysis: A hybrid approach of inductive and deductive coding and theme development. *International Journal of Qualitative Methods*, *5*(1), 80–92. https://doi.org/10.1177/160940690600500107

Ferreira, A., & Otley, D. (2009). The design and use of performance management systems: An extended framework for analysis. *Management Accounting Research*, *20*(4), 263–282.

Firth-Cozens, J., & Mowbray, D. (2001). Leadership and the quality of care. *BMJ Quality and Safety*, *10*(Suppl. 2), ii3–ii7.

Fitzgerald, L., Ferlie, E., Wood, M., & Hawkins, C. (2002). Interlocking interactions, the diffusion of innovations in health care. *Human Relations*, *55*(12), 1429–1449.

Flamholtz, E. (1996). Effective organizational control: A framework, applications, and implications. *European Management Journal*, *14*(6), 596–611.

Flamholtz, E. G. (1979). Toward a psycho-technical systems paradigm of organizational measurement. *Decision Sciences*, *10*(1), 71–84.

Flamholtz, E. G., Das, T. K., & Tsui, A. S. (1985). Toward an integrative framework of organizational control. *Accounting, Organizations and Society*, *10*(1), 35–50.

Fleig-Palmer, M. M., Rathert, C., & Porter, T. H. (2018). Building trust: The influence of mentoring behaviors on perceptions of health care managers' trustworthiness. *Health Care Management Review*, *43*(1), 69–78. https://doi.org/10.1097/HMR.0000000000000130

Flodgren, G., Eccles, M. P., Shepperd, S., Scott, A., Parmelli, E., & Beyer, F. R. (2011). An overview of reviews evaluating the effectiveness of financial incentives in changing healthcare professional behaviours and patient outcomes. *Cochrane Database of Systematic Reviews*, *7*, 1–90.

Floropoulos, J., Spathis, C., Halvatzis, D., & Tsipouridou, M. (2010). Measuring the success of the Greek Taxation Information System. *International Journal of Information Management*, *30*(1), 47–56. https://doi.org/10.1016/j.ijinfomgt.2009.03.013

Fonarow, G. C., Konstam, M. A., & Yancy, C. W. (2017). *The hospital readmission reduction program is associated with fewer readmissions, more deaths: Time to reconsider.* American College of Cardiology Foundation.

Chun Cheong Fong, S., & Quaddus, M. (2010). Intranet use in Hong Kong public hospitals. *International Journal of Accounting and Information Management*, *18*(2), 156–181. https://doi.org/10.1108/18347641011048138

Fornell, C., & Larcker, D. F. (1981). Evaluating structural equation models with unobservable variables and measurement error. *Journal of Marketing Research*, *18*(1), 39–50.

Franco-Santos, M., Lucianetti, L., & Bourne, M. (2012). Contemporary performance measurement systems: A review of their consequences and a framework for research. *Management Accounting Research*, *23*(2), 79–119. https://doi.org/10.1016/j.mar.2012.04.001

Franke, G., & Sarstedt, M. (2019). Heuristics versus statistics in discriminant validity testing: A comparison of four procedures. *Internet Research*, *29*(3), 430–447. https://doi.org/10.1108/IntR-12-2017-0515

Freidson, E. (2001). *Professionalism, the third logic: On the practice of knowledge.* University of Chicago press.

Friedland, R., & Alford, R. R. (1991). Bringing society back in: Symbols, practices and institutional contradictions. In W. W. Powell & P. J. Dimaggio (Eds.), *The new institutionalism in organizational analysis* (pp. 232–263). University of Chicago Press. http://www.citeulike.org/group/3317/article/262887

Friedman, L., Goes, J., Coddington, D. C., & Linenkugel, N. (2001). Why integrated health networks have failed/commentaries/Reply. *Frontiers of Health Services Management, 17*(4), 3.

Fuglsang, L. (2010). Bricolage and invisible innovation in public service innovation. *Journal of Innovation Economics, 5*(1), 67. https://doi.org/10.3917/jie.005.0067

Fukuyama, F. (1997). *Zaufanie: Kapitał społeczny a droga do dobrobytu.* PWN.

Galbraith, J. R. (1977). *Organization design.* Addison Wesley Publishing Company.

Gallouj, F., & Weinstein, O. (1997). Innovation in services. *Research Policy, 26*(4–5), 537–556. https://doi.org/10.1016/S0048-7333(97)00030-9

Garavand, A., Mohseni, M., Asadi, H., Etemadi, M., Moradi-Joo, M., & Moosavi, A. (2016). Factors influencing the adoption of health information technologies: A systematic review. *Electronic Physician, 8*(8), 2713–2718. https://doi.org/10.19082/2713

Garelick, A., & Fagin, L. (2005). The doctor-manager relationship. *Advances in Psychiatric Treatment, 11*(4), 241–250.

Geisser, S. (1974). A predictive approach to the random effect model. *Biometrika, 61*(1), 101–107. https://doi.org/10.1093/biomet/61.1.101

Getzen, T. E. (2022). *Health economics and financing* (6th ed.). John Wiley & Sons Inc.

Ghasemi, R., Habibi, H. R., Ghasemlo, M., & Karami, M. (2019). The effectiveness of management accounting systems: Evidence from financial organizations in Iran. *Journal of Accounting in Emerging Economies, 9*(2), 182–207. https://doi.org/10.1108/JAEE-02-2017-0013

Giddens, A. (1984). *The constitution of society: Outline of the theory of structuration.* University of California Press.

Giddens, A. (2013). *The consequences of modernity* (Wydane elektroniczne. Pierwsza publikacja 1990 r.). John Wiley & Sons.

Gille, F., Smith, S., & Mays, N. (2020). What is public trust in the healthcare system? A new conceptual framework developed from qualitative data in England. *Social Theory and Health, 19*(1), 1–20. https://doi.org/10.1057/s41285-020-00129-x

Glaser, B. G., & Strauss, A. L. (2009). *Odkrywanie teorii ugruntowanej. Strategia badania jakościowego.* Zakład wydawniczy "NOMOS".

Glasziou, P. P., Buchan, H., Del Mar, C., Doust, J., Harris, M., Knight, R., Scott, A., Scott, I. A., & Stockwell, A. (2012). When financial incentives do more good than harm: A checklist. *BMJ, 345,* (e5047), 1–5. https://doi.org/10.1136/bmj.e5047

Glinka, B., & Czakon, W. (2021). *Podstawy badań jakościowych.* Polskie Wydawnictwo Ekonomiczne.

Goes, J. B., & Park, S. H. (1997). Interorganizational links and innovation: The case of hospital services. *Academy of Management Journal, 40*(3), 673–696. https://doi.org/10.5465/257058

Goes, J. B., & Zhan, C. (1995). The effects of hospital-physician integration strategies on hospital financial performance. *Health Services Research, 30*(4), 507–530.

Gong, M. Z., & Ferreira, A. (2014). Does consistency in management control systems design choices influence firm performance? An empirical analysis. *Accounting and Business Research, 44*(5), 497–522. https://doi.org/10.1080/00014788.2014.901164

Goodhue, D. L. (1998). Development and measurement validity of a task-technology fit instrument for user evaluations of information system. *Decision Sciences, 29*(1), 105–138. https://doi.org/10.1111/j.1540-5915.1998.tb01346.x

Goodhue, D. L., Lewis, W., & Thompson, R. (2012). Does PLS have advantages for small sample size or non-normal data? *MIS Quarterly, 36*(3), 981. https://doi.org/10.2307/41703490

Goodhue, D. L., Lewis, W., & Thompson, R. (2017). A multicollinearity and measurement error statistical blind spot: Correcting for excessive false positives in regression and PLS. *MIS Quarterly, 41*(3), 667–684. https://doi.org/10.25300/MISQ/2017/41.3.01

Gordon, G., Gilley, A., Avery, S., Gilley, J. W., & Barber, A. (2014). Employee perceptions of the manager behaviors that create follower-leader trust. *Management and Organizational Studies, 1*(2), 44. https://doi.org/10.5430/mos.v1n2p44

Govindarajan, V., & Fisher, J. (1990). Strategy, control systems, and resource sharing: Effects on business-unit performance. *Academy of Management Journal, 33*(2), 259–285.

Govindarajan, V., & Gupta, A. K. (1985). Linking control systems to business unit strategy: Impact on performance. In C. Emmanuel, D. Otley, & K. Merchant (Eds.), *Readings in accounting for management control* (pp. 646–668). Springer. https://doi.org/10.1007/978-1-4899-7138-8_29

Graham, J. L., Shahani, L., Grimes, R. M., Hartman, C., & Giordano, T. P. (2015). The influence of trust in physicians and trust in the healthcare system on linkage, retention, and adherence to HIV care. *AIDS Patient Care and STDs, 29*(12), 661–667.

Greenberg, R., & Nunamaker, T. (1987). A generalized multiple criteria model for control and evaluation of nonprofit organizations. *Financial Accountability and Management, 3*(3–4), 331–342.

Greenwood, J. R., Pyper, R., & Wilson, D. J. (2002). *New public administration in Britain*. Psychology Press.

Greenwood, R., & Hinings, C. R. (1996). Understanding radical organizational change: Bringing together the old and the new institutionalism. *Academy of Management Review, 21*(4), 1022–1054.

Greenwood, R., Raynard, M., Kodeih, F., Micelotta, E. R., & Lounsbury, M. (2011). Institutional complexity and organizational responses. *Academy of Management Annals, 5*(1), 317–371.

Gregor, S. (2006). The nature of theory in information systems. *MIS Quarterly, 30*(3), 611–642.

Grigoroudis, E., Orfanoudaki, E., & Zopounidis, C. (2012). Strategic performance measurement in a healthcare organisation: A multiple criteria approach based on balanced scorecard. *Omega, 40*(1), 104–119. https://doi.org/10.1016/j.omega.2011.04.001

Groene, O., Arah, O. A., Klazinga, N. S., Wagner, C., Bartels, P. D., Kristensen, S., Saillour, F., Thompson, A., Thompson, C. A., & Pfaff, H. (2015). Patient experience shows little relationship with hospital quality management strategies. *PLOS One, 10*(7), e0131805.

Groenewegen, P. P., Hansen, J., & de Jong, J. D. (2019). Trust in times of health reform. *Health Policy, 123*(3), 281–287. https://doi.org/10.1016/j.healthpol.2018.11.016

Grol, R., & Wensing, M. (2020). Effective implementation of change in healthcare: A systematic approach. In M. Wensing, R. Grol, & J. Grimshaw (Eds.), *Improving patient care* (1st ed., pp. 45–71). Wiley. https://doi.org/10.1002/9781119488620.ch3

Gu, D., Deng, S., Zheng, Q., Liang, C., & Wu, J. (2019). Impacts of case-based health knowledge system in hospital management: The mediating role of group effectiveness. *Information and Management, 56*(8), 103162.

Gudergan, S. P., Ringle, C. M., Wende, S., & Will, A. (2008). Confirmatory tetrad analysis in PLS path modeling. *Journal of Business Research, 61*(12), 1238–1249. https://doi.org/10.1016/j.jbusres.2008.01.012

Gulati, R. (1995). Does familiarity breed trust? The implications of repeated ties for contractual choice in alliances. *Academy of Management Journal, 38*(1), 85–112. https://doi.org/10.5465/256729

Gupta, A. K., & Govindarajan, V. (1984). Business unit strategy, managerial characteristics, and business unit effectiveness at strategy implementation. *Academy of Management Journal, 27*(1), 25–41. https://doi.org/10.5465/255955

Hair Jr., J. F. (2020). Next-generation prediction metrics for composite-based PLS-SEM. *Industrial Management and Data Systems, 121*(1), 5–11. https://doi.org/10.1108/IMDS-08-2020-0505

Hair Jr., J. F., Sarstedt, M., Ringle, C. M., & Gudergan, S. P. (2018). *Advanced issues in partial least squares structural equation modeling* [epub]. SAGE Publications.

Hair, J. F., Hult, G. T. M., Ringle, C., & Sarstedt, M. (2016). *A primer on partial least squares structural equation modeling (PLS-SEM)*. SAGE Publications.

Hair, J. F., Ringle, C. M., & Sarstedt, M. (2011). PLS-SEM: Indeed a silver bullet. *Journal of Marketing Theory and Practice, 19*(2), 139–152. https://doi.org/10.2753/MTP1069-6679190202

Hair, J. F., Risher, J. J., Sarstedt, M., & Ringle, C. M. (2019). When to use and how to report the results of PLS-SEM. *European Business Review, 31*(1), 2–24. https://doi.org/10.1108/EBR-11-2018-0203

Hair, J. F., Sarstedt, M., Pieper, T. M., & Ringle, C. M. (2012). The use of partial least squares structural equation modeling in strategic management research:

A review of past practices and recommendations for future applications. *Long Range Planning, 45*(5–6), 320–340. https://doi.org/10.1016/j.lrp.2012.09 .008

Hair, J. F., Sarstedt, M., & Ringle, C. M. (2019). Rethinking some of the rethinking of partial least squares. *European Journal of Marketing, 53*(4), 566–584. https:// doi.org/10.1108/EJM-10-2018-0665

Hair, J. F., Sarstedt, M., Ringle, C. M., & Mena, J. A. (2012). An assessment of the use of partial least squares structural equation modeling in marketing research. *Journal of the Academy of Marketing Science, 40*(3), 414–433. https:// doi.org/10.1007/s11747-011-0261-6

Halachmi, A. (2002). Performance measurement and government productivity. *Work Study, 51*(2), 63–73.

Hall, M. (2008). The effect of comprehensive performance measurement systems on role clarity, psychological empowerment and managerial performance. *Accounting, Organizations and Society, 33*(2–3), 141–163.

Hall, M. A., Dugan, E., Zheng, B., & Mishra, A. K. (2001). Trust in physicians and medical institutions: What is it, can it be measured, and does it matter? *Milbank Quarterly, 79*(4), 613–639.

Hameiri, L., & Nir, A. (2016). Perceived uncertainty and organizational health in public schools: The mediating effect of school principals' transformational leadership style. *International Journal of Educational Management, 30*(6), 771–790. https://doi.org/10.1108/IJEM-05-2014-0060

Hammad, S. A., Jusoh, R., & Yen Nee Oon, E. (2010). Management accounting system for hospitals: A research framework. *Industrial Management and Data Systems, 110*(5), 762–784. https://doi.org/10.1108/02635571011044777

Hammad, S. A., Ruzita, J., & Ghozali, I. (2013). Decentralization, perceived environmental uncertainty, managerial performance and management accounting system information in Egyptian hospitals. *International Journal of Accounting and Information Management, 21*(4), 314–330.

Hass-Symotiuk, M. (2011a). *Koncepcja sprawozdawczości szpitali na potrzeby zintegrowanego systemu oceny dokonań* . Wydawnictwo Naukowe Uniwersytetu szczecińskiego.

Hass-Symotiuk, M. (2011b). *System pomiaru i oceny dokonań szpitala.* Wolters Kluwer.

Hatch, M. J. (2002). *Teoria organizacji.* PWN. http://www.empik.com/teoria-organizacji-hatch-mary-jo,280020,ksiazka-p

Haustein, E., Luther, R., & Schuster, P. (2014). Management control systems in innovation companies: A literature based framework. *Journal of Management Control, 24*(4), 343–382. https://doi.org/10.1007/s00187-014-0187-5

Haux, R. (2006). Health information systems–past, present, future. *International Journal of Medical Informatics, 75*(3–4), 268–281.

Håvold, J. I., & Håvold, O. K. (2019). Power, trust and motivation in hospitals. *Leadership in Health Services, 32*(2), 195–211. https://doi.org/10.1108/LHS-03 -2018-0023

Heinicke, A., Guenther, T. W., & Widener, S. K. (2016). An examination of the relationship between the extent of a flexible culture and the levers of control system: The key role of beliefs control. *Management Accounting Research*, *33*, 25–41.

Henri, J.-F. (2006). Management control systems and strategy: A resource-based perspective. *Accounting, Organizations and Society*, *31*(6), 529–558. https://doi.org/10.1016/j.aos.2005.07.001

Hensel, P. (2008). *Transfer wzorców zarządzania: Studium organizacji sektora publicznego*. Dom Wydawniczy Elipsa.

Henseler, J. (2017). Bridging design and behavioral research with variance-based structural equation modeling. *Journal of Advertising*, *46*(1), 178–192.

Henseler, J., Dijkstra, T. K., Sarstedt, M., Ringle, C. M., Diamantopoulos, A., Straub, D. W., Ketchen, D. J., Hair, J. F., Hult, G. T. M., & Calantone, R. J. (2014). Common beliefs and reality about PLS: Comments on Rönkkö and Evermann (2013). *Organizational Research Methods*, *17*(2), 182–209. https://doi.org/10.1177/1094428114526928

Henseler, J., Hubona, G., & Ray, P. A. (2016). Using PLS path modeling in new technology research: Updated guidelines. *Industrial Management and Data Systems*, *116*(1), 2–20. https://doi.org/10.1108/IMDS-09-2015-0382

Henseler, J., Ringle, C. M., & Sarstedt, M. (2015). A new criterion for assessing discriminant validity in variance-based structural equation modeling. *Journal of the Academy of Marketing Science*, *43*(1), 115–135.

Henseler, J., Ringle, C. M., & Sarstedt, M. (2016). Testing measurement invariance of composites using partial least squares. *International Marketing Review*, *33*(3), 405–431. https://doi.org/10.1108/IMR-09-2014-0304

Herman, R. D., & Renz, D. O. (1999). Theses on nonprofit organizational effectiveness. *Nonprofit and Voluntary Sector Quarterly*, *28*(2), 107–126. https://doi.org/10.1177/0899764099282001

Hernandez, S. E., Conrad, D. A., Marcus-Smith, M. S., Reed, P., & Watts, C. (2013). Patient-centered innovation in health care organizations: A conceptual framework and case study application. *Health Care Management Review*, *38*(2), 166–175. https://doi.org/10.1097/HMR.0b013e31825e718a

Herting, S. R. (2002). A curvilinear model of trust and innovation with implications for China's transition. *Chinese Public Administration Review*, *1*(3/4), Article 3/4. https://doi.org/10.22140/cpar.v1i3/4.34

Hodges, R., Wright, M., & Keasey, K. (1996). Corporate governance in the public services: Concepts and issues. *Public Money and Management*, *16*(2), 7–13.

Hoffer Gittell, J. (2002). Coordinating mechanisms in care provider groups: Relational coordination as a mediator and input uncertainty as a moderator of performance effects. *Management Science*, *48*(11), 1408–1426.

Hood, C. (1991). A public management for all seasons? *Public Administration*, *69*(1), 3–19. https://doi.org/10.1111/j.1467-9299.1991.tb00779.x

Hood, C. (1995). The "new public management" in the 1980s: Variations on a theme. *Accounting, Organizations and Society*, *20*(2–3), 93–109. https://doi.org/10.1016/0361-3682(93)E0001-W

Hood, C., James, O., Scott, C., Jones, G. W., & Travers, T. (1999). *Regulation inside government: Waste watchers, quality police, and sleaze-busters*. Oxford University Press.

Hopwood, A. G. (1972). An empirical study of the role of accounting data in performance evaluation. *Journal of Accounting Research*, *10*, 156–182.

Hovland, C. I., Janis, I. L., & Kelley, H. H. (1953). *Communication and persuasion*. Yale University Press.

Howell, R. D. (2013). Conceptual clarity in measurement—Constructs, composites, and causes: A commentary on Lee, Cadogan and Chamberlain. *AMS Review*, *3*(1), 18–23.

Hsia, D. C., Krushat, W. M., Fagan, A. B., Tebbutt, J. A., & Kusserow, R. P. (1988). Accuracy of diagnostic coding for Medicare patients under the prospective-payment system. *New England Journal of Medicine*, *318*(6), 352–355.

Hupe, P., & Hill, M. (2016). *Understanding street-level bureaucracy*. Policy Press.

Idemobi, E., Ngige, C. D., & Ofili, P. N. (2017). Relationship between organization reward system and workers attitude to work. *Journal of Business and Economic Development*, *2*(4), 247–254.

Institute of Medicine. (2021). *Six domains of health care quality*. http://www.ahrq .gov/talkingquality/measures/six-domains.html

Isaac, T., Zaslavsky, A. M., Cleary, P. D., & Landon, B. E. (2010). The relationship between patients' perception of care and measures of hospital quality and safety. *Health Services Research*, *45*(4), 1024–1040.

Ittner, C. D., Larcker, D. F., & Randall, T. (2003). Performance implications of strategic performance measurement in financial services firms. *Accounting, Organizations and Society*, *28*(7), 715–741.

Ives, B., Olson, M. H., & Baroudi, J. J. (1983). The measurement of user information satisfaction. *Communications of the ACM*, *26*(10), 785–793. https://doi.org/10 .1145/358413.358430

Jackson, D. L. (2003). Revisiting sample size and number of parameter estimates: Some support for the N: q hypothesis. *Structural Equation Modeling*, *10*(1), 128–141.

Janke, R., Mahlendorf, M. D., & Weber, J. (2014). An exploratory study of the reciprocal relationship between interactive use of management control systems and perception of negative external crisis effects. *Management Accounting Research*, *25*(4), 251–270.

Järvinen, J. T. (2016). Role of management accounting in applying new institutional logics. *Accounting, Auditing and Accountability Journal*, *29*(5), 861–886.

Jarvis, C. B., MacKenzie, S. B., & Podsakoff, P. M. (2003). A critical review of construct indicators and measurement model misspecification in marketing and consumer research. *Journal of Consumer Research*, *30*(2), 199–218. https://doi .org/10.1086/376806

Jaworzyńska, M. (2015). Zastosowanie Strategicznej Karty Wyników w szpitalu–studium przypadku. *Annales Universitatis Mariae Curie-Skłodowska, Sectio H Oeconomia*, *49*(4), 177–184.

Jenkins Jr., G. D., Mitra, A., Gupta, N., & Shaw, J. D. (1998). Are financial incentives related to performance? A meta-analytic review of empirical research. *Journal of Applied Psychology*, *83*(5), 777–787.

Jha, A. K., Orav, E. J., Li, Z., & Epstein, A. M. (2007). The inverse relationship between mortality rates and performance in the Hospital Quality Alliance measures. *Health Affairs*, *26*(4), 1104–1110.

Jiang, H. J., Lockee, C., & Fraser, I. (2012). Enhancing board oversight on quality of hospital care: An agency theory perspective. *Health Care Management Review*, *37*(2), 144–153. https://doi.org/10.1097/HMR.0b013e3182224237

Jin, Z., Hewitt-Dundas, N., & Thompson, N. J. (2004). Innovativeness and performance: Evidence from manufacturing sectors. *Journal of Strategic Marketing*, *12*(4), 255–266.

Johansen, S. T., Olsen, T. H., Solstad, E., & Torsteinsen, H. (2015). An insider view of the hybrid organisation: How managers respond to challenges of efficiency, legitimacy and meaning. *Journal of Management and Organization*, *21*(6), 725–740.

Johansson, T. (2018). Testing for control system interdependence with structural equation modeling: Conceptual developments and evidence on the levers of control framework. *Journal of Accounting Literature*, *41*, 47–62. https://doi.org/10.1016/j.acclit.2018.02.002

Johnson, R. B., & Onwuegbuzie, A. J. (2004). Mixed methods research: A research paradigm whose time has come. *Educational Researcher*, *33*(7), 14–26. https://doi.org/10.3102/0013189X033007014

Jones, R., & Pendlebury, M. (2000). *Public sector accounting*. Pearson Education.

Jöreskog, K. G. (1970). A general method for estimating a linear structural equation system. *ETS Research Bulletin Series*, *1970*(2), i–41. https://doi.org/10.1002/j.2333-8504.1970.tb00783.x

Kahn III, C. N., Ault, T., Potetz, L., Walke, T., Chambers, J. H., & Burch, S. (2015). Assessing Medicare's hospital pay-for-performance programs and whether they are achieving their goals. *Health Affairs*, *34*(8), 1281–1288.

Kamaruddeen, A. M., Yusof, N. A., & Said, I. (2010). *Innovation and Innovativeness: Difference and Antecedent Relationship*, *1*, 13.

Kanthi Herath, S. (2007). A framework for management control research. *Journal of Management Development*, *26*(9), 895–915. https://doi.org/10.1108/02621710710819366

Kaplan, R. S., & Norton, D. P. (1992). The balanced scorecard-measures that drive performance. *Harvard Business Review*, January–February, 71–79.

Kaplan, R. S., & Norton, D. P. (1996). *The balanced scorecard: Translating strategy into action*. Harvard Business Press.

Kaplan, R. S., & Porter, M. E. (2011). How to solve the cost crisis in health care. *Harvard Business Review*, *89*(9), 46–52.

Kaplan, R., & Norton, D. (2004). *Strategy maps. Converting intangible assets into tangible outcomes*. Harvard Business School Press.

Kastberg, G., & Siverbo, S. (2013). The design and use of management accounting systems in process oriented health care—An explorative study. *Financial*

Accountability and Management, *29*(3), 246–270. https://doi.org/10.1111/faam .12014

Kenny, D. A. (2018). *Categorical moderator and continuous causal variable*. http:// davidakenny.net/cm/moderation.htm

Kerpershoek, E., Groenleer, M., & de Bruijn, H. (2014). Unintended responses to performance management in Dutch hospital care: Bringing together the managerial and professional perspectives. *Public Management Review*, *18*(3), 417–436. https://doi.org/10.1080/14719037.2014.985248

Khandwalla, P. N. (1972). The effect of different types of competition on the use of management controls. *Journal of Accounting Research*, *10*(2), 275. https://doi .org/10.2307/2490009

Khandwalla, P. N. (1977). *The design of organizations* (713th ed.). Harcourt Brace Jovanovich. http://books.google.com/books?id=dwO3AAAAIAAJ

Khoo-Lattimore, C., Mura, P., & Yung, R. (2017). The time has come: A systematic literature review of mixed methods research in tourism. *Current Issues in Tourism*, 1531–1550. https://doi.org/10.1080/13683500.2017.1406900

Kim, T., Johansen, M., & Zhu, L. (2019). The effects of managers' purposeful performance information use on American Hospital performance. *Public Performance and Management Review*, *43*(1), 129–156. https://doi.org/10.1080 /15309576.2019.1638275

Kim, T.-Y., Wang, J., & Chen, J. (2016). Mutual trust between leader and subordinate and employee outcomes. *Journal of Business Ethics*, *149*(4), 945–958. https:// doi.org/10.1007/s10551-016-3093-y

Kimberly, J. R., & Evanisko, M. J. (1981). Organizational innovation: The influence of individual, organizational, and contextual factors on hospital adoption of technological and administrative innovations. *Academy of Management Journal*, *24*(4), 689–713.

Klag, M., & Langley, A. (2013). Approaching the conceptual leap in qualitative research. *International Journal of Management Reviews*, *15*(2), 149–166. https:// doi.org/10.1111/j.1468-2370.2012.00349.x

Klopper-Kes, A. H. J. (2011). *Mind the gap: Assessing cooperation between physicians and managers and its association with hospital performance* [PhD, University of Twente]. https://ris.utwente.nl/ws/portalfiles/portal/6067781

Kludacz-Alessandri, M., Baran, W., Cygańska, M., Macuda, M., & Raulinajtys-Grzybek, M. (2019). Stopień rozwoju rachunku kosztów w kontekście systemu informacyjnego szpitala. *Zeszyty Teoretyczne Rachunkowości*, *103*(159), 63–79.

Knezevic, B., Lewandowski, R., Goncharuk, A., & Vajagic, M. (2022). Studying the impact of human resources on the efficiency of healthcare systems and person-centred care. In D. Kriksciuniene & V. Sakalauskas (Eds.), *Intelligent systems for sustainable person-centered healthcare* (Vol. 205, pp. 145–164). Springer International Publishing. https://doi.org/10.1007/978-3-030-79353-1_8

Kobrin, S. J. (1991). An empirical analysis of the determinants of global integration. *Strategic Management Journal*, *12*(S1), 17–31. https://doi.org/10.1002/smj .4250120904

Kohli, R., & Kettinger, W. J. (2004). Informating the clan: Controlling physicians' costs and outcomes. *Mis Quarterly*, 363–394.

Kożuch, A., & Kożuch, B. (2008). Istota usług publicznych. *Współczesne Zarządzanie, nr 1*, 19–35.

Kristensen, T., Bogetoft, P., & Pedersen, K. M. (2010). Potential gains from hospital mergers in Denmark. *Health Care Management Science, 13*(4), 334–345.

Kroch, E. A., Duan, M., Silow-Carroll, S., & Meyer, J. A. (2007). *Hospital performance improvement: Trends in quality and efficiency* (pp. 1–46). Carescience Inc.

Kruis, A.-M. (2008). *Management control system design and effectiveness* [Nyenrode Business Universiteit]. https://papers.ssrn.com/sol3/papers.cfm?abstract_id=1441243

Kruis, A.-M., Speklé, R. F., & Widener, S. K. (2016). The levers of control framework: An exploratory analysis of balance. *Management Accounting Research, 32*, 27–44. https://doi.org/10.1016/j.mar.2015.12.002

Krumholz, H. M., Lin, Z., Keenan, P. S., Chen, J., Ross, J. S., Drye, E. E., Bernheim, S. M., Wang, Y., Bradley, E. H., & Han, L. F. (2013). Relationship between hospital readmission and mortality rates for patients hospitalized with acute myocardial infarction, heart failure, or pneumonia. *JAMA, 309*(6), 587–593.

Kuhlmann, E., & Burau, V. (2008). The 'healthcare state'in transition: National and international contexts of changing professional governance. *European Societies, 10*(4), 619–633.

Kuhlmann, E., Burau, V., Correia, T., Lewandowski, R., Lionis, C., Noordegraaf, M., & Repullo, J. (2013). "A manager in the minds of doctors:" A comparison of new modes of control in European hospitals. *BMC Health Services Research, 13*(1), 1. https://doi.org/10.1186/1472-6963-13-246

Kuhlmann, E., Burau, V., Larsen, C., Lewandowski, R., Lionis, C., & Repullo, J. (2011). Medicine and management in European healthcare systems: How do they matter in the control of clinical practice? *International Journal of Clinical Practice, 65*(7), 722. https://doi.org/10.1111/j.1742-1241.2011.02665.x

Lachmann, M., Knauer, T., & Trapp, R. (2013). Strategic management accounting practices in hospitals: Empirical evidence on their dissemination under competitive market environments. *Journal of Accounting and Organizational Change, 9*(3), 336–369. https://doi.org/10.1108/JAOC-12-2011-0065

Laffel, G., & Blumenthal, D. (1989). The case for using industrial quality management science in health care organizations. *JAMA, 262*(20), 2869–2873.

Laitinen, E. K. (2009). Importance of performance information in managerial work. *Industrial Management and Data Systems, 109*(4), 550–569. https://doi.org/10.1108/02635570910948669

Lambert, H., Gordon, E. J., & Bogdan-Lovis, E. A. (2006). Introduction: Gift horse or Trojan horse? Social science perspectives on evidence-based health care. *Social Science and Medicine, 62*(11), 2613–2620.

Lange, P. A. M. V., Rockenbach, B., & Yamagishi, T. (2014). *Reward and punishment in social dilemmas*. Oxford University Press.

Langfield-Smith, K. (1997). Management control systems and strategy: A critical review. *Accounting, Organizations and Society, 22*(2), 207–232.

Langfield-Smith, K. (2007). A review of quantitative research in management control systems and strategy. In C. S. Chapman, A. G. Hopwood, & M. D. Shields (Eds.), *Handbook of management accounting research* (pp. 753–783). Elsevier.

Larson, G. S., & Tompkins, P. K. (2005). Ambivalence and resistance: A study of management in a concertive control system. *Communication Monographs, 72*(1), 1–21. https://doi.org/10.1080/0363775052000342508

Larson, M. S., & Larson, M. S. (1977). *The rise of professionalism: A sociological analysis* (Vol. 233). University of California Press.

Lebas, M., & Weigenstein, J. (1986). Management control: The roles of rules, markets and culture. *Journal of Management Studies, 23*(3), 259–272.

Lee, N., & Cadogan, J. W. (2013). Problems with formative and higher-order reflective variables. *Journal of Business Research, 66*(2), 242–247.

Lee, N., Cadogan, J. W., & Chamberlain, L. (2014). Material and efficient cause interpretations of the formative model: Resolving misunderstandings and clarifying conceptual language. *AMS Review, 4*(1–2), 32–43.

Lega, F., & DePietro, C. (2005). Converging patterns in hospital organization: Beyond the professional bureaucracy. *Health Policy, 74*(3), 261–281. https://doi.org/10.1016/j.healthpol.2005.01.010

Leidner, D. E., Preston, D., & Chen, D. (2010). An examination of the antecedents and consequences of organizational IT innovation in hospitals. *The Journal of Strategic Information Systems, 19*(3), 154–170. https://doi.org/10.1016/j.jsis.2010.07.002

Lenik, P. (2017). *Zarządzanie ewolucyjnymi zmianami w szpitalach publicznych: Teoria i praktyka*. Wolters Kluwer.

Leotta, A., & Ruggeri, D. (2012). Changes in performance measurement and evaluation systems as institutional processes: The case of an Italian teaching hospital. In A. Davila, M. J. Epstein, & J.-F. Manzoni (Eds.), *Performance measurement and management control: Global issues* (Vol. 25, pp. 427–463). Emerald Group Publishing Limited. https://doi.org/10.1108/S1479-3512(2012)0000025019

Les MacLeod, M. P. H. (2012). The physician Leader's role in bridging the culture gap. *Physician Executive, 38*(6), 12–15.

Leung, P. W., & Trotman, K. T. (2005). The effects of feedback type on auditor judgment performance for configural and non-configural tasks. *Accounting, Organizations and Society, 30*(6), 537–553.

Levi-Strauss, C. (1966). *The savage mind*. University of Chicago Press.

Levy, A., DeLeon, I. G., Martinez, C. K., Fernandez, N., Gage, N. A., Sigurdsson, S. Ó., & Frank-Crawford, M. A. (2017). A quantitative review of overjustification effects in persons with intellectual and developmental disabilities: Overjustification and intellectual disabilities. *Journal of Applied Behavior Analysis, 50*(2), 206–221. https://doi.org/10.1002/jaba.359

Lewandowski, R. (2011). Will Russia cope with healthcare reform? *International Journal of Clinical Practice, 65*(4), 391–393. https://doi.org/10.1111/j.1742-1241.2010.02627.x

Lewandowski, R. (2013). Perspective of control in the light of professional and managerial role within health care organisations. *Przedsiębiorczoś ć i Zarządzanie, 14*(10, cz. 1), 215–227.

Lewandowski, R. (2014). Cost control of medical care in public hospitals – A comparative analysis. *International Journal of Contemporary Management, 13*(1), 125–136.

Lewandowski, R. (2017). Ideological control in public and business organizations. *Nowoczesne Systemy Zarządzania, 12*(2), 17–30.

Lewandowski, R. A., & Cirella, G. T. (2022). Performance management systems: Trade-off between implementation and strategy development. *Operations Management Research*. https://doi.org/10.1007/s12063-022-00305-4

Lewandowski, R., Goncharuk, A. G., & Fedorowski, J. J. (2020). Ideology, trust, and spirituality: A framework for management control research in industry 4.0 era. In P. Buła & B. Nogalski (Eds.), *The future of management: Industry 4.0 and digitalization* (pp. 72–91). Jagiellonian University Press.

Lewandowski, R., Lewandowski, J. B., Ekman, I., Swedberg, K., Törnell, J., & Rogers, H. L. (2021). Implementation of person-centered care: A feasibility study using the WE-CARE roadmap. *International Journal of Environmental Research and Public Health, 18*(5), 2205. https://doi.org/10.3390/ijerph18052205

Lewandowski, R., & Sułkowska, J. (2017). Levels of hybridity in healthcare sector. In J. Teczke & P. Buła (Eds.), *Management in the time of networks, cross-cultural activities and flexible organizations* (pp. 147–162). Cracow University of Economics.

Lewandowski, R., & Sułkowski, Ł. (2018). New public management and hybridity in healthcare: The solution or the problem? In A. B. Savignon, L. Gnan, A. Hinna, & F. Monteduro (Eds.), *Hybridity in the governance and delivery of public services* (Vol. 7, pp. 141–166). Emerald Publishing Limited. https://doi.org/10.1108/S2051-663020180000007004

Lewis-Beck, M. S. (1977). Influence equality and organizational innovation in a Third World nation: An additive-nonadditive model. *American Journal of Political Science, 21*(1), 1–11. https://doi.org/10.2307/2110444

Liedtka, S. L., Church, B. K., & Ray, M. R. (2008). Performance variability, ambiguity intolerance, and balanced scorecard-based performance assessments. *Behavioral Research in Accounting, 20*(2), 73–88. https://doi.org/10.2308/bria.2008.20.2.73

Liengaard, B. D., Sharma, P. N., Hult, G. T. M., Jensen, M. B., Sarstedt, M., Hair, J. F., & Ringle, C. M. (2021). Prediction: Coveted, yet forsaken? Introducing a cross-validated predictive ability test in partial least squares path modeling. *Decision Sciences, 52*(2), 362–392. https://doi.org/10.1111/deci.12445

Likert, R. (1958). Measuring organizational performance. *Harvard Business Review, 36*(2), 41–50.

Likert, R. (1960). Influence and national sovereignty. In J. G. Peatman & E. L. Hartley (Eds.), *Festschrift for gardner murphy* (pp. 214–227). Wiley.

Lill, P., Wald, A., & Munck, J. C. (2020). In the field of tension between creativity and efficiency: A systematic literature review of management control systems for innovation activities. *European Journal of Innovation Management* (ahead-of-print). https://doi.org/10.1108/EJIM-11-2019-0329

Lin, Z., Yu, Z., & Zhang, L. (2014). Performance outcomes of balanced scorecard application in hospital administration in China. *China Economic Review, 30*, 1–15. https://doi.org/10.1016/j.chieco.2014.05.003

Lincoln, Y. S., & Guba, E. G. (1985). *Naturalistic inquiry* (Vol. 75). Sage Publications.

Lioukas, C. S., & Reuer, J. J. (2015). Isolating trust outcomes from exchange relationships: Social exchange and learning benefits of prior ties in alliances. *Academy of Management Journal, 58*(6), 1826–1847. https://doi.org/10.5465/amj.2011.0934

Lipsky, M. (1971). Street-level bureaucracy and the analysis of urban reform. *Urban Affairs Quarterly, 6*(4), 391–409.

Lipsky, M., & Hill, M. (1993). Street-level bureaucracy: An introduction. *The Policy Process: A Reader* (pp. 381–385). Routledge.

Lisboa, A., Skarmeas, D., & Lages, C. (2011). Innovative capabilities: Their drivers and effects on current and future performance. *Journal of Business Research, 64*(11), 1157–1161. https://doi.org/10.1016/j.jbusres.2011.06.015

Lohmöller, J.-B. (1989). *Latent variable path modeling with partial least squares.* Physica-Verlag. https://doi.org/10.1007/978-3-642-52512-4

Long, C. P., & Sitkin, S. B. (2018). Control–trust dynamics in organizations: Identifying shared perspectives and charting conceptual fault lines. *Academy of Management Annals, 12*(2), 725–751. https://doi.org/10.5465/annals.2016.0055

Lonial, S. C., & Raju, P. S. (2001). The impact of environmental uncertainty on the market orientation—Performance relationship: A study of the hospital industry? *Journal of Economic and Social Research, 3*(1), 5–27.

Lounsbury, M. (2008). Institutional rationality and practice variation: New directions in the institutional analysis of practice. *Accounting, Organizations and Society, 33*(4–5), 349–361.

Lu, I. R., Kwan, E., Thomas, D. R., & Cedzynski, M. (2011). Two new methods for estimating structural equation models: An illustration and a comparison with two established methods. *International Journal of Research in Marketing, 28*(3), 258–268.

Luhmann, N. (2017). *Trust and power* (Wydanie elektroniczne. Pierwsza publikacja w 1973 r.). John Wiley & Sons.

Lynn Jr., L. E., Heinrich, C. J., & Hill, C. J. (2000). Studying governance and public management: Challenges and prospects. *Journal of Public Administration Research and Theory, 10*(2), 233–262.

Maarse, H., & Jeurissen, P. (2019). Low institutional trust in health insurers in Dutch health care. *Health Policy, 123*(3), 288–292. https://doi.org/10.1016/j.healthpol.2018.12.008

Madhok, A., & Osegowitsch, T. (2000). The international biotechnology industry: A dynamic capabilities perspective. *Journal of International Business Studies, 31*(2), 325–335. https://doi.org/10.1057/palgrave.jibs.8490909

Madorrán García, C., & de Val Pardo, I. (2004). Strategies and performance in hospitals. *Health Policy*, *67*(1), 1–13. https://doi.org/10.1016/S0168-8510(03)00102-7

Mak, Y. T., & Roush, M. L. (1996). Managing activity costs with flexible budgeting and variance analysis. *Accounting Horizons*, *10*(3), 141.

Malmi, T., & Brown, D. A. (2008). Management control systems as a package—Opportunities, challenges and research directions. *Management Accounting Research*, *19*(4), 287–300. https://doi.org/10.1016/j.mar.2008.09.003

Mangaliso, M. P. (1995). The strategic usefulness of management information as perceived by middle managers. *Journal of Management*, *21*(2), 231–250.

Manning, N. (2001). The legacy of the new public management in developing countries. *International Review of Administrative Sciences*, *67*(2), 297–312. https://doi.org/10.1177/0020852301672009

March, J. G., & Simon, H. A. (1958). *Organizations*. John Wiley & Sons.

March, J. G., & Sutton, R. I. (1997). Crossroads—Organizational performance as a dependent variable. *Organization Science*, *8*(6), 698–706.

Marcoulides, G. A., & Saunders, C. (2006). Editor's comments: PLS: A silver bullet? *MIS Quarterly*, *30*(2), iii. https://doi.org/10.2307/25148727

Marginson, D., McAulay, L., Roush, M., & Van Zijl, T. (2010). Performance measures and short-termism: An exploratory study. *Accounting and Business Research*, *40*(4), 353–370. https://doi.org/10.1080/00014788.2010.9995317

Marginson, D., McAulay, L., Roush, M., & van Zijl, T. (2014). Examining a positive psychological role for performance measures. *Management Accounting Research*, *25*(1), 63–75. https://doi.org/10.1016/j.mar.2013.10.002

Marinkovic, V., Rogers, H. L., Lewandowski, R., & Stevic, I. (2022). Shared decision making. In D. Kriksciuniene & V. Sakalauskas (Eds.), *Intelligent systems for sustainable person-centered healthcare* (Vol. 205, pp. 71–90). Springer International Publishing. https://doi.org/10.1007/978-3-030-79353-1_5

Martyn, P., Sweeney, B., & Curtis, E. (2016). Strategy and control: 25 years of empirical use of Simons' Levers of Control framework. *Journal of Accounting and Organizational Change*, *12*(3), 281–324. https://doi.org/10.1108/JAOC-03-2015-0027

Materna, G. (2010). Ewaluacja form wynagradzania pracowników ochrony zdrowia w Polsce. *Przedsiębiorstwo i Region*, *21*(1), 121–138.

Mayer, R. C., & Davis, J. H. (1999). The effect of the performance appraisal system on trust for management: A field quasi-experiment. *Journal of Applied Psychology*, *84*(1), 123–136.

Mayer, R. C., Davis, J. H., & Schoorman, F. D. (1995). An integrative model of organizational trust. *Academy of Management Review*, *20*(3), 709–734.

McAllister, D. J. (1995). Affect-and cognition-based trust as foundations for interpersonal cooperation in organizations. *Academy of Management Journal*, *38*(1), 24–59.

McConnell, C. R. (2005). Larger, smaller, and flatter: The evolution of the modern health care organization. *The Health Care Manager*, *24*(2), 177–188.

McEvily, B., Perrone, V., & Zaheer, A. (2003). Trust as an organizing principle. *Organization Science*, *14*(1), 91–103. https://doi.org/10.1287/orsc.14.1.91.12814

McHugh, M. D., & Stimpfel, A. W. (2012). Nurse reported quality of care: A measure of hospital quality. *Research in Nursing and Health, 35*(6), 566–575.

McMahon, J. T., & Perritt, G. W. (1973). Toward a contingency theory of organizational control. *Academy of Management Journal, 16*(4), 624–635.

McNeish, D., & Wolf, M. G. (2020). Thinking twice about sum scores. *Behavior Research Methods*, 1–19.

Mechanic, D. (1996). Changing medical organization and the erosion of trust. *The Milbank Quarterly, 74*(2), 171. https://doi.org/10.2307/3350245

Mechanic, D., & Schlesinger, M. (1996). The impact of managed care on patients' trust in medical care and their physicians. *JAMA: The Journal of the American Medical Association, 275*(21), 1693. https://doi.org/10.1001/jama.1996.03530450083048

Meissner, P., & Wulf, T. (2014). Antecendents and effects of decision comprehensiveness: The role of decision quality and perceived uncertainty. *European Management Journal, 32*(4), 625–635. https://doi.org/10.1016/j.emj.2013.10.006

Menon, N. M., Yaylacicegi, U., & Cezar, A. (2009). Differential effects of the two types of information systems: A hospital-based study. *Journal of Management Information Systems, 26*(1), 297–316.

Merchant, K. A. (1985). Organizational controls and discretionary program decision making: A field study. *Accounting, Organizations and Society, 10*(1), 67–85.

Merchant, K. A., & Otley, D. T. (2007). A review of the literature on control and accountability. In C. S. Chapman, A. G. Hopwood, & M. D. Shields (Eds.), *Handbooks of management accounting research* (Vol. 2, pp. 785–802). Elsevier.

Merchant, K. A., & Van der Stede, W. A. (2017). *Management control systems: Performance measurement, evaluation and incentives* (4th ed.). Pearson Education.

Merton, R. K. (1936). The unanticipated consequences of purposive social action. *American Sociological Review, 1*(6), 894–904.

Meyer, A. D., Brooks, G. R., & Goes, J. B. (1990). Environmental jolts and industry revolutions: Organizational responses to discontinuous change. *Strategic Management Journal, 11*, Special Issue: Corporate Entrepreneurship (Summer, 1990), 93–110. https://www.jstor.org/stable/2486672

Meyer, J. W., & Rowan, B. (1977). Institutionalized organizations: Formal structure as myth and ceremony. *American Journal of Sociology, 83*(2), 340–363.

Midttun, L., & Martinussen, P. E. (2005). Hospital waiting time in Norway: What is the role of organizational change? *Scandinavian Journal of Public Health, 33*(6), 439–446. https://doi.org/10.1080/14034940510005950

Miles, R. E., & Snow, C. C. (1978). *Organizational strategy, structure and process.* McGraw-Hill.

Miller, D., & Friesen, P. H. (1982). Innovation in conservative and entrepreneurial firms: Two models of strategic momentum. *Strategic Management Journal, 3*(1), 1–25. https://doi.org/10.1002/smj.4250030102

Milliken, F. J. (1987). Three types of perceived uncertainty about the environment: State, effect, and response uncertainty. *Academy of Management Review, 12*(1), 133–143. https://doi.org/10.5465/amr.1987.4306502

Miner, J. B. (2005). *Organizational behavior 2: Essential theories of process and structure.* ME Sharpe.

Mintzberg, H. (1980). Structure in 5s: A synthesis of the research on organization design. *Management Science, 26*(3), 322–341.

Mintzberg, H. (1993a). *Structure in fives: Designing effective organizations.* Prentice-Hall.

Mintzberg, H. (1993b). *Structure in fives: Designing effective organizations.* Prentice-Hall Inc.

Mintzberg, H. (1994). The fall and rise of strategic planning. *Harvard Business Review, 72*(1), 107–114.

Mintzberg, H. (1997). Toward healthier hospitals. *Health Care Management Review, 22*(4), 9.

Mintzberg, H. (2012). Managing the myths of health care. *World Hospitals and Health Services, 48*(3), 4–7.

Mintzberg, H., & Waters, J. A. (1985). Of strategies, deliberate and emergent. *Strategic Management Journal, 6*(3), 257–272.

Miszczyńska, K., & Antczak, E. (2020). *Uwarunkowania zadłużenia szpitali w Polsce.* Wydawnictwo Uniwersytetu Łódzkiego.

Moreira, M. R. A., Gherman, M., & Sousa, P. S. A. (2017). Does innovation influence the performance of healthcare organizations? *Innovation, 19*(3), 335–352. https://doi.org/10.1080/14479338.2017.1293489

Morgan, F. W. (1990). Judicial standards for survey research: An update and guidelines. *Journal of Marketing, 54*(1), 59–70. https://doi.org/10.1177/002224299005400104

Morrison, I. (2000). *Health care in the new millennium: Vision, values, and leadership.* Jossey-Bass Inc.

Morse, J. M. (2003). Principles of mixed methods and multimethod research design. In A. Tashakkori & C. Teddlie (Eds.), *Handbook of mixed methods in social and behavioral research* (Vol. 1, pp. 189–208). Sage.

Müller-Stewens, B., Widener, S. K., Möller, K., & Steinmann, J.-C. (2020). The role of diagnostic and interactive control uses in innovation. *Accounting, Organizations and Society, 80*, 101078. https://doi.org/10.1016/j.aos.2019.101078

Nahavandi, A., Mizzi, P. J., & Malekzadeh, A. R. (1992). Executives' type a personality as a determinant of environmental perception and firm strategy. *Journal of Social Psychology, 132*(1), 59–67. https://doi.org/10.1080/00224545.1992.9924688

Naranjo-Gil, D. (2016). Role of management control systems in crafting realized strategies. *Journal of Business Economics and Management, 17*(6), 865–881. https://doi.org/10.3846/16111699.2014.994558

Naranjo-Gil, D., & Hartmann, F. (2006). How top management teams use management accounting systems to implement strategy. *Journal of Management Accounting Research, 18*(1), 21–53. https://doi.org/10.2308/jmar.2006.18.1.21

Naranjo-Gil, D., & Hartmann, F. (2007). Management accounting systems, top management team heterogeneity and strategic change. *Accounting, Organizations and Society, 32*(7–8), 735–756. https://doi.org/10.1016/j.aos.2006.08.003

Nash, D. B. (2003). Doctors and managers: Mind the gap. *BMJ, 326*(7390), 652–653.

Neely, A. D., Adams, C., & Kennerley, M. (2002). *The performance prism: The score-card for measuring and managing business success*. Prentice Hall Financial Times.

Neely, A., Gregory, M., & Platts, K. (1995). Performance measurement system design: A literature review and research agenda. *International Journal of Operations and Production Management, 15*(4), 80–116.

Nguyen, N. P. (2018). Performance implication of market orientation and use of management accounting systems: The moderating role of accountants' participation in strategic decision making. *Journal of Asian Business and Economic Studies, 25*(1), 33–49. https://doi.org/10.1108/JABES-04-2018-0005

Nguyen, T. T., Mia, L., Winata, L., & Chong, V. K. (2017). Effect of transformational-leadership style and management control system on managerial performance. *Journal of Business Research, 70*, 202–213. https://doi.org/10.1016/j.jbusres.2016.08.018

NIK. (2014). *Działalnoś ć szpitali samorządowych przekształconych w spółki kapitałowe* (Informacja o Wynikach Kontroli KZ D-4101-004/2014; p. 54). Najwyższa Izba Kontroli. https://www.nik.gov.pl/plik/id,8411,vp,10488.pdf

NIK. (2016). *Restrukturyzacja wybranych samodzielnych publicznych zakładów opieki zdrowotnej korzystających z pomocy ze środków publicznych* (LOP.430.001.2016). Najwyższa Izba Kontroli, Delegatura w Opolu.

Nitzl, C. (2016). The use of partial least squares structural equation modelling (PLS-SEM) in management accounting research: Directions for future theory development. *Journal of Accounting Literature, 37*, 19–35. https://doi.org/10.1016/j.acclit.2016.09.003

Nolte, E., Pitchforth, E., Miani, C., & Mc Hugh, S. (2014). *The changing hospital landscape: An exploration of international experiences*. RAND Corporation.

Noordegraaf, M. (2020). Protective or connective professionalism? How connected professionals can (still) act as autonomous and authoritative experts. *Journal of Professions and Organization, 7*(2), 205–223. https://doi.org/10.1093/jpo/joaa011

Nyland, K., & Pettersen, I. J. (2004). The control gap: The role of budgets, accounting information and (non-) decisions in hospital settings. *Financial Accountability and Management, 20*(1), 77–102.

Oliveira Martins, J., & de la Maisonneuve, C. (2013). *Public spending on health and long-term care: A new set of projections* (OECD Economic Policy Papers no. 6). OECD.

Olsson, U. H., Foss, T., Troye, S. V., & Howell, R. D. (2000). The performance of ML, GLS, and WLS estimation in structural equation modeling under conditions of misspecification and nonnormality. *Structural Equation Modeling, 7*(4), 557–595.

Oreg, S. (2006). Personality, context, and resistance to organizational change. *European Journal of Work and Organizational Psychology, 15*(1), 73–101. https://doi.org/10.1080/13594320500451247

OECD. (2012). *Competition in hospital services* (DAF/COMP(2012)9). Competition Policy Roundtables. https://www.oecd.org/daf/competition/50527122.pdf

OECD. (2015). *Fiscal sustainability of health systems: Bridging health and finance perspectives*. OECD. https://doi.org/10.1787/9789264233386-en

OECD. (2020). *Reassessing private practice in public hospitals in Ireland: An overview of OECD experiences* (OECD Health Working Paper no. 118 DELSA/HEA/WD/HWP(2020)3).

OECD, & Eurostat (2019). *Oslo manual 2018: Guidelines for collecting, reporting and using data on innovation* (4th ed.). OECD. https://doi.org/10.1787/9789264304604-en

Østergren, K. (2009). Management control practices and clinician managers: The case of the Norwegian health sector. *Financial Accountability and Management, 25*(2), 167–195. https://doi.org/10.1111/j.1468-0408.2009.00473.x

Otley, D. (1999). Performance management: A framework for management control systems research. *Management Accounting Research, 10*(4), 363–382. https://doi.org/10.1006/mare.1999.0115

Otley, D. T., & Berry, A. J. (1980). Control, organisation and accounting. *Accounting, Organizations and Society, 5*(2), 231–244. https://doi.org/10.1016/0361-3682(80)90012-4

Ouchi, W. G. (1977). The relationship between organizational structure and organizational control. *Administrative Science Quarterly, 22*(1), 95–113.

Ouchi, W. G. (1978). The transmission of control through organizational hierarchy. *The Academy of Management Journal, 21*(2), 173–192.

Ouchi, W. G. (1979). A conceptual framework for the design of organizational control mechanisms. *Management Science, 25*(9), 833–848.

Ouchi, W. G. (1980). Markets, bureaucracies, and clans. *Administrative Science Quarterly, 25*(1), 129–141. https://doi.org/10.2307/2392231

Pache, A.-C., & Santos, F. (2013a). Embedded in hybrid contexts: How individuals in organizations respond to competing institutional logics. In M. Lounsbury & E. Boxenbaum (Eds.), *Institutional logics in action, part B (Research in the Sociology of Organizations, Vol. 39 Part B)* (pp. 3–35). Emerald Group Publishing Limited. https://doi.org/10.1108/S0733-558X(2013)0039AB014

Pache, A.-C., & Santos, F. (2013b). Inside the hybrid organization: Selective coupling as a response to competing institutional logics. *Academy of Management Journal, 56*(4), 972–1001.

Paulus, R. A., Davis, K., & Steele, G. D. (2008). Continuous innovation in health care: Implications of the Geisinger experience. *Health Affairs, 27*(5), 1235–1245. https://doi.org/10.1377/hlthaff.27.5.1235

Pešalj, B., Pavlov, A., & Micheli, P. (2018). The use of management control and performance measurement systems in SMEs: A levers of control perspective. *International Journal of Operations and Production Management, 38*(11), 2169–2191. https://doi.org/10.1108/IJOPM-09-2016-0565

Phelps, C. E. (2016). *Health economics*. Routledge.

Pierce, B., & Sweeney, B. (2005). Management control in audit firms—Partners' perspectives. *Management Accounting Research, 16*(3), 340–370.

Pitkänen, H., & Lukka, K. (2011). Three dimensions of formal and informal feedback in management accounting. *Management Accounting Research, 22*(2), 125–137. https://doi.org/10.1016/j.mar.2010.10.004

Pizzini, M. J. (2006). The relation between cost-system design, managers' evaluations of the relevance and usefulness of cost data, and financial performance: An empirical study of US hospitals. *Accounting, Organizations and Society, 31*(2), 179–210. https://doi.org/10.1016/j.aos.2004.11.001

Po, J., Rundall, T. G., Shortell, S. M., & Blodgett, J. C. (2019). Lean management and U. S. Public hospital performance: Results from a national survey. *Journal of Healthcare Management, 64*(6), 363–379. https://doi.org/10.1097/JHM-D-18-00163

Porter, M. E. (1980). *Competitive strategy: Techniques for analyzing industries and competitors.* The Free Press.

Porter, M. E. (2010a). What is value in health care? *New England Journal of Medicine, 363*(26), 2477–2481.

Porter, M. E. (2010b). What is value in health care? Appendix 2. *New England Journal of Medicine, 363*(26), 2477–2481.

Powell, W. W., & DiMaggio, P. J. (2012). *The new institutionalism in organizational analysis.* University of Chicago press.

Prajogo, D., Toy, J., Bhattacharya, A., Oke, A., & Cheng, T. C. E. (2018). The relationships between information management, process management and operational performance: Internal and external contexts. *International Journal of Production Economics, 199,* 95–103. https://doi.org/10.1016/j.ijpe.2018.02.019

Pratt, M. G., & Foreman, P. O. (2000). Classifying managerial responses to multiple organizational identities. *Academy of Management Review, 25*(1), 18–42.

Prendergast, C. (1999). The provision of incentives in firms. *Journal of Economic Literature, 37*(1), 7–63. https://doi.org/10.1257/jel.37.1.7

Price, J. L. (1997). Handbook of organizational measurement. *International Journal of Manpower, 18*(4/5/6), 305–558. https://doi.org/10.1108/01437729710182260

Professional Accountants in Business Committee. (2013). *Evaluating the costing journey: A costing levels continuum maturity model 2.0.* The International Federation of Accountants (IFAC).

Qingyue, M., Liying, J., & Beibei, Y. (2011). *Cost-sharing mechanisms in health insurance schemes: A systematic review.* The Alliance for Health Policy and Systems Research, WHO, 1–76.

Rahimi, H., Kavosi, Z., Shojaei, P., & Kharazmi, E. (2017). Key performance indicators in hospital based on balanced scorecard model. *Journal of Health Management and Informatics, 4*(1), 17–24.

Ramani, K. V. (2004). A management information system to plan and monitor the delivery of health-care services in government hospitals in India. *Journal of Health Organization and Management, 18*(3), 207–220.

Rampersad, H. (2004). *Kompleksowa Karta Wyników. Jak przekształcać zarządzanie, aby postępując uczciwie osiągać doskonałe wyniki.* Placet.

Ramsdal, H., & Bjørkquist, C. (2019). Value-based innovations in a Norwegian hospital: From conceptualization to implementation. *Public Management Review,* 1717–1738. https://doi.org/10.1080/14719037.2019.1648695

Raposo, V., Antonić, D., Nova, A. C., Lewandowski, R., & Melo, P. (2022). An overview of measurement systems and practices in healthcare systems applied to person-centred care interventions. In D. Kriksciuniene & V. Sakalauskas (Eds.),

Intelligent systems for sustainable person-centered healthcare (Vol. 205, pp. 119–143). Springer International Publishing. https://doi.org/10.1007/978-3-030-79353-1_7

Raulinajtys-Grzybek, M., Baran, W., Cygańska, M., Kludacz-Alessandri, M., & Macuda, M. (2019). Model oceny dojrzałości rachunku kosztów w szpitalu–koncepcja i empiryczne wykorzystanie. *Zeszyty Teoretyczne Rachunkowości, 102*(158), 131–154.

Reay, T., & Hinings, C. R. (2005). The recomposition of an organizational field: Health care in Alberta. *Organization Studies, 26*(3), 351–384. https://doi.org/10.1177/0170840605050872

Reay, T., & Hinings, C. R. (2009). Managing the rivalry of competing institutional logics. *Organization Studies, 30*(6), 629–652. https://doi.org/10.1177/0170840609104803

Reich, A. (2012). Disciplined doctors: The electronic medical record and physicians' changing relationship to medical knowledge. *Social Science and Medicine, 74*(7), 1021–1028. https://doi.org/10.1016/j.socscimed.2011.12.032

Reinartz, W., Haenlein, M., & Henseler, J. (2009). An empirical comparison of the efficacy of covariance-based and variance-based SEM. *International Journal of Research in Marketing, 26*(4), 332–344. https://doi.org/10.1016/j.ijresmar.2009.08.001

Rice, P. L., & Ezzy, D. (1999). *Qualitative research methods: A health focus.* Oxford University Press.

Rigdon, E. E. (2012). Rethinking partial least squares path modeling: In praise of simple methods. *Long Range Planning, 45*(5–6), 341–358. https://doi.org/10.1016/j.lrp.2012.09.010

Rigdon, E. E. (2014). Rethinking partial least squares path modeling: Breaking chains and forging ahead. *Long Range Planning, 47*(3), 161–167.

Rigdon, E. E. (2016). Choosing PLS path modeling as analytical method in European management research: A realist perspective. *European Management Journal, 34*(6), 598–605. https://doi.org/10.1016/j.emj.2016.05.006

Rigdon, E. E., Ringle, C. M., & Sarstedt, M. (2010). Structural modeling of heterogeneous data with partial least squares. In N. K. Malhotra (Ed.), *Review of marketing research* (Vol. 7, pp. 255–296). Emerald Group Publishing Limited. https://doi.org/10.1108/S1548-6435(2010)0000007011

Ringle, C. M., Wende, S., & Becker, J.-M. (2015). *SmartPLS 3.* SmartPLS GmbH. http://www.smartpls.com

Ritchie, W. J., Ni, J., Stark, E. M., & Melnyk, S. A. (2019). The effectiveness of ISO 9001-based healthcare accreditation surveyors and standards on hospital performance outcomes: A balanced scorecard perspective. *Quality Management Journal, 26*(4), 162–173.

Ritzer, G. (2020). *Classical sociological theory* (8th ed.). SAGE Publications Inc.

Roberts, J. (1990). Strategy and accounting in a UK conglomerate. *Accounting, Organizations and Society, 15*(1–2), 107–126.

Romney, M. B., & Steinbart, P. J. (2018). *Accounting information systems.* Pearson Education Limited.

Rönkkö, M., & Evermann, J. (2013). A critical examination of common beliefs about partial least squares path modeling. *Organizational Research Methods, 16*(3), 425–448. https://doi.org/10.1177/1094428112474693

Ross, S. A. (1973). The economic theory of agency: The principal's problem. *The American Economic Review, 63*(2), 134–139.

Rousseau, D. M., Sitkin, S. B., Burt, R. S., & Camerer, C. (1998). Not so different after all: A cross-discipline view of trust. *Academy of Management Review, 23*(3), 393–404. https://doi.org/10.5465/AMR.1998.926617

Rüsch, S. (2016). Cooperation between managers and the medical profession in the context of strategic decision-making in non-profit hospitals. In S. Salloch, V. Sandow, J. Schildmann, & J. Vollmann (Eds.), *Ethics and professionalism in healthcare: Transition and challenges* (pp. 138–147). Routledge. https://www.google.com/books?hl=pl&lr=&id=dw9qDAAAQBAJ&oi=fnd&pg=PA138&dq=R%C3%BCsch+Cooperation+between+managers+and+the+medical+profession+in+the+context+of+strategic+decision-making+in+non-profit+hospitals&ots=9uuaTEqcOq&sig=WzrRfEMd9Sc3McdhUNL2K9IJfY8

Rye, C. B., & Kimberly, J. R. (2007). The adoption of innovations by provider organizations in health care. *Medical Care Research and Review, 64*(3), 235–278. https://doi.org/10.1177/1077558707299865

Salaman, G., & Thompson, K. (1980). *Control and ideology in organizations* (Vol. 1). The MIT Press.

Salge, T. O., & Vera, A. (2009). Hospital innovativeness and organizational performance: Evidence from English public acute care. *Health Care Management Review, 34*(1), 54–67. https://doi.org/10.1097/01.HMR.0000342978.84307.80

Salter, B. (2007). Governing UK medical performance: A struggle for policy dominance. *Health Policy, 82*(3), 263–275. https://doi.org/10.1016/j.healthpol.2006.10.004

Saltman, R. B., Durán, A., & Dubois, H. F. (2011). Introduction: Innovative governance strategies in European public hospitals. In R. B. Saltman, A. Durán, & H. F. Dubois (Eds.), *Governing public hospitals. Reform strategies and the movement towards institutional autonomy* (pp. 1–11). European Observatory on Health Systems and Policies. http://www.academia.edu/download/9404229/e95981.pdf

Salvatore, D., Numerato, D., & Fattore, G. (2018). Physicians' professional autonomy and their organizational identification with their hospital. *BMC Health Services Research, 18*(1), 775. https://doi.org/10.1186/s12913-018-3582-z

Samuel, S., Dirsmith, M. W., & McElroy, B. (2005). Monetized medicine: From the physical to the fiscal. *Accounting, Organizations and Society, 30*(3), 249–278.

Sankowska, A. (2011). *Wpływ zaufania na zarządzanie przedsiębiorstwem: Perspektywa wewnątrzorganizacyjna*. Difin.

Sarstedt, M., Becker, J.-M., Ringle, C. M., & Schwaiger, M. (2011). Uncovering and treating unobserved heterogeneity with FIMIX-PLS: Which model selection criterion provides an appropriate number of segments? *Schmalenbach Business Review, 63*(1), 34–62. https://doi.org/10.1007/BF03396886

Sarstedt, M., Diamantopoulos, A., Salzberger, T., & Baumgartner, P. (2016). Selecting single items to measure doubly concrete constructs: A cautionary tale. *Journal of Business Research*, 69(8), 3159–3167. https://doi.org/10.1016/j.jbusres.2015.12.004

Sarstedt, M., Hair, J. F., Ringle, C. M., Thiele, K. O., & Gudergan, S. P. (2016). Estimation issues with PLS and CBSEM: Where the bias lies! *Journal of Business Research*, 69(10), 3998–4010.

Sarstedt, M., Ringle, C. M., Henseler, J., & Hair, J. F. (2014). On the emancipation of PLS-SEM: A commentary on Rigdon (2012). *Long Range Planning*, 47(3), 154–160.

Sasaki, L. (2003). Hospital offer unconventional services in hopes of attracting future patients. *Hospital Quarterly*, 6(3), 85–86.

Saunders, M. N. K., & Bezzina, F. (2015). Reflections on conceptions of research methodology among management academics. *European Management Journal*, 33(5), 297–304. https://doi.org/10.1016/j.emj.2015.06.002

Scandura, T. A., & Pellegrini, E. K. (2008). Trust and leader—Member exchange: A closer look at relational vulnerability. *Journal of Leadership and Organizational Studies*, 15(2), 101–110. https://doi.org/10.1177/1548051808320986

Schaefer, T., & Guenther, T. (2016). Exploring strategic planning outcomes: The influential role of top versus middle management participation. *Journal of Management Control*, 27(2–3), 205–249. https://doi.org/10.1007/s00187-016-0230-9

Schäffer, U., Strauss, E., & Zecher, C. (2015). The role of management control systems in situations of institutional complexity. *Qualitative Research in Accounting and Management*, 12(4), 395–424. https://doi.org/10.1108/QRAM-01-2015-0010

Schönemann, P. H., & Wang, M.-M. (1972). Some new results on factor indeterminacy. *Psychometrika*, 37(1), 61–91.

Schulz, A. K.-D., Wu, A., & Chow, C. W. (2010). Environmental uncertainty, comprehensive performance measurement systems, performance-based compensation, and organizational performance. *Asia-Pacific Journal of Accounting and Economics*, 17(1), 17–39. https://doi.org/10.1080/16081625.2010.9720850

Schut, F. T., & Van de Ven, W. P. (2011). Effects of purchaser competition in the Dutch health care system: Is the glass half full or half empty. Health Economics, Policy and Law, 6, 109–123.

Schwierz, C. (2011). Expansion in markets with decreasing demand-for-profits in the German hospital industry. *Health Economics*, 20(6), 675–687.

Schwierz, C. (2016). *Cost-containment policies in hospital expenditure in the European Union* (DISCUSSION PAPER 037; p. 76). European Commission.

Scott, A., Sivey, P., Ouakrim, D. A., Willenberg, L., Naccarella, L., Furler, J., & Young, D. (2011). The effect of financial incentives on the quality of health care provided by primary care physicians. *Cochrane Database of Systematic Reviews*, 9(9), 1–61.

Scott, W. R. (2014). *Institutions and organizations: Ideas, interests, and identities* (4th ed.). Sage publications.

Shao, B. (2019). Moral anger as a dilemma? An investigation on how leader moral anger influences follower trust. *The Leadership Quarterly, 30*(3), 365–382. https://doi.org/10.1016/j.leaqua.2018.10.002

Shapiro, D. L., Sheppard, B. H., & Cheraskin, L. (1992). Business on a handshake. *Negotiation Journal, 8*(4), 365–377. https://doi.org/10.1111/j.1571-9979.1992 .tb00679.x

Shen, Y.-C., Eggleston, K., Lau, J., & Schmid, C. H. (2007). Hospital ownership and financial performance: What explains the different findings in the empirical literature? *Inquiry: The Journal of Health Care Organization, Provision, and Financing, 44*(1), 41–68. https://doi.org/10.5034/inquiryjrnl_44.1.41

Shields, M. D., & Young, S. M. (1993). Antecedents and consequences of participative budgeting: Evidence on the effects of asymmetrical information. *Journal of Management Accounting Research, 5*(1), 265–280.

Shmueli, A., Stam, P., Wasem, J., & Trottmann, M. (2015). Managed care in four managed competition OECD health systems. *Health Policy, 119*(7), 860–873.

Shmueli, G. (2010). To explain or to predict? *Statistical Science, 25*(3), 289–310.

Shmueli, G., Ray, S., Velasquez Estrada, J. M., & Chatla, S. B. (2016). The elephant in the room: Predictive performance of PLS models. *Journal of Business Research, 69*(10), 4552–4564. https://doi.org/10.1016/j.jbusres.2016.03.049

Shmueli, G., Sarstedt, M., Hair, J. F., Cheah, J.-H., Ting, H., Vaithilingam, S., & Ringle, C. M. (2019). Predictive model assessment in PLS-SEM: Guidelines for using PLSpredict. *European Journal of Marketing, 53*(11), 2322–2347.

Shockley-Zalabak, P. S., Morreale, S., & Hackman, M. (2010). *Building the high-trust organization: Strategies for supporting five key dimensions of trust.* John Wiley & Sons.

Shockley-Zalabak, P., Ellis, K., & Winograd, G. (2000). Organizational trust: What it means, why it matters. *Organization Development Journal, 18*(4), 35.

Shortell, S. M., Blodgett, J. C., Rundall, T. G., Henke, R. M., & Reponen, E. (2021). Lean management and hospital performance: Adoption vs. implementation. *The Joint Commission Journal on Quality and Patient Safety, 47*(5), 296–305. https://doi.org/10.1016/j.jcjq.2021.01.010

Shortell, S. M., Gillies, R. R., Anderson, D. A., Erickson, K. M., & Mitchell, J. B. (2000). *Remaking health care in America: The evolution of organized delivery systems.* Jossey-Bass.

Shortell, S. M., & Kaluzny, A. D. (1997). *Essentials of health care management.* Delmar Publishers.

Simon, H. A. (1957). *Models of man, social and rational: Mathematical essays on rational human behavior in society setting.* John Wiley & Sons Inc.

Simons, R. (1987a). Planning, control, and uncertainty: A process view. In W. J. Bruns & R. S. Kaplan (Eds.), *Accounting and management: Field study perspectives.* Harvard Business School Press.

Simons, R. (1987b). Accounting control systems and business strategy: An empirical analysis. *Accounting, Organizations and Society, 12*(4), 357–374.

Simons, R. (1990). The role of management control systems in creating competitive advantage: New perspectives. *Accounting, Organizations and Society, 15*(1–2), 127–143.

Simons, R. (1991). Strategic orientation and top management attention to control systems. *Strategic Management Journal, 12*(1), 49–62. https://doi.org/10.1002/smj.4250120105

Simons, R. (1995). *Levers of control: How managers use innovative control systems to drive strategic renewal.* Harvard Business Press.

Simons, R. (2010). *Seven strategy questions: A simple approach for better execution.* Harvard Business Press.

Simons, R. (2014). *Performance measurement and control systems for implementing strategy.* Pearson Education Limited.

Simons, R., Dávila, A., & Kaplan, R. S. (2000). *Performance measurement & control systems for implementing strategy.* Prentice Hall.

Skelcher, C., & Smith, S. R. (2015). Theorizing hybridity: Institutional logics, complex organizations, and actor identities: The case of nonprofits. *Public Administration, 93*(2), 433–448. https://doi.org/10.1111/padm.12105

Smith, D., & Langfield-Smith, K. (2004). Structural equation modeling in management accounting research: Critical analysis and opportunities. *Journal of Accounting Literature, 23*, 49–86.

Smith, R. (2001). *Why are doctors so unhappy?* British Medical Journal Publishing Group.

Solstad, E., & Petterson, I. J. (2020). Middle managers' roles after a hospital merger. *Journal of Health Organization and Management, 34*(1), 85–99. https://doi.org/10.1108/JHOM-09-2018-0269

Soobaroyen, T., & Poorundersing, B. (2008). The effectiveness of management accounting systems: Evidence from functional managers in a developing country. *Managerial Auditing Journal, 23*(2), 187–219. https://doi.org/10.1108/02686900810839866

Sorrentino, R. M., & Roney, C. J. R. (2013). *The uncertain mind: Individual differences in facing the unknown.* Psychology Press.

Sosik, J. J., Kahai, S. S., & Piovoso, M. J. (2009). Silver bullet or voodoo statistics? A primer for using the partial least squares data analytic technique in group and organization research. *Group and Organization Management, 34*(1), 5–36.

Speckbacher, G., Bischof, J., & Pfeiffer, T. (2003). A descriptive analysis on the implementation of Balanced Scorecards in German-speaking countries. *Management Accounting Research, 14*(4), 361–388. https://doi.org/10.1016/j.mar.2003.10.001

Spitzer, D. R. (2007). *Transforming performance measurement: Rethinking the way we measure and drive organizational success.* Amacom Books.

Spreitzer, G. M., & Mishra, A. K. (1999). Giving up control without losing control: Trust and its substitutes' effects on managers' involving employees in decision making. *Group and Organization Management, 24*(2), 155–187. https://doi.org/10.1177/1059601199242003

Stadhouders, N., Kruse, F., Tanke, M., Koolman, X., & Jeurissen, P. (2019). Effective healthcare cost-containment policies: A systematic review. *Health Policy, 123*(1), 71–79. https://doi.org/10.1016/j.healthpol.2018.10.015

Stone, M. (1974). Cross-validatory choice and assessment of statistical predictions. *Journal of the Royal Statistical Society: Series B (Methodological), 36*(2), 111–133. https://doi.org/10.1111/j.2517-6161.1974.tb00994.x

Strong, E. P., & Smith, R. D. (1968). *Management control models.* Rinehart and Winston.

Sundmacher, L., Fischbach, D., Schuettig, W., Naumann, C., Augustin, U., & Faisst, C. (2015). Which hospitalisations are ambulatory care-sensitive, to what degree, and how could the rates be reduced? Results of a group consensus study in Germany. *Health Policy, 119*(11), 1415–1423.

Sušanj, Z. (2000). Innovative climate and culture in manufacturing organizations: Differences between some European countries. *Social Science Information, 39*(2), 349–361. https://doi.org/10.1177/053901800039002011

Swärd, A. (2016). Trust, reciprocity, and actions: The development of trust in temporary inter-organizational relations. *Organization Studies, 37*(12), 1841–1860. https://doi.org/10.1177/0170840616655488

Swedberg, K., Cawley, D., Ekman, I., Rogers, H. L., Antonic, D., Behmane, D., Björkman, I., Britten, N., Buttigieg, S. C., Byers, V., Börjesson, M., Corazzini, K., Fors, A., Granger, B., Joksimoski, B., Lewandowski, R., Sakalauskas, V., Srulovici, E., Törnell, J., Wallström, S., Wolf, A., & Lloyd, H. M. (2021). Testing cost containment of future healthcare with maintained or improved quality—The Costcares project. *Health Science Reports, 4*(2). https://doi.org/10.1002/hsr2.309

Sztompka, P. (1999a). Kulturowe imponderabilia szybkich zmian społecznych: Zaufanie, lojalnoś ć, solidarnoś ć. In P. Sztompka (Ed.), *Imponderabilia wielkiej zmiany. Mentalnoś ć, wartości i więzi społeczne czasów transformacji.* PWN.

Sztompka, P. (1999b). *Trust: A sociological theory.* Cambridge University Press.

Sztompka, P. (2007). *Zaufanie: Fundament społeczeństwa.* Wydawnictwo znak.

Szymańska, K. (2008). Makroekonomiczne przyczyny zadłużenia polskiej służby zdrowia. *Współczesna Ekonomia, 2*(2), 5–17.

Tak, H. J., Curlin, F. A., & Yoon, J. D. (2017). Association of intrinsic motivating factors and markers of physician well-being: A national physician survey. *Journal of General Internal Medicine, 32*(7), 739–746.

Tannenbaum, A. S. (1956). The concept of organizational control. *Journal of Social Issues, 12*(2), 50–60.

Tannenbaum, A. S. (1962). Control in organizations: Individual adjustment and organizational performance. *Administrative Science Quarterly, 7*(2), 236–257. https://doi.org/10.2307/2390857

Tasso, K., Behar-Horenstein, L. S., Aumiller, A., Gamble, K., Grimaudo, N., Guin, P., Mandell, T., & Ramey, B. (2002). Assessing patient satisfaction and quality of care through observation and interview. *Hospital Topics, 80*(3), 4–10. https://doi.org/10.1080/00185860209597996

Taylor, F. W. (1903). *Shop management.* New York Harper. https://archive.org/details/shopmanagement06464gut

Taylor, F. W. (2004). *Scientific management.* Routledge. https://dspace.gipe.ac.in/xmlui/bitstream/handle/10973/41111/GIPE-191173.pdf?sequence=3

Tenenhaus, M., Vinzi, V. E., Chatelin, Y.-M., & Lauro, C. (2005). PLS path modeling. *Computational Statistics and Data Analysis, 48*(1), 159–205. https://doi.org/10.1016/j.csda.2004.03.005

Tessier, S., & Otley, D. (2012). A conceptual development of Simons' levers of control framework. *Management Accounting Research, 23*(3), 171–185. https://doi.org/10.1016/j.mar.2012.04.003

Thakur, R., Hsu, S. H. Y., & Fontenot, G. (2012). Innovation in healthcare: Issues and future trends. *Journal of Business Research, 65*(4), 562–569. https://doi.org/10.1016/j.jbusres.2011.02.022

Thomas Craig, K. J., McKillop, M. M., Huang, H. T., George, J., Punwani, E. S., & Rhee, K. B. (2020). U.S. hospital performance methodologies: A scoping review to identify opportunities for crossing the quality chasm. *BMC Health Services Research, 20*(1), 640. https://doi.org/10.1186/s12913-020-05503-z

Thompson, C. R., & McKee, M. (2011). An analysis of hospital capital planning and financing in three European countries: Using the principal–agent approach to identify the potential for economic problems. *Health Policy, 99*(2), 158–166.

Thompson, J. D. (2003). *Organizations in action: Social science bases of administrative theory.* Transaction Publishers.

Thornton, P. H. (2004). *Markets from culture: Institutional logics and organizational decisions in higher education publishing.* Stanford University Press.

Thornton, P. H., Ocasio, W., & Lounsbury, M. (2012). *The institutional logics perspective: A new approach to culture, structure, and process.* Oxford University Press on Demand. https://www.google.com/books?hl=pl&lr=&id=xPlagJzF-m2AC&oi=fnd&pg=PP1&dq=The+Institutional+Logics+Perspective:+A+New+Approach+to+Culture,+Structure+and+Process&ots=xMDcfdqR7T&sig=gasPJLgXplyLhkR3Hm0WUBSSL5U

Tiemann, O., & Schreyögg, J. (2009). Effects of ownership on hospital efficiency in Germany. *Business Research, 2*(2), 115–145.

Tkotz, A., Munck, J. C., & Wald, A. E. (2018). Innovation management control: Bibliometric analysis of its emergence and evolution as a research field. *International Journal of Innovation Management, 22*(03), 1850031. https://doi.org/10.1142/S1363919618500317

Toivonen, M., Tuominen, T., & Brax, S. (2007). Innovation process interlinked with the process of service delivery: A management challenge in KIBS. *Economies et Sociétés, 41*(3), 355.

Townley, B., Cooper, D. J., & Oakes, L. (2003). Performance measures and the rationalization of organizations. *Organization Studies, 24*(7), 1045–1071.

Tsai, T. C., Joynt, K. E., Orav, E. J., Gawande, A. A., & Jha, A. K. (2013). Variation in surgical-readmission rates and quality of hospital care. *New England Journal of Medicine, 369*(12), 1134–1142.

Tsai, Y. (2013). Health care industry, customer orientation and organizational innovation: A survey of Chinese hospital professionals. *Chinese Management Studies*, 7(2), 215–229. https://doi.org/10.1108/CMS-Oct-2011-0086

Tucker, B., Thorne, H., & Gurd, B. (2009). Management control systems and strategy: What's been happening? *Journal of Accounting Literature*, 28, 123.

Tung, Y.-C., Chou, Y.-Y., Chang, Y.-H., & Chung, K.-P. (2020). Association of intrinsic and extrinsic motivating factors with physician burnout and job satisfaction: A nationwide cross-sectional survey in Taiwan. *BMJ Open*, 10(3), e035948.

Tuomela, T.-S. (2005). The interplay of different levers of control: A case study of introducing a new performance measurement system. *Management Accounting Research*, 16(3), 293–320. https://doi.org/10.1016/j.mar.2005.06.003

Unsworth, K. L., & Clegg, C. W. (2010). Why do employees undertake creative action? *Journal of Occupational and Organizational Psychology*, 83(1), 77–99. https://doi.org/10.1348/096317908X398377

Valls Martínez, M. D. C., & Ramírez-Orellana, A. (2019). Patient satisfaction in the Spanish national health service: Partial least squares structural equation modeling. *International Journal of Environmental Research and Public Health*, 16(24), 4886.

van der Ark, L. A. (2005). Stochastic ordering of the latent trait by the sum score under various polytomous IRT models. *Psychometrika*, 70(2), 283–304. https://doi.org/10.1007/s11336-000-0862-3

Van der Stede, W. A., Young, S. M., & Chen, C. X. (2005). Assessing the quality of evidence in empirical management accounting research: The case of survey studies. *Accounting, Organizations and Society*, 30(7–8), 655–684. https://doi.org/10.1016/j.aos.2005.01.003

Van Peursem, K. A., Prat, M. J., & Lawrence, S. R. (1995). Health management performance: A review of measures and indicators. *Accounting, Auditing and Accountability Journal*, 8(5), 34–70. https://doi.org/10.1108/09513579510103254

VanHeuvelen, J. S. (2020). Professional engagement in articulation work: Implications for experiences of clinical and workplace autonomy. In E. H. Gorman & S. P. Vallas (Eds.), *Research in the sociology of work* (pp. 11–31). Emerald Publishing Limited. https://doi.org/10.1108/S0277-283320200000034005

Veen, M. (2021). Creative leaps in theory: The might of abduction. *Advances in Health Sciences Education*, 26(3), 1173–1183. https://doi.org/10.1007/s10459-021-10057-8

Venkatraman, N., & Ramanujam, V. (1987). Measurement of business economic performance: An examination of method convergence. *Journal of Management*, 13(1), 109–122.

Vera, A., & Kuntz, L. (2007). Process-based organization design and hospital efficiency. *Health Care Management Review*, 32(1), 55–65.

Villers, R. (1964). *Research and Development: Planning and control*. Financial Executives Research Foundation.

von Knorring, M., de Rijk, A., & Alexanderson, K. (2010). Managers' perceptions of the manager role in relation to physicians: A qualitative interview study of the top managers in Swedish healthcare. *BMC Health Services Research*, 10(1), 1.

Voorhees, C. M., Brady, M. K., Calantone, R., & Ramirez, E. (2016). Discriminant validity testing in marketing: An analysis, causes for concern, and proposed remedies. *Journal of the Academy of Marketing Science, 44*(1), 119–134.

Waldman, D. A., Ramirez, G. G., House, R. J., & Puranam, P. (2001). Does leadership matter? CEO leadership attributes and profitability under conditions of perceived environmental uncertainty. *Academy of Management Journal, 44*(1), 134–143.

Waldman, J. D., & Cohn, K. H. (2007). Mending the gap between physician and health executives. In K. H. Cohn & D. E. Hough (Eds.), *The business of healthcare: Leading healthcare organizations* (2nd ed, pp. 27–59). Praeger Publishers. https://citeseerx.ist.psu.edu/document?repid=rep1&type=pdf&doi=4c9841a15be a982155ef4fe1259b7c723ff5f9a2

Walker, R. M. (2014). Internal and external antecedents of process innovation: A review and extension. *Public Management Review, 16*(1), 21–44. https://doi.org /10.1080/14719037.2013.771698

Walkey, A. J., Shieh, M.-S., Liu, V. X., & Lindenauer, P. K. (2018). Mortality measures to profile hospital performance for patients with septic shock. *Critical Care Medicine, 46*(8), 1247.

Waller, N. G., & Jones, J. A. (2010). Correlation weights in multiple regression. *Psychometrika, 75*(1), 58–69. https://doi.org/10.1007/s11336-009-9127-y

Wang, T., Wang, Y., & McLeod, A. (2018). Do health information technology investments impact hospital financial performance and productivity? *International Journal of Accounting Information Systems, 28*, 1–13. https://doi.org/10.1016/j .accinf.2017.12.002

Weber, M. (2009). *The theory of social and economic organization* (Pierwszy raz wydane w 1924 r.). Simon and Schuster.

Weinert, D. J. (2013). *Environment for innovation: Exploring associations with individual disposition toward change, organizational conflict, justice and trust* [Doctor of Philosophy, University of Iowa]. https://doi.org/10.17077/etd .wzjeued4

Wheat, H., Horrell, J., Valderas, J. M., Close, J., Fosh, B., & Lloyd, H. (2018). Can practitioners use patient reported measures to enhance person centred coordinated care in practice? A qualitative study. *Health and Quality of Life Outcomes, 16*(1), 1–14.

Widener, S. K. (2007). An empirical analysis of the levers of control framework. *Accounting, Organizations and Society, 32*(7–8), 757–788. https://doi.org/10 .1016/j.aos.2007.01.001

Wilkes, M. S., Srinivasan, M., & Flamholtz, E. (2005). Effective organizational control: Implications for academic medicine. *Academic Medicine, 80*(11), 1054–1063.

Willaby, H. W., Costa, D. S. J., Burns, B. D., MacCann, C., & Roberts, R. D. (2015). Testing complex models with small sample sizes: A historical overview and empirical demonstration of what Partial Least Squares (PLS) can offer differential psychology. *Personality and Individual Differences, 84*, 73–78. https://doi .org/10.1016/j.paid.2014.09.008

Williams, I. (2011). Organizational readiness for innovation in health care: Some lessons from the recent literature. *Health Services Management Research, 24*(4), 213–218. https://doi.org/10.1258/hsmr.2011.011014

Williamson, O. E. (1975). *Markets and hierarchies: Analysis and antitrust implications: A study in the economics of internal organization.* University of Illinois at Urbana-Champaign's academy for entrepreneurial leadership historical research reference in entrepreneurship.

Williamson, O. E. (1993). Calculativeness, trust, and economic organization. *The Journal of Law and Economics, 36*(1), 453–486.

Witman, Y., Smid, G. A. C., Meurs, P. L., & Willems, D. L. (2010). Doctor in the lead: Balancing between two worlds. *Organization, 18*(4), 477–495. https://doi.org /10.1177/1350508410380762

Wold, H. O. A. (1982). Soft modeling: The basic design and some extensions. In K. G. Jöreskog & H. O. A. Wold (Eds.), *Systems under indirect observation* (Vol. 2, pp. 1–54). Elsevier Science Ltd.

Wolf, C., & Floyd, S. W. (2013). Strategic planning research: Toward a theory-driven agenda. *Journal of Management, 43*(6), 1754–1788.

WHO. (2008). *Guidelines: Incentives for health professionals.* http://www.whpa.org/ sites/default/files/2018-11/WHPA-positive_practice_environments-guidelines-EN .pdf

Wren, D. A., & Bedeian, A. G. (2009). *The evolution of management thought* (6th ed.). John Wiley & Sons.

Wren, D. A., Bedeian, A. G., & Breeze, J. D. (2002). The foundations of Henri Fayol's administrative theory. *Management Decision, 40*(9), 906–918.

Wysocka, M., & Lewandowski, R. (2017). Key competences of a health care manager. *Journal of Intercultural Management, 9*(4), 165–184. https://doi.org/10 .1515/joim-2017-0026

Yalcinkaya, G., Calantone, R. J., & Griffith, D. A. (2007). An examination of exploration and exploitation capabilities: Implications for product innovation and market performance. *Journal of International Marketing, 15*(4), 63–93. https:// doi.org/10.1509/jimk.15.4.63

Yang, C.-W., Yan, Y.-H., Fang, S.-C., Inamdar, S. N., & Lin, H.-C. (2017). The association of hospital governance with innovation in Taiwan. *International Journal of Health Planning and Management, 33*(1), 246–254. https://doi.org/10.1002/ hpm.2441

Yeşilbaş, İ., & Çetin, Ş. (2019). Trust in military leader: Scale development and validation. *Military Psychology, 31*(2), 147–159. https://doi.org/10.1080/08995605 .2019.1578150

Yetano, A., Matsuo, T., & Oura, K. (2020). Diagnostic and interactive use of PMM by Japanese local governments: Does the context affect the fitness of use? *Public Performance and Management Review, 44*(1), 28–57. https://doi.org/10.1080 /15309576.2020.1817108

Yi, Y., Liu, Y., He, H., & Li, Y. (2012). Environment, governance, controls, and radical innovation during institutional transitions. *Asia Pacific Journal of Management, 29*(3), 689–708.

Yokoe, D. S., Avery, T. R., Platt, R., Kleinman, K., & Huang, S. S. (2018). Ranking hospitals based on colon surgery and abdominal hysterectomy surgical site infection outcomes: Impact of limiting surveillance to the operative hospital. *Clinical Infectious Diseases, 67*(7), 1096–1102.

Yoon, S. N., Lee, D., & Schniederjans, M. (2016). Effects of innovation leadership and supply chain innovation on supply chain efficiency: Focusing on hospital size. *Technological Forecasting and Social Change, 113*, 412–421. https://doi.org/10.1016/j.techfore.2016.07.015

Young, G. J., Charns, M. P., & Shortell, S. M. (2001). Top manager and network effects on the adoption of innovative management practices: A study of TQM in a public hospital system. *Strategic Management Journal, 22*(10), 935–951. https://doi.org/10.1002/smj.194

Yu, C.-L., Wang, F., & Brouthers, K. D. (2016). Competitor identification, perceived environmental uncertainty, and firm performance. *Canadian Journal of Administrative Sciences / Revue Canadienne des Sciences de l'Administration, 33*(1), 21–35. https://doi.org/10.1002/cjas.1332

Yu, Y., Baird, K. M., & Tung, A. (2018). Human resource management in Australian hospitals: The role of controls in influencing the effectiveness of performance management systems. *The International Journal of Human Resource Management*, 1–26. https://doi.org/10.1080/09585192.2018.1511618

Zábojník, J. (2014). Subjective evaluations with performance feedback. *The RAND Journal of Economics, 45*(2), 341–369.

Zhang, M. (2018). When the principal knows better than the agent: Subjective evaluations as an optimal disclosure mechanism. *Journal of Economics and Management Strategy, 28*(4), 631–655.

Zilber, T. B. (2008). The work of meanings in institutional processes. *The SAGE handbook of organizational institutionalism, 18*, 151–168.

Zmud, R. W. (1982). Diffusion of modern software practices: Influence of centralization and formalization. *Management Science, 28*(12), 1421–1431. https://doi.org/10.1287/mnsc.28.12.1421

Zwanziger, J., Melnick, G. A., & Bamezai, A. (2000). The effect of selective contracting on hospital costs and revenues. *Health Services Research, 35*(4), 849–867.

Annexes

Appendix 1 Characteristics of the Hospitals Included in the Qualitative Study

By the Law of March 23, 2017, the Primary Hospital Care System, the so-called hospital network, was established (Table A1.1). The system distinguishes six levels of hospitals: Level I hospitals, Level II hospitals, Level III hospitals, oncology or pulmonology hospitals, pediatric hospitals, and general hospitals. The levels are determined by the types of services provided and defined by indicating the profiles or types of organizational units (Article 95l (2) of the SLE). In the author's opinion, this division does not reflect well the categories of hospitals in terms of their complexity, which was taken as the main criterion for classification in the context of the management control topic undertaken. For example, a pediatric hospital in the law is defined as "the level of pediatric hospitals – all profiles of the security system for children for inpatient treatment," which means that a large, specialized hospital, as well as a small hospital with two or three departments, qualifies for this category. A similar situation exists at the level of nationwide hospitals. For example, in the Pomeranian Voivodeship, this category includes both the 115th Military Hospital in Hel, with a budget of about PLN 10 million, and the University Clinical Center in Gdansk, with revenues of about PLN 700 million. Therefore, the paper uses the usual classification of hospitals dividing them into monospecialty, general, specialized, and university hospitals. In this classification, there is considerable overlap in terms of complexity between specialized and university hospitals. The latter were separated as a separate category due to, in the author's opinion, the greater autonomy of a significant proportion of professionals in university hospitals. The increased autonomy is due to two reasons. First, from the specific relationship between professionals (academics) and the hospital as their

Table A1.1. Levels of the primary hospital health-care system

Level name	Number of hospitals	Share %	List of profiles qualifying for the level
Level I hospitals	281	47%	general surgery, internal medicine, obstetrics and gynecology (one of the reference levels), neonatology (one of the reference levels), pediatrics.
Level II hospitals	96	16%	pediatric surgery, plastic surgery, cardiology, neurology, ophthalmology, orthopedics and traumatology of the musculoskeletal system, otorhinolaryngology, rheumatology, urology.
Level III hospitals	62	10%	thoracic surgery, thoracic surgery for children, vascular surgery (one of the reference levels), lung diseases, lung diseases for children, infectious diseases, infectious diseases for children, cardiac surgery, cardiac surgery for children, cardiology for children, nephrology, nephrology for children, neurosurgery, neurosurgery for children, neurology for children, ophthalmology for children, orthopedics and traumatology for children, otorhinolaryngology for children, clinical toxicology, clinical toxicology for children, clinical transplantology, clinical transplantology for children, urology for children.
Nationwide hospitals	91	15%	all profiles of the security system In terms of hospital treatment.
Cancer hospitals	19	3%	brachytherapy, gynecologic oncology, chemotherapy hospitalization, oncology surgery, pediatric oncology surgery, hematology, pediatric oncology and hematology, clinical oncology, radiation therapy, isotope therapy, clinical transplantology, clinical transplantology for children.
Pediatric hospitals	12	2%	all profiles of the security system For children in hospital treatment.
Pulmonology hospitals	31	5%	chemotherapy hospitalization, thoracic surgery, thoracic surgery for children, lung diseases, lung diseases for children.
Total	**592**	**100%**	

Source: Act of health-care services financed from public funds (Journal of Laws of 2021, item 1285, as amended).

employer, as academics often sit on the senate of the medical university, which owns the hospital, and to some extent exercise oversight over their place of employment. Second, from the higher status of professionals with academic degrees, who are likely to be proportionately more numerous in university hospitals.

SzO1, SzO2, SzO3, and SzO4 hospitals fall under the category of general hospitals. SzO1 is a small district hospital providing services in four departments: general surgery, internal medicine, pediatrics, and day orthopedics, as well as three outpatient clinics: general surgery, dermatology, and orthopedics. It has been classified as a level I hospital in the primary care hospital system. SzO1, at the time of the study, had a total of 175 employees, including 14 doctors and 48 nurses (Table 4.1). The hospital had 120 inpatient beds. Noteworthy is the fact that the value of the contract with the National Health Fund steadily increased, which in 2019 amounted to 12 million zlotys. The contract with the National Health Fund was the main source of funding for the hospital's operations. Other revenues were of marginal importance. The hospital certified its quality management system for compliance with ISO 9001:2015; however, it did not approach the acquisition of accreditation from the Ministry of Health (CMJ accreditation).

The hospital recorded a loss of 250 thousand zlotys in the fiscal year preceding the audit, which was, however, a much smaller loss than the annual depreciation, which amounted to 472 thousand zlotys. The director was an economist by training and employed an experienced surgeon as his deputy for treatment, who also provided services in the surgical ward and emergency room.

The SzO2 city hospital is larger, but it is still categorized as a general hospital in the typology adopted in the monograph and classified as a level I hospital in the "network," as it provides services in the following nine profiles of the security system: anesthesiology and intensive care, general surgery, internal medicine, infectious diseases, neonatology, orthopedics and musculoskeletal traumatology, pediatrics, obstetrics and gynecology, and hospital emergency department and in 11 associated outpatient clinics. In addition, outside the network, the hospital has three departments: general rehabilitation, neurological rehabilitation, and day rehabilitation, which are located in a separate location. It has 302 beds, with 109 doctors and 184 nurses working there. This hospital's main source of revenue is also a contract with the National Health Service, although the hospital performs laboratory tests for private patients for a fee and rents space for a general pharmacy and a hospital store and catering service. The hospital has not only certified its quality management system for compliance with ISO 9001:2015, but has also been accredited by the Ministry of Health (CMJ accreditation). The chief executive officer at the time of the study was a physician, a specialist in anesthesiology, while the treatment director was an internist. The hospital also recorded a loss in 2019 that was less than depreciation.

Similar to the SzO2 hospital and also qualified in the "network" for Level I is the SzO4 provincial hospital, except that SzO4 does not have rehabilitation, but instead it has a dialysis station and a general and oncology dermatology department. The slightly changed structure influenced the higher number of nurses at this hospital. In contrast, the approach to the bottom line of the directors of these hospitals differed significantly. While the director of SzO2 allowed a negative financial result, the director of SzO4, a lawyer by training, adhered to the principle of strict attention to the financial result in this regard, which gave the hospital more investment opportunities. The hospital was also ISO 9001 certified and accredited by the Ministry of Health (CMJ).

Another general and Level I-qualified hospital is SzO3, which had a ward structure similar to SzO2 and SzO4, except that, on average, the wards had a lower number of beds and provided services in similar areas, but, unlike the previous two hospitals, only in the least complex medical cases, resulting in significantly lower revenues and a lower number of employees. The SzO3 structure also includes a home oxygen treatment center and sanitary transport. The hospital has been showing losses for many years but, of course, not exceeding the value of depreciation, which, according to the Law on Medical Activities, would result in significant legal consequences. The SzO3 and SzO4 hospitals operated as IPHIs, while the SzO1 and SzO2 hospitals operated as limited liability companies with 100% public ownership of the local government.

Due to the unclear boundaries between the different levels of hospitals in their description from the quantitative survey, intermediate levels such as SzO/S were used, which means that the hospital is on the border between general and specialized hospitals. And it is to this group of hospitals that SzO/S1 and SzO/S2 can be classified. The SzO/S1 hospital admittedly has only ten departments, but among them are such specialized departments as hematology and bone marrow transplantation and neurosurgery; moreover, in principle, all departments also receive appeal patients from other hospitals. In addition to hematopoietic cell transplantation, SzO/S1 also carries out treatment programs for malignant lymphomas, acute lymphoblastic leukemia with Filadelfi chromosome (Ph+), neurogenic displacement hyperreactivity, primary immunodeficiencies, and chronic lymphocytic and myeloid leukemia, among others. The high degree of referentiality of the departments means that the hospital has additional laboratories and laboratories. SzO/S2 is under the authority of the provincial government but does not have the adjective "provincial" in its name. Although it is a specialized hospital by name, it does not legitimize as specialized wards as SzO/S1, but it has a significant number of wards, as many as 19. This is due to the fact that it has extensive psychiatry and rehabilitation. The significant number of conservative wards means that despite its large number of beds (540), larger than many provincial hospitals, its budget is at a moderate level (Table 3.6). Both hospitals have been classified as Level II hospitals in the primary hospital health-care system. These hospitals regularly record negative financial results, however, not exceeding the amount of depreciation.

The SzS1 and SzS2 specialty hospitals within the "network" have been classified as Level III hospitals. SzS1 is a provincial specialty hospital that has 23 departments in its structure, including a number of Level III referral departments, such as neonatology and obstetrics and gynecology. Outpatient services are provided there in 21 outpatient clinics. In addition, SzS1 has a much broader treatment program for various types of cancer than SzO/S1. The SzS2, which is subordinate to the mayor, provides services in a slightly smaller number of departments, but it has more outpatient clinics, with 26. The difference between the hospitals is also evident in the number of employees and the amount of revenue, as well as in financial performance. SzS1 regularly shows a profit, while SzS2 shows a loss. The hospitals are managed by a doctor and a non-doctor, respectively, with several years of experience as hospital directors. It is noteworthy that while the difference in revenue between the large general and general/specialist hospitals was not significant, the increase in the budget of the specialty hospitals compared to the general/specialist hospitals is almost double. Both hospitals make their treatment facilities available to medical universities for student training. All Polish hospitals surveyed had a very similar management structure.

Another hospital qualified for the field study was a specialized provincial SzS/U hospital. Here, too, a combined category was used – specialized and university. This hospital does not differ much in its structure from other specialized hospitals, with 23 departments and 24 outpatient clinics, but it stands out for its commitment to scientific activities, from which it has made a major component of its strategy. Jat pointed out the hospital's director, more than half of the doctors hold at least a doctorate in medicine, and many of them participate in Polish and international research teams. The hospital had been showing losses for years, but, the hospital director said, at such a level that some of the money from depreciation could be had for the hospital's own share in projects. At the time of the study, the SzS1, SzS2, and SzS/U hospitals had current ISO 9001 and Ministry of Health accreditation certificates.

The next facility studied was the SzU hospital, which belongs to a medical university. It was by far the largest Polish hospital that took part in the qualitative research. The structure of this hospital included 26 clinics and departments, 36 outpatient clinics, and 8 departments, such as laboratory diagnostics, gastroenterology endoscopy, clinical microbiology, etc. (it is worth noting the different nomenclature in university hospitals, e.g., "department" rarely appears in non-university hospitals, there are mostly "laboratories"). At the time of the study, the hospital was facing serious financial difficulties. It had maturing liabilities and was generating a loss every year, although previous restructuring efforts were already bearing fruit and the financial situation was steadily improving.

Two single-named hospitals were also included in the field study. SzM1 is a psychiatric hospital, and SzM2 is a rehabilitation hospital, with one pediatric ward, and therefore classified in the "network" as a pediatric hospital. Both hospitals report to provincial governments and are managed by directors with economic training. SzM1 balances on the edge of profit and loss from year to year, while SzM2 has consistently posted a small positive financial result for years.

Four foreign hospitals also participated in the study, providing a kind of reference point, allowing us to see to what extent the phenomena observed in Polish hospitals have a universal, international character. SzGB is a hospital/trust in northern England. In addition to 1,159 beds, it has a well-developed network of day services and outpatient clinics. The Trust has a divisional structure, headed by a chief executive officer (CEO) who handled strategy and outreach. The trust's board of directors also included a chief financial officer, chief operating officer, chief medical officer, chief human resources officer, and chief nurse, responsible for the "patient experience at the hospital" (Chief Nurse & Director of Patient Experience). It can be said that these directors constituted the hospital's staff. Clinical operations, on the other hand, were divided into three divisions (divisions): general medicine, cancer surgery, diagnostics and clinical support, and the women's and children's services division. Each division was managed by a director who had a deputy for medical and nursing affairs. Within the divisions were business units, e.g., the surgery division had business units such as the Head, Neck, Eyes and Plastics Business Unit, or the General Surgery & Urology Business Unit, managed by general directors or clinical directors, except that at this level, general directors usually had medical training, which cannot be said of senior directors.

Noteworthy in the British hospital was a separate department within the "staff" for Business Development, Transformation & Operational Performance (Business Development, Transformation & Operational Performance). The hospital also had a dedicated strategy and improvement (improvement) unit, headed by a director (Executive Director of Strategy & Improvement), who had two directors reporting to him – Strategy and Improvement. The structure of this hospital indicated a very strong orientation toward the introduction of "business" management, one could say management logic. In 2016, the hospital recorded a loss of £15 million. According to the hospital's CEO, the reason for the loss was that the hospital's building and ancillary services, such as cleaning, security, nutrition, and infrastructure maintenance, were provided by an external company, the owner of the property. This is because the hospital was built as a public-private partnership. This hospital definitely differs from Polish and Lithuanian hospitals in the number of staff employed, in particular the proportionally lower number of doctors compared to the total staff employed (Table 4.1).

A similar management structure, but far less extensive (with fewer directors), was presented by a hospital in Ireland. Despite the relatively small number of beds, this hospital provided services in a wide range of medical specialties, such as orthopedics, rehabilitation, cardiology, women's health, urology, cardiac surgery, vascular surgery, plastic and reconstructive surgery, ENT, neurology, general surgery, comprehensive oncology care, and emergency medicine. The hospital made a small positive financial result every year.

The next facilities surveyed were a university hospital and a city hospital in Lithuania. The former is the largest hospital in the Baltics. With 2,300 beds and more than 7,000 employees, it provides services in virtually every medical field available today. The city hospital provided services on more than 800 beds, employing less than 2,000 people. The management structure of Lithuanian hospitals was very similar to that of Polish hospitals.

Appendix 2 Formalization of Performance Indicators – Limits on Overruns (Excerpt from the Director's Order)

Order No. 33/2017

The director of the hospital obliges the managers of organizational units to implement contracts with the National Health Fund in accordance with the established limits (determined monthly in the information on the implementation of contracts) with the following indicators of their permissible overruns in the below departments, outpatient clinics and laboratories for each type of health services:

1. Internal diseases – up to 3%
2. Cardiology and cardiac intensive care:
   a. E11-E14 procedures – unlimited
   b. hospitalizations – up to 5%,
3. Hematology – up to 5%
   a. oncology care – unlimited,
   b. transplantation procedures – unlimited
4. ITM (Intensive Medical Care) – limiting admissions of patients from other hospitals to "emergency" cases in order to reduce the level of overruns,
5. General oncological and vascular surgery – up to 3%
   a. oncology care – unlimited
6. Neurology – up to 3%
7. Neurosurgery – up to 3%
   a. oncology care – unlimited
8. Trauma and orthopedic: general procedures – up to 3%
   a. Excluding endoprosthetic surgery, unlimited
9. General urology and oncology – up to 3%
   a. oncology care – unlimited

Appendix 3 Rules for Ordering Diagnostics and Admitting Patients to the Hospital (Excerpt from the Director's Order)

Order No. 15/2017

Physicians of individual specialties consulting in the Emergency Room are advised to limit the ordering of laboratory tests to the following:

Internal Medicine Physicians:
Abbreviated morphology, sodium, potassium, creatinine, glucose, urinalysis, CRP, blood gas, toxicology tests, bilirubin, ALAT, amylase, INR, troponin.

Cardiologists
Abbreviated morphology, sodium potassium, creatinine, glucose, troponin, blood gas, INR, APTT, CRP.

Physicians Surgeons
Abbreviated morphology, sodium, potassium, creatinine, glucose, amylase, bilirubin, ALAT, ASPAT, urinalysis, INR, APTT.

Neurology Doctors
Abbreviated morphology, sodium, potassium, creatinine, glucose, ALAT, 1 NR.

Orthopedic Doctors
Abbreviated morphology, sodium, potassium, creatinine, glucose.

Urology Doctors
Abbreviated morphology, sodium, potassium, creatinine, glucose, general urinalysis, CRP.

Hematologic Physicians
Morphology with smear, sodium, potassium, creatinine, glucose, CRP, bilirubin, ALAT, INR; APTT, uric acid and LDH.

Neurosurgical Physicians:
Abbreviated morphology, sodium, potassium, glucose, INR, APTT, creatinine.

Other laboratory tests can be ordered only after a thorough evaluation of the patient's condition and the need for diagnostics at the emergency room level and the approval of the chief duty officer. If diagnostics become more extensive and costly, the patient should be left for observation within the department concerned. This also applies to patients who have had a CT scan in the emergency room.

Appendix 4 Control of Cooperation between Medical Departments

Order No. 41/2019

The Director of [...] establishes the following rules for cooperation between medical departments:

1. If it is necessary to hospitalize a patient in patient rooms of other wards than the one to which the patient was admitted (a situation of lack of free beds), medical care for these patients is provided by doctors of the ward to which the patient was referred. In turn, nursing care is provided by the staff of the ward where the patient is temporarily (until the beds are free) hospitalized. Medicines, dressing materials and other medical supplies are secured by the staff of the ward to which the patient has been referred.

2. In order to shorten the length of a patient's stay (and thus reduce the cost of their hospitalization) in orthopedic departments after hip and/or knee endoprosthesis procedures and in neurosurgery after surgical procedures requiring rehabilitation, as well as patients hospitalized in the neurology department in order to ensure continuity of treatment for this group of patients, when determining the number and timing of scheduled admissions of other patients to rehabilitation departments, the needs of patients hospitalized in the departments of our hospital should be taken into account first (with equivalent medical considerations).

3. For patients in the orthopedic department, the provision of a minimum of 4 beds per week in the rehabilitation department (subject to prior notification by doctors in the trauma and orthopedic department).

4. I entrust control of the implementation of the order to the Medical Director.

Index

Printed in the United States
by Baker & Taylor Publisher Services